Spectrum Guide to
INDIA

Camerapix Publishers International

Spectrum Guide to India

First published 1998 by
Camerapix Publishers International,
PO Box 45048,
Nairobi, Kenya

© 1998 Camerapix

ISBN 1 874041 96 2

This book was designed and produced by
Camerapix Publishers International,
PO Box 45048,
Nairobi, Kenya

Fax: (254-2) 448926/7
Tel: (254-2) 448923/4/5

Website:http//www.camerapix.com
E-mail: info@camerapix.com

The **Spectrum Guides** series provides a comprehensive and detailed description of each country they cover together with all the essential data that tourists, business visitors, or potential investors are likely to require.

Spectrum Guides in print:
African Wildlife Safaris
Eritrea
Ethiopia
Jordan
Kenya
Madagascar
Maldives
Mauritius
Namibia
Nepal
Oman
Pakistan
Seychelles
South Africa
Sri Lanka
Tanzania
Uganda
United Arab Emirates
Zambia
Zimbabwe

Colour separations: Universal Graphics Pte Ltd, Singapore.
Printed and bound: UIC Printing & Packaging Pte Ltd, Singapore.

Publisher and Chief Executive: Mohamed Amin
Projects Director: Rukhsana Haq
Editorial Director: Brian Tetley
Consultant Editor: Salim Amin
Picture Editor: Duncan Willetts
Editor: Ruth Davidar
Contributors: Dr Sahai, Geetan Batra, Dr Mohinder Singh, Jaya Jaitly, Miel Sahgal, Madhulita Mohapatra and Zothanpari
Cartographer: Terry Brown
Production Editor: Gail Porter
Graphic Designer: Calvin McKenzie
Editorial Assistant: Rachel Musyimi
Photographic Researcher: Abdul Rahman

Editorial Board

Spectrum Guide to India is the latest in the popular series of high-quality, lavishly and colourfully illustrated *Spectrum Guides* to exotic and exciting countries, cultures, flora and fauna.

Spectrum Guides are the creation of the three-man travel book team of world-famous photographer and cameraman **Mohamed Amin**, Publisher and Chief Executive, equally renowned photographer **Duncan Willetts**, Picture Editor, and Editorial Director **Brian Tetley**.

India is one of the most spectacular tourist destinations, a rich, many-faceted country that needs to be rediscovered over and over again. Though there are many guides to India, this new *Spectrum Guide* gives exciting and hitherto unseen dimensions to this vast and fascinating nation.

Spectrum Guide to India took shape under a panel of distinguished national contributors, each an expert in their chosen subject.

Prominent among them are editor and author **Ruth Davidar, Dr Sahai, Geetan Batra, Dr Mohinder Singh, Jaya Jaitly, Miel Sahgal, Madhulita Mohapatra** and **Zothanpari**. Their lyrically written essays on the regions, states and principal cities take residents and prospective travellers alike, along colourful and sometimes little-known pathways as they explore the wonders of one of the world's most complex and exciting nations.

Information on India's past and present, the country's physical features, flora, fauna and cuisine, provides the necessary backdrop to the travel section.

Nandini Lal has written a scholarly and fascinating account of India's 5,000-year-old civilization, while **Sharda Nayak** compiled the material on the country's museums and the innumerable festivals.

Gillian Wright contributed the section on wildlife and natural history, and **Sumir Lal** clarifies the intricacies of Indian business, economy, investment and taxation. Finally, the section on Facts at your Fingertips meticulously details the practical knowledge travellers require to make their journey trouble free.

Many of the photographs in the guide are by **Kamal Sahai**, a well-known photographer and intrepid traveller, whose visual documentation of the mountains, rivers and forests, the coast and the desert, the people and their vibrant lifestyles adds spectacular colour to the written word.

Overall supervision of the complex logistics and liaison was by *Spectrum Guides* Projects Director **Rukhsana Haq.**

In Nairobi and London, *Spectrum Guides* in-house teams also laboured long and hard, particularly Production Editor **Gail Porter** who checked and double-checked facts, house style, syntax and clarity, while London-based Graphic Designer **Calvin McKenzie** unknotted some distinctly mystical Indian designs. Typography and typesetting was the contribution of Editorial Assistant **Rachel Musyimi**.

TABLE OF CONTENTS

Half-title: A quiet moment, Porbandar. Title: Camels on the outskirts of a village near Jaisalmer. Overleaf: Flamingos at Sultanpur.

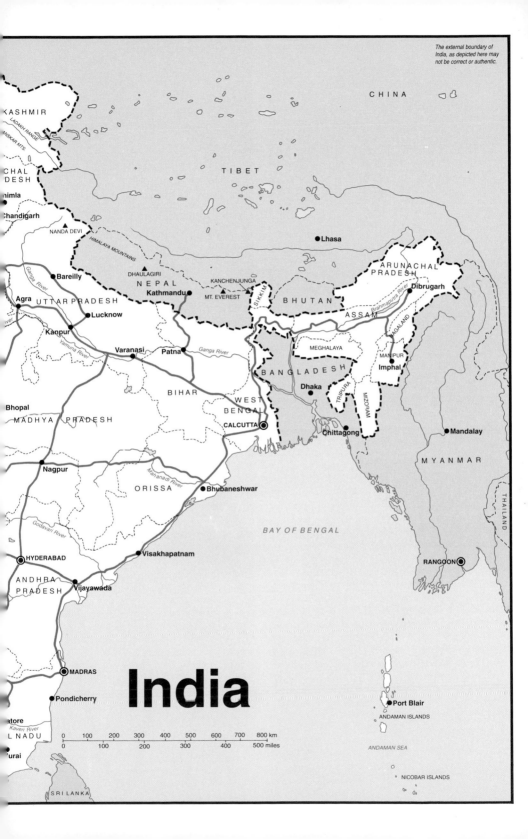

India

The India Experience

There is more to India than meets the eye. It has a cultural tradition dating back 4,000 years. Unlike the ancient — and younger — civilizations of Egypt and Greece, India's most significant attribute, in large part, has been her ability to retain her own identity despite numerous foreign invasions. No analogy of this experience exists elsewhere in the world.

The first to come were the Aryans in 1500 BC. Then Alexander the Great and his conquering armies in 32 BC brought to bear a Greek influence on Hindu art, architecture and philosophy. During the classical age of Indian civilization (AD 319-540), under the Gupta dynasty, not only did the arts flourish, but also advanced metallurgy, mathematics and science, including astronomy. The Rashtrakuta dynasty of the eighth century AD exerted its influence in the Deccan and in south India. The 10th- and 11th-century Chola rulers of the south and the Indo-Aryan Chandellas of central India were patrons of temple architecture. Muslim rule in India under the Mughals was firmly established in the 13th century up until the beginning of the 18th century when the British dominated the subcontinent for a century and a half. Through all these influences the fundamental institutions of Indian culture survived, even though change was often imposed by the rulers of the time. It is this remarkable resilience that accounts for her unity and stability amid what might appear to the unprepared visitor as 'chaotic diversity'. In other words, nothing was too big or too insignificant to find acceptance in this vast, accommodating land.

An attempt to understand the collective Indian psyche would necessarily confront the function of religion and caste in everyday life. All the world's major religions are represented in India, and Hinduism, Sikhism, Jainism and Buddhism actually have their origins there. With spiritualism as a way of life, it is not surprising that religion has even engaged political affairs, and the persistence with which each successive government maintains a fragile, secular balance is credit to the Indian state.

India's principal lure lies in its cultural and natural wealth. Besides, it is one of the cheapest destinations to travel to with immense value for money. There is an astonishing range of palaces, fortresses, *ashrams* or hermitages, temples, wildlife sanctuaries, beaches, mountains and desert tracts, besides an exotic cuisine and hand-woven Indian silks and carpets, and local handicrafts, gems and jewellery at ridiculously low prices. The best of traditional art (including tribal works, each a masterpiece in vegetable dyes and pigments), theatre, dance and music also find expression in Bharat, the more correct name for India.

India's contrasts are many. Luxurious hotels and shopping malls exist cheek by jowl with shabby hutments, and the roads are clogged with fancy cars jostling for space with ancient bullock carts, cows and pedestrians unmindful of traffic.

Bureaucratic red-tape is dished out in equal measure to native and foreigner alike, and a good bargain is a sparring session between two players where neither loses. Pollution of every sort is high and so is the abundance of hospitality and friendliness of the people. What explains the traveller, who swears there is no worse destination for a holiday, to return at the first possible opportunity? It is, very simply, something that gets better with each sampling. For this unique experience, plan a visit to this land of mesmeric charm that will hold you long after your aircraft climbs into the skies.

So, in the words of greeting used by all Indians, *Namaste* — Welcome.

Opposite: Four of the many faces of India.

Travel Brief and Social Advisory

Some dos and don'ts to make your visit more enjoyable.

Getting There

Besides the regular programmes on offer, you might choose an itinerary to indulge a pet whim — visiting the national parks in India, for instance. Make doubly sure in advance what facilities you might expect at the other end — airport transfers, acceptable credit cards, facilities for foreign exchange. Not all small town banks have this facility, and when they do, there could be a limit on the amount you can change.

Visas

All tourists must have a valid passport and a tourist visa to enter the country. Tourist visa requests for one to six months are entertained. If you plan to visit any neighbouring country, opt for a multiple-entry visa.

Arrival

International flights, except for Asian airline services, arrive at an unearthly hour. Therefore, it is important to clarify everything with your travel agent before you leave your home country, as touts are a frequent pest at all destinations and can take advantage of your uneasiness, disorientation and the late hour of arrival.

On arrival in India, first convert some money at the airport then head for the prepaid taxi service, usually administered by the police or state government, if you are not being met. Ensure that you register with them before you leave the building and remember to collect a receipt which will serve as evidence should you meet with a demand to pay again. This receipt is usually handed over to the driver at your destination. Some cities have efficient airport-to-city bus services. The Ex-servicemen's Air Link Transport Service operates in the major metros. Check before leaving the airport. In Mumbai (Bombay), it takes around 20 minutes to get from the international to the domestic terminal. A courtesy bus is available for about Rs 20.

Customs

Customs checks are thorough and do not have to be troublesome. A Tourist Baggage Re-Export form (TBRE) has to be filled in for dutiable goods that are allowed into the country untaxed, as they have to be carried back with the traveller.

Leaving the country with Rs 2,000 worth of gold and ornamental jewellery and precious stones valued at Rs 10,000 is not taxable. Be prepared to produce bills, if asked, to provide proof of a purchase. India is a signatory of CITES (Convention on International Trade in Endangered Species) so the sale of ivory, animal and snake skin goods is banned. The government has banned taking antiques over 100 years old out of the country.

Taxes

Airport tax is Rs 300 for foreigners and Rs 100 for Indian residents.

If the duration of your stay exceeds the visa limit for whatever reason, an income-tax clearance certificate will have to be produced at the point of departure.

Currency

India's currency is the rupee, with 100 paise to a rupee. Foreigners are allowed to bring in US$10,000 without declaration. All hotel bills that exceed Rs1,200 (US$50) carry a 20 per cent entertainment tax (ET).

Retain all encashment certificates. It is possible to reconvert rupees to dollars to the value of these certificates at the airport just before leaving. List all credit card and traveller's cheque numbers in a diary to report loss, if any.

Security

Airport security throughout India is very strict and even camera batteries have to be packed into baggage that goes into the hold. Frequently, tape recorders, radios, nail scissors and pocket knives are disallowed — anything that looks like potential hijack material. All hand baggage is inspected by x-ray. Where this facility does not exist, physical checks will be conducted.

It is advisable to keep all valuables, money, passport and tickets on your person. If this is not possible, use the hotel's safe deposit lockers. Never leave them behind in hotel rooms, even if your baggage can be locked. In public places take particular care. A good padlock is indispensable, especially to secure baggage to the luggage rack on trains.

Report any theft immediately and file a First Information Report (FIR) necessary to settle insurance claims. The consular offices of your country (not embassies) are responsible for your welfare in India, so their addresses and telephone numbers are an essential part of your baggage (see listings).

Getting Around

Restricted areas

You can travel freely in India, except to the north-east, Sikkim, parts of Himachal Pradesh and the Andaman and Nicobar islands, where permits are necessary. Sporadic political disturbances in certain volatile regions portend danger to visitors. Check in advance with the travel agent.

Domestic travel

If you choose to pick your way through India, efficient road, rail or air services link even the remotest parts of the country to the larger towns.

By road

The Automobile Association of India has branches in the four metropolitan cities of Delhi, Mumbai, Calcutta and Chennai, and in major towns, and publishes a series of road maps of India and individual route charts of the various regions with comprehensive details of motorable roads, restaurants and so on. Distances are indicated in kilometres. Though the country is well served with filling stations,

ninety-three octane is seldom available outside the metropolitan cities. However, Indian traffic conditions are unpredictable and alarming, as even the ancient bullock cart shares the same road, and rarely does road travel progress as planned. Car hire is limited to the big cities. The car papers and the various permits necessary to cross interstate borders will have to be checked if you are driving yourself. A car with a driver is preferable, and often cheaper, as the driver frequently acts as a guide.

Personal papers that must be produced include a valid international or Indian driving licence, a copy of your passport and passport-size photographs.

Driving is on the left and other quaint norms, such as flashing headlamps at on-coming traffic to indicate right of passage, will take getting used to. Travel within the city by taxi can be arranged on (usually) an eight-hour, 80-kilometre (50-mile) basis for a pre-determined fee at most big hotels and is very economical.

Bus travel is an alternative worth considering. Some states are better served by their state corporations and private bus companies than others. The trip can be fast and efficient or nightmarish, depending on what you pick. Luxury bus services usually cater to local tastes in entertainment, and video shows and loud film music are the norm.

Avoid video coaches, especially if you are travelling through the night and want a good night's rest. All services have a stop or two along the way for a simple, wholesome Indian meal. Soft drinks are usually available too. Stick to known brands and avoid sodas and flavoured waters poured out of old-fashioned bottles with marble-tops. Mineral water is usually available everywhere. Ensure that the seal is unbroken. Otherwise, carry sterilizing tablets and purify water available locally.

Public toilets are virtually non-existent except for those in luxury hotels and at airports. Elsewhere, if rest room facilities are available, they take the form of the Indian toilet which has to be tackled on one's haunches. Toilet paper is not an Indian concept so you will have to carry your own. A good precaution is to ensure that the toilet has a bucket full of water before you enter. Men, naturally, have it easier.

By rail

India is served by a remarkably well-connected rail system that criss-crosses the country in a bewildering maze of lines. Four classes — second, first, A/C (air-conditioned) sleeper, II A/C — are available on most trains. A/C chair is available only in certain sectors. The first-class service is comfortable and reasonably priced. Bedding is available for a nominal charge. Air-conditioned travel is wise in the blistering Indian summer.

Food is available on most trains either through the canteen car or by way of the railway catering service, which serves meals at important stations en route. The meals are Indian except perhaps breakfast on some trains. Some popular and fairly luxurious trains have meals worked into the ticket cost. A wide range of foods, ranging from biscuits to bananas, are sold on the platform. Ask your fellow travellers for help or the uniformed Train Ticket Examiner (TTE), who will provide information on the duration of each halt, time of arrival and so on.

All foreign-exchange-paying tourists can make their reservations at a separate counter at major stations to avoid the interminable queues. A quota exists at all times.

Booking 48 hours in advance should be sufficient, unless the tourist season — October to April — is on or the destination is a popular tourist spot. Railway interlinking systems are unreliable except on computerized networks. Travel in such a way that you have sufficient time to make your booking, particularly if you move away from well travelled routes and do not use a travel agent.

An Indrail Pass can be bought with foreign exchange. Enquire casually about the luggage allowance (weight in kilos) for your class of travel. Checks are rare but do not be the one inconvenienced. Watch your luggage and do not entrust it to anyone.

Porters are present at every station, but try not to engage them as the rate (per piece of luggage) displayed on their armbands rarely applies. If their services cannot be avoided, agree on a price before you surrender your goods to them.

By air

Dual tariff applies in India, and foreigners are expected to pay at the dollar rate. However, with the government introducing the 'Open Sky' policy, private air taxis relieve one's dependency on the domestic airline systems of Indian Airlines. Vayudoot Air India, the national airline, also flies to a few destinations within the country. Boeings, Airbuses and Dorniers comprise the carriers of major fleets. With increased options, efficiency and service have taken giant strides forward. But it is important to physically identity your luggage after checking in for a domestic flight. Otherwise your luggage will not be loaded.

Local transport

Buses, trains, trams, the Metro (Calcutta), taxis and the three-wheeled autorickshaws, comprise public transport in all cities and major towns. All rates are predetermined.

However, when travelling by taxi or autorickshaw, ensure that the meter is turned to the basic fare, which varies from city to city. At the destination, pay by the meter. If your money is refused, ask to see the taxi-autorickshaw card, that has to be produced by law until the meter is calibrated to the new hike in rates. If they are still adamant, walk away (remember the meter is still ticking). You will be called back and the card will have appeared from somewhere. Carry lots of change. If the driver declares he has none, you will never get back the difference. Avoid tipping.

In smaller towns, which do not have a regular taxi service, more expensive tourist taxis can be hired. Fix the price in advance and take into account waiting time, overnight journeys and driver's charges.

Opposite: The snow-capped Himalayas tower above the Garhwal Valley.

Above: The narrow-gauge Nilgiri Blue Mountain Railway, Ooty.

Women and handicapped travellers

Women should avoid travelling alone in India. Any foreigner is a curiosity and women attract greater attention. Unfortunately, it is not possible to discern when the undue attention a woman receives is plain friendliness or seduction. In a nation where mothers, sisters, wives and daughters are fiercely protected, a woman outside this circle is considered fair game. However, if you delight in living on the edge, you will be pleased to know that the railways, in particular, and most bus services have compartments or seats set aside for women.

One exception to this rule is a woman with a child. Indians love children and consider them a gift from God. A mother is respected and will receive much considerate attention. Women also have certain rights. If a woman is taken into police custody, she can refuse interrogation if a female police officer is not present. She is also allowed one phone call and has to be provided with a lawyer and produced before a magistrate within 24 hours.

The handicapped must travel to India with a companion. There are few facilities provided for them.

The people

Indians are intensely curious and what may be viewed as downright nosey by the average foreigner is probably just the Indian way of breaking the ice. How old are you? How much do you earn? Are you married? How many children do you have? These questions are asked with unblinking candour. Though life in the cities and towns reached by satellite television is more tolerant of Western social mores, it is assumed in India that a man and woman travelling together are married. Couples travelling through India would be wise to refrain from amorous gestures.

Etiquette

The traditional form of greeting is the *namaste*, where the hands are neatly folded together in a prayer-like gesture. However, handshakes are now common, though most women will refrain from physical contact.

Indians have a curious non-verbal way of agreeing with you. They shake their

Above: Various modes of transport vie for space on a crowded street in south India.

heads from side to side when they mean 'yes', so be careful how you interpret their signals. Incredibly hospitable, Indians are easily offended if refused. Even unexpected visitors will be invited to share in a meal. Otherwise, tea or coffee will be forced on you. Some special functions call for use of the banana leaf plate and you will have to sit cross-legged on the floor.

Sit as comfortably as you can because you will have to eat with your fingers. Use your right hand only, even if you are a southpaw. It is considered unclean to use the left hand.

Similarly, never give or receive anything with your left hand. In Indian etiquette it is not done. In many homes, footwear is left outside the door to keep out the dirt of the street. However, socks may be kept on.

Begging and giving of alms is a religious obligation for most Indians, but restrain yourself and do not encourage this practice. Indians also are fascinated by all things 'phoren'.

Many travellers carry extra ballpoint pens, cigarette lighters, chocolate bars, soap, pins and duty-free cigarettes. Your gifts will endear you to the recipients and many a bribe can thus be saved.

Language
Though Indians speak myriad languages and dialects, English is the lingua franca. Someone will always be willing to act as an interpreter if you are stuck. English-language newspapers and magazines are widely available.

Clothes
The national dress for women is the *saree*, though the loose pyjama suit called the *salwar kameez* is (now) acceptable everywhere. Women should dress modestly unless they wish to invite unwelcome stares. Vests, halter-neck tops and shorts will never meet with approval. Shirts with long sleeves and trousers or mid-length skirts make good sense.

Many of India's monuments are also places of worship, so bare heads and arms must be covered. However, there are some spots beside the safe confines of five-star hotels which are havens to sunbathers, like Goa on the west coast.

Above: Babies strapped to their mothers' backs, Manipur.

Personal necessities
India is often mistakenly described as part of the Third World, but its consumer industry is not.

Almost everything is available there from toiletries and cosmetics to cigarettes, mosquito repellent and modern drugs — most medicines can be bought over the counter without a prescription. Do not waste valuable baggage space bringing these along.

Health
Tourists will not be admitted into the country without a valid yellow-fever vaccination. Inoculation against typhoid and cholera must be taken before you leave for your holiday.

An anti-malarial prophylactic beginning two weeks before your arrival and continued for six weeks after your departure is recommended.

Gamma globulin injections offer some protection against hepatitis, and tetanus jabs and an anti-rabies vaccine are advisable. More injections are mandatory if an animal bites you, however.

Carry sufficient stocks of prescription drugs for the duration of the trip and the prescription, too. Write down the generic title and composition of the drug in a diary for double security.

A simple medical kit with medication for upset stomachs, cuts and wounds, allergies and analgesics is recommended. Most foreigners will probably experience a tummy problem upon arrival. Heat and exhaustion are likely to blame rather than the food and water. However, persistent trouble needs medical attention.

Do not drink tap water unless first purified with sterilizing tablets. All travellers are advised to exert some restraint when indulging in the delicious local cuisine in the initial stages of their stay.

Larger hotels assist with medical help in case of an illness. Otherwise, emergency health facilities cannot be relied upon in a crisis. Injury caused in an accident requires police intervention by law and immediate medical assistance can only be provided by a government hospital. Take out travel insurance at the same time you make your travel plans.

Above: A woman from the tribal belt, Saurashtra.

Photography

Photographing bridges, airports and military establishments is forbidden by law. Take these warnings seriously or your film may be confiscated and you will lose more than that photograph was worth. A small charge is sometimes levied on still cameras carried into Indian monuments where photography is allowed. However, if you wish to use a tripod, flash or video camera, make sure you obtain written permission from the Archaeological Survey of India (ASI) in New Delhi before proceeding on your travels. It takes a good deal of energy and perseverance to get one, but it will be your only refuge if your intentions are ever questioned. Film is available in most major towns but only a few studios have acceptable E6 or B&W processing. For printing, opt for computerized processing

When to go

Winter (October to March) is the best time to visit the plains of India, though landlocked north India can be bitterly cold. Southern India is pleasantly cool at this time. The mountains of the north are snow-bound in winter and the hills of the south frost-bitingly chilly. But in summer — April to mid-June — the plains are shimmering hot and sticky, and the mountains great getaways. Those interested in the monsoon should visit between June-September.

Where to stay

India has luxury hotels of various grades — from one to five-star — in the larger towns and cities, and cheaper places elsewhere. Let your travel agent know your budget. See listings for 'Hotels'. Also check with the Tourist Development Authority of each state for details.

Cheap, wholesome accommodation is provided by the YMCA and YWCA guesthouses. Facilities are better in the cities but the demand for them is tremendous. Youth hostels are less comfortable but cheap. Book well ahead of time and seek early confirmation. The railway retiring rooms are also surprisingly clean and comfortable in a few places, though the facilities are minimal. However, unless reservations are made well in advance, the

Above: A typical village in rural Bihar.

chances of staying in them are slim. Never go in search of hotels after dark. Even in broad daylight it is hard work to ward off touts and at night they can be unbearably persistent.

Sports
Sports opportunities are generally restricted to a few exclusive clubs, which can be accessed only through membership or as a member's guest, and to the facilities provided by large hotels. However, cricket is a national passion and all life comes to a standstill when the Indian team is playing at home or abroad. A little knowledge of this sport will advance your immediate acceptance even among strangers. Backyard and street teams abound.

Shopping
Before you buy, walk into a 'fixed-price' shop to check their rates. Then step out and shop around. Goods' prices will invariably be many times the actual worth. Start by slashing them by half and then settle for something in between.

Government shops and emporia are best for authentic handicrafts. Retain all bills to produce before the customs if questioned. These bills are also necessary if your purchases are to be sent on ahead by freight.

Reputable shops often offer to ship goods on home for you. However, it is best to post or courier them yourself. Those shopping for Western clothes in India will come across a number of 'export-surplus goods' available from pavement markets in large cities.

If you spot college kids wearing clothes you like, ask them. They will probably take you there themselves. Driving a hard bargain will land you *haute couture* garments for a fraction of the cost.

If you are not on a budget, a number of fashionable boutiques offer top-of-the-line clothes at fancy prices.

Parting shot
The Indian atmosphere grows on you. It can be a hugely enjoyable experience if you can forget what you left behind and fully partake of the place and circumstance. So pack your bags and head east where a warm *namaste* awaits you.

PART ONE: HISTORY, GEOGRAPHY AND PEOPLE

Above: Carved stone panel, Konarak.

Five Thousand Years of Civilization

Hidden deep beneath the snows of the Himalayas, buried in the fertile soils of its great plains and carried along by its great rivers to the sun-kissed shores of its sparkling beaches, are the many secrets that make India's story unlike any other.

And today India is still alive with a sense of history. A history that divides into three — ancient, medieval and modern: namely the Hindu period or the Vedic Age until the advent of Islam; the Muslim period from 1200 to 1707; and the British period between 1707 and 1947 respectively.

Ancient India covers the Harappan civilization (3000-1500 BC), the Vedic Age (1500-300 BC), the rise of Buddhism and Jainism (600-400 BC), the Mauryas (321-185 BC), the post-Mauryan invasions (200 BC-AD 300), the Gupta Age (AD 320-606), and the smaller kingdoms (AD 500-800).

Medieval India starts with the advent of Islam and comprises the Delhi Sultanate (1206-1526), the Vijayanagara (1336-1565) and Bahamani (1345-1565) kingdoms, and religious movements (15th century) by Kabir, Nanak (Sikhism) or the Bhakti and Sufi cults.

Modern India includes the Mughal dynasty (1526-1707), the Marathas under Shivaji and the Peshwas, the advent of Europeans and the East India Company (1498-1754), British expansion and administration (1757-1857), cultural awakening (the 1857 revolt onwards), and the Indian Nationalist Movement until Independence.

Ancient India

Indus Valley civilization

When archaeologists Banerjee and Marshall discovered the Indus Valley civilization in 1921-22, they pushed back the dawn of Indian history thousands of years. Previously it was believed to have started with the Vedic Age when the Aryans made India their home. Ruins were revealed of two urban centres dating from 3000-1750 BC. One was at Mohenjodaro on the Indus

in Sind (present-day Pakistan), and the other was at Harappa on the River Ravi in Punjab. Subsequent excavations unearthed six more cities — Ropar near Chandigarh, Lothal near Ahmedabad, Kalibangan in Rajasthan, Kot Diji and Chanhudaro in Sind, and Banwali in Haryana.

This vast civilization was distinctly urban. Mohenjodaro and Harappa were perfectly planned cities with walled garrisons, granaries (perhaps tributes were paid in the form of grain), and clearly demarcated residential and citadel areas with well-organized drainage and sanitation systems. Mohenjodaro is famous for its public bath.

Surprisingly, neither temples nor palaces were discovered, though the houses of varying sizes seem to indicate class differences. Their interests were predominantly mercantile and agricultural. The presence of accurately graded measures and weights, besides Harappan stamps in Mesopotamia and a dockyard in Lothal (a port, perhaps), all point to their flourishing maritime trade.

The Indus Valley was not the desert it is today, but was once humid, with good rainfall and forest cover, so crops were easily grown. Wheat and barley were the staples (though rice was later introduced in Lothal); peas, dates, mustard and sesame were also grown. The Indus Valley people were the earliest users of cotton.

Few weapons were discovered, suggesting they were a peaceful race. Yet the fact that these were walled cities proves they knew the art of defence.

They were skilled in the use of many metals, including bronze, but strangely not iron. While a number of animals from goats to elephants were domesticated or trained, the horse was not known. A certain toy reveals the use of wheeled carts for transport. Trinkets suggest a fondness for jewellery. Pictographs, engraved human and animal images and inscribed seals recapture wide-ranging activities, like pottery, weaving, metalcraft, stockbreeding, cultivation and international commerce. Worship of the bull and the *pipal* tree was common. Urns and graves containing household items show that they believed in life after death.

The sculptures were stylized, geometric and stereotyped. The humped buffalo seals, the terracotta figurine of the Earth Mother Goddess symbolizing fertility, and the stone seal of the meditating male god surrounded by animals that resembled Pashupati Mahadeva are well-known relics.

Floods, war or the expansion of the desert are some of the reasons ascribed to the mysterious disappearance of this civilization. Besides natural calamities, the Aryan invasion could well have been a partial factor. Though there is no evidence of a mass confrontation, skeletons with sharp injuries have been found in a heap. Whatever the reason, their culture faded out so completely that not even traces of art forms or town planning have survived elsewhere.

The coming of the Aryans

The word 'Arya' means noble. The tall, fair-skinned Aryans of Indo-European stock came over the Hindukush Pass from Central Asia around 1500 BC and settled around the Indus and its tributaries (Sapta Sindhva). They gradually spread towards the east and drove the indigenous, dark-skinned Dravidian tribes, whom they contemptuously called *dasyus* or *dasa* — pirates and servants — further southwards, establishing the Vedic Age.

The Indus people were city dwellers, while the Aryans were a semi-nomadic, pastoral race who reared cattle and tilled the land. Though the cow was holy it was a barter symbol, signifying a man's wealth.

The Aryan government was essentially tribal and based on kinship. The seeds of democracy can be traced to this system.

The king (*rajan*) was the ruler of the state (*rashtra*). He was aided by a council of elders (*sabha*) and the tribal assembly (*samiti*). The king also consulted the village headman (*gramani*) and the military commander (*senani*). Each tribe (*jana*) was composed of several clans (*vish*), which, in turn, consisted of many villages (*grama*), where several heads of families came together. The Aryans were originally divided into *panchajana* or five tribes. The people made voluntary offerings (*bali*) but there were no taxes.

In the early Vedic Age, where women were given prominence in Hindu society, they even participated in religious rituals and political *sabhas*, which had not become a male domain up until then. Many were educated enough to write hymns in the *Rig-Veda*. The caste system was still fluid and based on the division of labour. People were divided into groups (*jatis*) depending on colour (*varna*), but there were no taboos against intermingling.

Professions were still not hereditary. Untouchability did not exist. Religion was a simple affair celebrating the communion of people with nature. Prayers and offerings were made to Indra, Varuna, Vishnu, Surya and Agni. Significantly, they all symbolized the different forces of nature. Initially the gods were worshipped out of fear or for personal favour, not because of *bhakti* or devotion. Hymns were sung in Sanskrit, the language of the Aryans.

By the later Vedic Age, certain changes had taken place in the Aryan lifestyle. By now they were settled in the Doab — the confluence of the Ganga and Yamuna rivers — region. They began to chop forests with axes — iron was freely in use by 800 BC — to create fields and moved from a pastoral to an agricultural economy. While cattle were still most precious to them, the idea of land as private property also began to take shape. Trade received a boost with the appearance of various craftsmen.

Kingship was now hereditary. The king no longer ruled over tribes but over territories. As royal power increased, popular assemblies declined. The *sabha* and *samiti* came to be dominated by princes and nobles. The king's officers began to include the *singrihitra* (treasurer) and the *purohit* (chief priest). Now there were taxes, instead of voluntary offerings. Several kingdoms were established. Towns like Hastinapur and Kausambhi had their beginnings then. The great battle between the Pandavas and Kauravas in the *Mahabharata* is said to have been fought around this time.

Society became more patriarchal. Women were forced to take a back seat in domestic and public life. The fourfold hierarchical division of society into *Brahmins* (priests and scholars), *Kshatriyas* (warriors and kings), *Vaishyas* (merchants and artisans) and *Shudras* (menials and labourers) had by now crystallized into its familiar rigid form. Intermarriages were frowned upon.

The Brahmins, who enjoyed exclusive knowledge of the Hindu religious texts, and the Kshatriyas, who had control over political and military affairs, became all-powerful. The Vaishyas, who amassed wealth through trade but were denied social prestige, formed the tax-paying class. The Shudras, usually of mixed Aryan-Dravidian origin, were expected to serve the other varnas but, unlike slaves, were not owned by the upper classes.

The Vedic texts — *Rig, Sama, Yajur* and *Atharva* — are the main sources of information on Aryan society. The *Vedantas*, or post-Veda religious literature, included the *Upanishads* and *Brahmanas*. Many more changes took place in Hinduism, most of them for the worse. Idol worship was introduced. New gods like Prajapati, Rudra and Vishnu came to replace the earlier ones. To justify the bewildering plurality of the Hindu pantheon, it was held that god is one, but his manifestations are many. Similarly, the law of *karma* or rebirth was used to vindicate casteism, which meant that everyone had predetermined positions in society from their birth. References to holy texts were cited to justify discrimination against women and the lower castes. *Yajnas* or rituals, often involving sacrifices, became a complicated and expensive business. The details of the ceremonies began to overshadow the spirit behind them. This increased dependence on the intervention of the priest, which suited the Brahmins. The lofty ideals of the *Upanishads* and the simplicity of early Vedic society were abandoned. In their place arose an unjust, caste-conscious system. Buddhism and Jainism, the offshoots of Hinduism, were born out of a reaction against these evils.

Buddhism
The Buddha, born Gautama or Siddhartha in 566 BC, left home at the age of 29 and, after seven years of spiritual quest, attained enlightenment while meditating under a *pipal* tree at Bodhgaya. He founded the philosophy of Buddhism which spread across much of Asia even after his death in 486 BC.

Jainism
Vardhamana Mahavira, a contemporary of the Buddha, left a wealthy home in quest of enlightenment in 510 BC. Called Jina or conqueror, he led his followers, the Jains, until his death in 468 BC. However, Jainism remained within the bounds of the Indian subcontinent.

The Mauryas
In the sixth century BC, there were the Mahajamapadas, or the 16 great kingdoms. Of these, the four most powerful kingdoms, Magadha, Kosala, Vatsa and Avanti, kept up a hundred-year-long battle for power till Magadha finally won. Magadha in Bihar, which had first Rajgir and then Pataliputra as its capital, became the political hub under Bimbisara (542-493 BC) and Ajatashatru (493-461 BC). The Shishunaga and Nanda dynasties followed, until a young adventurer, Chandra Gupta Maurya, conspired with a Nanda minister, Chanakya, to take over the throne and founded the famous Maurya dynasty. The rise of Magadha in a sense meant the rise of monarchy. The ruler was considered God's representative on earth, the protector of the people and the owner of the land. Two seminal literary works serve as important source material of the Mauryan period. One is Kautilya's *Arthashastra* and the other is *Indica* by Megasthenes, the Greek ambassador of Seleukos Nicator. The former is an effective guide to *realpolitik* by Chanakya, the wily prime minister of Chandra Gupta Maurya. The latter is an account of contemporary social and court life. Chandra Gupta Maurya (321-297 BC) was the first ruler of an all-India empire. His son Bindusara (297-272 BC) was

Opposite: Carved stupa, Nalanda.

succeeded by the famous Ashoka (268-231 BC) who in 260 BC fought the Battle of Kalinga, the horrors of which converted him to Buddhism. He is known for his belief in paternal kingship and *dhamma*, a universal faith based on the ideals of peace and virtue. Many edicts, pillars, capitals and stupas (like the one at Sanchi) were built at his behest. The two great socio-religious epics, Valmiki's *Ramayana* and Vedavyasa's *Mahabharata*, were written later, between 200 BC and AD 200.

Post-Mauryan invasions

Other invaders of the pre-Christian era included Alexander the Great — Sikander Shah to Indians — remembered for the Battle of Hydaspes against Poros, ruler of the Jhelum. Kanishka started the Kushana era in AD 78 and helped Taxila become the centre of art.

Both the Shakas and the Kushanas belonged to the Scythian race. The greatest contribution has been the Greco-Buddhist influence on art (the schools of Gandhara and Mathura) and religious thinking.

Christianity first came to India in the first century AD along the Malabar coast.

All these invasions led to the opening up of trade routes, increasing commerce between India and the rest of the world, and allowing foreigners to rule this land.

The Gupta age

The classical or golden age of India started with the ascension of Chandra Gupta I to the throne in AD 320. Samudra Gupta (AD 335-375), Chandra Gupta II or Vikramaditya (AD 375-415), Kumara Gupta (AD 415-454) and Skanda Gupta (AD 454-467) succeeded him and ruled until the empire collapsed, largely owing to the onslaught of the Huns. The *Puranas*, sacrosanct Hindu documents by Brahmins, were rewritten in classical Sanskrit at this time. They are a record of tradition and history, beginning with creation, and delineating dynasties, customs and sects. The works of Chandra Gupta Vikramaditya's court poet Kalidasa (*Abhijnan Shakuntalam, Meghduta, Raghuvamsham, Kumarasambhava* and *Ritusamhara*), Shudraka's *Mrichchakatika*, Vishakhadutta's *Mudrarakshasa*, Bhasa's 13 plays, the *Panchatantra* (fables) and Amarasimha's *Amarakosa* (lexicon) were the main literary works of this age. Most plays were romantic comedies in which the upper classes spoke in Sanskrit and the lower classes used the Prakrit tongue.

Numerals and decimals were already in use in the Gupta Age. Aryabhata and Varahamihira were famous astronomers who arrived at conclusions and calculations far ahead of their time.

Their advanced knowledge in metallurgy is evident from the finely engraved coins of this era, the copper life-sized standing image of the Buddha, and the 70-metre (230-feet) iron pillar in Delhi (Qutb Minar), which has shown no trace of rust for over 15 centuries.

Remains of Gupta paintings in unfaded colours depicting events in the Buddha's life may be seen in the caves of Bagh, Ajanta and Badami. The cult of Shiva was confined to *lingam* (phallic symbol) worship, but Vishnu's incarnations allowed for the exercise of sculptural imagination. Temples of stone began to replace those in brick and wood.

Post-Gupta kingdoms

The next important ruler after the decline of the Gupta empire was Harshavardhana (AD 606-647), who belonged to the Pushyabhukti family of Thaneswar.

His reign can be reconstructed from the account of the Chinese pilgrim, Hsuan Tsang and *Harshacharita*, his biography by his court poet Bana Bhatta.

In the Deccan, the Satavahanas emerged as a force in the first century AD. Further south, the Cholas of Tanjore (now Thanjavur), the Pandyas of Madurai and the Cheras of Malabar battled incessantly for power. Later, from AD 608 to 757, it was the Chalukyas (who built their empire on the ruins of the Vakatakas, successors of Satavahanas) of Badami, the Pallavas of Kanchipuram, and the Pandyas of Madurai, who kept fighting among themselves over the conquest of Vengi.

Of them, the most famous was the Chalukya king, Pulakeshin II, who defeated both Harshavardhana and the Pallavas led by Mahendravarman. The Chalukya

Above: Pillars and Temple of the Sun, Konarak.

empire had come to an end by the mid-12th century. This led to the rise of the Yadavas of Devagiri (Deccan), the Kakatiyas of Warangal (Andhra), and the Hoysalas of Dwarasamudra (Mysore). The kingdoms lasted until overthrown by the Turkish sultans in the 14th century.

In religion, the Advaita (monoism) Movement was started by Shankaracharya. In the 11th century, Ramanujan refuted Shankaracharya's emphasis on knowledge and said true devotion was more important.

This period saw a surge in sacred art and architecture. The most impressive temples of the Chalukya reign are the Elephanta Island Caves, the white marble Jain temples at Dilwara in Mount Abu, the Buddhist Cave Shrines at Ajanta and the Hindu, Buddhist and Jain temples of Ellora. The massive rock-cut Kailash temple at Ellora, open to the sky, is ascribed to the eighth-century Rashtrakutas, and the seven *rathas* or chariots, the shore temple at Mamallapuram and the temples at Kanchipuram to the Pallavas. The Hoysaleshwara Temple at Halebid is in the Chalukyan style, as are the free-standing temples at Aihole and Badami. The temples at Bhubaneswar, Puri and Konarak are representative of the eastern Indian group. The Khajuraho temples are the finest monuments built by the Chandellas in Bundelkhand.

The typical Dravidian concentric style of the temples of the south reached its peak under the Chola chieftains of Tamil Nadu in the first century AD — lofty temple gate towers and high walls surrounding a passage around the audience hall for public ceremonies, which went around the inner sanctum with roof and pillars containing the deity. The fine standard sculpting attained during the Chola period is evident from objects as diverse as the giant statue of Gomateshwara at Sravanabelagola and the bronze figurines of Nataraja (dancing Shiva). Between AD 750 and 1000, three powers tried to wrest control of Kannauj and hence of north India. They were the Pratiharas of Rajasthan, the Rashtrakutas of the Deccan and the Palas of Bengal and Bihar. The three occupied Kannauj in turns. As the threesome went into decline, the Rashtrakutas were replaced by the later

Chalukyas, the Palas by the Senas and the Pratiharas by some Rajput chieftains. Besides the Chandravanshis and the Suryavanshis the four major Rajput clans of this period going back to the fire family (Agnikula), were the Pariharas, Chauhans, Solankis and Pawars or Paramaras.

Medieval India

The Delhi sultanate
Barely a century after the death of the Prophet Mohammed, the Muslims invaded Sind. However, it was only some centuries later that Mahmud of Ghazni led several sorties into north-western India (997-1030) looting the temples of Somnath, Mathura and Kannauj. These raids, more for short-term gain than a thrust for long-term power, were followed by fresh flocks of invaders, who were also from central Asia.

Finally, in 1206, Qutb-ud-din Aibak, who was the first of the Slave or Mamluk Sultans, came to stay and head the Delhi Sultanate. He proclaimed Islam as the state religion and Delhi as his capital. Thus was laid the nucleus of a new political entity, known as the Delhi Sultanate (1206-1526), which was to survive for three centuries. The dynasties established were the Slave Sultans (1206-90), the Khaljis (1290-1320), the Tughluqs (1320-99), the Sayyids (1414-51) and the Lodis (1451-1526). The Slave Sultans after Aibak were Iltutmish (1211-27), Razia (1236-39) and Balban (1265). Jalal-ud-din Khalji (1290-96) and Ala-ud-din Khalji (1296-1316) of the Khalji dynasty were followed by some insignificant kings.

By this time, Delhi was a shadow of its former self due to recurrent Mongol raids. The Sayyids, who followed, functioned as nominees of that infamous Turkish invader, Timur (Tamurlane). The Lodis, who were of Afghan origin, then took over. The most famous of them was Sikandar Lodi (1488-1516), who moved the capital to Agra. The weakest was the unpopular Ibrahim, the last of the Lodis, whose army plotted with Babur, King of Kabul, to overthrow Ibrahim. Lodi's defeat in the first battle of Panipat (1526) paved the way for the Mughal empire, founded by Babur. The source material for this period includes Al Beruni's *Tahqik-i-Hind*, Iltutmish's *Tabaqat-i-Nasiri*, the many literary and documentary works of Amir Khusrau (a poet who was patronized by Ala-ud-din Khalji), Zia ud-din Barani and Firoz Shah; and the Moroccan traveller Ibn Batuta's account of Muhammad bin Tughluq's reign.

Society was very different under the Muslims. The three chief village officials were the headman (*muquaddam*), accountant (*patwari*), and revenue collector (*mushrif*). The main court officials were the chief minister (*wazir*) and the judge and religious adviser (*qazi*).

This period saw the burgeoning of Turko-Afghan architecture, which meant the input of three chief features: arches, domes and minarets. The decorations remained Indian; yet this unique synthesis portrayed the artistic culmination of Hinduism and Islam in architecture during the Mughal era.

Sufi and Bhakti movements
A breakaway Islamic group, the Sufis believed faith was the focus of their religion, not fasts and prayers. On the other hand, the Bhakti movement led by Kabir (1440-1518), which flourished at this time, resisted discrimination against women and the lower castes.

Sikhism
Guru Nanak (1469-1539) rebelled against casteism and idol worship to establish the Sikh religion. By the time he died, the religion was well established in Punjab.

Modern India

The Mughal empire
The Mughal emperors were Babur (1526-30), Humayun (1530-40 and 1555-56), Akbar (1556-1605), Jahangir (1605-27), Shah Jahan (1627-58) and Aurangzeb (1658-1707). Sher Shah, an ambitious Afghan adventurer, ruled successfully (1540-55) after forcing Humayun to flee. Between 1707 and the 1857 revolt, 15 incompetent

Above: A finely carved terracotta panel from Vishnupur, West Bengal.

successors to the throne carried on the name of the Mughal dynasty, until the last, Bahadur Shah, was dethroned by the British.

The blood that flowed through both Asian terrors, Chengez Khan (Mongol) and Tamurlane (Turk), was in the veins of Zahir-ud-din Mohammed Babur — which means tiger — the founder of the Mughal empire. After conquering both Kabul and Samarkand, he led four successful expeditions that helped him to overrun India — the first battle of Panipat in 1526 against Ibrahim Lodi; the battles of Kanwaha in 1527 against Rana Sanga of Mewar, aided by Afghan chiefs Mahmud Lodi, Hasan Khan Mewati and Silahadi, Chanderi in 1528 against the Rajputs of Malwa; and Ghagra in 1529 against the Rajputs of Bihar and Bengal.

Babur's generalship and his lively memoirs on life in India (*Tuzuk-i-Baburi*) apart, he is remembered as the pioneer of a famous dynasty. Unfortunately, his son Humayun inherited an unwieldy empire and an empty treasury. He led the life of a wandering exile in Lahore, Persia and Kabul (1540-55) after his throne was usurped by Sher Shah, who defeated him in the battles of Chausa and Kannauj. When Sher Shah died, Humayun returned, but he was not destined to rule for long, as he tumbled down a staircase to his death months later.

Sher Shah — so known for having once killed a tiger or *sher* — or Farid Khan who rose from a humble fiefdom in Sasaram to become emperor of Delhi by grit and craft, and formed the short-lived Suri dynasty, is known for his various conquests and administrative reforms. After his death, the Mughal dynasty was re-established with the accession of 14-year-old Akbar, son of Humayun. After quelling the rising power of Hemu, general of the Afghan, Adil Shah, in the second battle of Panipat (1556), Akbar set about completing his grandfather's good work.

It is Akbar who is regarded as the true founder of the Mughal empire, which he sought to preserve and extend by a wise policy of aggrandizement coupled with conciliation. The powerful Rajputs turned into staunch allies. Only the legendary Rana Pratap of Mewar held out. Akbar

31

founded Din-i-Illahi, a pan-Islamic faith. He was an enthusiastic patron of the arts, especially painting, poetry and music. The 'nine gems' of his court were geniuses like Abul Fazl, Faizi, Raja Todarmal, Raja Bhagwan Das, Raja Man Singh, Mirza Aziz Koka, Abdur Rahim Khan-i-Khana, Birbal and Tan Sen.

During his reign, the new capital of Fatehpur Sikri, Humayun's tomb, various forts, and his own mausoleum at Sikandra were either built or the plans for them approved. He brought large parts of India, including the Deccan, under his sway.

Jahangir or Salim, who succeeded his father, Akbar, was given over to wine and women, and allowed his wife Nur Jahan to meddle in political affairs. Both William Hawkins and Thomas Roe, English representatives, visited his court and wrote vivid accounts of his reign, beset by rebellions, extravaganzas, court intrigue and general inefficiency. Portrait painting was greatly encouraged by him.

His son Shah Jahan was a good ruler who had a peaceful reign and left behind great works of art. Monuments like the Taj Mahal, Jama Masjid, Moti Masjid, Musamman Burj, Red Fort, the Peacock Throne, various tombs and pleasure gardens and the seventh Delhi township of Shahjahanabad were all built during his reign. Of these, the Taj Mahal — the white marble mausoleum built in memory of his wife, Mumtaz Mahal, on the banks of the River Yamuna — which took 20,000 men and twenty-two years to complete and remains one of the wonders of the world, is perhaps the greatest contribution by any ruler to India's history. Aurangzeb, the next emperor, was unpopular due to his bigotry and his religious persecution of the Hindus. His anti-Rajput offensives and his disastrous Deccan policy proved his ruin. He managed to provoke both the Marathas and the Sikhs. The Mughal line petered out and the later emperors became puppet rulers as the British influence grew stronger.

The British in India

It all started with Vasco da Gama's discovery of India in 1498. Initially, Portuguese, Dutch, French and English trading companies came to India for its fabled silks, spices and saltpetre. The French, though initially strong, were expelled after their defeat in the three Carnatic wars in India that echoed Anglo-French rivalries on the continent in the Seven Years and Hundred Years wars of the mid-18th century.

Though the Portuguese ruled over Goa, Daman and Diu until 1961, and the French were a strong influence over Chandannagar and Pondicherry until 1954, the British made a lasting impression nationwide.

Victory over the French and Bengal

The East India Company's aspirations gradually changed from purely mercantile to political, as was already evident in their taking advantage of the hostility between the Nawab of Arcot and the Nizam of Hyderabad during their Carnatic offensives against the French under Dupleix and his able generals La Bourdonnais and Lally.

Robert Clive's similar machinations, which led to his victories over Siraj-ud-daulah at Plassey in 1757 and over Mir Kasim at Buxar in 1765, made this transition from trader to ruler a cakewalk for the British. The East India Company secured all the revenue rights (*dewani*) to Bengal, Bihar and Orissa; the Nawab of Oudh was reduced to a puppet; and the Mughal emperor became their virtual prisoner.

The Maratha, Mysore and Sikh wars

Between 1765 and 1818, the British were busy with the Anglo-Maratha, Anglo-Mysore and Anglo-Sikh wars.

The Marathas were no longer the force they had been in the days of Shivaji (1627-80), the famous 'Mountain Rat' who bested the Sultan of Bijapur; Aurangzeb's wily commander Afzal Khan; the governor of the Deccan Shayista Khan, and even Aurangzeb himself with his guerrilla tactics, and then had the nerve to proclaim himself *Chhatrapati* (king) in 1674, right under the Mughal emperor's nose, and establish a line of Peshwas. The Marathas had restored their fortunes after their devastating defeat by the Afghans under Ahmad Shah Abdali in the third battle of Panipat in the year 1761.

Above: The Gumbaz, Tipu Sultan's Mausoleum, at Srirangapatnam.

The successive Peshwas and the powerful chiefs of the Maratha confederacy (Scindia, Gaekwad, Holkar and Bhonsle) alternately wrangled among themselves and patched up, while the British played one against the other. The able statesman, Nana Fadnavis, put up a brave front until he died in 1800. The treaty of Bassein in 1802 made the Maratha State a subsidiary ally of the British. The chiefs either followed suit or were isolated. In 1818, the last-ditch attempt at freedom by the Marathas ended in failure and the Peshwa was dethroned and his territories annexed, thus ending the Anglo-Maratha wars. On the Mysore front, too, Haider Ali and his son Tipu Sultan were formidable foes of the British until the humiliating Treaty of Seringapattam in 1792. Mysore became a subsidiary ally after Tipu Sultan was defeated and killed in the fourth Anglo-Mysore war in 1799.

The Sikhs were a force to contend with, first under Maharaja Ranjit Singh (1780-1839), the 'Lion of Punjab', and then under his son Dalip Singh from 1845 until Punjab was captured in 1849. Nepal (1811), Burma (1826), Sind (1843) and Sikkim (1850) were similarly annexed to the British empire through wars. Afghanistan was the only place to resist the British. Lord Auckland's ambitious Afghan policy ended in failure.

British policy of conquest

Besides outright war, a great instrument for extending the British empire was the Subsidiary Alliance, created by Lord Wellesley. Any Indian ruler who entered into this alliance had to acknowledge the East India Company as the paramount power, keep an English Resident in his state, and agree to neither employ non-English Europeans nor make any political decisions without British appproval.

The ally, moreover, had to give money or territory to the British for the permanent maintenance of a British contingent in the state. This was supposed to protect him from external danger and internal disorder; but, in effect, it meant the signing away of independence. The Nizam of Hyderabad was the first to accept this in 1798, followed by the Nawab of Oudh (1801), Peshwa Baji Rao II (1802), the new ruler of Mysore, Raja

Krishnan, after Tipu's death (1799), and the Maratha chiefs Gaekwad, Scindia and Bhonsle (1803). Lord Dalhousie's Doctrine of Lapse was a master-stroke of British imperialist policy in India. If the ruler of a dependent state died without leaving a natural heir, his property would not pass to his adopted son but 'lapse' into the East India Company's custody unless the company granted special sanction.

This policy claimed Satara (1848), Jaipur (1850), Sambhalpur (1850), Baghat (1850), Udaipur (1852), Nagpur (1853) and Jhansi (1854). The ploy to legitimize aggrandizement made many enemies, and Rani Laxmibai of Jhansi became a rallying point of the 1857 Sepoy Mutiny.

The only state taken on grounds of misgovernment was Oudh (1856), then under Nawab Wajid Ali Shah. Another step by Lord Dalhousie that reduced the expense to the British but cost them dearly during the Great Revolt of 1857 was removing titles and pensions of the new rulers of Poona, Tanjore and Surat, and the dire warning that they would do so to the last Mughal emperor Bahadur Shah's successor, too.

Growth of British influence

On the administrative front, the East India Company consolidated itself through the reforms of various governors-general. The police, army and judiciary were organized and strengthened. Railway and telegraph services were started. Trade and industry received a fillip but British efforts to buy cheap and sell dear resulted in a drain on the Indian economy and ruined indigenous artisans and craftsmen.

In 1793, Lord Cornwallis enforced the Permanent Settlement, which increased the oppression of the peasantry, who were reduced to landless labourers. The British revolutionized Indian society by introducing social reforms like the banning of *sati* (self-immolation) by Lord Bentinck (1829) and female infanticide by Hardinge, and the encouragement of widow remarriage (1856). The development of Western education through English-medium schools and colleges bred a new class of intellectuals.

Christian missionaries and progressive thinkers — Ishwarchandra Vidyasagar, Swami Vivekananda and others — and societies (Ram Mohan Roy's Brahmo Samaj, Derozio's Young Bengal Movement, Swami Dayananda's Arya Samaj, the Ramakrishna Mission, Sayyid Ahmed Khan's Aligarh School and others) helped in this cultural awakening.

The Mutiny of 1857

Paradoxically, these changes led to the revolt. The people felt India's religions would not survive such Westernization. Lord Dalhousie's policy of aggression; the high-handedness of the British towards Indian rulers, particularly the Mughal emperor and dispossessed big landlords; the disbanding of their huge armies and retainers, leading to loss of livelihood; increasing economic exploitation; inequitable appointments and pay between Britishers and Indians; the General Services Enlistment Act requiring Indian soldiers to go overseas (against Hindu religion); widespread conversions by Christian missionaries; all these made the British unpopular.

The immediate cause of unrest was the greased cartridges that the Indian soldiers had to bite to fit them into their rifles. The rumour gained ground that the English were deliberately using the fat of pigs and cows, taboo to Indians, to grease them. A *Brahmin sepoy* (soldier) in Barrackpore, Bengal, Mangal Pandey, refused to do so and thus the great uprising of 1857 began. It spread from Meerut and Delhi across central and north India. But the British, who had the upper hand in men, materials and communication, quashed these spontaneous and sporadic rebellions in which the Sikh, Gorkha and Rajput battalions did not participate.

Tantia Tope (dispossessed Maratha Peshwa Nana Sahib's commander) and Rani Laxmibai of Jhansi died fighting. The revolt sounded the death-knell of the East India Company. By the act of 1858, India became the jewel in Victoria's crown.

Above: Nehru at the Commonwealth Prime Ministers Conference, London, 1948.
Top: Nehru with Lord Mountbatten 1948.

Growth of nationalism

The proliferation of the local press and public reactions to Lord Lytton's Vernacular Press Act (1878) and Lord Ripon's Ilbert Bill (1883) increased political awareness and discontentment with British rule and the Indian National Congress (1885) was formed.

Some of its great presidents, Dadabhai Naoroji, Surendranath Banerjee and Gopal Krishna Gokhale, were moderates. They asked for constitutional reforms — greater representation, Indianization of the services and an end to poverty and famine. But this policy proved ineffective.

So a new group of extremists led by the Lal-Bal-Pal trio, Aurobindo Ghose and others, started popular *hartals* (general strikes) and Hindu festivals to promote patriotism.

Lord Curzon's partition of Bengal (1905) on the pretext of administrative convenience made the public suspicious of the motives of Britain, and there were mass meetings and strikes. Everywhere the people began using *Swadeshi* (Indian) goods and boycotting British goods.

The Muslim League (1906) and such leaders as Maulana Mohammed Ali and Abul Kalam Azad, encouraged Muslim nationalism. The British reacted by banning the press, arresting and deporting leaders and playing 'divide and rule' between Hindus and Muslims, but the partition had to be revoked (1911).

In 1915, two Home Rule Leagues were started under Tilak and Annie Besant. As the movement became militant, revolutionaries such as Chaki and Savarkar took over. Secret terrorist societies, like Dacca's Anushilan Samiti, were formed. Many youths like Khudiram Bose became martyrs. But violence was not the answer.

At this juncture Mohandas Karamchand Gandhi took over as leader. He taught that victory could be achieved by converting others through truth and sacrifice. His attempt to erase untouchability and encourage the use of the spinning wheel to produce indigenous cloth brought patriotism to the people in the village.

The fight for independence became a mass-based movement. Gandhi came to be hailed as *Bapu*, the father of the nation.

In 1919, Gandhi launched his *Satyagraha* or Non-violent Movement against the Rowlatt Act, which authorized the British to imprison any Indian without right to trial, and was himself incarcerated. In April 1919, 20,000 people gathered in Amritsar in protest. The police, under General Dyer, opened fire.

Thousands died. Martial law was imposed in Punjab. In protest, Gandhi began the Non-cooperation Movement in 1920 and there were country-wide demonstrations. Foreign cloth was burnt. Schools and colleges were shut down, and many gave up government posts and English titles.

The Muslims, under the Ali brothers Shaukat and Mohammed, started the Khilafat Movement against the British war with Turkey. Soon they merged with the movement for *swaraj* (self rule).

By 1921, all major leaders were in jail. The violence by Indians in Chauri Chaura, Bihar, led Gandhi to call off the Non-violent Movement in disgust. In 1930, thousands braved *lathis* (batons) and bullets to join Gandhi as he resumed Civil Disobedience with his famous Dandi March to prepare salt against the salt laws. The movements, Congress sessions, government pacts and prison terms carried on until the Quit India Movement of August 1942.

The fight for freedom now came under leaders like Jawaharlal Nehru, Sardar Patel and Netaji Subhash Chandra Bose. Arson and riots had already become common with Muslim League leader Jinnah's call for a separate Muslim nation.

The British finally partitioned India and Pakistan on 15 August 1947. India has, since then, established itself as a stable democracy, rare among Third World countries. Nehru's socialism and non-alignment helped put post-colonial India on its feet.

In 1996, a programme of economic liberalization was introduced. India has survived ethnic strife in the border states, communal tension as the fallout of its Partition, three wars with Pakistan and one with China, and three assassinations with remarkable control.

At the threshold of the 21st century, the future of India shines bright.

The Land: Diamond of the East

A dominating presence in south Asia, India derives its name from the River Indus which flows through present-day Pakistan. The seventh largest country in the world, it occupies 2.4 per cent of the world's surface and is about one-third the size of the US and slightly less than half that of Australia. Located in the tropical zone between latitudes 8° 4'N and 37° 6'N, and longitudes 68° 7'E to 97° 25'E, the country stretches 3,214 kilometres (1,993 miles) from north to south and 2,933 kilometres (1,819 miles) from east to west. It is almost neatly bisected through the middle by the Tropic of Cancer, thereby ensuring that the entire country enjoys some form of tropical or sub-tropical climate.

The country is bounded to the west by Pakistan, to the north by China and to the east by Myanmar (Burma). It also shares long boundaries with the smaller nations of Nepal and Bhutan in the north, and Bangladesh, which it almost encloses, to the east. Peninsular India has a long coastline of nearly 7,000 kilometres (4,340 miles) and is bounded on the east, south and west by the Bay of Bengal, the Indian Ocean and the Arabian Sea. India possesses the island territories of Lakshadweep in the Arabian Sea, and the Andaman and Nicobar islands in the Bay of Bengal.

Politically, the country is divided into 26 states, the largest of which is Madhya Pradesh. There are six union territories administered directly by the federal government. India is essentially a land of villages — over 5.5 million of them — but also boasts some of the largest cities in the world, including Delhi, Mumbai and Calcutta, each hosting a population of around 10 million.

Physical regions

A subcontinent that possesses virtually all nature offers, from spectacular mountains to flat deserts and giant river systems to tropical jungles, this diamond-shaped country can be divided into three main geographical regions: the Himalayan Mountains, the northern plain and the peninsula.

Northern India is dominated by the Himalayas, the highest mountain range in the world, though only its western and eastern limits are within Indian territory. These mountains form an impenetrable physical and climatic, and indeed historical and cultural, boundary that has shut India off from China and central Asia.

Strung out over 2,400 kilometres (1,488 miles), with 92 peaks over 7,500 metres (24,608 feet), the two tallest within India being Kanchenjunga, 8,598 metres (28,210 feet), the third highest mountain in the world, and Nanda Devi, 7,817 metres (25,648 feet), the Himalayas are the world's mightiest mountain range.

Geographers divide the Himalayas into five parallel zones. The southernmost comprises the Shivaliks, a chain of low sandstone hills which run along the foot of the main range. Behind this lie the Lesser Himalayas, a zone 80 to 100 kilometres (50 to 60 miles) broad where the mountains average 1,800 metres (5,900 feet) in height and where many of India's more popular hill resorts are located. The next zone is of dissected spurs, averaging a height of 4,500 metres (14,800 feet). Behind this are the Greater Himalayas, a 25-kilometre-broad (16-mile) and 2,500-kilometre-long (1,550-mile) band of the world's loftiest peaks, beginning with Nanga Parbat, 8,126 metres (26,661 feet) in the west and including Everest, 8,848 metres (29,030 feet), Kanchenjunga, Makalu, 8,481 metres (27,826 feet) and Dhaulagiri, 8,172 metres (26,812 feet). The fifth zone comprises the Trans-Himalaya or Tibet Himalayas, a watershed region between rivers flowing to the north and those flowing southwards. At 3,500 to 4,000 metres (11,484-13,124

Overleaf: The dramatic Zoji La Pass on the road from Srinagar to Leh.

feet) it contains the headwaters of two of the subcontinent's greatest rivers, the Indus and Brahmaputra. The Himalayan system includes certain important branch ranges as well, such as the Karakoram and Zanskar to the west, and Pathkoi, Lushai and Garo to the east.

A more popular segmentation of the Himalayas occurs on a regional basis. Thus the Punjab Himalayas extend for 582 kilometres (361 miles) from the River Indus to the Sutlej; the Garhwal and Kumaon Himalayas for 320 kilometres (200 miles) from the Sutlej to the Kali; the Himalayas in Nepal, with the highest peaks, for 800 kilometres (500 miles) from the Kali to the Teesta; and finally, the Assam Himalayas extend a farther 750 kilometres (465 miles) east of the Teesta up to the Brahmaputra.

Geologically, the Himalayas are among the youngest mountains in the world and are still growing in some areas — though they contain some of its oldest rocks. Their formation is believed to have been caused by the thrusting of peninsular India, once a part of the supercontinent of Gondwanaland, against the Asian landmass, a process that still continues.

The second major physical region of India is its great northern plain, also known as the Indo-Gangetic Plain, which extends immediately south of the Himalayas and parallel to it from west to east. This is the heartland of India, containing the bulk of its population, the fount of much of its popular culture, home to its granaries, big cities and industries, the playfield of its major river systems (the Indus and Ganga-Brahmaputra) and the scene of pivotal events of its history.

The plain is believed to have its origins in a deep downfold in the earth's crust, caused by the same movements that thrust up the Himalayas. Over millions of years, this depression was filled over with silt and other deposits carried by the rivers flowing down from the mountains. The Himalayan rivers, led by the Ganga, hold an exalted status in the Indian consciousness and continue to perform this task today, depositing hundreds of tonnes of alluvium daily and making the plain among the most fertile farming regions in the world. The triangular-shaped peninsula to the south forms the third great physical region of India. Geologically, it is of immense interest as, unlike the Himalayas and the northern plain, it has remained stable for aeons. For this reason, it contains some of the world's oldest rocks and continuously weathered land surfaces, and has provided much of the evidence for the Gondwanaland theory.

The peninsula is almost entirely occupied by the Deccan Plateau which is cut off from the northern plain by the Vindhya Mountains. It rises off the west coast, from which it is set apart by a very narrow plain and the 1,500-metre-high (4,900-feet) Western Ghats that run parallel to the coast.

It slopes gently towards the east, where it ends in a low, broken range called the Eastern Ghats. Further east is a somewhat broader coastal plain. To the south, the two Ghats converge to form the picturesque Nilgiri Hills (Blue Mountains).

The peninsula also has its share of big (and holy) rivers such as the Godavari, Krishna, Kaveri and Mahanadi, which flow eastwards into the Bay of Bengal, and the westward flowing Narmada and Tapti, which empty into the Arabian Sea. Compared to the alluvium of the north, the Deccan is largely composed of ancient granite and gneisses, but lava flows, up to 3,000 metres (9,850 feet) thick, to the west to form the basis for a tract of black-soil, cotton-growing country. To the north-east of the plateau is a rich mineral belt, including abundant seams of coal.

Climate
The highlight of the Indian climate is the monsoon or rainy season. The wait for the year's first shower, the beauty of the billowing, grey clouds, sheets of cool rain and the smell of wet earth, and the sheer joy of the season are ingrained in the collective Indian memory. On the mercy of the rain gods depend the crop, the well-being of the farmer and the general prosperity of the nation, besides floods and cyclones with their power to disrupt life and devastate. The arrival of the monsoon is thus a most awaited event, and its success or failure the most discussed subject every year.

Above: The verdant forests of Kerala's Silent Valley.

The climate can be divided into four seasons, with the monsoons playing the pivotal role. But the weather is not uniform all over the country and there are strong regional variations. For example, the hot, humid north-east receives over 1,000 centimetres (394 inches) of rainfall while the Thar Desert in the west and the cold desert plateau of Ladakh in the north receive less than 10 centimetres (four inches) annually.

Similarly, the higher reaches of the Himalayas experience very low temperatures while plain and peninsula become unbearably hot. In winter (December-February), it becomes colder the further north inland one travels. The Himalayas act as a cold-air source. The wind blows offshore and this season is thus cool and dry. In the north, daytime temperatures hover pleasantly around 25ºC (77ºF) but nights are often cold and frosty. In the south, especially coastal areas, the climate remains moderate.

There is a brief, pleasant and colourful spring during February-March, after which the weather grows hotter. The movement of the sun towards the Tropic of Cancer heralds a hot, dry period. Summer is at its peak in south India in April-May, and in the northern plain in May-June. Away from the moderating influence of the sea, the extreme is once more in the north and inland, with temperatures soaring to 43ºC (109ºF) in parts of the Gangetic plain.

The heat of summer is relieved by the monsoon, which flows in two currents from the Bay of Bengal and the Arabian Sea. After crossing the Andaman and Nicobar islands in late May, it reaches the mainland in early June and eventually covers the entire subcontinent by mid-July.

However, its intensity and punctuality depend on a host of global, climatic and environmental factors, and thus it remains unpredictable, temperamental, partial to different regions in different years — and utterly romantic. Some areas are subject to variations in this pattern because of topographical and oceanographic factors. Bengal is hit by storms in February-March, while Tamil Nadu receives rain in winter as well. Between the retreat of the monsoon and the onset of winter, the eastern coast is prone to devastating cyclones.

Above: Terraced fields, Uttar Pradesh.

Agriculture

Agriculture is the backbone of India's economy, its essential lifestyle and folk culture. It provides livelihood to almost 70 per cent of the country's work-force and supports about three-quarters of the total population.

Though there is an extensive network of both conventional and modern irrigation systems, agriculture remains, by and large, dependent on the monsoon.

After accounting for forest cover, wasteland, fallow land and built-up areas, some 47 per cent of India's land area is given over to cultivation.

The rich alluvial soil, deposited by the major rivers of the northern plain and in the coastal belts, occupies a quarter of India's land area. Other major natural soils are the black soil of the Deccan, the red soil of the southern peninsula, lateritic soils, forest soils and arid soils.

Crops in India are classified on the basis of the cropping season. *Kharif* crops are sown in summer, between May and July, and harvested after the rains in September-October. The important kharif crops are rice, millet, cotton and jute. *Rabi* crops are sown at the beginning of winter, during October-November, and harvested between February and April. Wheat, barley, oilseeds and pulses are the major rabi crops.

There are exceptions, of course. Long-duration crops like sugarcane, which take 10 to 18 months to mature, and such short-duration crops as vegetables automatically fall out of these categories.

Similarly, there is no such distinction in well-irrigated areas, which grow three or four crops a year, or in parts of the south, which are able to undertake sowing in winter, being blessed with rain and moderate temperatures at that time of the year.

Rice is the most important crop, ranking first in both acreage and output, followed by wheat.

Other major crops are maize, millets, sugarcane, cotton, jute, oilseeds and pulses. India is a major supplier of tea to the world market and coffee, rubber, silk, tobacco and spices are other products.

Opposite: Waterfalls, central India.

The People and Religion

Religion, ingrained in the national psyche for centuries, casts its long shadow on every Indian's life from the moment of their birth. To understand Indian religion is to understand India.

Religion is a national preoccupation dictating mindsets and lifestyles ever since Valmiki, the bandit-turned-*bhakt* (devotee), dipped his quill in ink to pen the opening invocation of the *Ramayana*, the story about Rama and Sita.

India is a curious circus of myriad religions: Hinduism, Islam, Christianity, Buddhism, Jainism, Sikhism, Judaism, Zoroastrianism and a rash of minor sects. All these have influenced one another and the course of history. Though Hinduism is the faith of the majority, the Indian Constitution honours all others equally.

Hinduism

Hinduism, the religion of 82 per cent of India's people, is so amorphous that no single text or tenet can sum up its philosophy. The routes to enlightenment are conveniently many. You can believe in Shiva, Brahma or Vishnu, plants or planets, the god of rain or the goddess of snakes, heroes based on recent history or local lore, all or none.

Hinduism, therefore, is not so much a religion as a way of life. Its tolerance and resilience has helped to preserve its sanctity under a succession of foreign invasions and to embrace alien beliefs in its purview.

Its richness can be gauged from the Hindu pantheon of deities whose variety is simply a manifestation of one divine principle: God is one, but his *avatars* (incarnations) are many. This makes Hinduism at once profound and flexible, and enhances its appeal among followers of other faiths.

Hinduism has no single spiritual source, such as the Bible, the Qur'an or *Granth Sahib*. The commandments can be said to be equally inscribed in the *Vedas*, *Upanishads* or *Puranas*. While the *Vedas* are hymns in praise of different gods, the *Upanishads* are discourses between a spiritual guide (*guru*) and a disciple (*shishya*), which stress the unity of the godhead, the concept of the soul (*atman*) surviving the human body after death, and the law of *karma*, which ascribes happiness in this life to good deeds in a previous life.

Even if you bypassed them all, it would still be possible to be a committed Hindu. Hindu philosophy can be culled from a vast corpus of extant holy literature.

The ultimate goal of a Hindu is to gain *moksha* — deliverance from the cycle of birth and rebirth. This depends on the law of *karma*. The three immediate aims in this life are pleasure (*kama*), money or fame (*artha*) and truth (*dharma*). The paths to self-realization are also three: knowledge (*jnana*), devotion (*bhakti*) and work (*karma*).

Hindus were split into four castes based on *varna* (colour) and division of labour: priests (*Brahmins*), soldiers (*Kshatriyas*), traders (*Vaishyas*) and unskilled labourers (*Shudras*). The last group performed menial jobs. Considered untouchables they were not allowed to drink from a communal well or pray at temples. Their plight improved with social awareness and with Mahatma Gandhi pronouncing them as *Harijans* (God's own people).

A Hindu's life is split into four stages (*ashramas*) of being: student and bachelor (*brahmacharya*), householder (*grihasthya*), meditator in the forest (*vanaprasthya*) and finally, renunciant of material life for the spiritual (*sanyas*). Hinduism has spawned a number of movements (Bhakti, Advaita), societies (Keshab Chandra Sen's Brahmo Samaj, Swami Dayanand Saraswati's Arya Samaj, Ramakrishna's mission), social thinkers (Kabir, Shankaracharya, Vidyasagar), cults (Vaishnavs, Shaivites), icons (*lingams, nandis*), festivals (Jagannath Rath Yatra in Puri), even reforms (widow remarriage, abolition of *sati*) and breakaway religions (Buddhism, Jainism, Sikhism).

Opposite: A monk pays homage to the Bodhi Tree, Bodhgaya.

Buddhism

Gautama or Siddhartha (566-486 BC), later known as the Buddha or 'The Enlightened One', was born into a wealthy Shakya family of *Kshatriyas* in Lumbini, in the foothills of Nepal. He found true wisdom under a *pipal* tree at Bodhgaya.

In his first address at the Sarnath Deer Park in Benaras, Buddha spoke of 'four noble truths' — the world is full of suffering; suffering is caused by desire; suffering can be removed; one must overcome desire. To do this, one must follow the 'eightfold path': right view, right thought, right speech, right action, right livelihood, right effort, right mindfulness and right concentration. The goal of Buddhism is *nirvana* — state of bliss — or spiritual liberation from the cycle of birth and rebirth.

Buddhism questioned Hindu practices like elaborate ceremonies, image worship, the elevation of *Brahmins* and the subordination of women.

Buddhism also taught equality which attracted the oppressed classes who bore the brunt of Hindu bigotry. The law of impermanence (nothing lasts) and the law of causation (nothing happens by chance) are at the centre of its philosophy. The existence of God is irrelevant to its doctrine.

Four general councils of the Buddhist church were held at Rajgriha, Vaishali, Pataliputra and Kashmir. At the first, the Buddha's teachings were compiled in the Pali canon as the *Tripitakas*. The second council in 387 BC was followed by the one at Pataliputra in 250 BC during the reign of Ashoka, one of the faith's chief proponents, when the decision to send missionaries abroad was made. Stupas and beautiful paintings of the Buddha's life in the Ajanta and Ellora caves still survive.

The fourth council, in the early second century, officially recognized the schism in Buddhism between the *Hinayanas* (travellers by the lesser vehicle) and the *Mahayanas* (travellers by the greater vehicle). Hinayana is a simple faith without religious paraphernalia though likenesses of the Buddha are also erected. Hinayana Buddhism flourished in Sri Lanka, Burma and south-east Asia, while Mahayana Buddhism has its stronghold in India, China, Japan, Tibet and central Asia.

The Buddha created monasteries (*viharas*) for both praying and preaching. The schools at Nalanda and Vikramshila in Bihar and Valabhi in Gujarat were famous. Ashwaghosha and Nagarjuna were largely responsible for the spread of Buddhism after Buddha's death.

Jainism

Vardhamana Mahavira or 'The Great Hero' (540-468 BC) was a contemporary of the Buddha. His father was head of a famous *Kshatriya* clan and his mother was a Lichchhavi princess. Mahavira became an ascetic at the age of 30 and attained perfect knowledge (*kaivalya*) at 42. He came to be known as the Jina (conqueror), and his followers, Jains. He died at Pavapuri near Rajgir. The Jain philosophy urges total renunciation. The three jewels (*ratnas*) of good living, according to Mahavira and the 23 *Tirthankaras*, are based on 'right faith, right knowledge and right action'.

Jainism is based on non-violence (*ahimsa*), so killing is forbidden. Most Jains are vegetarian and cover their mouths to avoid inadvertently swallowing germs or insects. Jain philosophy also urges self-control, asceticism and renunciation from all worldly bonds. Jain teachings had an oral tradition until the third century BC when they were collated and recorded at a council in Pataliputra. The final version of the *Angas* (Jain treatises) was edited in the fifth century AD.

The Jains have two sects — the *Digambaras* (sky-clad) and the *Shvetambaras* (white-clad). The Digambaras refuse to recognize the rearranged version of the 12 *Angas* as authentic. Unlike Buddhism, Jainism is largely confined to the trading community of western India.

Sikhism

Guru Nanak (1469-1539) founded Sikhism in India which draws elements from both Hinduism and Islam. His followers, under a succession of 10 *gurus* (spiritual guides) after his death, came to be known as Sikhs and worshipped in *gurudwaras* (abodes of the *gurus*). He preached the importance of *Satnam* (worshipping the true name, or one God) and the indispensability of the right *guru* for self-realization. He believed in the role of *karma* in the attainment of *moksha*, the highest bliss and did not favour idol worship, casteism or asceticism. When his son tried to form a sect of *Udasis* he was discouraged. Nanak introduced the concept of a common kitchen (*langar*) to feed the poor. His follower Guru Angad popularized the Gurmukhi script. Guru Ram Das founded Amritsar. Guru Arjun Dev made the *Granth Sahib* their holy book.

It was the tenth guru, Govind Singh, who made Sikhs into a militant group and started the Sikh canon (*khalsa*). He decreed that the Sikhs always carry the five Ks as identification: long hair tied in a turban (*kesh*), comb (*kangha*), iron bracelet (*kara*), dagger (*kirpan*) and underwear (*kachcha*). The Sikhs under him fought the Mughals in the first and second battles of Anandpur.

Islam

The period from 1200 to 1707 represents Muslim domination of India. First introduced by Arab traders, conversions to Islam were of two types — those that were forced by foreign invaders, and those that took place voluntarily by members of the lower castes and other oppressed sections. A third category traces its lineage to foreigners who came and settled there in the wake of invasions. The first Muslim invasion occurred in the eighth century, but the first real clash between Hinduism and Islam came in the 12th century when Mahmud of Ghazni and Mohammed Ghuri carried out a succession of raids.

Qutb-ud-din Aibak formed the Slave Dynasty, which launched the 300-year-old Sultanate that ruled over India from Delhi. The Khaljis, Tughluqs, Sayyids and Lodis were followed by the Mughals. The Hindus and Muslims, in the face of the British threat, made a stormy alliance until Independence in 1947 and the unhappy division of the nation into India and Pakistan. The Muslims, who now form 11 per cent of the population, are India's second largest community and are scattered all over the country. The Hindu-Muslim interaction has produced an extraordinarily rich culture in music, architecture, cuisine and literature.

Sufi and Bhakti movements

The Sufis maintained that fasts or prayers could not replace true faith. They were considered heretics by the orthodox Muslims. At Sufi gatherings *Qawwalis* were sung. There were several orders under different *pirs* or sheikhs, of which those of Salim Chishti, Suhrawardy and Firdausi, were most important. Another popular saint was Nizam-ud-din Auliya, respected by Hindus and Muslims alike.

The Bhakti movement received a fresh fillip under the Sufi influence. It tried to resist discrimination against women and lower castes. The most significant contributions were made by Kabir (1440-1518) and Nanak (1469-1539). Kabir's beautiful couplets (*dohas*) express his philosophy of brotherhood and tolerance. His followers came to be known as Kabirpanthis.

Christianity

There are 30 million Christians in India. They are peaceful, forward-looking and the third largest community in India, primarily from the southern states of Tamil Nadu, Kerala and Karnataka, and Goa. Some say Christianity came to India with St Bartholomew, others insist it was St James. But they became a force to reckon with when the Europeans and the English, affiliated to different churches, began missionary work. St Francis Xavier, who came to India in the 16th century, and whose body lies in a church in Goa, spearheaded Christian missionary activity in the country. Their good work in the fields of reform and education continues to be admired.

Zoroastrianism

The Parsis are mostly clustered in and around Mumbai. They came years ago from Persia to avoid persecution and to trade with India. They are worshippers of the sun and the earth with fire and water central to their religion. Their Sun and Fire temples, Towers of Silence and Navroz ceremonies are well known.

Judaism

There were 30,000 Jews in India at independence in 1947. Though many left, the

Above: Temples at Amarkantak, the source of the Narmada River.

remaining few are the Kochi Jews of Kerala and the Bene Israel of Mumbai, a close-knit minority, mostly professionals.

Racial groups

India is a multi-hued, multi-lingual swarming milieu best described as many nations rolled in one.

The racial groups are the Negritos (Andamans), Proto-Austroloids (Indus Valley civilization and most modern tribals), Mongoloids (Ladakh, Sikkim and the north-eastern hills), Paleo-Mediterraneans or Dravidians (south), Mediterraneans (Punjab, Rajasthan and Uttar Pradesh), Western Bradrychycephals (parts of West Bengal, Orissa, Gujarat, Maharashtra and the south, besides Coorgs and Parsis), and the Nordics or Indo-Aryans (Jammu and Kashmir, Punjab, Haryana, Rajasthan and the Gangetic area).

Tribal groups

With more than 50 tribal groups the important ones are the Abhors (north-east), Adivasis (Bastar, Madhya Pradesh), Angami (Manipur), Bhils (Dravidians of central India), Garos, Khasis and Jaintiyas (Assam and Meghalaya), Lushai (Tripura), Nagas (Nagaland), Santhals (West Bengal, Bihar and Orissa) and Todas (Nilgiri Hills, Tamil Nadu).

Population

The population in 1996 was over 830 million. Calcutta is the most populated city.

Languages

Indian languages belong to four major groups — Indo-Aryan, (Hindi, Sanskrit, Bengali, Marathi, Gujarati, Punjabi, Oriya, Assamese, Kashmiri and Urdu) spoken by three-fifths of the population; Dravidian, (Tamil, Telugu, Kannada and Malayalam); Sino-Tibetan; and Austro-Asiatic.

The Indian Constitution recognizes 15 languages, the 14 mentioned above and Sindhi.

Hindi (Devnagari script) is the official language, but English is the language of commerce, federal government, higher courts, science, technology and higher education.

PART TWO: PLACES AND TRAVEL

Above: An elaborately decorated truck, Karnataka.

Delhi: Mosques, Temples and Tombs

Delhi, the capital of modern India, is one of the ancient cities of the world. As narrated in the *Mahabharata*, Delhi is identified with Indraprastha, the city founded by the Pandavas in the sixth century BC.

The five towns claimed by the Pandavas — Inderpat, Sonipat, Panipat, Tilpat and Baghpat — still exist under their original names in the vicinity of Delhi. The growth of cities like Mathura, Kannauj and Patiliputra relegated Delhi to oblivion until the Tomaras established Dhillika in AD 736 around the ancient Indraprastha. Later they moved to Anangpur near Surajkund and finally built Lal Kot, Delhi's first extant fort near the Qutb Minar. Delhi's recorded history begins from this point in the 12th century. The traditionally mentioned seven cities of Delhi are, in fact, the seven citadels of the medieval period — Lal Kot, Siri, Tughluqabad, Jahanpanah, Firuzabad, Dinpanah, Shahjahanabad. Indraprastha was, perhaps, the first Delhi, as New Delhi is the most recent.

Getting there
The Indira Gandhi International Airport receives flights from every corner of the world. Express and luxury trains connect Delhi to the rest of India. Convenient buses, some air-conditioned, ply to the major Indian cities, and to the north Indian hill-stations and surrounding tourist sites.

When to go
The summer months between April and August are best avoided.

Where to stay
Hotel Ashok, Centaur Hotel, Holiday Inn, Crown Plaza, Hotel Sofitel, Hyatt Regency, Le Meridien, Oberoi Inter-Continental, the Taj Mahal, the Taj Palace Inter-Continental and Maurya Sheraton are some of the luxury hotels. Claridges Hotel, Imperial Hotel, Siddhartha Hotel and hotels run by the Indian Tourist Development Corporation, namely Kanishka, Samrat and Qutb provide five-star accommodation.

Ambassador, Diplomat, Hans Plaza, Janpath, Marina, Nirula's Hotel, Oberoi Maidens and Park Hotel are other options. Ashok Yatri Niwas, Central Point, Fifty-Five, Lodhi (ITDC), President, Ranjit (ITDC), Vikram, YMCA International Guest House and YMCA Tourist Hotel are budget hotels.

Sightseeing
To be able to see the most important monuments in Delhi it is best to visit the better known ones in clusters. The Rajput and rulers of the Delhi Sultanate are responsible for the **Qutb area,** girdled by the walls of **Lal Kot,** and its later southern extension, the **Qila Rai Pithora.** The large tank called the **Anang Tal** was enlarged by successive rulers, who used it for building the **Qutb Minar** and the **mosque.**

Under the shadow of the Qutb, the exquisitely sculptured pillars of the corridors once belonged to the Tomar and Rajput temples. At the back of the arched screen stands the sanctum of the Vishnu Temple, the core of Lal Kot. Today, the defaced sculptures speak of the superior craftsmanship of those Hindu artisans. The seven-metre (23-feet) **Iron Pillar** in the courtyard belongs to the Gupta period (AD 320-606).

The inscription records the victorious exploits of Chandra Gupta II. Amazingly the column has remained free of rust through 1,600 years of sun and shower. The *garuda* (vehicle of Vishnu) crowning the pillar has since been removed. Visitors are asked by local guides to stand with their backs to the shaft and encircle it with their arms. The successful will win a kingdom, so the story goes.

The mosque, Delhi's first, was built in 1193 by Aibak, Muhammad Ghuri's slave general and deputy. Though work on the Qutb Minar began in 1199, it was completed by Iltutmish, Aibak's successor. Originally built in four storeys, the thrice repaired 73-metre (240-feet) tower has alternating semi-circular and angular fluting. The stalactite ornamentation below the projected balconies and the superbly

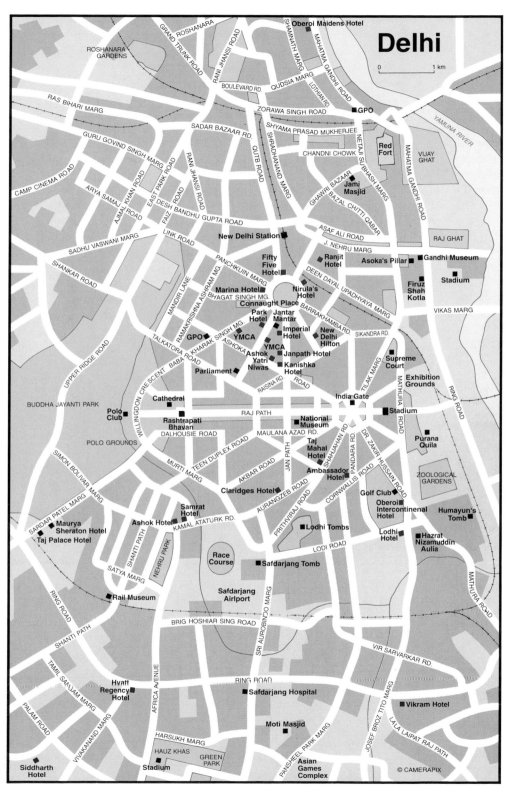

51

Above: A devotee at Tirupati, Andhra Pradesh.

calligraphed bands of Qur'anic inscriptions are examples of sheer perfection in stonecraft.

In 1368, Firuz Shah Tughluq removed the damaged fourth storey and replaced it with two circular storeys of lavishly carved white marble.

The tower was once crowned with a highly incongruous **pavilion**, which now rests in the south-east quarter of the garden. Iltutmish also built the wing of arches west of the Qutb. Behind the mosque lies the small but lavishly sculptured **Tomb of Iltutmish**. The huge but unfinished core of a tower is the **Alai Minar,** an attempt by Ala-ud-din Khalji to dwarf the Qutb which was brought to a halt by his sudden death in 1316. However, **Alai Darwaza,** a splendid gateway southeast of the Qutb, with elegant alternating bands of calligraphy in marble and red sandstone, was completed before his death.

The arches are perfect and the squinch dome a marvel of architecture. His **tomb**

Opposite: Delhi's Qutb Minar.

and *madrasah* (school) at the Qutb are also worth a visit. Beside the Qutb stands the 16th-century **Jamali Kamali Mosque**. The small tomb of the poet-saint has the most spectacular stucco ornamentation in blue and turquoise geometrical and floral patterns. If it is closed, find the caretaker and insist on being shown Delhi's most gorgeously decorated ceiling.

Near the Mehrauli bus terminus are two stepped-wells — the **Gandak ki Baoli**, built by Iltutmish, and the **Rajon ki Baoli** of the Lodi period. The octagonal Mughal **Tomb of Adham Khan** stands on a high platform near the Rajon ki Baoli. **Qutb Sahib ki Dargah** is the tomb and shrine of the Sufi saint Qutb-ud-din Bakhtiyar Kaki, patron saint of Iltutmish. The **Yog Maya Temple,** on the way back to the Qutb, gave Delhi one of its earlier names, Yoginipura.

The ruins of Aibak's **White Palace** have emerged from centuries-old debris at the excavation site within the Lal Kot area. The ruins of a mammoth fort, **Tughluqabad,** built within four years (1321-25) and then abandoned, lies 10 kilometres (six miles) south-east of the Qutb. The **Tomb of Ghiyas-ud-din Tughluq** stands within a small fortress opposite the fort. This red sandstone tomb crowned with a marble dome, has splendidly buttressed walls, typical of Tughluq architecture, and an overall rugged character. The tomb is well preserved.

The haunting ruins of **Adilabad,** a fortress built by Muhammad Tughluq, son of Ghiyas-ud-din, are certainly worth a visit, but even the adventurous should only go as a group.

The **Hauz Khas** area, lying roughly between the **Safdarjang Hospital** and the Qutb, has some interesting monuments. An austere work with buttressed walls, the **Tomb of Firuz Shah Tughluq,** is surrounded by small structures of a school for religious instruction. The monuments overlook a huge reservoir called **Hauz-i-Alai** or **Hauz Khas** built by Ala-ud-din Khalji. In recent years, the rustic looking **Hauz Khas Village**, on the way to the monuments, has come up as Delhi's sophisticated and high-priced market for ethnic 'designer wear' and exotic restaurants. The setting there is ideal for an evening's entertainment. The

Village Bistro and **Delhi Tourism** organize two package tours in the afternoon and evening which include sightseeing and shopping. The evening package has the added attraction of folk dances performed against a backdrop of floodlit monuments. **Duke's Place** in the Village is Delhi's only restaurant that serves up jazz with the food.

A short distance from Hauz Khas is the **Siri Fort Auditorium** and **restaurant complex** primarily used for international film festivals. Founded by Ala-ud-din Khalji in 1303, Siri's ruins are still in evidence. **Badi Manzil**, a palace in utter ruins atop a prominence, the grand **Begampuri Mosque** with a stately court, arched cloisters and a high pylon built by Firuz Shah Tughluq, the **Khirki Masjid**, another Tughluq creation with a covered court, battered walls and a large number of domes, are all worth a visit. The **Chor Minar**, an intriguing tower built by Ala-ud-din Khalji to display the severed heads of Mongol offenders as a warning against crime is, despite its gruesome history, an interesting monument. Lady Willingdon Park, the present **Lodi Gardens**, is a spectacular setting for a cluster of modest tombs of the Sayyid and Lodi rulers. The octagonal tomb of Muhammad Shah, the double-domed garden **Tomb of Sikandar Lodi** and the square tombs of the Lodi nobles, are splendid in their simplicity. In 1504 Delhi was abandoned by the Lodis for Agra.

Close by, the last Mughal monument of remarkable splendour, the **Safdarjang Tomb**, stands on a high platform amid extensive gardens. Built in 1753-54 by the Nawab of Avadh for his father, the tomb and gardens were modelled after the Humayun Tomb.

Undoubtedly Delhi's most beautiful and finest garden tomb is the **Humayun Tomb** in the **Nizamuddin Area**. Built in 1565 by his widow, the tomb was designed by the Persian architect Mirak Mirza Ghiyas, and served as a model for the Taj Mahal. The high-walled garden laid out in the typical Islamic pattern of a *charbagh* is still maintained in its original plan. Rising 43 metres (141 feet) from the terrace, the tomb is crowned with a 'double-dome' in white

Above: A detail of carved façade, Qutb Minar.

marble. The inner dome forms the vaulted ceiling and the outer shell creates the soaring effect. The cenotaph lies under the dome while the grave itself lies in the basement below. The red sandstone structure is discreetly ornamented with white marble and the four corner *chattris* or canopies add a touch of the Orient. On the high terrace are the graves of the less fortunate Mughals — Dara Shikoh, Farrukhsiyar and Alamgir II.

A host of smaller monuments stand in the vicinity — **Arab ki Serai,** where the 300 Persian craftsmen engaged in building Humayun's Tomb were housed; **Isa Khan's Tomb** and **Mosque**, a noble at Sher Shah's court; **Nila Gumbad**, outside the garden of the Humayun Tomb, with its blue tile decoration and exquisite ceiling; the lovely stucco work of the **Subz Burz** at the junction of Mathura Road and Lodi Road — are noteworthy. The **dargah** (shrine) of Nizam-ud-din, a Chishti saint who lived through the Balban and Ala-ud-din Khalji dynasties,

attracts thousands of admirers and devotees all through the year, especially during the saint's death anniversary ceremonies, the annual *Urs*.

Sharing the same courtyard with the saint are the **graves** of his disciple and friend **Amir Khusro Muhammed Shah** and **Jahanara Begum**, who was Shah Jahan's eldest daughter. Her grass-filled, open-to-the-sky grave carries a humble epitaph which she wrote herself: 'Let naight (sic) cover my grave save the green grass, for grass suffices as the covering for the lowly.' The *baoli* or stepped-well at the southern corner of the enclosure is still in use.

Through the narrow market lane overflowing with people, lesser known, but nonetheless exquisite, tombs wait to be appreciated — **Atagha Khan's Tomb** is small but profusely decorated with tiles and white marble; **Chausath Khamba** is a uniquely designed white marble hall with grand columns joined by superbly executed *jali* (lattice) screens; and **Kalan Masjid**, one of the seven grand mosques built by Firuz Shah Tughluq. If you have accepted the crowds at Delhi's monuments, you will miss them at **Purana Qila** (Old Fort), built by Humayun in 1539. Humayun founded a new city called Dinpanah and had hardly completed the ramparts and mammoth gateways when he was toppled by Sher Shah, who built a magnificent mosque and a few palaces in the new city of Sher Garh. In 1555, Humayun reclaimed his lost kingdom, using **Sher Mandal**, the octagonal tower built by Sher Shah, as his library. He met his death when one day he tumbled down its steep stairs.

While neither Dinpanah nor Sher Garh can be traced, the magnificent **Qila-i-Kuhna Mosque** stands testimony to the unfulfilled architectural plans of Sher Shah.

Outside the Purana Qila is the mammoth **Lal Darwaza**, on the boundary of Sher Garh. **Khooni Darwaza**, another gateway of Sher Shah's city, stands near Kotla. The **Khairul Manzil Masjid**, adjacent to the Lal Darwaza, was built in 1561. The **National Zoological Park** lies south of Purana Qila.

Pragati Maidan, on the Mathura Road beside Purana Qila, is a sprawling exhibition ground drawing millions of visitors to the International Trade and Book Fairs every year. All the 26 Indian states have permanent pavilions there. A pool-side restaurant, markets, cinema halls, open-air theatres and **Appu Ghar**, a children's park, complete the complex. The Nehru Pavilion, the Atomic Energy and Defence Pavilions and the Hall of Nations, an architectural marvel, are also of interest.

The **Crafts Museum** at Pragati Maidan houses more than 20,000 specimens of traditional Indian tribal and folk crafts from all over the country, and includes rich collections of terracotta, bronzes, enamel work, wood carving, jewellery and textiles. Master craftsmen are invited to hold their art demonstrations at Craft Fairs, open between 0930 and 1700 every day, except Mondays.

Firuz Shah Kotla, the fifth city of Muslim Delhi, stands today on Bahadur Shah Zafar Marg. All its fabulous palaces were destroyed by Timur in 1398 and the stones plundered for building the city of Shahjahanabad in 1648. The greatest attraction at the Kotla is the **Ashokan Pillar**, brought from Meerut by Firuz Shah. Untarnished even after more than 2,000 years, the pillar carries Ashokan injunctions against religious schisms. The great **mosque** at Kotla stands in utter ruins except for a *baoli*. Another **Ashokan Pillar,** from Ambala, stands at the northern ridge, near the hunting lodge of Firuz Shah, the present **Bada Hindu Rao Hospital**.

Rajghat, the black marble *samadhi* (memorial) of Mahatma Gandhi, set amid sprawling gardens on the Ring Road, is nearby. On the same road, towards the Red Fort, are the *samadhis* of former Indian prime ministers. The **Gandhi Memorial Museum** stands across the road.

The **Red Fort** is the most splendid example of Mughal architecture. Completed in 1648, it is Shah Jahan's greatest gift to Delhi. Entry is through the Lahori Gate. **Chatta Chowk**, with an impressive Gothic arch and an octagonal open court, now a bustling market for tourist bric-à-brac, antiques, miniature paintings and fake ivory carvings, was once the royal bazaar.

The **Diwan-i-Aam** (Hall of Public Audience), where Shah Jahan held court, stands beyond the **Naqqar Khana**. The splendid marble canopy over the royal throne is inlaid with precious stones and decorated with exquisite *pietra dura* panels behind the throne. Of particular beauty is the Orpheus Panel, the work of Austin de Bordeaux. These panels were removed and sold to a London museum during the British occupation of the fort, but Lord Curzon had them restored to their original setting.

The harem palaces on the river front are also worth a visit. The **Rang Mahal** has a lotus-shaped fountain fashioned out of a single block of marble. **Mumtaz Mahal** now houses the museum. The magnificent lattice screen below the Scales of Justice at the **Khwabgah**, the emperor's exclusive quarters are splendid artistry.

The fabulous **Peacock Throne**, a solid gold frame studded with rubies, emeralds and diamonds, once stood in the **Diwan-i-Khas** (Hall of Private Audience). The pure silver ceiling added to its splendour. Amir

Khusro's verse 'If there is a Paradise on the face of the earth, it is here, it is here, it is here' is inscribed on two panels over the engraved marble arches. The Diwan-i-Khas witnessed both the splendour of Shah Jahan's court and the decline of Mughal power when Nadir Shah, the Persian invader, humiliated the Mughal king, Muhammad Shah II in 1739 and made off with the Koh-i-Noor diamond and the Peacock Throne. The present wooden ceiling was painted by the British.

Moti Masjid, built by Aurangzeb, is an architectural gem. The glass mosaics in the crumbling **Shah Burj** are still gorgeous. The desolate marble pavilions — **Sawan and Bhadon** — stand over water channels in the **Hayat Baksh Garden**. The other royal garden — Mahtab Bagh, was completely destroyed by the British to make room for barracks.

Built of red sandstone, **Jami Masjid**, Shahjahanabad's chief congregational mosque is the pride of Mughal architecture. The arched corridors around the grand courtyard, the five-arched façade of screens on the western front and the central ablution tank, speak eloquently of its impeccable proportions.

The slender 40-metre (131-feet) minarets are distinctively Mughal. Their three onion-shaped domes dominate the city. For a small fee it is possible to climb a minaret to catch a glimpse into the maze of alleys and congested markets behind the mosque. **Chandni Chowk** (Silver Square), the market and cultural centre of Shahjahanabad, was built by Jahanara Begum. It remains one of India's most fascinating bazaars.

Though the various ancient cities of Delhi and their monuments carry the distinctive stamp of the dynasties which built them, the British chose the new Imperial style for their buidings when **New Delhi** became the capital of the British Raj in 1911. Two architects, Lutyens and Baker, created the masterpieces in sandstone on Raisina Hill. Lutyens' Viceroy's House, now called **Rashtrapati Bhawan**, has a grand 36-column façade topped by a majestic copper dome, recalling the dome of the Sanchi Stupa and its splendid stone railing. Its 340 palatial rooms include a Darbar Hall, a dining room and various reception rooms. The Mughal Garden is complete with lotus fountains and a circular pool, open to visitors in February every year.

The 44-metre (144-feet) Jaipur column, with a glass star sprouting from a bronze lotus, stands sentinel in the forecourt. The high grill gates deserve a closer look for their lace-like workmanship. Visits inside Rashtrapati Bhawan can be arranged on prior application to the Public Relations Officer, Rashtrapati Bhawan.

Baker's twin **Secretariat Blocks** recall the dome of St Paul's Cathedral in London. The view of Rajpath from this end of Raisina Hill is panoramic. The circular building of the Imperial Legislative Council, the present-day **Parliament House**, is Baker's work of Lutyens' design. The All India War Memorial, better known as **India Gate**, is set amid acres of lawns, fountains and canals around which traffic flows in a ceaseless whirl. Two churches built by Henry Medd, the **Cathedral Church of Redemption** and the **Cathedral Church of the Sacred Heart**, stand near Parliament House.

Connaught Place is New Delhi's prestigious shopping centre. Close by, **Jantar Mantar**, the observatory built by Sawai Jai Singh in 1725 to revise the calendar and correct the astronomical tables used by contemporary priests, is an intriguing set of huge masonry instruments. The largest instrument, the Samrat Yantra, is a huge right-angled, triangular sundial.

The **Baha'i (Lotus) Temple** in south Delhi is the latest addition to Delhi's places of worship. Shaped like a lotus in bloom — three sets of nine petals, nine arches, nine pools — the temple sits in the middle of 24 acres (10 hectares) of lush landscape. There are no rituals, no priests, no idols and no lectures. The interior is austere, merely a place for meditation.

The Ashokan rock edict in **Srinivaspuri**, which has only recently come to light, takes our knowledge about the city's origin to the third century BC.

The **National Museum** at Janpath was formed from the nucleus of the Exhibition of Indian Art in London (1947). Today it has grown into one of the country's most prestigious museums providing a comprehensive review of ethnological objects, from prehistoric archaeological finds to art objects of medieval India. It has India's richest collection of ancient sculptures, miniature paintings, illustrated manuscripts, arms and textiles. Open from 1000 to 1700 except Mondays. A small fee is charged for entrance and camera.

The **Rail Museum** in Chanakyapuri, the first of its kind in India, has on permanent exhibition 26 vintage locomotives, 17 carriages and saloons, plus a complete armoured train. The star attractions are the Fairy Queen (1855), the oldest functioning locomotive; a small Darjeeling-Himalayan railway engine; a four-wheeled saloon used by the Prince of Wales in 1876; the Mysore Maharaja's Saloon, made of seasoned teak with gold and ivory embellishment, built to run on both metre and broad gauges and, the eight-wheeled Viceregal dining car, complete with upholstery and a kitchen fitted with a refrigerator. The museum, set in a 10-acre (four-hectare) garden, also offers joy train rides. It is open from Tuesday to Sunday from 0930 to 1730. Closed on Mondays.

Shopping

Connaught Place, in the heart of the city, is the centre for most markets. **Palika Bazaar, Central Cottage Industries Emporium** and the **Janpath Tibetan stalls** are a treasure trove of exotic Indian crafts. The **State Emporia Complex** on Baba Kharak Singh Marg makes available the choicest *objets d'art* from all the Indian states. Bargaining over prices is not allowed, though frequently the shops offer authentic discounts. Open 1000 to 1900, but closed on Sundays.

Chandni Chowk in Old Delhi is a true oriental market selling an amazing variety of goods — antiques, gold and silver jewellery, paintings, bronze and brass goods, cotton and silk, brocades and leather items.

In fact, almost anything you fancy can be bought there. **Sunder Nagar Market** is worth visiting for real and fake antiques, miniature paintings and precious stones. **Khan Market**, **South Extension** and the **Greater Kailash markets** are for the rich and trendy, where boutiques and department stores sell expensive fashion garments, jewellery and the like.

Excursions from Delhi

Beyond Tughluqabad, 16 kilometres (10 miles) south of Delhi, **Surajkund** (in Haryana) is the site of the historic amphitheatre sunpool dating back to the 11th century. The sun temple, now in utter ruins, once stood on the western side of the reservoir. Surajkund was part of the Tomar settlement before they moved to the Qutb area. In February, the **Surajkund Crafts Fair**, is a wonderful opportunity to watch master craftsmen at work — weavers, potters, block-makers, marble and metal workers, embroiderers and enamel artisans, acrobats and folk dancers.

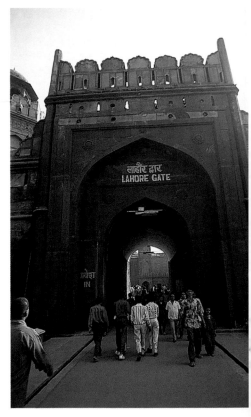

Above: The splendid Red Fort is Shah Jahan's greatest gift to Delhi. Entry is through the Lahore Gate.

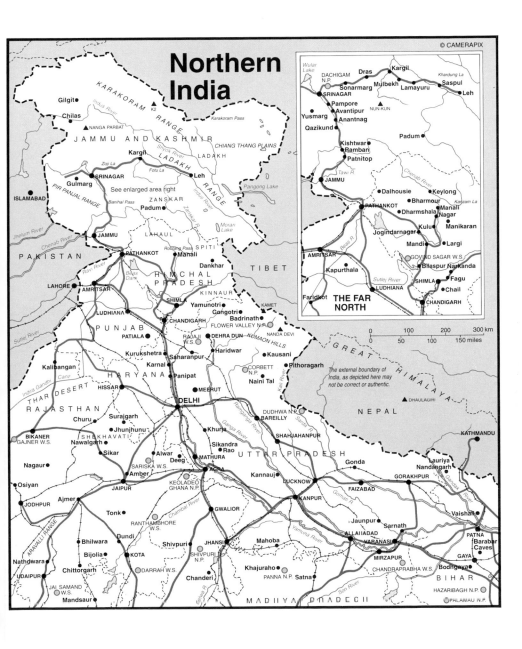

© CAMERAPIX

Northern India

THE FAR NORTH

0   100   200   300 km
0   50   100   150 miles

The external boundary of
India, as depicted here may
not be correct or authentic.

Jammu and Kashmir

Jammu: Charm and Culture

Most people miss Jammu in their hurry to escape the heat of the plains and reach the Kashmir Valley, but Jammu has its charms — a history of valiant kings, important contributions to art and religion, and lakes, rivers and forests tucked away in its rugged regions. The first settlement of Jammu is said to have been established by King Jamulochan in the ninth century BC when he was struck by the sanctity of a spot where a tiger and a goat were drinking from the same pond. In 1730, Dogra rule brought about a flourishing of art and culture.

Getting there
Jammu is connected by air with Delhi, Chandigarh and Srinagar. The two quickest trains to Jammu from Delhi are the Jammu Mail and the 172 Up Superfast Express. Buses ply regularly from Delhi, Srinagar, Chandigarh, Pathankot, Dharamsala and Shimla.

When to go
The summers are hot and dusty as in most of northern India. September to March is the best time to visit Jammu.

Where to stay
For an overnight's stay, the Tourist Reception Centre is best. Otherwise many hotels and lodges, of which the more luxurious are the Asia Jammu Tawi, Hotel Jammu Ashok, Vardan Hotel, Mansar Hotel and Airlines Lodge, are available. See listings for 'Hotels'.

Sightseeing
If you plan to spend a day in Jammu en route to Kashmir, visit the **Bahu Fort** built on the rock-face overlooking the Tawi River, five kilometres (three miles) from the heart of town. It houses a temple of the goddess Kali and, although Dogra rulers repaired the fort during their reign, the original construction dates back almost 3,000 years. The **Amar Mahal Palace Museum** and **Dogra Art Gallery** display fine miniatures of the Pahari, Jammu and Basohli schools, sculptures and excavated artefacts. Both displays are closed on Mondays. The **Raghunath** and **Ranbireshwar** temples are important landmarks.

Excursions from Jammu
For those who wish to venture out of Jammu, **Mansar Lake**, surrounded by hills, is 80 kilometres (50 miles) east, and is connected by bus. Accommodation at tourist bungalows or family huts. The **Vaishnu Devi Shrine**, 62 kilometres (38 miles) north, is an important place of pilgrimage reached by bus, car or helicopter, with the last stretch by pony or on foot.

Kashmir: Paradise on Earth

Bounded by Pakistan and China in its northern regions and by Punjab, Himachal Pradesh, Tibet and China in the south and east, Jammu and Kashmir have been a constituent state of India since 1947.

Today, parts of Jammu and Kashmir are occupied by Pakistan and China. It comprises the rugged rustic Jammu division, Kashmir, the 'Paradise on Earth' and awe-inspiring Ladakh. Each has its own history and culture and reflects Hindu, Muslim and Buddhist influences which have contributed to eras of philosophical, religious, literary and artistic enlightenment.

According to legend, the sea goddess Sati once covered the entire valley of Kashmir. Sati, who was Lord Shiva's wife, was also known as Parvati. An ascetic named Kashyap prayed that the lake should dry up. When it happened, the habitable land came to be known as Kashmira and later Kashmir. In the third century BC, the great

Previous pages: Fishing on the Dal Lake, Srinagar.

Above: An indigenous boat, commonly seen in Srinagar.

Mauryan emperor, Ashoka, sent Buddhist missionaries to Ladakh and Kashmir when the first town was established at Srinagar.

The region became a great centre of Hindu culture, and was ruled by successive Hindu dynasties until the 14th century, when it came under Muslim rule. Kashmir was annexed to the Sikh kingdom of Punjab in 1819 and came under Dogra rule in 1846.

It was under the Dogra ruler Hari Singh that Kashmir acceded to India in 1947, retaining a special status under Article 370 of the Indian Constitution. It has its own constitution, adopted in 1956.

According to Persian history, Jammu saw political power in AD 900. Evidence of Neolithic settlements in Burzahom in Kashmir indicates that this area was inhabited between 2300 and 1500 BC.

Evidence of a primitive culture in Jammu exists in the form of Stone Age tools and pottery unearthed at Akhnoor and Ambaran. The first inhabitants of Ladakh were nomadic shepherds who lived in black, animal-skin tents. Even today, in the Chiang Thang plains, these dwellings are used. The Chiang tribes earlier practised an animistic form of religion called *Bon Pa*, and despite the arrival of Buddhism with Ashoka's missionaries, it was only when the Tibetans conquered Ladakh between the seventh and 10th centuries AD, that the culture became feudal and the people took to Buddhism.

Islam was introduced around 1675 and Sikh patronage in Jammu between 1819 and 1846 saw the establishment of well-known schools of miniature painting.

With valleys, rivers and lakes the state boasts some of the most majestic mountain vistas in the world. The Pir Panjal and the Himalayas, with K2 the world's second-highest peak, Ladakh, a high-altitude desert at over 3,353 metres (11,000 feet), and snow-covered slopes and icy glaciers, pine forests and mountain trails all offer a variety of moods and experiences.

Above: View of Alchi and Saspool, Ladakh, Jammu Kashmir.

Srinagar and the Valley

Srinagar, located in the heart of the valley, is the summer capital of the government. At a height of 1,730 metres (5,676 feet), summer temperatures range from 30°C (86°F) to 10°C (50°F). Winters are cold with temperatures of 7°C (45°F) during the day, and minus 2°-3°C (28°-27°F) at night. Apart from a spring full of cherry, apple and almond blossoms, and a golden-red autumn when the grand *chinar* trees shed their maple-like leaves, the valley also gets the last of the south-west monsoons between July and September. The sunny summers are ideal for swimming or water-skiing while winter is perfect for snow-sports. The present Srinagar city was founded by Pravarasena II. Hsuan Tsang, who visited it in AD 631, described it at its present location. King Lalitaditya was among the more illustrious Hindu rulers, who in the eighth century built the grand Sun Temple in Martand. King Zain-ul-Abedin, 1420-70, introduced highly skilled artisanship and contributed greatly to the flowering of the arts. Akbar, the Mughal king, endowed Srinagar with its captivating gardens and mosques. Carpet weaving, fine silk and woollen embroideries, walnut wood carving, engraved copperwork and basketry demonstrate centuries-old talent. Today, Srinagar is the hub of both handicrafts production and the tourism industry.

Getting there

The Valley is connected by daily flights to Delhi, Amritsar, Jammu, Chandigarh, Leh, Ahmedabad and Mumbai. Flights to Leh are occasionally cancelled in winter because

Opposite: Women of Kashmir Valley.

of bad weather. The Delhi-Srinagar flight takes an hour, while Jammu-Srinagar is a half-hour hop. Travelling by train, the nearest railhead is Jammu Tawi, 305 kilometres (189 miles) from Srinagar. Jammu Tawi is well connected to all parts of the country by the Jammu Mail, Super fast Express, Sealdah Express, Shalimar Express, Jhelum Express, Himgiri and Himsagar Express, and Pathankot passenger train. Trains connect with bus services to the valley. It takes about eight hours, driving through the picturesque Patnitop, Batote and Banihal Tunnel. All these stops have comfortable tourist facilities.

Taxis ply between Jammu and Srinagar. If you travel by road from Delhi, plan to spend the night at Jammu, or in cooler climes, at Patnitop, before the second lap to the valley. The well maintained highway is closed occasionally for a few hours between Ramban and Qazikund, particularly after heavy rain or snowfalls.

When to go
Srinagar is at its most beautiful in late April, May and early June. After a warm spell, September and October becomes very pleasant. For those who like winter sports and plenty of snow, January to March at Gulmarg is the best time.

Where to stay
Srinagar's hotels and the unique house-boats on the Jhelum River, and the Dal and Nagin lakes, are graded according to their tariffs and facilities as de luxe, A, B, C and D categories. Hotel Oberoi Palace and Centaur Lake View Hotel offer stunning views and comfort. Broadway, nearer town, has a swimming pool.

There are many A-grade hotels on the Boulevard overlooking the Dal Lake, with plenty of handicraft shops within reach. Hotel Dar es Salaam, and Lake Isle Resort are on the Nagin Lake, a quieter locality near the famed Hazaratbal Shrine. Category-B hotels are on Shervani Road, Sonwar, Lambert Lane, Residency Road and on the Boulevard. Lal Chowk and Dal Gate bring you into the bazaar area with lower tariffs and easy access to shops, transport and crowds. Houseboats have living rooms, bedrooms with hot and cold water, well equipped dining rooms, a cook and a waiter, and a *shikara* taxi to get about. The boats are decorated with ornate wood carving, walnut wood furniture and carpets, and have wonderful decks and balconies for sunbathing or relaxing at sunset. Huts on the Chashma Shahi can be booked for an entire family on a monthly basis and the Tourist Reception Centre at the Tourist Hotel in Srinagar has short-stay facilities for trekkers and budget groups.

Sightseeing
A serene pace underlies all sightseeing if you choose to make the shikara your mode of transportation to see the gardens, waterways, famous mosques and old Srinagar. Boarding at **Dal Gate**, the shikara will wind past apiaries, floating vegetable gardens, tiny residential hotels, majestic house-boats, old wooden houses with wide overhanging balconies and provide glimpses of the people of Kashmir whose lives revolve around the lakes.

The shikara will emerge at **Nagin Lake** and stop at the **Nagin Club**. A short walk away are willow basketry shops and the famed **Hazaratbal Mosque** with its single minaret. It is specially revered, as a sacred hair of the Prophet Mohammed is preserved there. It is displayed on special occasions. Across Nagin Lake is **Hari Parbat Fort**, built by an Afghan governor in the 18th century. The wall around the hill was raised in the 16th century by Emperor Akbar. Facilities on Nagin Lake include water-skiing and swimming off special swimming boats.

Another shikara ride, off the tourist track, follows the Jhelum River. It starts from **Zero Bridge** and passes through the heart of the city.

Srinagar has seven bridges over the Jhelum and the Zero Bridge gets its name because it is located before the first or **Badshah Bridge**. A halt at the **Shah**

Opposite: The sun sets over the Dal Lake.

Hamdan Mosque, one of the oldest in the city, is worthwhile because it has Kashmir's famous papier mâché work on its ceiling. **Pather Masjid**, built of stone by Nur Jahan, is opposite the Shah Hamdan Mosque. At the third bridge, the handicraft centre hums with shawl embroidery and carpet weaving activities. Narrow alleyways, wooden houses, children playing cricket and old people smoking hookahs, and tiny shops piled with copper vessels, transport you to the atmosphere of Srinagar. It is best to spend a day on each trip, carrying a packed lunch on the shikara for a truly moveable feast.

A taxi ride to the **Moghul Gardens** starts at Dal Gate and goes along the boulevard. **Chashma Shahi** was originally laid out by Shah Jahan, who also built the Taj Mahal in 1632. It has a cool mineral water spring and a well laid garden. Two kilometres (one mile) ahead is **Pari Mahal**, once a Buddhist monastery, later converted to a school of astrology by Dara Shikoh, Emperor Shah Jahan's son. It is illuminated at night and overlooks the lake and surrounding mountain ranges.

Farther on, **Nishat Bagh** stands on the banks of **Dal Lake**, against the backdrop of the **Zabarwan Range**. Four kilometres (three miles) on is the grandest garden of them all — **Shalimar Bagh** built by Emperor Jahangir for his wife Nur Jahan. It has four rising terraces, a central canal and a *son-et-lumière* show run by the India Tourism Development Corporation (ITDC) from May to October, which recreates the history and romance of the Mughal Courts.

Take the full run-up to **Harwan,** where Srinagar's reservoir is located. Remains of ancient tile pavements, with costumes, flora, fauna and geometric designs of the Buddhist period, are also found there.

The first part of the **Shankaracharya Temple**, just above the boulevard overlooking Dal Lake, was said to have been built by Jaluka, son of Emperor Ashoka, around 200 BC. The present temple was built during the reign of Emperor Jahangir. The view from the top is beautifully reproduced on an embroidered shawl displayed among other textiles and old artefacts at the **Shri Pratap Singh Museum** at Lal Mandi. Open from 1000 to 1700, closed on Mondays. Walks along the Bund from the Kashmir Government Handicrafts Emporium, **Abi Guzar**, take you past some of Kashmir's best handicraft shops. Residency Road and Polo View in the same vicinity offer good shopping, especially for made-to-order suede leather shoes.

Excursions from Srinagar

Mid-distance outings from Srinagar are not more than 60 kilometres (37 miles) away, which makes road travel leisurely and pleasant, allowing for picnics on the way. **Chirari-Sharif**, 30 kilometres (19 miles) south-west of Srinagar on the road to **Yusmarg**, has a stunning **wood-latticed shrine** of the patron saint of Kashmir, Nund Rishi. The town is also renowned for its pottery and willow *kangri* held beneath one's garments for warmth. Seventeen kilometres (11 miles) on is a small open valley surrounded by fir and pine.

Burzahom excavations, 24 kilometres (15 miles) north of Srinagar, has an impressive array of objects dating back to 2500 BC. **Ganderbal** and **Manasbal** are picturesque towns, 19 kilometres (12 miles) and 32 kilometres (20 miles) north. Ganderbal offers camping sites on the banks of the Sindh River amid giant *chinar* trees and Manasbal is perfect for lazy afternoon shikara rides, bird-watching and enjoying a prolific array of lotus plants in summer. Tourist huts are available for an overnight stay.

For an unrivalled view of mountain ranges and the lake, head 56 kilometres (35 miles) due west from Srinagar, through poplar fields, to **Tangamarg, Gulmarg** and then to **Khilanmarg** by pony, into the snows. Gulmarg is a flower-laden, rolling meadow and valley. Wonderful walks, good hotels and winter sports facilities of international standard, have great touristic appeal. **Alpather Lake**, 13 kilometres (eight miles) away, remains frozen until mid-June and is approachable by pony. Hotels and a tourist bungalow provide accommodation. Highlands Park, Asia Gulmarg, Pine Palace and Zum-Zum are the most comfortable. Trekking, walks, pony rides, golf, tennis and winter sports make it idyllic.

Pahalgam, 96 kilometres (60 miles) east

of Srinagar, can be reached via **Pampore**, through Asia's only saffron-growing area, which blooms in November. You have to travel south first, so stop at **Avantipur** to see the ninth-century temple ruins, and **Martand**, just beyond **Avantrag**, for the splendid eighth-century Sun Temples. **Kokernag** and **Verinag**, within a radius of 15 kilometres (nine miles), have springs, gardens and quiet huts.

Meet the crystal-clear, rushing **River Lidder** before entering Pahalgam, an ideal place for trekking, picnics, trout fishing, pine forests and pony rides. There is also a bustling bazaar with hotels and shops.

An invigorating, 47-kilometre (29-mile), three-day trek from Pahalgam takes you to the pilgrimage shrines of **Amarnath Cave** at 3,962 metres (12,999 feet), said to be the abode of Lord Shiva, and the brilliant blue **Sheshnag Lake** at 2,895 metres (9,499 feet), where a stalactite in the cave waxes and wanes with the moon. During July and August pilgrims camp along the way.

Kolahoi Glacier and **Aru Meadow**, 36 kilometres (22 miles) along a pony track, have rest houses and breathtaking views. Trekking and fishing are run by the state tourist agency, complete with permits, guide maps and equipment.

Shopping

Kashmir is perfect for hand-knotted wool and silk carpets in traditional Persian designs. But buy walnut carving, papier mâché, *pashmina* and *shahtoosh* shawls with or without fine embroidery, silver-ware, semi-precious stones and leather goods in Srinagar.

Because of the political situation in Kashmir, travel in the region was not recommended in 1996. Therefore, check before making plans to visit.

Ladakh: Land of Passes

Ladakh means 'The Land of Passes'. Fa-Hsien, the famed Chinese traveller, wrote of its great beauty after his journeys in the fifth century AD. Opened to tourists only in the mid-1970s, its virgin, high-altitude desert, majestic and awe-inspiring mountain ranges and a culture of practising Buddhism hold a fascination hard to resist.

The road from Srinagar to Kargil begins with the Zoji-La Pass. Beyond is Fotu-La, at 4,267 metres (14,000 feet). Between Leh and Pangong Lake is Khardung-La, a pass at the breathtaking height of 5,486 metres (18,000 feet). **Leh**, at 3,597 metres (11,800 feet), is one of the highest mountain capitals in the world. The average elevation of Ladakh is 3,500 metres (11,484 feet) and this vast area of 97,000 square kilometres (37,452 square miles) has one of the lowest population densities in the country.

From Assam to Nepal and Garhwal, the Himalayas divide into three sections in Jammu and Kashmir, its northernmost point. The Karakoram Mountains pass through China and Pakistan, the Ladakh Range to the north of the Indus and the Zanskar Range to the south. The high mountain barriers limit summer rain and winter snow to nine centimetres (four inches). Sunshine 330 days of the year keeps the atmosphere extremely dry even when temperatures are below zero. **Dras**, which is situated between Sonamarg and Kargil has the greatest extremes of temperature — minus 40°C (minus 9°F) in winter and 40°C (104°F) in summer. Both altitude and temperature variations have a distinct effect on the lifestyles of the people. The first inhabitants of Ladakh were nomadic shepherds who lived in black animal-skin tents.

The Chiang tribes once roamed the pastures of central Asia and later became settled farmers, who practised an animist religion called *Bon Pa*, rich in ritual and superstition. In the second century AD, Ladakh was part of the Kushan empire. Despite the Buddhist missionaries sent by Ashoka, it was when the Tibetans conquered Ladakh, between the seventh and 10th centuries AD, that Tibetan and Indian influences began to change the essentially tribal culture into a feudal one.

Tibetan culture was associated with the religious and liturgical aspects of Vajrayana Buddhism, which was, in turn, linked to the flourishing Buddhist centres in India of the time. Ladakh became a historical trading centre in the heart of the

Asian continent, served as a gateway between the Punjab and the Indo-Gangetic plain and lay on the Silk Route of central Asia. Traders from Khotan, Yarkand, Kashgar and other trading posts between China and the Mediterranean passed through Ladakh.

Caravans of merchants traded in silk, shawls, wool, carpets, spices, silver, turquoise, salt, tea and tobacco, and these trade routes also became passageways for cultural exchange. In 1675, the Mughal governor of Kashmir helped the rulers of Ladakh turn back invaders from Tibet, leading to the acceptance of Islam.

In Punjab, Ranjit Singh expanded the Sikh empire to include Jammu by 1810, and annexed Kashmir by 1819. His loyal Dogra warrior Gulab Singh gradually gained independent strength and through General Zorawar Singh established his authority over Baltistan and Ladakh. In 1842, the British entered into an agreement with Gulab Singh, granting him independently Kashmir, Ladakh and Jammu, and sent a mission to demarcate the frontier with China. This remains in dispute until today.

In 1947 Jammu and Kashmir chose to merge with India. The maharaja, who was a Hindu reigning over a Muslim majority population, vacillated, which led to the first Indo-Pakistani conflict. Various border disputes around Kashmir and Ladakh between India, Pakistan and China restrict travel. Tensions in certain sectors still exist but these areas are well demarcated and tourists should encounter no problems.

Getting there

Indian Airlines operates flights from Delhi, Srinagar and Chandigarh to Leh. Some are daily, others less frequent. Book well in advance during the tourist season, and always be prepared throughout the year for delays and cancellations because of adverse weather conditions. While flights are quicker and take you over breathtaking mountain peaks, it is wise to rest completely on the first day as the rarefied air could cause respiratory problems that come on suddenly. Army and civil authorities provide good medical facilities. The road journey allows gradual acclimatization to altitude and temperature changes. The 230 kilometres (143 miles) of well-maintained state highway between Srinagar and Kargil is best covered the first day by jeep, car or bus. Leh is 434 kilometres (269 miles) from Srinagar. Many hotels of various categories or the tourist bungalow at Kargil are convenient for a night halt. On the way, similar facilities at Sonamarg, Dras, Mulbek and Saspol are available. Heavy snows at Zoji-La block the highway between October and May.

For information on road conditions, contact the Traffic Police Headquarters at Srinagar. For bus and jeep travel, contact the State Transport authorities at the Tourist Reception Centre at Srinagar or book through competent travel agents in Delhi.

For travel within Ladakh, tourist taxis and jeeps can be hired through the Tourist Office at Leh or the Ladakh Taxi Operators Union. Ponies and mules are there for those who enjoy trekking and exploring mountain trails. Transport costs are higher because fuel is brought over long distances.

When to go

You can visit Ladakh at any time of the year depending on how willing you are to endure the dry cold. Winter lasts seven months, from October to April. Daytime temperatures vary from 15°-20°C (59°-68°F).

A short spring lasts from April to May. Sometimes evening temperatures fall to 0°C (32°F) and, within 10 days, rise to 28°C (82°F). Summer lasts until September, with high temperatures in the day making cotton clothes sufficient. But the night temperatures necessitate a blanket. Low humidity and constant sunshine create temperature variations from 8°C (46°F) in the morning to 37°C (99°F) by mid-afternoon. Autumn is as short as spring, with leaves turning golden before they fall. The melting snows, streams and the Indus, Shyok, Zanskar, Nubra and Surn rivers provide water for irrigation where hardly

Opposite: Lamayuru Gompa, Ladakh.

one per cent of the land is cultivated due to climatic extremes and low rainfall. People live as high as 4,500 metres (14,765 feet) above sea-level.

Where to stay
Since the influx of tourism the people of Leh have converted their homes into paying-guest-style rooms and lodges. Camping sites for trekkers, tents, caravans — anything goes. Classified hotels ensure electricity and hot water. There are a number of top-range and mid-range hotels with telephone booking facilities. Budget hotels are many. Reservations for government tourist bungalows are made through the Assistant Director, Tourism, at Leh.

Sightseeing
One of the few Shangri-Las left in the world, Ladakh, with its crystal-clear air and brilliant blue skies, deserves more than a cursory visit. Strolls in the Leh bazaar and its by-lanes, treks to far-flung monasteries, long jeep rides across vast stretches reminiscent of the moon's surface, fishing by the Indus or studying various aspects of Tibetan Buddhism, and enjoying murals, ancient manuscripts and other art treasures, leave an indelible impression.

Lamayuru, 125 kilometres (78 miles) short of Leh on the main highway to Ladakh, is a marvel created by people and nature, where the 10th-century **Lamayuru Monastery**, mere caves carved out of the mountain, are surrounded by a vast basin and rugged mountains indicative of ancient earth movements and drained ocean beds. The *thangkas*, carpets and carved wooden tables lend an aura of rich meditative silence to the monastery.

The **Leh Palace**, built in the late 16th-century by Sengge Namgyal, overlooks the town and contains murals depicting the Buddha's life. A two-storeyed statue of a seated Chamb Buddha is housed in the **Tsemo Gompa**, a royal monastery nearby. To exhibit the supremacy of the spiritual king, the **Namgyal Tsemo** towers over the palace and the town. It has a gilded statue of the Buddha, scrolls, manuscripts and murals.

The **Leh Mosque,** built by Delden Namgyal in the mid-17th century as a tribute to the king's Muslim mother, is a fine example of Turko-Iranian architecture. Bookshops, outdoor cafés and handicraft bazaars in town, provide ample reason to spend leisure time between excursions to soak up the atmosphere.

A visit to the monasteries is a day-long exercise. Begin the day early. Start with the **Shey Palace** and **monastery**, 15 kilometres (nine miles) from Leh. A summer palace of the erstwhile rulers of Leh, it was built in 1620. It has the largest victory stupa topped with pure gold. Its seated Sayamunni Buddha, made of copper and brass, gilded with gold and silver, and studded with precious gems, is the most fabulous feature. It rises to a height of two storeys.

Farther up, the **Stok Palace Museum**, 17 kilometres (11 miles) along the Indus Valley, is open from 0700 to 1800. Picturesque surroundings, well renovated architectural features, and a pleasant atmosphere, more homely than museum-like. The well displayed collections of coins, royal costumes and regal paraphernalia, precious stones, thangkas and prayer instruments make a visit there a must.

Thiksey Monastery, 19 kilometres (12 miles) beyond the Palace Museum, has 12 storeys of eight temples where 250 monks reside. Butter lamps illuminate a wonderful collection of statues, stupas, thangkas, swords and Tantric wall paintings. Detailed explanations may not be forthcoming, so just enjoy the experience unless you are a research scholar. Wading in the side streams or fishing in the Indus is a pleasant outdoor diversion during the monastery tour.

The approach to **Hemis Gompa**, the most famous monastery, is not the most spectacular as the road veers right off the main Indus Valley and climbs around a small ravine before arriving at the foot of the monastery. While every monastery has its own festival, many of them in winter, Hemis celebrates the birthday of Guru Padmasambhava in June. Because of its timing, tourist attendance is heavy.

Monastery dances celebrate the ancient battles and victories of good over evil, the troublesome influence of demons and the

Above: The colourful Hemis festival.

benign divine powers. Elaborate colourful costumes and masks create a larger-than-life impression, as dancers glide and jump in a slow, measured tempo accompanied by powerful drums, long bugle-like horns and chanting monks. The display is spectacular. The largest thangka within the monastery is displayed once every 12 years; the next will be in the year 2004. Monks take visitors around, pointing to the gilded statues, thangkas and stupas decorated with precious stones.

Other monasteries organize archery competitions and other such events on their festival days.

Another excursion from Leh takes you to the **Likir** and **Alchi monasteries,** both within a distance of 70 kilometres (43 miles) from Leh, located off the national highway to Srinagar. The Likir Gompa was founded in the 12th century, the first royal monastery to be established in Ladakh under Tibetan influence. It has numerous large clay statues of the Buddha.

Life in Likir is expressed in clay, as many houses have elaborate clay stoves and the local potter still fashions tea

kettles, lamps, jars and teacups on a minute potter's wheel that is totally dismantled after use.

Surrounded by mountains it also has a pleasant camping site for tourists.

The Alchi Monastery requires crossing the river and driving into a secluded village nestling among rocks, fruit trees and barley fields. Its innocuous appearance belies the wealth of art in its 1,000 year-old architecture and wall paintings depicting the life of the Buddha, monks and musicians. The monastery has six temples, each special in its own right, revealing the contribution of Kashmiri artists and artisans to Buddhist culture. A makeshift restaurant and tea stall are the only facilities. Visitors are left to absorb history and culture in its most natural state.

If you have not had your fill of monasteries, make a brief stop at the **Spituk Monastery,** a 500-year-old structure, nine kilometres (six miles) short of Leh which boasts a huge statue of the goddess Kali, whose many faces are unveiled only once a year, and an ancient collection of masks and some magnificent thangkas. For those who are not culture buffs and prefer to hit the mountain trails with knapsacks and trekking boots, Ladakh offers among the world's best experiences.

For the sports enthusiast, polo played in traditional dress on small ponies is a special Ladakhi sport which can be seen in Leh in the summer months. For the more adventurous, white-water rafting events organized on the Indus and its tributaries by tourist agencies are popular.

Many trekking trails have been laid out ranging from short weekend treks to 11-day journeys spreading in all directions to include the **Zanskar**, **Ladakh** and **Karakoram** mountain ranges.

Mountain climbing can be organized through the Indian Mountaineering Foundation in New Delhi. For equipment and advice for treks from Leh, contact the Leh Tourist Office.

Excursions from Leh

Kargil, mid-way between Srinagar and Leh, is an important district headquarters. The population is largely Muslim, with the Buddhist-dominated villages beginning 45 kilometres (28 miles) east of Kargil at Mulbekh, noted for its nine-metre (30-feet) rock statue of the Maitreya Buddha. Its village homes welcome visitors and reveal the typical gentle rural style of living which endears Ladakh to those interested in cultural studies. Kargil is a good starting point for treks into the Zanskar region.

Suru Valley is the home of Tibeto-Dard descendants, and the Nun-Kun peaks which are over 7,000 metres (22,967 feet) high. A beautiful fertile valley and many trekking routes make it popular with those who want to escape.

Zanskar, remote and isolated, full of monuments, monasteries and many trek routes to Manali, Kishtwar and the Indus Valley is perfect for those who seek nature at its most rugged and beautiful. From the **Padum** base, it is a two-hour trek to **Karsha**, the largest and wealthiest of Zanskar's monasteries, dating back to the 16th century. Twelve kilometres (seven miles) from Padum, **Burdan** is another monastery with a fine collection of idols. On the Padum-Kishtwar trek is

Zong-Khul, a cave monastery built around two caves in the steep rock-face of a gorge. Padum, the base point for most expeditions to the Zanskar Valley, is served by an economy class hotel.

Shopping

The Leh bazaar is just one long, winding street with some back lanes, all dotted with shops. Vegetables, camera film and all types of handicrafts vie for attention with medicines, groceries, tailoring shops and artisans fashioning gold jewellery. Good buys are the thick soft *pashmina* shawls woven locally, coral, turquoise and seed pearl jewellery, carved wooden tables, fashion garments, locally knitted sweaters and socks, thangkas, brass prayer accessories and traditional costumes.

Local food comprises a mixture of Ladakhi noodle soups, steamed dumplings, Chinese food, German breads and Indian cuisine with its more spicy flavour. A visit to Ladakh is one of the more unforgettable experiences in life. Tourists should return nature's favour by not discarding litter.

Above: Dachigam National Park, near Srinagar.
Opposite: A mountain gorge.

Himachal Pradesh: Skiing, Sanctuaries and Shrines

For those with a spirit of adventure, Himachal Pradesh is a veritable paradise. Just a short plane ride away from the capital Delhi, this small mountain state in north India, with lofty peaks, rugged rocks, fierce waterfalls and sparkling streams, is a favourite with all kinds of tourists. A combination of ski resorts, wildlife sanctuaries, trekking and fishing adventures, ancient monuments, religious shrines and handicrafts makes the tiny state an all-season destination where two important rivers, the Sutlej and the Yamuna, wend their way through the five mountain ranges down to the plains.

A holiday in Himachal begins with a ride up the mountains, whether by road or by the 'toy' train. Until recently, the more remote parts of the state were closed to tourists.

The first reliable accounts of the state were found in the travel writings of Hsuan Tsang, the Chinese traveller who visited India during the peaceful and prosperous reign of King Harshavardhana around AD 630. After the collapse of the Vardhan empire, petty chiefs known as *ranas* and *thakurs* carved out territories for themselves.

There was continuous civil strife, but it was difficult for any one ruler to take control of the entire area due to the rugged terrain. Even the Mughals, later on, failed to establish their complete suzerainty over the state. It was in 1695 that the Sikhs managed to wrest control of the hill area.

When the local lords, with the Gurkhas of Nepal, failed to drive out the Sikhs, they turned to the British for help. After the Anglo-Sikh wars of the mid-19th century, the British took charge of the area.

To escape the summer heat down on the plains, the British established a string of hill-stations in this state. Today, these stations are as 'with it' for the Indians as they were for the British during the Raj. Initially, after the partition, Himachal became a centrally administered unit with 31 hill provinces. The local chieftains of these provinces gave up their right to rule after independence, and it was then known as the Simla and Punjab Hill State.

In 1966, the hilly areas of Punjab were included and it came to be called Himachal Pradesh, a union territory of the Central Government. It was granted statehood in 1971.

The people of Himachal are hospitable, simple mountain folk. In the remoter parts of the state, still untouched by tourism, communities still gather at dusk to break into self-expressive *Pahari* melodies. Song, dance and rhythm are a part of everyday life in Himachal.

Shimla

Shimla, the capital, was also the summer capital of the British when they ruled India. Today 'The Queen of Hill Stations', despite its rundown and overused condition, is still evocative of the Raj.

Spread over a 12-kilometre (seven-mile) crescent-shaped ridge, the western arm of the **Jakhu** Hills, Shimla, at 2,215 metres (7,267 feet), is like a big amusement fair. A road encircles the base of the town, beyond which traffic is restricted.

The grand houses and country cottages built by British officers are more prominent features of Shimla's skyline. Auckland House, the residence of the governor-general, Bentinck's Castle (now the Grand Hotel), Barnes Court (today the residence of the Governor) and the Viceregal Lodge (which houses the Indian Institute of Advanced Studies) are proof of the lives of splendour lived by the British.

Getting there

A daily flight from Chandigarh or a bus journey up the winding 110-kilometre (68-mile) road are popular ways of getting there. The drive is cool and invigorating. Those at leisure and romantically inclined can take the Himalayan Queen, a narrow gauge railway built in 1903-04, which starts at Kalka, 14 kilometres (nine miles) from Chandigarh. The 96-kilometre-long (60-mile) track passes through 103 tunnels and 24 overbridges. It stops at 18 tiny stations which radiate an old-world charm, and bewitching mountain scenery, straight out of picture books, comes into view at every turn in the track.

When to go

The best months are April to June, when a profusion of flowers, especially irises and lilies, bloom in the meadows. The start of the monsoon in July makes travelling risky due to landslides. It is pleasant again between September and October, before the snow spreads out its white blanket in December, which continues to lie until mid-March. The trip can be planned to indulge a sports whim, such as skiing.

Where to stay

Oberoi Clarks, Cecil Hotel, Chapeslee, Woodville, Hotel Holiday Home, Grand Hotel, Asia the Dawn and a host of privately managed tourist bungalows and inns offer a comfortable stay. Water is scarce, and a necessary precaution would be to clarify the situation before checking in. See listings for 'Hotels'.

Sightseeing

Everywhere in Shimla there is a sight to behold. The most spectacular view of the town itself can be had from the top of the **Jakhu Hills**, at 2,445 metres (8,022 feet). It is a steep climb from the ridge, and a temple dedicated to the monkey god Hanuman stands on the summit. It is said that at this point Hanuman rested while on his way to look for the magical herb, the *sanjivini booti*, which alone could save the life of Lakshmana, Lord Rama's brother. This fact is documented in the *Ramayana*. Aptly, a large number of monkeys live around the temple. On the ridge stands the Gothic **Christ Church**, complete with murals and stained glass windows. The ridge is a popular place for honeymooning

couples and tourists. The point where the ridge meets **The Mall** is called **Scandal Point** — apparently because it was there, many years ago, that the Maharaja of Patiala abducted the daughter of a British officer and took her to Chail.

Nearby, the famous **Gaiety Theatre** is more like a club now and **Davico's Ballroom** evokes the old Garrick of London. The road going downhill from the ridge leads to **Lakkar Bazaar**.

There, as the name implies, carved wooden walking sticks and other hand-crafted wooden items, are available.

Excursions from Shimla

Annandale, a grassy glen five kilometres (three miles) from the ridge, is a lovely picnic spot. The **Glen** nearby, through which runs a stream, is quieter and less frequented. Slightly farther up are the **Chadwick Falls**. With a 66-metre (217-feet) drop, they are an impressive sight during the monsoons.

Kufri, 18 kilometres (11 miles) north of Shimla, is a beautiful winter ski resort. About 65 kilometres (40 miles) farther on, **Narkanda**, at 2,700 metres (8,859 feet), is another famous ski resort. The Himachal Pradesh government runs ski camps there. **Fagu**, between Kufri and Narkanda, offers some spectacular views of the surrounding mountains and valleys.

Tattapani, 51 kilometres (32 miles) away, on the banks of the River Sutlej, has hot sulphur springs. Near Kufri, along another route at **Mashobra**, is the famous **Wild Flower Hall**, once the residence of Lord Kitchener, the Commander-in-Chief of the Imperial forces in India. The beautiful hotel-resort with landscaped pine forest gardens, was partially destroyed by fire, but some log huts and rooms were still open to tourists in 1996.

The **Sipi Fair** is held at Mashobra every June. **Naldhera**, 23 kilometres (14 miles) from Shimla, has a nine-hole golf course. The deep gorge of the **Sutlej River** is visible from there. **Kasauli**, at 1,850 metres (6,070 feet) above sea level, is the first hill-station on the Chandigarh-Shimla route. It is an army cantonment, a slight diversion from the main road. It is 35 kilometres (22 miles) from Kalka, and 65 kilometres (40 miles) from Chandigarh. Kasauli is a quiet and restrained place after the holiday crowds of Shimla.

Long walks and treks, and clean, uncluttered surroundings, are the hallmarks of Kasauli. A walk up to **Monkey Point** is well worth it, especially at dusk, to see the flat, well-planned city of Chandigarh as it slowly switches on its lights as darkness falls and the meandering Sutlej becomes a silver ribbon in the moonlight. The **Upper** and **Lower Mall** encircle the entire town, and with traffic restricted to these roads, Kasauli is free of any noise or pollution.

The **Tibetan Stalls** just above the bus-stand offer good-quality woollen bargains. Three main shops — Gupta's, Jakki Mull's Drapers and Daily Needs provide good-quality everyday merchandise. Hotel Alasia is the best place to stay in Kasauli.

At a height of 1,850 metres (6,070 feet), 45 kilometres (28 miles) east of Shimla, **Chail** is one of the smallest hill-stations. Developed by the royal family of Patiala to compete with Shimla it is surrounded by lush forests and offers a magnificient view of the Himalayas.

Nearby, a **bird sanctuary** boasts many hill species. The maharajas constructed a palace with extensive gardens and sports facilities and made it a sort of social centre for India's royalty. Chail's **cricket pitch** is one of the highest in the world.

Later, the Patiala family sold the palace, and it is now managed by the Himachal Pradesh Tourism Development Corporation (HPTDC) as a luxury hotel.

Accommodation to suit all budgets is available at the Chail Palace Complex, as beside the main hotel, there are new and old cottages and an economy block. Himreel Hotel is another place to stay. See listings for 'Hotels'.

Kulu Valley

In the heart of Himachal, the Kulu Valley is considered 'The Valley of the Gods'. About 200 local deities are worshipped there. Kulu is one of the oldest provinces of the Punjab. The people of the valley are warm and amiable, perhaps the result of having lived a life of plenty. The valley is a centre for apple and cannabis cultivation.

Folklore has it that the original valley was called Kulantapith, meaning 'The End of the Habitable World'. This name would be appropriate if one viewed the desolate starkness of Lahaul on one side of the Rohtang Pass, and the fertile, inhabited Kulu Valley on the other.

Geographically, the narrow Kulu Valley runs from Mandi in the north through Kulu and Manali to the majestic heights of the Rohtang Pass. The valley nestles between the Dhauladhar and Pir Panjal ranges. It is 80 kilometres (50 miles) long and hardly more than two kilometres (one mile) wide. The Beas River runs through this fertile, terraced valley, where carpets of paddy fields are visible during the monsoons, and golden wheat fields sway in the late winter sun.

Though a well-developed tourist destination, the Kulu Valley is still unspoilt. This is probably because the locals are not economically dependent on tourism. They work their orchards and looms, and live in traditional stone and wooden houses.

Kulu shawls, with their geometrically patterned borders, are now being produced on a commercial basis, and the flat, colourful Kulu cap is popular with tourists, too.

The lower storeys of the houses serve as cattle sheds and are often stacked with hay and cattle feed. The fair-skinned Gaddis, nomadic shepherds, who appear on the mountain slopes between March and September, are believed to be descendants of Alexander the Great. In the winters they move back to Bharmour with their long-haired goats.

Getting there
There are regular flights from Delhi via Chandigarh and Shimla to Bhuntar, which is 10 kilometres (six miles) south of Kulu. The flights are unreliable and overbooked, especially in summer. Taxis and buses (including luxury coaches) are available from Delhi, 512 kilometres (317 miles) away. Similarly, Shimla, 235 kilometres (146 miles) and Chandigarh 270 kilometres (167 miles), have an efficient bus service to

Above: A view of Shimla.

Kulu. For those with time on their hands, take a train to Pathankot and change there to the narrow gauge railway to Joginder-nagar, and then take a bus to Kulu.

When to go

In April and May the valley is full of blossoming trees and flowers, and in September and October, the dazzling autumn colours, local fruit, clear air, fairs and dances hold a special attraction.

Where to stay

Cottages at the Kulu Valley Resort Hotel, Himachal Pradesh Tourism Development Corporation-run Sarvari, Hotel Silver Moon, Ashoka Travellers Lodge, hotels Ramneek and Rohtang are good places to seek accom-modation. See listings for 'Hotels'.

Sightseeing

Kulu, at a height of 1,220 metres (4,000 feet), is the largest settlement in the valley. The southern part of the town is a wide expanse of grassy land called the **Dhalpur Maidan**, and it is there that the famous **Kulu Dusshera** is held every year in September or October. The Kulu Dusshera is different from the one celebrated in the rest of India. The festival there begins on Vijayadashmi, the day it ends everywhere else. Over 100 local deities gather near the palace at the **Raghunathji Temple**, dedi-cated to Rama (as Raghunathji) and Sita. Images from this temple lead the Dusshera procession.

Just above the Maidan, along the main road, is **Sultanpur**, the 17th-century capital of Raja Jagat Singh. The descendants of the raja still own the **Rupi Palace**. There are several other temples in Kulu namely **Jagannath Devi, Vaishno Devi** and **Basheshar Mahadev**.

The **Bijli Mahadev Temple**, 14 kilo-metres (nine miles) from Kulu, has an 18-metre-high (60-feet) staff to attract divine blessings in the form of lightning, which shatters the *Shivalingam* (phallic symbol)

into a thousand pieces. The pieces are then put together by the priest until the next bolt of lightning.

Excursions from Kulu
Apart from the temples around Kulu, one can make a trip to **Manikarna**. At 1,737 metres (5,700 feet), this was where Parvati, the consort of Lord Shiva, lost her earring (*manikaran*).

A hot spring bubbled up from the place where she eventually found it, today a sulphur bath. Lentils and rice are cooked in the boiling water by devotees lowering their pots directly into it.

For those keen on fishing, the small hamlet of **Largi**, 34 kilometres (21 miles) away, is a delight. The stunningly located **Rest House** at the meeting point of two Himalayan streams has the best trout fishing spots in the state. **Raison**, 12 kilometres (seven miles), and **Katrain**, 20 kilometres (12 miles) from Kulu, are also on the main road to Manali. There are trekking base camps and orchards there.

Another route runs from Kulu to Manali, along the eastern bank of the Beas River. Along the way, opposite Katrain, at **Naggar** 1,770 metres, (5,807 feet), a 500-year-old **wood and stone castle** stands despite frequent earth tremors. The castle is now a small hotel with a spectacular view. A short walk away is the **Roerich Gallery**, a large white house with many beds of roses, displaying the works of Nicholas Roerich, a Russian painter who made India his home.

There are some interesting temples in Naggar which is halfway between Kulu and Manali. There are two ancient temples in **Jagtashukh** on the way to Manali.

Manali

Straddling the Beas River to the extreme left of the Kulu Valley, Manali is a place of legends. Close to the snows of the Rohtang Pass, at an altitude of 1,830 metres (6,000 feet), it never becomes warm there, unlike Kulu and Mandi. Manali means 'The Home of Manu', father of humanity.

When to go
From April to August this is a great getaway from the summer heat. The best time to see a display of nature's colours is autumn. In November the snow arrives and stays until late February.

Where to stay
Ashoka Traveller's Lodge, Hotel Ambassador Resort, John Bannon's Hotel, Hotel Piccadilly and Mayflower Guest House are good places to stay. The Himachal Pradesh Tourism Development Corporation (HPTDC) runs self-catering Log Huts, Hotel Rohtang Manalsu and Hotel Beas. See listings for 'Hotels'.

Sightseeing
Away from the market, a couple of kilometres north, you can find refuge in the quiet hillsides. Marijuana, which made Manali a haven for hippies, still grows wild. The **Hidimba Temple** in the **Doongri forest** is above the Manali village. The four-tiered, pagoda-shaped temple, built around a natural cave, enshrines the footsteps of the female demon of the same name, who was married to Bhima, the strongest of the Pandava brothers in the epic *Mahabharata*. Finally she was adopted as the patron goddess of the Kulu royal family. Towards the north, stone steps lead toward the **old village** and the **Temple of Manu**.

Tibetans have a base camp at Manali which includes a large, **modern temple**, and a handicrafts outlet, near the busstand. The collection of Tibetan jewellery found there is a treat. Five kilometres (three miles) from Manali is the **Arjuna Gufa**. It is said that this is the cave where Arjuna, one of the heroes of the Mahabharata, did penance. The **Mountaineering Institute**, on the left bank of the river, offers trekkers expert advice. The **hot springs** of the **Vashisht Village** are located three kilometres (two miles) from Manali.

Opposite: The densely forested Kulu Valley.

Excursions from Manali

Fifty-one kilometres (32 miles) beyond Vashisht, the road leads to the **Rohtang Pass** and into the **Lahaul Valley**. It is open from June to November. Unpredictable snowfall can pose a threat to the traveller. Beyond the pass lies the **Sonapani Glacier** and **Beas Kund Lake**, the source of the **Beas River**. Towards the north-west, **Salong Pass**, the glacier closest to Manali, is a distance of 13 kilometres (eight miles). The **Rahalla Falls**, 15 kilometres (nine miles) from Manali, are worth a visit.

Mandi

The old, princely capital of Mandi is on the way to the Kulu Valley as all the roads from Shimla, Delhi and Chandigarh meet near the Govind Sagar Reservoir at Bilaspur. Along the road, the half-submerged temples of the valley of Sundernagar are visible. The valley narrows again as it reaches Mandi. New construction and decaying old buildings make it a peculiar mix of ancient and modern. Mandi is known for beautiful stone carvings in the old temples of **Bhutnath, Triloknath, Panchvaktra** and **Shyamalkoli** on the Tarna Hills.

Sightseeing

The places around Mandi are almost untouched by tourism — the **Sundernagar Valley**, the floating reed islands in **Rewalsar Lake**, and the Buddhist, Hindu and Sikh shrines at **Junjheli**. There are verdant apple orchards at **Karsog**.

Lahaul and Spiti

Lahaul, Spiti and Kinnaur are the three tribal regions of Himachal Pradesh, and make up a third of the state. Lahaul and Spiti, at 2,750 metres (9,023 feet), border Tibet and Zanskar. Compared with the Kulu Valley, they are dry and barren.

Getting there

Buses ply from Kulu and Manali in summer when the Rohtang Pass is open. The buses go on to Ladakh, weather permitting.

When to go

Spiti is best in summer. While Lahaul is accessible throughout the year, entry can be made only when the Rohtang Pass is open.

Where to stay

A Public Works Department (PWD) rest house and a tourist bungalow at Keylong are the best, and should be used as a base to explore Lahaul and Spiti. Keylong, 117 kilometres (73 miles) from Manali, is the district headquarters.

Sightseeing

Spiti is located on the leeward side of the lofty mountains which the monsoons never reach. During the cool, short summers, the valley is covered with grass and alpine flowers. Seed potato is grown in summer. Small clusters of huts, laid out along glacial streams, are juxtaposed with shocks of green potato fields in a brown landscape.

Spiti experiences one of the harshest climates in the world. In winter, when the land is totally snow covered, the people stay indoors, spinning and weaving. Spiti was part of the western Tibetan kingdom of Guge. It retains its Tibetan character and Buddhist heritage. Most festivals and marriages are celebrated in winter, when the community gathers to sing and dance. Few amenities, dirt roads, and the rarefied air at this very high altitude discourage the casual traveller from exploring Spiti. It is, in any case, closed to tourists.

For those who do make it, there are a number of unnamed and unconquered peaks of over 6,096 metres (20,000 feet). The highest Himachal peak, **Gya,** is still unclimbed. For the trekker, there are walks along the **Mane** or **Dhankar Lakes**, or through the pastures of **Langza** and **Demulor** up the **Paraiho** stream. In the **Pin Valley National Park**, the snow leopard and the ibex may be seen. Medicinal herbs are also found in abundance. For the adventurous, white-water rafting and hang-gliding are available. Worth seeing is the 11th-century **Gompa** at **Tabo** which houses the remains of Rinchen Tsangpo, a great scholar and translator. It is one of the holiest places for Tibetan Buddhists. Exquisite frescos adorn the mud roof of the monastery. The other

Above: The Lahaul Valley is ringed by the Zanskar, the Greater Himalayas and the Pir Panjal mountains.

monasteries in the valley belonging to different Buddhist sects are **Key**, **Dhankar**, **Tanguid** and **Kungri**.

Open all the year round to tourists, **Lahaul** lies west of Spiti. It forms the upper catchment of the Chenab River and is ringed by the Zanskar, the Greater Himalayas and the Pir Panjal mountains. Even though it is only 2,438 metres (8,000 feet) high, Lahaul can be reached only by crossing over a few high passes. It lies in a narrow gorge formed by the Chenab as it cuts through the Pir Panjal range. The Rohtang Pass offers the easiest access, but is closed for nearly six months a year. It is said that the people of Lahaul learnt about the easier life elsewhere in the world through the birds, and prayed to Lord Shiva, who then created the Rohtang Pass.

Lahaul, too, was influenced by Buddhism, first under the dominance of the Guge of Tibet, and later under Ladakh. In the sixth century, the Kulu rulers took over Lahaul before it fell to the British.

There are many monasteries around Keylong. The **Kharding Monastery**, three kilometres (two miles) away, overlooks the town and stands on the spot of the former capital. The **Tiayal Monastery**, six kilometres (four miles), and the **Gurughantal Monastery**, 11 kilometres (seven miles) away at the confluence of Chandra and Bhaga, streams of the Chenab River, are worth a visit. The rest of Lahaul and Spiti has to be experienced.

The **Bara Shigri Glacier**, the biggest in Himachal Pradesh, lies on the left bank of the Chandra. It is first seen on entering Lahaul from Kulu. The road leads on to Spiti before reaching the **Kunzum Pass**. There are villages along the road on the right bank of the Chandra River and **Gondhla**, one of the larger villages, has an **old fort** belonging to the Thakurs. On the opposite bank, sheer rock-faces drop 1,524 metres (5,000 feet).

Haryana: the Green State

A state that literally means 'Land of Greenery and Vegetation' Haryana came into existence in 1966 as a result of a reorganization of Punjab on a linguistic basis. Like Punjab, Haryana is also a seat of pre-historic and historic cultures. Various pilgrim centres dot the state. Haryana is predominantly agricultural.

Getting there
Based on the geographical fact, an imaginative scheme has been framed so that most roads out of Delhi snake through Haryana. Haryana is also served by rail.

When to go
Avoid the summer months of May, June and July for the tourist complexes of Haryana have become the weekend getaway for people from Delhi and other neighbouring states.

Sightseeing
Sacred as the wellspring of the holy *Bhagwad Gita* scriptures, **Kurukshetra**'s other claim

to fame is that it also witnessed the Mahabharata war.

The city is full of Hindu, Muslim and Sikh pilgrimage centres; famous Hindu ones are Brahmsarovar, Sannihit Sarovar, Banganga and Nabhikamal, the source of the universe. There are *gurudwaras* (abodes of the gurus) to commemorate the visits of Sikh *gurus* (spiritual guides).

Of historical importance in **Panipat**, 100 kilometres (62 miles) from Delhi, are the **mausoleum** of Hazrat Bu-Ali-Shah-Qalandar, the **tomb** of Ibrahim Lodi, Chabutra-e-Fateh Mubarik and **Kabuli Bagh Mosque**.

Hissar is crowded with Harappan and pre-Harappan sites. The minarets of Jama Masjid and Firoz Shah's Palace are some important historical monuments. Flamingo Tourist Resort provides rest and camping facilities.

Another tourist attraction in Haryana is **Badkhal Lake**, 32 kilometres (20 miles) from Delhi. A natural depression in the Aravalli Hills has encouraged the formation of a lake fed by rain water and a small rivulet. The expansive lawns, terraced gardens and flowering trees and shrubs add charm to the lake and its surroundings. The Minivet Huts are built to provide every tourist comfort. The Grey Falcon and Mayur are two centrally air-conditioned restaurants which serve both continental and Indian dishes. Garud is a magnificent motel in the complex.

Surajkund, eight kilometres (five miles) from Delhi in the Faridabad area, is an historic site where a Sun Temple once stood. A Crafts Mela held every February is a splendid occasion to appreciate arts and crafts from all over India. The annual Bougainvillea Show in April is a visual feast.

Karna Lake, near Karnal town on the main highway, is 124 kilometres (77 miles) from Delhi. It has a centrally air-conditioned restaurant and a luxuriously furnished motel overlooking the lake.

Above: Jami Masjid Mosque. Opposite: Photographs depicting religious themes.

GOLDEN TEMPLE AMP

Punjab: Land of Five Rivers

Punjab, or land of 'the Five Rivers', is one of the most prominent provinces of modern India. Its geographical boundaries have changed in time. Most of present-day Pakistan and the Indian states of Punjab, Haryana, Himachal and Delhi formed ancient Punjab.

Because of its location, Punjab bore the brunt of foreign invasion which awakened the martial instincts of the people, who are traditionally known as defenders of the land.

Primarily an agricultural state, almost 86 per cent of the land is under cultivation and 76 per cent of the population are farmworkers. Known as the 'Fruit Basket' and the 'Granary of India', hard-working Punjabis have transformed it into one of India's wealthiest states.

Punjab is dotted with numerous shrines connected with the lives and times of important Sikh *gurus* (spiritual guides). The Golden Temple, in **Amritsar**, is the most important. Apart from Patiala, there are palaces and forts in the erstwhile princely cities of Kapurthala, Nabha and Faridkot. Fatehgarh Sahib, a Punjabi district, has many *gurudwaras* (abodes of the gurus) in memory of Guru Gobind Singh's mother, Mata Gujri, and his two younger sons.

Chandigarh

Getting there
Today, Chandigarh is the capital for both Punjab and Haryana and is also a union territory. It is 260 kilometres (161 miles) from Delhi. By air, rail (air-conditioned trains) and road (buses), Chandigarh is linked with Shimla and Amritsar.

When to go
Avoid the midsummer months.

Where to stay
Tourist accommodation is available in the city. See listings for 'Hotels'.

Sightseeing
Named after Chandi Devi, the goddess of Shakti whose **temple** stands 15 kilometres (nine miles) outside the city, **Chandigarh** was built as the alternative capital of Punjab, in lieu of Lahore, which went to Pakistan after partition.

Chandigarh, considered India's most beautiful town, was designed by French architect Le Corbusier. Apart from being well planned and well designed, Chandigarh has various tourist attractions.

The **Rock Gardens**, about four kilometres (three miles) from the city centre, are a fantasy land created by Nek Chand from 20th-century urban waste: discarded sanitary ware, fuses, broken bangles, pottery, and so on.

There is a **Darbar-i-Aam** or 'Hall of Public Audience', **Darbar-i-Khas** or 'Hall of Private Audience', marching armies, parading schoolboys and girls, hookah-smoking elders and dancing dolls.

Sukhna Lake, an artificial reservoir, is for boating and water-skiing. The Lake Restaurant, on a tiny island is reached by boat.

The **Rose Garden** is Asia's largest, and the fragrance of thousands of varieties lingers long after the visit.

Excursions from Chandigarh
Morni Hills, so named because of the abundance of peafowl, lies 35 kilometres (22 miles) away from **Pinjore** and 44 kilometres (27 miles) from Chandigarh at 1,220 metres (4,000 feet) above sea-level. The hills can be visited throughout the year. The **Mountain Quail Complex** at Morni is a motel and restaurant. The area is ideal for trekking.

Yadavindra Gardens in Pinjore, said to have been originally planned by Nawab Fidai Khan in the 17th century, were patterned after the Shalimar Gardens in Srinagar, Kashmir. They were renamed Yadavindra Gardens in memory of the late Raja Yadavindra Singh, the Maharaja of the state's capital Patiala.

Patiala

Getting there
Patiala is 250 kilometres (155 miles) from Delhi and linked by road and rail to Chandigarh.

When to go
The best time to visit Patiala is October to November or between February and March.

Sightseeing
Capital of a once princely state, **Patiala** has world-famous forts, palaces and extensive gardens. Baba Ala Singh laid the foundation of **Patiala Fort** and named it Qila Mubarak. Located in the centre of the city it houses an impressive collection of chandeliers and an armoury.

The **Moti Bagh Palace**, a copy of the Shalimar Gardens in Lahore, built by Maharaja Narendra Singh in 1847 has terraces, fountains and canals. Its Sheesh Mahal (Palace of Mirrors) is full of exquisite murals and paintings of Sikh *gurus*. These paintings came to be known as the Patiala School of Painting. **Baba Ala Singh's** *samadhi* (memorial), the **Bara Dari Palace**, now houses the Punjab State Archives. The **10 gates** of the city and the new **Moti Bagh Palace** are other landmarks of Patiala also known for its footwear, gold embroidered clothes and crafts.

Amritsar

Known as the 'Reservoir of Nectar', Amritsar is one of Punjab's oldest and most important cities.

The spiritual capital of the Sikhs, Amritsar was founded by Guru Ram Dass in 1577 on a piece of land which, according to some sources, was gifted to Bibi Bhani, wife of the Guru, by the Mughal emperor, Akbar.

Iksvak, a Kshatriya king and predecessor of Lord Rama, performed sacrificial rituals there according to the *Ramayana*. It is also believed that Lord Rama's consort, Sita, stayed at Ram Tirath near Amritsar during her exile and gave birth to two sons who unknowingly fought against their father, wounding him in battle where the Dukh Bhanjani Beri now stands. When the identity of their injured father was disclosed, they quickly brought *amrit* (nectar) from the pool nearby and revived him. The rest of the nectar was poured in the pond, which became famous as a centre of healing. It regained its significance during the era of the Sikh gurus.

Legend says the leper husband of Rajni, the daughter of Rai Duni Chand, was healed in the sacred tank. Guru Ram Dass, upon hearing about the pool's healing powers, named it a place of pilgrimage.

Getting there
Amritsar, 500 kilometres (310 miles) from Delhi, is connected by air with Delhi, Chandigarh and Srinagar. Many fast trains, notably, the Dadar-Amritsar Express, the Frontier Mail and the Paschim Express, link Amritsar to Delhi and Mumbai.

When to go
The cooler months, October-November and February-March, are the best times to visit. Dusshera and Diwali provide the opportunity for festival celebration.

Where to stay
For those keen on staying outside the Golden Temple complex, there are air-conditioned hotels, restaurants and guesthouses to suit every budget. See listings for 'Hotels'.

Sightseeing
In 1606, Guru Hargobind built the **Akal Takht**, adjacent to the main entrance of the **Golden Temple**. Ever since he declared it the seat of the Sikhs' temporal authority, all political matters concerning the Sikh community are decided there, and the chief of the Akal Takht directs religio-political issues.

During the seventh invasion of Ahmad Shah Abdali, the Akal Takht and the Golden Temple were levelled to the

Overleaf: Golden Temple, Amritsar.

Above: Farmers in rural Punjab.

ground, but were rebuilt in 1764 by the then Sikh chieftains. The main structure anchored by a 52-metre (171-feet) square base rises from the centre, approached by a causeway about 60 metres (197 feet) long.

During Maharaja Ranjit Singh's rule (1799-1838), the Golden Temple was redecorated by master craftsmen. Covered with gold-plated copper sheets, it came to be called Swaran Mandir (Golden Temple).

The stone inlaid work and floral decoration were executed by Muslim artisans, and the murals by painters from the famous Kangra School of Art. Indeed, the architectural style of the Golden Temple is unique among the shrines of India.

Outside the temple the information office provides free literature and other useful information to tourists.

Other historic shrines in the vicinity of the Golden Temple, are the **Gurudwara Tharha Sahib**, **Gurudwara Manji Sahib**, **Gurudwara Guru Ke Mahal**, **Gurudwara Baba Atal Sahib** and **Gurudwara Mai**

Kaulan Da Asthan. Apart from Sikh *gurudwaras,* the city has other attractions, the most important of them being **Jallianwala Bagh**, which marks the site where Britain's General Dyer ordered the killing of thousands of Indians on the festive day of Baisakhi in April 1919.

A central **memorial** in the **Old Garden**, on the way to the **Golden Temple**, commemorates the atrocity. **Durgiana Mandir**, modelled after the Golden Temple, is a famous place of Hindu pilgrimage.

Constructed in the early 1920s outside the **Hathi Gate** in Amritsar, the idols of worship in the central structure are beautifully draped and profusely ornamented.

Maharaja Ranjit Singh, who had the Golden Temple redecorated, was a frequent visitor to Amritsar. The beautiful garden and palace he built, known as **Ram Bagh**, was also used as a state guest-house for the maharaja's European guests and other English travellers. Ram Bagh now houses the **Punjab Government Museum**.

Uttar Pradesh: Rich in Culture

Uttar Pradesh, bigger than many European countries, has something for every visitor, from snow-clad peaks to the Taj Mahal, from famous pilgrim centres to those forgotten capitals of ancient kingdoms.

Culturally and geographically, Uttar Pradesh is the richest state, presenting a cultural mosaic of foreigners who invaded northern India, particularly Muslims of the Afghan and Turkish armies and people from the other Indian states.

Geographically, Uttar Pradesh is divided into the northern Himalayan belt, with splendid snow-covered peaks, thick forests and great rivers, like the Ganga and Yamuna which originate from perennial glaciers in the high mountains. It is home to shy tribes, who stay within their snow-bound villages. The lower Indo-Gangetic plain is a fertile region where many an illustrious kingdom rose and fell.

Fed by the rivers Ganga, Yamuna, Gomati, Ramganga, Ghaghra, Chambal and Gandak, Uttar Pradesh was the seat of the kingdoms of Nanda, Magadha, Sunga, Sakas and Kushanas, primarily because of the state's strategic location.

Between the fourth and seventh centuries AD, the Guptas created an age of great splendour matched only by the Mughals 12 centuries later.

Kashi (Varanasi), Kosal (Avadh), Vatsa (Allahabad), Surasena (Mathura), Panchala (Ahichchattra in Bareilly) and Kuru (Hastinapur near Meerut), all important cities today, were great principalities in the past.

Furthermore, Uttar Pradesh is the setting for two great Indian epics, the *Ramayana* and the *Mahabharata*.

Sightseeing

The northern region, the sacred abode of the gods, is today explored for its scenic mountains and exciting treks through sleepy villages, rippling streams, torrential rivers, awesome glaciers and enchanting peaks. **Badrinath** and **Kedarnath**, time-honoured pilgrim centres, are located amid India's most magnificent mountains. One of the holiest Hindu shrines **Badrinath Temple**, dedicated to Vishnu, at 3,122 metres (10,243 feet), is guarded by the snow-clad **Nar** and **Narayana** peaks and the tumbling **Alaknanda River**. It is closed to tourists from November to April. En route to Badrinath is **Govindghat**, from where treks lead to the world-famous **Valley of Flowers** — a riot of gorgeous blooms between July and August — at 3,352 metres (10,998 feet) above sea level. **Hemkund Gurudwara**, the sacred Sikh shrine, lies close by, surrounded by spectacular mountains and a lake.

High in the mountains at 3,581 metres (11,749 feet) is **Kedarnath**, a Shiva temple with a most venerated *jyotirlingams* (Shiva's image of great importance). It was built by the Pandavas in atonement for their sins after the war of Mahabharata. A huge *nandi* (Shiva's bull-vehicle) guards the temple on the bank of the **Mandakini River**. Closed from November to April, it is a 15-kilometre trek (nine-mile) from **Gaurikund**.

Known for its spectacular scenery, **Uttarakhand** also provides trekking opportunities, notably to **Gangotri**, 4,138 metres (12,577 feet) high, the source of the holy River Ganga and **Yamunotri**, 3,323 metres (10,903 feet), the source of the Yamuna River in the heart of these mountains. The road is motorable to within 15 kilometres (nine miles) of these sacred spots. The Garhwal Mandal Vikas Nigam Limited, Rishikesh, organizes exciting treks through the unforgettably splendid mountains.

Uttar Pradesh also offers daring and challenging adventure sports, started by Sir Edmund Hillary's trail-blazing 'Ocean to Sky' rafting expedition, which begins at the mouth of the **Ganga** and goes on to the higher reaches of the **Alaknanda River**.

The Bhagirathi and Alaknanda rivers now draw international sports enthusiasts for adventure expeditions in treacherous streams that thunder and froth through narrow gorges. The **Kumaon Hills**, immortalized by Jim Corbett and his man-eating

tigers, have much to offer visitors.

Pithoragarh, Almora, Kausani and **Nainital** offer enchanting views of the mountains and wonderful treks through pine and rhododendron forests. These mountains are only for those keen to step into a world of unimaginable natural splendour, but with many discomforts.

Hardwar, the gateway to the mountains on the River Ganga, is an ancient pilgrim centre. **Har ki Pauri,** the most sacred *ghat* in Hardwar, has footprints of Vishnu in stone. The evening devotion, or *aarti*, is a memorable experience and the tone is set with the chanting of *mantras*, floral offerings and myriad tiny earthen lamps, or *diyas*, bobbing on the Ganga River. The great **Kumbha Fair** there is held every 12 years. More picturesque **Rishikesh**, 24 kilometres (15 miles) upstream, is the base for travel to Badrinath, Kedarnath, Gangotri and Yamunotri. There, *ashrams* (hermitages) for transcendental meditation once attracted some famous Hollywood stars.

Mathura, of equal religious importance as Hardwar, stands on the **Yamuna**. It is particularly venerated as the birthplace of Krishna, an incarnation of Vishnu. Once a prosperous city and a Buddhist and Jain centre, all its ancient temples were demolished by Muslim invaders during the 11th and 12th centuries, and later in the 17th century by Aurangzeb, when he built a **mosque** on the ruins of the ancient fort. **Vishram Ghat** is the main ghat on the river. It is believed that Krishna rested there after killing his tyrant uncle Kansa.

Annually the **Dwarkadhisha Temple** attracts millions of devotees. The 11-kilometre (seven-mile) circular walk around Mathura is regarded a must for every devotee. **Vrindaban**, the neighbouring town, is associated with Krishna's childhood and **Barsana Village** was home to Krishna's consort, Radha. There are about 1,000 temples in the neighbourhood. The boisterous festival of **Holi** in March is the best time to see the villagers dousing each other in dappled powders and water. The great rivers Ganga and Yamuna meet at **Allahabad**, 135 kilometres (84 miles) from Varanasi. Known as Prayag in ancient times, Allahabad, like Hardwar, draws millions of devotees to the mammoth **Kumbha Mela** held once every 12 years in January to February. **Akbar's Fort** stands on the river. Of interest is a single Ashokan pillar inside. Visitors are not allowed into the fort.

Khusrau Bagh in the city has some splendid Mughal tombs. **Kausambi**, 51 kilometres (32 miles) south-west of the ancient capital city of Allahabad, has a formidable fort, ascribed to Parikshit, son of Arjuna, the hero of the *Mahabharata*.

The home of Buddhism, Uttar Pradesh has some notable places of Buddhist pilgrimage. **Piprahwa**, 96 kilometres (60 miles) from Gorakhpur, has recently been identified as the ancient Kapilvastu or the native place of the Buddha. Lumbini in Nepal, easily reached from Gorakhpur, is the birthplace of Lord Buddha. At **Sravasthi**, Buddha performed the miracle of sitting in a 1,000-petalled lotus. Sravasthi is now called **Saheth-Maheth** in the Gonda district of Uttar Pradesh. **Kushinagar**, 55 kilometres (34 miles) east of Gorakhpur, is the site of the Buddha's *Parinirvana* during the 80th year. Ashoka built a grand stupa there which lies buried.

The **Mata Kunwar ka Kot** enshrines a large sculpture of the Buddha in the state of *nirvana* (salvation). **Sankasya** (now called **Sankisa** in Farrukhabad district) is the place where the Buddha is said to have descended to earth after preaching the Abhidharma to his mother and the gods in the Trayastrimsa Heaven. The place is rich in sculptural finds, especially the **Ashokan pillar** with a sculptured elephant.

Agra and **Fatehpur Sikri** are known for their wealth of ancient monuments, in particular palaces and mausoleums.

Uttar Pradesh is a treasure trove of arts and crafts. Agra's marble craft in stylized floral and geometrical arabesques set with precious and semi-precious stones, in a dazzling array of table-tops, trays, vases and paper weights, make outstanding gifts. Descendants of artisans who worked on

Opposite: Uttar Pradesh, where the traditional merges with the modern.

the Taj Mahal still practise carving marble. *Durrie*-weaving is another craft. This flat-weave cotton rug is cherished for its most splendid designs and riotous colour schemes.

Mirzapur, **Bhadoi** and **Shahjahanpur** are famous for their hand-knotted carpets in Persian or naturalistic designs. **Varanasi** silk and brocades have a legendary reputation for their enchanting colours and their luxurious feel. The *chikan* (shadow-work embroidery) work of **Lucknow**, done with white silk or cotton threads on white muslin, is internationally acclaimed. Nur Jahan, Jahangir's queen, is reputed to have created this form of embroidery. Pottery from **Khurja** and **Chinhat** is well known abroad for its silk-smooth finish. Elegant wooden folding screens with intricate geometrical designs are works of art from **Saharanpur**.

Agra

Agra was established as the capital of the Mughal kingdom in 1526 after the reign of the Lodis. Situated 223 kilometres (138 miles) south-east of Delhi, it was there that the famed Koh-i-Noor diamond was presented to Humayun by the Raja of Gwalior. Called 'Akbarabad' after Emperor Akbar, Agra enjoyed a flourishing trade in Persian carpets, Arabian horses, precious stones and fabrics.

Getting there
There are regular flights to Agra from Delhi and Jaipur. Excellent train services connect Agra to major Indian cities. The Shatabdi Express and the Taj Express are the two most convenient trains from Delhi, with air-conditioned coaches. The Taj Express makes it possible to visit Agra and return the same day. Tickets for coach tours within Agra are issued on the train before arrival. The coach will return you to the station before the Taj Express departs for Delhi.

When to go
Avoid the months of May, June and July when it can be frightfully hot. October to March is the best season to visit.

Where to stay
Hotel Agra Ashok, Hotel Clark's Shiraz, Taj View Hotel and Welcomgroup Mughal Sheraton are luxury hotels. Budget hotels include the Agra Hotel, Hotel Amar, Grand Hotel, Khanna Hotel, Mayur Tourist Complex, Mumtaz Hotel and the Government tourist bungalow run by the Uttar Pradesh Tourism Development Corporation. See listings for 'Hotels'.

Sightseeing
The mammoth **Agra Fort** in red sandstone was built by Akbar in 1565 over the crumbling mud-brick edifice of the Lodis. The first and greatest fort built by the Mughals, its lofty crenellated battlements are visible from all along the river bank. The entrance through the **Amar Singh Gate** is over-shadowed by high towers and a gateway where a hairpin bend and a steep ramp served as an effective barrier against the invading enemy in the past.

Beyond the ramp, the royal residential area begins. Seventy-six by 91 metres (250 by 300 feet), the red sandstone façade of the **Jahangiri Mahal** on the right, decorated with ornamental niches and lotus-bud fringes, was built by Akbar. A gigantic stone cup stands in the middle of the vast **courtyard**.

The surrounding palace halls bear heavily carved, gilded brackets and serpentine beams reminiscent of Man Mandir in Gwalior. This is the only original Akbari structure at the fort.

Shah Jahan's white marble palace, **Khas Mahal**, epitomizing Mughal opulence, is vastly different from the Akbari palaces in their sombre red sandstone. The architectural style is distinctly Persian. The two lovely **pavilions** with copper-covered Bengali-roofs and the formal garden, **Anguri Bagh**, prepared from soil brought from Kashmir, are in the foreground.

Closed to public viewing, the 'Royal Bath', or **Sheesh Mahal**, has glass mosaics, fountains and cisterns. Its inlaid colonnade was removed by Hastings and presented to the Prince Regent (later George IV). It is now a proud possession of the Victoria and Albert Museum in London. The romantic **Musamman Burj** (Jasmine Tower) was

Above: Kumbha Mela, Hardwar.

home to the two most beautiful of Mughal queens — Nur Jahan and Mumtaz Mahal. The columns of the small but ornate structure in marble, the **Diwan-i-Khas**, were once covered with *pietra dura* work. On the terrace outside, are the two **marble thrones** of Shah Jahan (white) and Jahangir (black). The emperor and prince would watch elephant fights staged on the *reti* (sand) below from there.

Beneath the Diwan-i-Khas stand the harem quarters, **Machchi Bhawan**, beside which a decorative gate opens to **Meena Bazaar**, the market of the royal ladies and their entourage. The first floor of Machchi Bhawan leads to the royal canopy overlooking the columned hall of **Diwan-i-Aam**, where the emperor received his courtiers. The triple-arched ornamental *pietra dura* canopy, is a much altered version of the Akbari original.

The architecturally perfect **Moti Masjid,** built by Shah Jahan, can be viewed across the open court. A mere five kilometres (three miles) beyond **Delhi Gate** in Agra, on the Agra-Delhi Road, stands Akbar's magnificent **tomb** at **Sikandara**. The tomb is approached through a well laid out Mughal garden. The entrance through the white marbled southern gateway bears four minarets worked in flawless floral and geometrical arabesques of coloured marble inlaid in red sandstone.

The pyramidal structure of the tomb is an architectural curiosity. Inspired by Buddhist structures, perhaps, the cenotaph chamber in the basement has a remarkable austerity. The stucco vestibule is still resplendent with gold and blue ornamentation. The Jats, who plundered the tomb in 1681, carried away gold jewels, the emperor's armour, clothes and books kept close to the sarcophagus. The first three storeys in red sandstone were built by Akbar and the white marbled upper floors were completed by his son Jahangir in 1613. The open court on the uppermost terrace has exquisite *jali* (lattice) screens. The cenotaph, a duplicate of the original in the basement, is carved with the 99 names of Allah and Allaho Akbar (Great is His Glory). The **tomb** of Itimad-ud-Daula was built by Jahangir's chief queen, Nur Jahan, for her father in 1626. Situated on the **Yamuna**

River's edge and enclosed within a high-walled garden interrupted by four magnificent gateways, the *pietra dura* tomb bears exquisite Persian floral and geometrical ornamentation in lapis, onyx, jasper, topaz and cornelian. Structured like a jewel in a casket, this tomb is topped by a small pavilion of delicate jali screens. The cenotaphs, of greenish-yellow marble, stand over a floor of mosaics inlaid to resemble Persian carpets. Beside the tomb of Itimad-ud-Daula stands **Chini ka Rauza**, the tomb of Shah Jahan's Prime Minister, with its decaying glazed tiles and stucco ceiling.

Overlooking the river, Agra's first garden **Aram Bagh** is laid out with a number of terraces, pools, pavilions and fruit trees and is a favourite picnic spot.

Built in 1648, the **Jama Masjid** has no minarets but squat domes in red sandstone ornamented with zigzag lines in white marble. The mosque stands in a crowded locality and is the most frequented in Agra.

The greatest love story ever told in stone is epitomized in the **Taj Mahal**. It was built for Mumtaz Mahal, who died giving birth to Shah Jahan's 14th child in 1631. The emperor vowed not to remarry and to build the world's most magnificent mausoleum in her memory.

Work on the tomb began in 1632 and, if the contemporary account of Tavernier is to be believed, it was completed over 22 years by some 22,000 artisans.

The massive **arched entrance**, 33 metres (108 feet) high, is topped with 22 cupolas symbolical of the years taken to complete the Taj. A Qur'anic inscription on the gate reads: 'So enter as one of His servants; and enter into His garden'. Worked to perfection, this calligraphic ornamentation has letters bigger at the top, so that when viewed from a distance, the size of the transcription looks uniform. When the original solid silver **door**, studded with 1,100 silver nails topped with silver coins, was plundered by the Jats, it was replaced by the wooden one seen today. The **dome** rising 98 metres (322 feet) into the sky is a purely Islamic concept, uniting heaven and earth. It represents the throne of God in paradise. The four water channels and quadripartite section of the large garden stand for the abode of God. Through his chief architect Ustad Ahmad Lahori, Shah Jahan realized in marble the image of paradise. The **cenotaph** of Mumtaz lies in the centre of the hall and **Shah Jahan's** to its left, the only asymmetrical work at the Taj.

In the **crypt chamber**, the 99 names of Allah decorate the eastern and western sides of Mumtaz's grave. A boat ride to view the Taj from the other side of the river will confirm what Tagore said of the world's most magnificent mausoleum: 'One solitary tear . . . on the cheek of time'.

Shopping

For centuries, artisans in Agra have been specializing in inlaid work in marble. Countless shops in **Tajganj**, near the Taj, practise their craft with mother-of-pearl. The best pieces are available at the **Crafts Palace** on the Mall. **Daresi**, near the Jama Masjid, is a thriving market for inlaid items and mini replicas of the Taj. Agra is also known for brassware, ivory and wood carving, carpets and *durries* (cotton rugs). Avoid the touts and shopkeepers' invitations to tea. Head for the **Taj Complex,** where the **State Emporia** sell genuine stuff at fixed prices.

Excursions from Agra

Thirty-seven kilometres (23 miles) west of Agra, **Fatehpur Sikri** was founded in 1571 as a thanksgiving to the Muslim saint, Sheikh Salim Chishti, who prophesied that the Mughal emperor Akbar would have three sons. Approaching the royal enclosure from the Delhi Gate side, the **Diwan-i-Aam** (Hall of Public Audience) is an open court where the royal balcony is secured by large lattice screens.

There Akbar sat cross-legged in audience to ambassadors and courtiers and to listen to the petitions of nobles and commoners. Behind the Diwan-i-Aam rises the magnificent central octagonal pillar of the **Diwan-i-Khas**, which has four passages

Opposite: Taj Mahal, perfection in marble.

radiating from its high circular seat, supported on 36 elegantly sculptured brackets. In all likelihood, this was the **Ibadatkhana**, where Akbar sat for religious consultations with leaders of different faiths that led to the formulation of the syncretic faith Din-i-Illahi.

Ankh Micholi is a set of three interconnected rooms believed to be the royal treasury, outside which the **Astrologer's Seat** stands with elaborate foliate *toranas* (ornate arches) typical of the Jain temples at Dilwara, Mount Abu.

The spacious **Pachisi Court** represents a grand chessboard, where live models once served as chessmen. The curious-looking, five-storeyed **Panch Mahal** is a Persian wind tower or *badgir*. Its 176 sculptured columns were once joined by screens but these have since been removed to expose the skeleton of the grand structure.

The ornamental tank, **Anup Talao** and the **Turkish Sultana's Palace**, with its amazing dado carvings of animals, birds and forests, are other interesting features.

The emperor's frescoed, spartan private apartments, called **Daulat Khana-i-Khas,** have been home to some precious manuscripts. From a window there, Akbar used to appear for the ritual *jharokha darshan* (window appearance) to present a glimpse of his good health and sovereignty to his citizens. **Jodha Bai's Palace,** with its ornamental brackets, niches and vast courtyard, and **Mariam's Palace** or Sunehra Makaan, with its barely visible gilded frescos and painted ceilings, stand near the emperor's apartments. The residence of Akbar's witty minister, **Birbal's House**, is part of the complex. An exclusive garden near **Panch Mahal** adjoins the seraglio.

Guarded by two much-damaged stone elephants, **Hathia Pol**, the formal entrance to the Sikri Palaces, stands behind the harem. It leads to a lake, now dry, and the **Hiran Minar**, a 21-metre (70-feet) pillar with a thousand stone elephant tusks.

Some splendid ruins of magnificent caravanserais, stables, schools and the porticoed mansion of the court historian Abu'l Fazl and his poet brother Faizi also remain. Built in 1571, the **Jama Masjid Mosque**, the site of Sheikh Salim Chishti's *tomb,* stands within a majestic courtyard. It contains some gorgeous floral and geometrical arabesques in turquoise, brown, red and black. The original red sandstone of the tomb was later replaced with white marble lattice screens and serpentine brackets carved out of single blocks of marble by Gujarati craftsmen.

The small cenotaph chamber glows with mother-of-pearl ornamentation on the ebony frame. Millions of devotees visit this *dargah* (shrine) every year, particularly childless women. To show that faith is stronger than force, myriad multi-coloured threads flutter in the breeze from the jali screens.

The great southern triumphal arch, **Buland Darwaza**, was built in 1575 to celebrate Akbar's victory in Gujarat. When Akbar moved to Lahore, Fatehpur Sikri became India's most splendid ghost city.

Lucknow

Lucknow, the capital of Uttar Pradesh, emerged as a prominent political and cultural centre when Mughal power declined in Delhi and the nawabs of Avadh moved from Faizabad to Lucknow in 1774. It is believed that Lucknow was founded by Rama, the hero of the *Ramayana*, who gave it to his brother Lakshmana as landed property.

Getting there
Regular flights connect Lucknow to Delhi, Mumbai, Patna, Varanasi and Calcutta.

Excellent train services link Lucknow to Delhi, Mumbai, Calcutta and all the other major cities in the country, beside convenient bus services.

When to go
The cooler months between September and March are recommended.

Where to stay
Hotel Gomti, Carlton Hotel, Clark's Avadh, Hotel Kohinoor, Hotel Capoor, Deep Hotel, Ellora Hotel, Tourist Hotel and Gulmarg Hotel offer a broad spectrum of accommodation. See listings for 'Hotels'.

Above: Water-pool reflecting the shrine of Salim Chisti.

Sightseeing

Asaf-ud-Daula built the Lucknow we see today. Only a *baoli*, or stepped-well, and the derelict ruin of **Asafi Kothi** remain of **Macchi Bhawan**, which bears the fish motif crest of his predecessor, Sadaat Khan, who formalized his break from Delhi in 1728.

Built in 1784, the **Asafi Imambara** is the largest vaulted hall in the world. It is supported without a single pillar, steel girder or wooden beam, and the roof is a maze of narrow passages and 489 doors arranged in a cleverly conceived labyrinth between two 55-metre (181-feet) long verandahs, which distributes its weight evenly. Do not venture in without a guide. In the vast courtyard stands a grand **mosque** and massive triple-arched gateways.

A little beyond the Imambara stands the **Rumi Darwaza**, an ornamental gateway, 18 metres (59 feet) high, topped with an octagonal umbrella. This conch-shaped gate was modelled along the lines of a gate in Constantinople.

Beyond the Rumi Darwaza, Muhammad Ali Shah (1837-42) built a burial place for himself, the **Hussainabad Imambara**. It is a gilded, highly ornate dome with small turrets and minarets. Inside, huge *tazias* (large paper and wood models of the tomb of Imam Hussain) and chandeliers fashioned from colourful Belgian glass are on display. The two splendid life-sized statues of women holding chains suspended from the doorway are lightning conductors. Two miniature Taj Mahals, flanking the central pool, house the tombs of his daughter and son-in-law.

Jami Masjid, with its tall minarets and onion-shaped domes, was built by Malika Jahan Begum. Towards **Asafi Imambara**, a big **clock tower** in a meadow beside a stream reflects the **Baradari,** or pillared pavilion, which was built by Muhammad Ali Shah. Today, it houses portraits of the nawabs. A **mosque** built by Aurangzeb stands near Asafi Imambara.

Overlooking River Gomti, the battle-scarred **Residency**, set in 33 acres (13 hectares) of sprawling lawns and gardens, was witness to the First War of Independence between the Indians and the British in 1857. It had previously been the pleasure palace of Asaf-ud-Daula.

The Central Drug Research Institute is housed in **Chattar Manzil**, with its spacious halls and underground channels and tunnels (now closed), built by the French adventurer Claude Martin.

The two, gilt-domed **mausolea** built by Ghazi-ud-Din Haider for his parents stand in the **Hazrat Mahal Park** nearby. The gardens around these mausolea lead to the fabulous **Qaiser Bagh Palaces,** which is where Wajid Ali Shah, the last nawab, housed wives and concubines.

The **Safed Baradari**, the **China Bazaar Gate** towards Hazratganj, the **Roshan-ud-Daula Kothi,** acquired by Wajid Ali Shah for his paramour, and **Lal Baradari** or the Throne Hall are all part of the palace complex and are still well preserved. Chandeliers from Britain adorn the **Shahnazaf** or **Nazaf-e-Ashraf** named after the Iraqi city Nazaf, where the tombs of Hazrat Ali, Ghazi-ud-Din Haider and his wives stand.

The architecturally curious **Constantia**, now a school, was built in Italian style with gargoyles atop corinthian columns. It faces an artificial lake from which rises a fluted masonry column, 38 metres (125 feet) high. Other places of interest are the **Archaeological Museum** in Qaiser Bagh and the **National Botanical Research Institute**, once Wajid Ali Shah's harem quarters.

Shopping

Hazratganj is a fully Westernized market. **Chowk**, near the **Medical College**, is the place for the most exquisite *chikan* work — delicate shadow-work embroidery, worked with white cotton threads on cotton or polyester fabric — for which Lucknow is renowned.

At **Aminabad**, you can buy the heady, exotic Lucknowi *attar* (perfumes) from Asghar Ali Muhammad Ali's perfumery.

Nakhas Market, near Chowk, is the place to separate gems from junk. It also has a well-known bird market, and cocks, once bred to indulge the nawabs' sporting fancy, are still sold there.

Varanasi (Benaras)

After many changes from Muhammadabad to Benaras, the 'City of Light', Kashi, is now known as Varanasi. Situated at the confluence of the Varuna and Asi rivers, Varanasi, on the western bank of the River Ganga, has been a religious centre since 2000 BC.

It is mentioned in the *Mahabharata* and the records of two Chinese travellers, Fa-Hsein (AD 405-411) and Hsuan Tsang (AD 630-644), seem to indicate that it was a flourishing Buddhist centre. However, Varanasi has always been the most venerated of Hindu pilgrim centres.

To die in Varanasi, the city blessed by Shiva, the Creator of the Universe, from whose locks the great River Ganga flows, cleansing away all sin, is the ambition of every Hindu. Daily, acres upon sloping acres of people converge on the waterfront *ghats* to ritually bathe, offer prayers and flowers, cremate their dead and go through the day's ablutions without inhibition.

Getting there

There are daily flights from Delhi and Khajuraho. Fast trains like the Neelachal Express, the Kashi Vishwanath Express, the Howrah Express and the Delhi-Calcutta Rajdhani Express connect Varanasi with all the major Indian cities. Buses to neighbouring cities are frequent and convenient.

When to go

October to March is the best time to visit.

Where to stay

Luxury hotels include Clark's, Taj Ganges and Hotel Varanasi Ashok. Hotel de Paris, Hotel Hindustan International, Pallavi International Hotel, KVM Hotel, Ajay Hotel and the tourist bungalow offer comfort at affordable rates. See listings.

Sightseeing

Life at the *ghats* begins before dawn. A boat ride from the southern end will afford

Opposite: Sarnath, where the Buddha preached his first sermon.

Above: Bathers at the ghats on the Ganga at Benaras.

a camera-perfect view of the ghats, with their thronging priests, pilgrims and tourists. The centrally located **Dasaswamedha Ghat** draws the thickest crowds, as it is hallowed for the legendary sacrifice of 10 horses by Brahma on this spot. The **Manikarnika Ghat** preserves Vishnu's footprints, the *charanpaduka*, in stone. It is said Vishnu created a well with his discus and filled it with his perspiration. This is a burning *ghat*, where people cremate their dead. Sometimes half-burnt bodies are removed to accommodate the next in line. But nobody seems to mind, not least the Dom Raja, major domo of the funeral rites, who makes a packet from relieved relatives.

In the teeming street behind the Dasaswamedha Ghat and the **Vishwanatha Temple**, dedicated to Shiva, hundreds of small shops sell the simple traditional breakfast of *puri* (fried unleavened bread) and potatoes. Non-Hindus are not allowed into the Vishwanatha Temple but can look through the silver-plated doorway or from the balcony of a house opposite. The present temple was rebuilt by Rani Ahalya Bai of Indore in 1776, after the original was

demolished by Aurangzeb who built a mosque over the ruins. The **Gyanvyapi Well** may be found behind the temple, where allegedly the original *Shivalingam* is hidden. A huge *nandi* beside it is always smothered in vermilion.

Aurangzeb's **Alamgir Mosque** with its 71-metre (233-feet) minarets stands on a prominence overlooking the Ganga. The city's other notable monuments include a small observatory built by Sawai Jai Singh II on the terrace of **Man Mandir**. A cluster of smaller and newer shrines crowds the southern end of the city. The **Durga Temple** is infested with boisterous monkeys that snatch food from you. The **Tulsi Manas Mandir** in white marble has the whole epic, the *Ram Charita Manas*, inscribed in black relief. **Sankat Mochan** is dedicated to the monkey god Hanuman, and **Shakshi Vinayak** to Ganesh, the elephant god. The latest temple, **Birla Mandir,** is in the university complex which also houses the **Bharat Kala Bhawan** museum with its collection of Mughal miniatures.

The **Ramnagar Fort**, occupied by the last maharaja, displays exquisite pieces of

Above: A floating wares shop on the Ganga at Varanasi.

old silver and brocade, palanquins and silver elephant howdahs in its small museum. From there you can see the Ganga sweep round the bend below the ghats.

Shopping

Varanasi is famous for its magnificent brocades embroidered with gold and silver threads called *zari*. Silk sarees are sold in bulk at the **Chowk, Golghar** and **Godaulia** markets and are much cheaper.

Excursions from Varanasi

Sarnath, 10 kilometres (six miles) away, is a great pilgrim centre for visitors from Sri Lanka, Japan and China because Gautama Buddha preached his first sermon to five disciples in the **Deer Park** there. The monastery was destroyed in 1394. Though the **Ashoka pillar** is now broken, the Chunar stone of which it is made has retained a fine polish. The four-lion capital which once crowned this 15-metre (49-feet) column is kept in the **Archaeological Museum** nearby. The **Dhamekh Stupa** marks the site of the sermon. The floral and

geometrical ornamentation on the stupa belongs to the Gupta period but the brickwork core is of Mauryan origin (200 BC).

The empty niches once contained small images of Buddha. The **Dharamrajika Stupa** was ransacked for hidden treasures by the British. The **Chaukhandi Stupa**, built about the fifth century AD, is crowned with an octagonal tower which was built by the Mughals. **Chunar**, about 37 kilometres (23 miles) from Varanasi, is a ruined fort that was of strategic importance in the 16th-century Mughal wars, when Humayun lost to Sher Shah. **Jaunpur**, 58 kilometres (36 miles) away, was a famous stronghold of the Sharaqui rulers who built splendid mosques as well as tombs in the Afghan style. Today, Jaunpur is famous for its incense and perfumes.

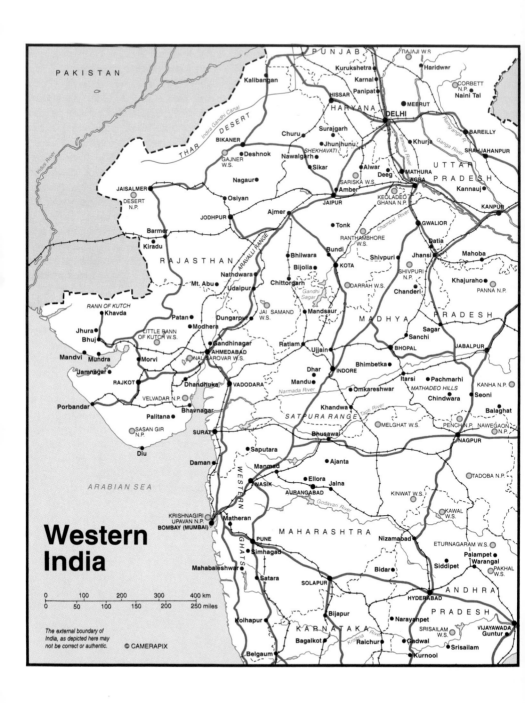

Western India

ARABIAN SEA

The external boundary of
India, as depicted here may
not be correct or authentic.

© CAMERAPIX

| 0 | 100 | 200 | 300 | 400 km |
| 0 | 50 | 100 | 150 | 200 | 250 miles |

Rajasthan: Medieval Charm

To the foreign visitor, Rajasthan is a land of maharajas, magnificent forts and palaces, romantic ruins and fascinating art and crafts. Despite the changes brought about by modernization, Rajasthan still retains its quintessence of fabled medieval charm.

Rajasthan has two distinct regions divided by the Aravalli Range of hills running south-west to north-east. The northern area is part of the Thar desert — arid and harsh — which, millions of years ago, lay under the sea. The southern part has dense, forested hills, lakes and lush greenery.

Rajasthan saw the dawn of civilization quite early. Traces of pre-Harappan culture can still be seen at Kalibangan.

Much later the original inhabitants of the land were baptized through a fire ritual and the ferocious warriors, the Rajputs, governed by a strict code of chivalry and honour, came into being.

They built up various principalities in the early medieval period and it was then Rajasthan came to be known as the princely state of the country.

Through the Muslim invasions in the 11th to the 13th centuries and later against the British, the legendary Rajput valour asserted itself until the different states merged in the Indian Union after independence.

Of compelling interest is the riotous burst of colour in the dress of the people — women in swirling skirts of dazzling red, pink, mustard and blue topped by multi-hued *chunnis* (veils) in dotted patterns or stripes, fringed with silver lace; and men in sparkling white *dhotis* (sarongs drawn up between the legs) and shirts with flamboyant turbans in stunning pink, mustard, red and indigo, which distract from the dullness of the monochromatic landscape.

Rajasthan is justifiably proud of the tie-dye fabric called *bandhini*, in which patterns are created from many tiny knots before the cloth is dipped in colour.

Lehariya (wavy stripes) is another kind of colour dyeing. The stunning hand-painted and block-printed textiles from Sanganer and Bagru, near Jaipur, are much in demand abroad. The mirror-embroidery of Barmer, south-west of Rajasthan, led to the revolutionary revival of the ethnic look in sophisticated fashionwear.

The ingeniously crafted silver jewellery derives from a rich heritage with beginnings in the Indus Valley civilization. Necklaces, earrings, anklets or those armfuls of heavy bone bangles form part of the daily dress of village womenfolk.

Richer and more sophisticated is *minakari*, the art of enamelling metal and gold jewellery studded with rubies, diamonds, emeralds and sapphires.

Characteristic of Rajasthani jewellery are *lac* bangles with precious stones on one side and enamel inlaid work on the reverse. Gift items like elephants and peacocks bring out the splendour of this craft, initiated by five craftsmen from Lahore brought to Amber by Raja Man Singh, Akbar's general.

These hardy people also create works of art on the leather *jutis* (unlaced shoes) worn by the common man. The Jodhpur *juti* is sturdier and brighter in ornamentation than the Jaipur juti. Small images in purest Makrana marble and the iridescent turquoise and ultramarine blue pottery, introduced by the Persians and Mughals and developed by local artisans, are much sought after. Hand-beaten brassware from Jaipur is another local craft.

The folk paintings from Rajasthan now adorn lobbies of luxury hotels in India and abroad.

Pabuji ki Phad is a narrative scroll which was once carried by native balladeers when they gave virtuoso musical performances. Playing on their stringed *ravanhatha* — an archaic musical instrument — legends about the exploits of the legendary folk hero Pabuji were sung.

Today the colourful and dramatic effects of these stories are reproduced as *phads*, folk art which are a speciality of Bhilwara in the south-west of Rajasthan. *Pichwai*, from Nathdwara, near Udaipur, is

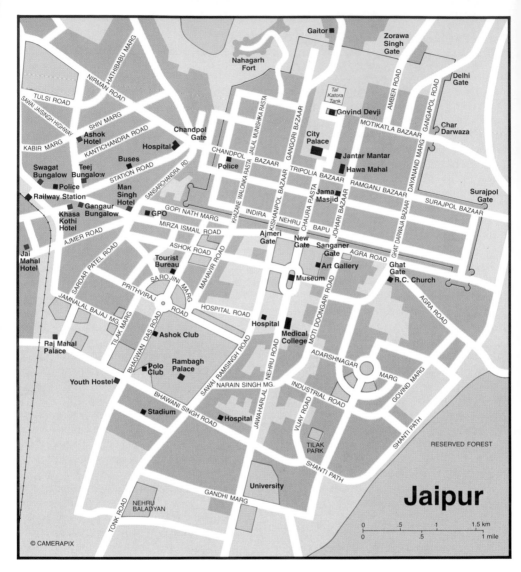

Jaipur

© CAMERAPIX

an equally rare work of art. Used as a backdrop for the image in the Nathdwara shrine, the painting depicts the frolics of the Lord Krishna. Originally the art was handed down from father to son, but now these backdrop paintings with their strong devotional character are reproduced by others.

Sightseeing

Not even the most elaborate coverage of Rajasthan can do justice to the wealth of places to visit. Among the lesser known gems are **Alwar** and **Bharatpur** in the north of the state. **Alwar**, 170 kilometres

(105 miles) south-east of Delhi, a medieval city with splendid ruins of a **fort** perched on a hill overlooking the **Aravalli ranges**, is also a quaint town with a magnificent **tank** and **cenotaphs**. The **Sariska Sanctuary**, 37 kilometres (23 miles) from Alwar, has thick forests with tigers in their natural habitat. The impressive battle-scarred **fort** of **Bharatpur**, 184 kilometres (114 miles) south-east of Delhi, was built by Jat rulers in the 18th century. The **Keoladeo Ghana National Park**, close to Bharatpur, is one of the most enchanting waterfowl sanctuaries in India. **Deeg**, between Bharatpur and Alwar, is known for its complex of exquisitely

planned gardens and palaces recreating the ambience of Mughal luxury. The **marble swing** in the garden complex belonged to Nur Jahan, the Mughal empress, and was brought there from the Agra Fort.

The two small states of **Bundi** and **Kota** lie south-east of Jaipur. Bundi is splendid and **Taragarh Fort** dominates the city. The Chitrashala in the fort has frescos typical of the medieval tradition which combined warring skills with the pursuit of excellence in the arts. Bundi and Kota are also known for their fine miniature paintings, romantic in tone and vibrant in colour. **Kota**, 38 kilometres (24 miles) from Bundi, has a **fort** and fabulous **palaces**. Kota is famous for its fine meshed muslin. Forty-eight kilometres (30 miles) from Bundi, in wooded seclusion on the road to Chittorgarh, north-west of Kota, stand the **Menal Temples**. Though much ruined, they exude splendour and eloquence in sculpted stone.

Bijolia, a further 16 kilometres (10 miles) away, is another cluster of ruined **temples**. Of the original 100 temples, only a few survive. The **Karni Mata Temple** at **Deshnok**, 26 kilometres (16 miles) south-east of Bikaner, is dedicated to the tutelary deity of the Bikaner rulers, but now more famous for the hundreds of freely scampering rats. Twice a year, in April-May and October-November, grand fairs are held there to honour the deity.

The magnificent **Ranakpur Jain temples** stand in the Aravalli Hills. These carvings equal those at the Dilwara temples. The main **Chaumukha Temple** has 80 domes and 1,444 columns, each differently carved. Ranakpur, which is 160 kilometres (99 miles) north-east of Udaipur, can be reached by bus or taxi. At **Kiradu**, in the south-western corner of Rajasthan, stands the finest of **12th-century temples**.

When to go

Rajasthan is cool and pleasant between September and March when the Rajasthan Tourism Development Corporation (RTDC) organizes a great number of fairs for tourists. These include breathtaking dances, gorgeous costumes and arts and crafts. Among them are: Nagaur Cattle Fair, at Nagaur, January-February; Desert Festival at Jaisalmer, January-February; Baneshwar Fair at Baneshwar (near Dungarpur), January-February; Hadoti Festival at Kota, February; Braj Festival at Bharatpur, March; Mewar Festival at Udaipur, March-April; Elephant Festival at Jaipur, March-April; Marwar Festival at Jodhpur, October; Pushkar Cattle Fair at Pushkar, November; and Bikaner Festival, November. It is advisable to book well in advance through the RTDC offices in Delhi and other major cities in India.

Jaipur

The extremely lovely city of Jaipur was made to order. In 1727, Sawai Jai Singh II, an illustrious Kachhwaha Rajput, ordered the building of Sawai Jainagar or Jaipur. Jaipur, one of the loveliest cities in the world, owes much of its grandeur to its brilliant architect, Vidyadhar Bhattacharya, who fastidiously executed Jai Singh's ideas and his own plans. Vidyadhar built the new city on a grid plan with nine auspicious squares divided by magnificent straight and wide roads, protected by high

Above: A young Bishnoi woman.

Above: Camels lead a colourful procession in Jaipur.

crenellated walls and guarded by seven splendid gateways. The city's main thoroughfare stretched for three kilometres (two miles) between Chand Pol and Suraj Pol, and was lined on both sides with shops. The main buildings within the royal square, temples and thoroughfares were completed within six years.

Getting there
Well connected by air from Delhi, Jodhpur, Udaipur and Mumbai, Jaipur enjoys daily flights from these cities. The fastest train to Jaipur from Delhi is the Pink City Express. Jaipur lies on the Delhi-Ahmedabad route and has convenient train connections to Agra, Ajmer, Udaipur and Ahmedabad. Buses leave at half-hour intervals from Bikaner House and the Inter State Bus Terminal (ISBT) in Delhi. The Rajasthan Tourism Development Corporation (RTDC) operates de luxe buses between Jaipur and the other cities in Rajasthan.

Distances from Jaipur: Agra-230 kilometres (143 miles); Ajmer-131 kilometres (81 miles); Bikaner-321 kilometres (199 miles); Jaisalmer-654 kilometres (406 miles); Jodhpur-332 kilometres (206 miles); Udaipur-374 kilometres (232 miles) and Delhi-261 kilometres (162 miles).

When to go
Rajasthan on the plains is pleasant between September and March.

Where to stay
Many former palaces have been converted into luxury hotels where you can soak up the grandeur of the past, among them Rambagh Palace Hotel, Jai Mahal Palace Hotel, Hotel Man Singh and Clark's Amer. Hotel Jaipur Ashoka is a first-class hotel. Budget hotels include Narain Niwas Palace, Gangaur Tourist Bungalow, Teej Tourist Hotel, Swagatam Tourist Bungalow, Hotel Khas Kothi, Hotel Mandawa House, Mandawa, and the Samode Palace Hotel, Samode. See listings for 'Hotels'.

Sightseeing
Jai Niwas was the first royal edifice to be built to house the image of Govindevji which the *Sawai* (one-and-a-quarter, or superior) brought from Mathura. Today it

is Jaipur's most frequented shrine.

Chandra Mahal, a seven-storeyed palace, freely combines Rajput and Mughal architectural features. It has an air of openness with a very pleasing arrangement of balconies and a pavilion. Entry through the **Gainda Ki Deorhi** leads to **Mubarak Mahal**, the former guest-house of the royal household, a double-storeyed structure with slender marble columns which houses a **textile museum** today.

Guarded by two marble elephants, the **Sarhad Ki Deorhi** leads to the **Diwan-i-Khas** (Hall of Private Audience), a pillared hall built on a platform which was used by the royal court. The two huge silver urns in this hall, each weighing 350 kilos (770 lbs), are in the *Guinness Book of World Records*. Madho Singh II, the first Jaipur ruler to set foot on foreign shores, carried these urns filled with the holy water of the Ganga to the coronation of Edward VII in 1902, so that he could purify himself at all times.

The magnificent **Ridhi-Sidhi Pol** gateway, to the left of the Diwan-i-Khas, leads to the splendid **Pritam Chowk** courtyard with its four exquisitely frescoed portals. The **Peacock Door** is the most captivating. Royal celebrations for the seraglio were held here.

Ticket holders are allowed entry to the ground floor, a hall with small curios and some paintings on display. The former maharaja occupies most of the palace, so you can only see the fabulously ornate upper floor from the courtyard.

The extreme corner of the courtyard is occupied by the **Diwan-i-Aam** (Hall of Public Audience), which is crammed with rare carpets, miniatures and howdahs.

Of particular interest are copies of Akbar's Persian translation of the *Mahabharata* called *Razmnamah*. This veritable Eldorado of art objects cries out for a better display.

Built by Sawai Jai Singh for his astronomical studies in 1728, the **Jantar Mantar**, mentioned in the *Guinness Book of Records* as the largest sundial in the world, stands outside the **City Palace**. Until recently, Jaipur's time was based on amazingly correct readings from this gnomon. Jai Singh built four other observatories in

Delhi, Mathura, Ujjain and Benaras. The 1799 **Hawa Mahal** (Palace of Winds) at the Badi Chaupad is to Jaipur what the Qutb Minar is to Delhi.

It is a bold architectural experiment, with a five-storeyed façade, tattooed with 953 latticed windows, which enabled the ladies of the seraglio to witness the grand processions that passed below.

There are beautifully sculptured ceilings and marble panels on superb *chattris* (canopies) over the royal cenotaphs at **Gaitore**.

The **Lake Palace**, amid **Man Sagar Lake**, looks charming from a distance. It was built by Madho Singh II as a blind for duck shooting and was never a pleasure palace. The renovated **Kanak Vrindavan Temple** is located on the road that leads to the Lake Palace and is set in a verdant garden at the foot of the barren **Dhundar Hills**.

Excursions from Jaipur

From Jaipur, a visit to the **Amber Palace** to the extreme north of Jaipur is memorable. The magnificent pillars of its **Diwan-i-Aam** once had to be plastered over to conceal their beauty.

The **Sheesh Mahal** has entire walls and the ceilings covered in the most splendid glass mosaics. The chief attraction in the towering fortifications of **Jaigarh Fort** on top of a hill is **Jaivan**, the largest cannon in the world, cast at the Jaigarh foundry in 1720. Three **storage tanks** are still popularly believed to conceal the ancient Kachhwaha treasures, which eluded the government excavators in 1976. On another hill, **Nahargarh**, a cool retreat for the Jaipur queens, offers a fine view of Jaipur.

The well laid-out **Sisodia Rani** and **Vidyadhar Gardens** lie south of Jaipur. The road from Jaipur passes through rugged terrain and leads to the **Temple of Surya** and some ruined *havelis* (mansions with inner courtyards) with fabulous frescoed ceilings on the summit of the Galta Hill. The foreign hand in Jaipur's architecture is best seen in Moti Doongri, the Rambagh Palace and Albert Hall. Built as an imitation of a Scottish castle, the **Moti Doongri** or 'Scottish Folly' looks terribly out of place. The **Rambagh Palace**, now a luxury hotel, and **Albert Hall**,

Above: Hanumana, the Monkey God, painted on a wall.

designed by Sir Swinton Jacob, show an admirable synthesis of Rajput and Mughal architectural styles. Albert Hall, now the **City Museum**, is renowned for its collection of Rajasthani miniatures of various styles.

When Stanley Reed, the editor of the *Times of India*, visited Jaipur in 1905, he described it as 'pink' as it is built out of local quartzite stone covered with terracotta. Sandstone and marble are rare. Hence the term 'Pink City' which conjures up images of a delightfully enchanting Jaipur.

Shekhavati

In a triangle formed by Jaipur, Bikaner and Delhi lies Shekhavati, famous for its magnificent frescos. The two districts of Sikar and Jhunjhunu form the core of Shekhavati. Named after Rao Shekhaji (1433-88), a scion of Jaipur's Kachhwaha rulers, Shekhavati became home to Rajasthan's richest businessmen when excessive taxation by the East India Company drove them out of their villages.

They left only to make enormous wealth in trade away from home. Whenever they returned, they embellished their *havelis* (mansions with inner courtyards) with extravagantly painted frescos. In the earlier phase, between 1830 and 1900, traditional themes dominated — gods and goddesses, hunting and everyday life.

Later, from 1900 to 1930, as interaction with the British grew and European lithographs and etchings became available, the themes also included Europeans, trains, bicycles, ships, aeroplanes and telephones.

The splendour and novelty of these frescos, originally worked in wet plaster, have only been realized recently, and visitors with an eye for the different choose to travel through the two districts, each within an hour's drive of the other.

Getting there
The Shekhavati Express is the most convenient train from Delhi to both Sikar and Jhunjhunu. Delhi is 231 kilometres (143 miles) from Jhunjhunu and 299 kilometres (185 miles) from Sikar.

When to go
Avoid midsummer months when the heat can prove a bit too much.

Where to stay
At Nawalgarh: Hotel Castle Mandawa, Dundlod Fort, Roop Niwas and Jangid Haveli. Hotel Shiv Shekavati at Jhunjhunu. Accommodation is excellent to modest, but this is a chance to explore unspoilt desert country. See listings for 'Hotels'.

Sightseeing
At Sikar, the frescos on the **Gopinath, Raghunath** and **Madan Mohan temples** are excellent. There is a haveli painted only in blue, a kind of status symbol for the *nouveau riche*. Portraits of Queen Victoria can be seen at the **Sikar Fort**. Beside the lovely frescoed walls of the fort, an aerial view of Jaipur is painted on the ceiling of a dome. The havelis of the Poddars and Ruias at **Ramgarh**, and the Singhania, Goenka and Sarogi havelis at **Fatehpur** are particularly interesting. The **Nand Lal Devra Haveli** has portrait medallions — from Jahangir to a European with a dog. The **Kedia Haveli** has enchanting frescos all over the walls. The Ganeriwali **Char-Chowk Haveli** at Lakshmangarh is magnificent and built to a plan like the city of Jaipur.

Nawalgarh has been justly proud of the richest merchant families in Rajasthan, which include the Poddars, Bhagats and Dangaichs. One haveli displays a marriage party on a spectacular 12-metre-long (40-foot) panel. The **Telephone Exchange** in Nawalgarh is completely covered with frescos. The **Saat Haveli** complex and the **Shiva Temple** with a multi-faced *lingam* (phallic symbol) are also worth a visit.

Jhunjhunu has a chain of frescoed havelis at Khetri, Baggar and Chirawa. The frescos at **Tibrewala Haveli** depict carpenters and accountants at work, trains and soldiers. Floral motifs dominate **Nuruddin Farukhi's Haveli**. The **Kothari Haveli** in Churu is exquisite. The **Kanahya Lal Bugla Haveli** has impressive frescos of the legendary lovers Dhola and Maru, Sassi and Punnu. **Surajgarh, Alisar, Malsisar, Bissau** also have beautiful specimens. The **Sone-**

Chandi ki Haveli and the **Raghunath Temple** at Mahensar, both built by the Poddars, are particularly grand.

Contained within a fort, **Mandawa** has some splendid havelis. Note the erotica at **Saraf Haveli**, a gramophone at **Sneh Ram Ladia Haveli** and a boy making his first telephone call at the **Bansidhar Haveli**. The havelis of the **Chokhanis, Goenkas** and **Sarafs** are profusely ornamented. The **Mandawa Castle** terrace offers a spectacular view of the town. Also worth seeing is the royal collection of costumes and arms.

The **Lodhuram Goenka Haveli** has grand frescos of elephants and horses, the traditional symbols of power and status. The **Chokhani Haveli** shows a helmet-wearing European riding a cycle without pedals. The **Newatia Haveli** depicts the Wright brothers and their magnificent flying machine in a curious way — one of the brothers stands suspended in mid air.

Mandawa town has nearly 120 havelis, maintained by retainers, tenants or poor relatives of the big business magnates of India. The havelis preserve a kaleidoscope of life in these remote parts in Rajasthan.

Ajmer

Ajmer was founded by Raja Ajai Pal Chauhan in the seventh century and named after the mountain Ajaimaru. Rajputs, Mughals and Marathas fought for possession of the city because it held immense strategic importance for campaigns in Rajasthan and the south. When the last Chauhan king, Prithvi Raj III, was defeated and killed by Ghuri in 1192, this provincial capital became part of the Delhi Sultanate.

Ajmer is the holiest Muslim city in India because the *dargah* or shrine of the renowned saint Sheikh Muin-ud-din Chishti, who died in 1235, is enshrined there. The Sufi saint on pilgrimage in Madinah had a vision to spread Islam in Ajmer. Akbar, the third Mughal emperor, visited the dargah to invoke the saint's blessings for a male heir and built a mosque within the mausoleum precincts when his wish was granted.

Later, Shah Jahan also built a mosque in white marble and Princess Jahanara added

Above: A village in the Rajasthan desert.

the splendid portico called Begami Dalan after her. In 1888, the Nizam of Hyderabad added the Mehfilkhana for pilgrims who flock to celebrate seven-day *Urs* (death anniversary) of the saint. Noted *Qawwali* singers perform and visitors offer roses and rich floral tapestries.

Getting there
Jaipur is the nearest airport, 138 kilometres (86 miles) away. There are convenient train connections from Jaipur, Udaipur, Delhi and Agra. Frequent, regular buses run between Ajmer and Jaipur, Delhi, Agra and all the other major towns in the state.

When to go
September to March are the coolest months and travel is pleasant.

Where to stay
Khadim Tourist Bungalow, managed by the Rajasthan Tourism Development Corporation (RTDC), Hotel Mansingh Palace, Bikaner Hotel and Champa Mahal Hotel offer accommodation for visitors. See listings for 'Hotels'.

Sightseeing
The **Taragarh Fort**, built at a height of 244 metres (800 feet), commands the desert for miles around Ajmer and offers a spectacular view of the city.

Adhai-din-ka-Jhopra, within the city, has great architectural significance. Built as a Jain temple in AD 660, it was converted into a Sanskrit college in 1153 by the Chauhan king Vishaldev. Qutb-ud-din Aibak destroyed the college and built a mosque with splendid calligraphic ornamentation over the screen-like arches. The *mihrab* (niche in the wall which points in the direction of Mecca) was built in 1199 by Aibak, and Iltutmish built the exquisitely carved screen in 1213.

Ana Sagar, an artificial lake of immense beauty with **four marble pavilions** built by Jahangir, was created by Anaji (1135-50) and completed by Shah Jahan. Yet another tourist attraction is the architecturally interesting but little known **Chashma-i-Nur** (Hafiz Jamal) in the hills west of Ajmer. The stepped structure was built by Rao Maldeva of Mewar in 1535 to conduct water upwards and Jahangir improved

Above: Dazzling Anup Mahal, the jewel of Bikaner's Junagadh Fort.

upon it in 1615. The masonry gateway stands in a defile between two hills. Within the city of Ajmer stands the **Daulat Khana**, the residential palace of Akbar, now a museum of Mughal and Rajput armoury.

Sir Thomas Roe, emissary from the court of James I of England, presented his credentials there to Jahangir in 1616.

Excursions from Ajmer

Pushkar is separated by the Nag Pahar from Ajmer, which is only 11 kilometres (seven miles) away. It is the holiest and most ancient of Hindu pilgrim centres.

Pushkar has the **Brahma Temple**, the only one in India, where the creator of the universe is enshrined and worshipped. It is regarded even holier than the four *dhams* (places of pilgrimage for Hindus) Badrinath, Jagannath Puri, Dwarka and Rameshwaram. According to legend, Brahma was in search of a place to perform his *yajna* (religious self-mortification). Three lotus petals fell from his hand at Pushkar and three lakes — **Jayeshta**, **Madhya** and **Kanishtha Pushkar** — came into being. During the last five days before

Kartika Purnima (full moon night in the month of October-November) a dip in the holy lake of Jayeshta assures *moksha* (salvation) to the repentant. There is yet another twist to the Pushkar legend. It is told that Brahma was anxious to perform the yajna rites at the most propitious time, but Savitri, his consort, took her own time to come. Not to miss the hour waiting for Savitri, Brahma married a *gopi* (milkmaid), Gayatri, and named her his consort. Savitri was enraged at the humiliation. She cursed Brahma, ordaining that Pushkar would be the only place on earth where he would be worshipped.

She then went away to the **Ratnagiri mountains** nearby, where a temple dedicated to her still stands. Ironically, a **Gayatri Temple** stands on the opposite hill and both overlook the Pushkar Lake. A *parikrama* (circular trip) around the three lakes of Pushkar completes the pilgrimage. The Jayeshta Pushkar is girdled with 52 bathing *ghats* built mostly by the princely families of Rajasthan and includes one built for Queen Mary of England in 1911. Behind the ghats rises a charming cluster

113

Above: A canopy decorated with blue tiles.

of **temples**, **priestly houses** and *serais* (accommodation) for pilgrims. The **Brahma Temple**, built atop a flight of stately steps, overlooks a long winding road. The temple is the culmination of a spiritual odyssey. The present image of Brahma was installed in 1809 after Aurangzeb broke the original.

Pushkar has more than 100 temples. The important ones are dedicated to Savitri, Varaha, Shiva and Badrinarayana. During Kartika Purnima, right after the Hindu festival of Diwali, Pushkar attracts not only pilgrims but thousands of village folk to the biggest cattle fair in the region.

The **Pushkar Cattle Fair** provides the desert folk with a rare opportunity to buy and sell camels, and have a little fun. On the dunes opposite the **Tourist Village** set up by the RTDC, hundreds of camels are paraded, examined, prodded and raced before prospective buyers. The fair is a riot of colours. It is a long-awaited annual event for the womenfolk as a vast market of *bric-à-brac*, clothing, colourful camel covers, and local handcrafted leather shoes, miniature paintings, puppets and stringed musical instruments.

The circus, Ferris wheel and magic shows are great crowd pullers. For hundreds of villagers there is no outing until the next Pushkar Fair. Camel races held at the open stadium are hugely popular. Even foreigners participate.

Ludnooth, a rural sport, draws eager entrants. Turbaned villagers clamber onto a camel till it can carry no more. The team with the largest number emerges the winner. It is a hilarious sight as occasionally the whole team tumbles down from their high perch and colourful turbans lie scattered in the sand.

Photography at the bathing ghats is strictly prohibited and police and volunteers take their job seriously and your movements and camera are always under scrutiny. Do not get lured into photographing young village girls who dress up in typical Rajasthani finery and pose seductively. They are out to make a quick buck. They know the value of such photographs in magazines and make capital out of the few days at the fair.

Evenings at the lake are enchanting as groups sing *bhajans* (devotional songs) and women carrying baskets of roses, marigolds, coconuts and *diyas* (earthen lamps) converge on the ghats to make their offerings.

With the ghats enveloped in the fading light of day, the myriad of lighted diyas afloat on the shimmering lake waters is a sight to behold.

Vedic *mantras* are broadcast over loudspeakers to create an aura of devotion, which is special to Pushkar. From the temples float the wail of conch shells, bells and gongs as devotees register their presence in the abodes of the gods.

At the RTDC Tourist Village, the evening includes cultural shows with performances by famous folk dancers and musicians, a feast to the ears and eyes. The lake, dunes and camels make a visit to Pushkar memorable. Pushkar can also be visited between September and March, the cooler months. Jaipur is the nearest airport and Ajmer the nearest railhead. The RTDC-run Sarovar Tourist Bungalow and Pushkar Palace Hotel offer board and lodging.

Jodhpur

Situated on the edge of Thar desert, 275 kilometres (171 miles) from Udaipur and 300 kilometres (186 miles) from Jaipur, Jodhpur is famous primarily for the impregnable Mehrangarh Fort perched on a 122-metre-high (400-feet) natural bluff.

The old town of Jodhpur lies below the Fort, girdled by a strong battlemented wall with eight mammoth gateways. It was a prosperous trading centre because of its strategic location on the trade route that lies between central Asia and China, and northern India and Gujarat.

Getting there

Two flights from Delhi daily and one each from Udaipur and Mumbai provide the air link to Jodhpur. Trains such as the Jodhpur Mail from Delhi and the Agra-Barmer Express and convenient bus services connect major cities in Rajasthan and Jodhpur.

When to go

September to March are the most pleasant months to visit Jodhpur.

Where to stay

Umaid Bhawan Palace, Ajit Bhawan Palace, Marudhar International Hotel and the Ghoomer Tourist Bungalow, run by the Rajasthan Tourism Development Corporation (RTDC), offer accommodation across a wide spectrum. See listings for 'Hotels'.

Sightseeing

Rao Jodha abandoned Mandore, the Rathore capital, and built **Mehrangarh Fort** in 1459. The first gate, **Jai Pol**, is the tourist entrance to the Fort. The palace lies beyond **Suraj Pol**. The palaces within the Mehrangarh Fort were built by different rulers, yet they form a compact and homogenous group. **Moti Mahal,** with its delicately carved lattice screens, is part of the *zenana* complex. The gilded ceiling and elaborate **Shringar Chowki**, the throne of Jodhpur rulers, with peacock-shaped armrests and gilded elephants, creates an ambience of royal splendour and opulence.

Functionally, **Jhanki Mahal,** a long gallery with glorious lattice screens, is meant for the seraglio to watch royal functions and celebrations in the courtyard below.

Chandan Mahal contains A H Muller's mural depicting Durga Das, a Jodhpur hero, honoured for rescuing King Jaswant Singh's son from Delhi. **Sardar Vilas** has exquisite wood carving and **Umaid Vilas** fascinating Rajput miniatures. **Takth Vilas** is famous for its glorious murals on the Radha-Krishna and Dhola-Maru themes.

The large *pankha* (fan), which kept the royal apartments cool in summer, and the lacquered ceiling provide a glimpse into the lives of the royals in days gone by. A collection of royal costumes is on display at **Ajit Vilas.**

The high standard of Jodhpuri painting may be viewed at **Phool Mahal.** The **Hall of Private Audience** or Diwan-i-Khas has some fascinating goldwork and exquisite depictions of the 36 musical notes (*ragas* and *raginis*). Below the Phool Mahal lies the **Tent Room** which displays the Imperial Mughal Campaign Tent, now pride of the **Mehrangarh Fort Museum**. Made of silk and velvet, embroidered with gold thread, the tent was once used by Shah Jahan for his *darbars* (royal courts) when he was out on his campaigns. It was plundered from Aurangzeb's camp by Jaswant Singh.

At Mehrangarh the collection of howdahs, palanquins and folk musical instruments is of immense cultural value. Of particular beauty is a silver howdah, Shah Jahan's gift to Jaswant Singh in 1657. It has carved figures of a lion, a fish, a peacock and a woman surrounded by flowers. Also on display are nine howdahs from the former Rathore states. Notable among them is the golden **Mahadol** palanquin from Gujarat and a peacock-shaped **Tam Jham** palanquin. The collection of cradles at **Ajit Vilas** and the Jodhpur armoury at **Man Vilas** is also worth a visit.

Umaid Bhavan on Chittar Hill was built by Umaid Singh in 1929 to provide relief employment to his famine-ravaged people.

It is the largest private house in the world and, with 347 rooms, numerous courtyards, sweeping marble staircases, fountains, swimming pools, a tennis court and a cinema hall, took 15 years to complete. Inspired by the Viceroy's House in New Delhi, Rashtrapati Bhawan, the architect H V Lanchester designed Umaid Bhawan in the *beaux-arts* tradition to meet the Westernized taste of the ruler. A large portion is now a five-star hotel. The former maharaja occupies one section and a **museum** is housed in the rest of the palace.

Shopping
Back in Jodhpur, the maze of narrow lanes around the **clock tower** and **Sajoti Gate** hum with the activities of local craftsmen engaged in making *kathputlis* (marionettes), tie-dye, shoes, flasks and lacquer bangles.

Excursions from Jodhpur
Mandore lies nine kilometres (six miles) to the north of Jodhpur. The old capital of the Parihars and later of the Rathores up to 1459, cenotaphs of six Rathore rulers, landscaped gardens, the **Hall of Heroes** with a rock surface carved with statues of Rathore heroes and the **Shrine of Thirty-Three Crore Gods** — wildly exaggerated for those good with numbers — attest to its ancient heritage. Returning to Jodhpur, a detour worth taking is to **Balsamand**, an artificial lake created in 1159. Realizing its

potential as a pleasure resort, a **palace** was built there in 1936. **Mahamandir**, famous for its 100 carved pillars, is close by.

Nagaur, 135 kilometres (84 miles) northwest of Jodhpur, has a **Mughal fort** and **mosque** built by Akbar. The annual **Cattle Fair** in February, similar to the Camel Fair at Pushkar, can be a delightful experience. Thousands of cattle and a greater number of colourfully dressed villagers from different parts of Rajasthan converge on this town for business and fun. The **Bishnoi Villages** in the neighbourhood provide a glimpse into the simple and honest living style of these people, who preserve plant and wildlife with religious dedication.

The ruins of eighth to tenth-century Hindu and Jain temples make **Osia**, 65 kilometres (40 miles) away, an interesting place to visit. **Harihara**, the oldest, is the largest and most beautiful of the temples. The architecturally important **Surya** and **Mahavira Jain Temples** (AD 770-780) in the same village, are also enchanting. The latter, particularly, has a ceiling of inverted concentric rings decorated with figurines of celestial beauties. The **Sachiya Mata Temple** on the hill, much repaired and enlarged, is also fascinating.

Jaisalmer

Jaisalmer, atop majestic Trikuta Hill, was founded in 1156 by the Bhatti Rajput chieftain, Rawal Jaisal, in fulfilment of Lord Krishna's prophecy that a scion of his Yadav clan would build a great kingdom there.

Getting there
The Palace on Wheels is a luxurious train to Jaisalmer, stopping at Agra, Bharatpur, Jaipur and Jodhpur. There is also a direct daily train from Jodhpur to Jaisalmer. Direct buses operate between Jaisalmer and Bikaner, 324 kilometres (201 miles) away.

When to go
Between September and March.

Where to stay
Jaisal Castle, Hotel Jaisal Palace, Hotel Moomal Palace, run by the Rajasthan

Tourism Development Corporation (RTDC), Hotel Jai Niwas Palace and Hotel Sri Narayana Vilas offer a range of accommodation. Besides these hotels in Jaisalmer accommodation is no problem. Anyone who can spare two decent rooms in his house calls it a palace and everyone is keen to make a living from this business, especially during the three-day Desert Festival.

Sightseeing

The **Fort of Jaisalmer,** with its four gateways **Akhai Pol** (Ganesh Pol), **Suraj Pol, Bhuta Pol** and **Hawa Pol**, is the heart of the city. Cobbled stone pathways and hairpin bends combine to form an intriguing defence against the enemy.

The five main palaces, **Sarvottam Vilas, Akhai Vilas, Gaj Mahal, Rang Mahal** and **Moti Mahal,** are hidden behind the seven-storeyed façade. The courtyards are protected from the fierce desert heat and dry wind by lattice screens, and the *jharokhas* or projected balconies have an unsurpassed ethereal quality which earned the artisan from Jaisalmer much repute.

Rang Mahal, on the uppermost floor, with its exquisite arches painted with murals and spandrels, witnessed many a music and dance soirée, that entertained the seraglio in days gone by. The view of the mammoth ramparts from its balconies is breathtaking. The balconies of **Gaj Mahal** are also wonderful works of art.

One-third of the city's population lives within the fort. Many of the houses provide accommodation to the budget-conscious and also house curio shops. The palace courtyard is a world in itself. The three **Jain Temples** within the palace complex are elaborately sculptured, and one of them has an emerald icon of Mahavira. Jaisalmer is one of those towns where it is impossible to get lost. Every road will return you to the fort. Not to be missed are the *havelis* (mansions with inner courtyards) the pride of Jaisalmer's architecture and a national heritage. One can only marvel at the splendour of **Salim Singh's Haveli** at the eastern corner of the city, with its large balconies upheld by sculptured peacocks, slender pillars and dainty arches.

Patwon ki Haveli, built between 1800 and 1860 by a family dealing in brocades and gold and silk embroidery, stands near the city centre. It is a fine showpiece of Jaisalmer's legendary stonecraft. The arches and the balconies, and the finesse of craft is simply incredible. **Nathmal ki Haveli**, built in 1885, has two identical portions joined by a common façade. Again the workmanship of these balconies is superb.

Among the few other buildings of remarkable architectural splendour are the **Jai Niwas Palace**, now a hotel, and the **Tazia Tower**, an artisan's gift to his ruler.

Shopping

The market is concentrated along the narrow strip of road that runs through the entire length of the city. Small shops are filled with indigenous art objects: bedspreads and fabrics decorated with appliqué, glass-work embroidery, camel-hair blankets and rugs, and miniature paintings.

During the annual **Desert Festival** in January-February — the dates change every year — shopkeepers from Jodhpur, Bikaner and Barmer set up shop there.

The festival itself is a riot of colours, with women swirling *ghaghras* (knee-length skirts) of multi-hues and *odhnis* (cotton shawls) and men in their flamboyant turbans. Buses, camel carts, jeeps and every other conceivable mode of transport bring people from far-flung villages to the fair. Renowned artists participate in cultural shows and dances organized by the Rajasthan Tourism Department. When the festival is on, conducted tours to the **Sam** and **Khuri villages**, in the heart of the desert on the Pakistan border, are made available by the RTDC. Romantic plays of valour and chivalry are staged under a full moon on the rippling sands. A makeshift stage sets the ambience for stunning performances of the **Gher, Dhap, Ghoomar, Moria** and **TerehTal** folk dances. Wild wolf calls and thundering applause announce the entry of the **Kalbelia** dancers garbed in black ghaghra lined with silver

Overleaf: Jaisalmer, the desert citadel.

Above: Lake Palace, Udaipur.

lace. They perform with electrifying gusto to the lilting rhythms of the Langa and Manganiyar musicians. After the show you could have a problem locating your vehicle, but, as always, the Jaisalmer Fort looms with lighthouse-like reassurance.

Excursions from Jaisalmer

To experience the rigours of a treeless desert, go on one of the **camel safaris**, arranged by the RTDC, but remember to take plenty of water along. Jeeps hired from the RTDC office can take you to outlying villages. Seventeen kilometres (11 miles) away, **Lodurva** has a magnificent **Jain Temple** with exquisite lattice screens, a high ornate arch or *torana* and a model of the *kalpavriksha* (wish fulfilment tree).

Lodurva also has ruins and peacocks. **Bada Bagh**, six kilometres (four miles) away, has a cluster of **royal cenotaphs** amid an oasis of shady trees and a stream.

Garhisar, close to the **Jaisalmer Fort**, has an artificial reservoir, Jaisalmer's main source of water. The arched gateway was built by a courtesan. During winter people throng the temples and the trees come

alive with the songs and colours of birds.

Seventeen kilometres (11 miles) down the Barmer Road, the **Akal Wood Fossil Park** has rare 180-million-year-old fossils which were under the sea nearly 35 million years ago until it receded, slowly turning the land mass into the arid Thar desert.

Kiradu, a five-hour bus journey from Jodhpur or Jaisalmer, is the least publicized destination in Rajasthan, 45 kilometres (28 miles) from Barmer. The skeleton of the Ranga Mandap at the **Vishnu Temple** and the heavily ornamented columns of the **Somesvara Temple** speak of a Gupta influence. The *shikhara* (tower) has *urusringas* (turrets) clinging to the main body, a feature of north Indian temples.

Udaipur

Unlike the other cities in Rajasthan, which are perennially besieged by vast sandy stretches on all sides, Udaipur, with its enchanting lakes and lush green hills, looks every bit the 'Venice of the East'. Udaipur was built by the Sisodia Ranas after they lost Chittorgarh to Akbar in 1568-69. These Suryavanshi rulers, who claim to be descendents of Lord Rama of the *Ramayana* epic, ruled Vallabhi in Gujarat for centuries before moving north to Chittorgarh. Udai Singh chose the hilly eastern bank of Lake Pichola to build a grand new city and named it Udaipur after himself.

Getting there
There are daily flights between Udaipur and Delhi, Jodhpur, Jaipur, Mumbai and Aurangabad, convenient express trains from Ahmedabad, Jodhpur, Jaipur and Delhi and excellent de luxe coaches between Udaipur and major cities in Rajasthan and its neighbouring states.

When to go
September to March is the best time.

Where to stay
Lake Palace Hotel, Shivniwas Palace, Lakshmi Vilas Hotel, run by the India Tourism Development Corporation (ITDC), and budget hotels like Hotel Lakend, Saheli Palace Hotel, Alka Hotel and Lake Pichola Hotel offer comfortable accommodation. See listings for 'Hotels'.

Sightseeing
Udaipur has spectacular royal palaces. It is well worth making the **City Palace**, a complex of palaces on the Pichola, your first stop in Udaipur. Through the **Hathipol** and **Tripolia**, the triple-arched grand gateway, the visitor is ushered into **Rai Angan**, the royal courtyard in the **Badal Mahal Zenana** complex. The palaces there are interlinked with galleries, and though constructed by different rulers, bear a striking homogeneity in architectural design.

Chandra Mahal was the coronation palace of the Sisodias up to 1710. Each new ruler was weighed against gold and silver to be distributed to the poor at the coronation.

Dilkushal Mahal, a suite of four 17th-century rooms, is enchantingly decorated with glass, tiles and murals. **Bari Mahal** or 'Garden Palace' is built around a 17-metre (56-foot) natural hill which rises suddenly from within the royal enclosure. It now

boasts an elegant garden. **Krishna Vilas**, built in memory of a princess who chose to end her life to avert a clash between rival princes from Jaipur and Jodhpur who sought her hand in marriage, displays Jodhpur miniatures. **Manak Mahal** houses a collection of fine Chinese porcelain. A visit to **Surya Gokhala** at **Bhim Vilas** is a must, if only to enjoy a glorious view of Lake Pichola and its embankments. Every morning from this window the Ranas paid their ritualistic obeisance to the sun.

Also within the palace complex, the gorgeous glass mosaics of the **Peacock Courtyard** depict the plumage of the bird. The **Shrine of Dhuni Mata**, the spiritual centre of the palace, stands on the spot where the fugitive Udai Singh was blessed by an ascetic to found the city of Udaipur.

Certain sections of the palace still occupied by royalty are closed to visitors. However, if you have a penchant for royal comfort, the **Shivniwas Palace**, converted into a luxury hotel recently, offers you a memorable stay, the ultimate in style.

Jag Niwas and **Jag Mandir**, the two islands on Lake Pichola, have charming summer palaces. **Jag Niwas** is a luxury hotel. **Jag Mandir** has an ancient **temple**, dedicated to Lord Jagannath. There, Karan Singh built a **palace** in red sandstone with an elegant dome to provide refuge to Prince Khurram, the future Shah Jahan, who rebelled against his father, Jahangir, in 1623. Mosaic floors inlaid with coloured stones evoke the ambience of Mughal palaces. There is also an elegant **marble throne** and an exquisite **mosque** on the island. A boat ride will get you there.

The **Jagdish Temple** within the city is a remarkable landmark. It stands on a prominence and its stately *shikhara* (tower) is visible from miles around. You won't miss the road. The temple is dedicated to Lord Vishnu and Lord Jagannath.

Sahelionhki Bari or 'Garden of Maidens' is a private royal garden impeccably laid out with elegant fountains, *chattris* (canopies) and elephant statues. The fountains create the sound of rain in a land which lacks only that one blessing. An ideal spot for those last souvenir photographs.

The **Bhartiya Lok Kala Museum** has

a fabulous collection of folk jewellery, puppets, masks, musical instruments and magnificent folk paintings.

For a spectacular bird's-eye view of Udaipur, a trek or a jeep ride to the **Moti Magri Hill** is well worth the effort. The **equestrian statue** of Maharana Pratap, the greatest Sisodia warrior, whose undaunted courage in battle was respected even by his victor Akbar, crowns the top. **Sajjan Garh Palace** is built on a 305-metre-high (1,000-feet) hill opposite the other.

Khas Odi or **Shikarbadi**, an arena for animal combat, provided entertainment for the royalty in bygone years. The view from these magnificent hills leaves no doubt why Udaipur remains Rajasthan's most romantic city.

Shopping

To feel the pulse of the people and the city take a leisurely stroll through the meandering narrow lanes and the two thriving markets, **Bada Bazaar** and **Bapu Bazaar**, will be a rewarding experience. Curios, traditional folk paintings or a colourful Rajasthani turban are just a few of the wonderful souvenirs you can carry home.

Excursions from Udaipur

Short excursions to the ancient temple towns around Udaipur make you realize the Rajputs venerated their Maharanas next only to their gods.

The Shiva shrine in the eighth-century **Eklingji Temple**, 22 kilometres (14 miles) away, built by the Sisodia ancestor, Bappa Rawal, was destroyed twice by invaders and was rebuilt each time in greater splendour.

Kailashpuri, this walled city, at one time, had 108 temples in it. The twin temples of **Sas-Bahu,** 23 kilometres (14 miles) away at **Nagda,** have superb sculptures. **Nathdwara**, 48 kilometres (30 miles) from Udaipur, is among India's richest temples. It enshrines a reincarnation of Lord Krishna, Shrinathji. The black stone image is decorated with fabulous diamonds and jewellery. The Krishna shrine, in the **Dwarkadhisha Temple** at **Kankroli**, 65 kilometres (40 miles) away, is venerated by the Vallabhacharya sect.

Haldighati, scene of an epic battle between Rana Pratap and Akbar in 1567, is 40 kilometres (25 miles) away. A cenotaph stands there in memory of Rana Pratap's valiant steed which collapsed from mortal wounds on the battlefield.

A visit to the impenetrable fortress of **Kumbhalgarh**, 84 kilometres (52 miles) away, which ranks next in importance to Chittorgarh, is memorable. It was built by Rana Kumbha in the 15th century over the ruins of a second-century fort.

History buffs should also visit **Ahar**, three kilometres (two miles) away. Nineteen cenotaphs of the Sisodia ancestors stand guard on the sacred **Gangabhar Kund**.

Relics of a 4,000-year-old Harappan civilization lie buried in a mound called **Dhulkot**, which might be the legendary Tambavati Nagari. Ahar was the alternate capital of the Sisodias whenever they were forced to desert Chittorgarh.

On lonely, deserted mountain roads beware of the Bhils, the aboriginal settlers of the land, who materialize without warning to demand money. A refusal could mean broken windows, punctured tyres, physical injury and much wasted time. Accept your defeat with a smile.

Chittor

Chittorgarh, the most illustrious fort in Rajasthan, has a history steeped in chivalry and romance. Its battle-scarred stones speak eloquently of a past when every Rajput preferred death to defeat.

Chittor acquired its legendary reputation after Bappa Rawal annexed the fort from the ruling Mori Rajputs in AD 734.

Many successive Sisodia rulers embellished the fort with palaces and temples, strengthening defences and building tanks to ensure a permanent water supply.

Getting there
Chittor is 112 kilometres (69 miles) northeast of Udaipur, with hourly buses.

When to go
Avoid May and June.

Where to stay
Janta Avas Grih and the Panna Tourist Bungalow, run by the Rajasthan Tourism Development Corporation (RTDC), Natraj Tourist Hotel and Hotel Sanvaria offer comfortable accommodation. See listings.

Sightseeing
The **Chittor Fort** commands the town. The ten-arched grey limestone **bridge** over the Gambhiri River is still in use nearly 700 years after it was built. The winding road to the top of the fort passes through seven magnificent **gateways** and the **cenotaphs** of three valiant soldiers — Jaimal, Kalla and Patta — who died resisting Akbar's soldiers, are visible from the road.

Kumbha, a legendary 15th-century Rajput warrior king, is credited with 32 forts in Rajasthan, in which in the vaulted cellars of one — the grim and imposing **Rana Kumbha's Palace** — Rani Padmini, the legendary beauty, committed *johar* (mass immolation) with thousands of womenfolk to escape dishonour at the hands of the Khalji soldiers. **Padmini's Palace** stands in a lake.

The palace was part of the royal complex, and the *zenana* was housed within the Kumbha Palace. The gates of this royal pavilion were carried away to Agra by Akbar as war booty. The palace of the heir apparent stands close to Kumbha Palace.

A magnificent nine-storeyed, 37-metre (121-foot) 'Tower of Victory', **Kumbha's Vijai Stambha**, is believed to commemorate Kumbha's victory over the Sultan of Malwa in 1440. The 157 steps that lead to balconies afford a spectacular view of the ruins and across the hillside.

The **Kirti Stambha,** or 'Tower of Fame', is dedicated to Adinatha, the first Jain Tirthankara. Seven storeys and 22 metres (72 feet) high, the tower is decorated with exquisite sculpture. Built in 1150, the **Samidheswara Shiva Temple** was restored by Rana Mokul of Chittor in 1428. **Mahasati**, a vast open courtyard, was the site of another great *johar* in 1533, when Rani Karnavati led 13,000 women to burn themselves rather than surrender to Gujarat's Sultan Bahadur Shah. The eighth-century **Kalika Mata Temple**, the 15th-century **Kumbha Shyam Temple**, dedicated to Vishnu in the *varaha* (boar) incarnation, the **Palace of Patta**, **Naukatha Magazine** (arsenal) and **Naulakha** (royal Chittor treasury) are all worth a visit. The newly built **Fateh Prakash Palace** houses sculptures from the ruins at Chittor.

Mount Abu

Mount Abu, 184 kilometres (114 miles) south-east of Udaipur, is steeped in mythological glory. According to legend, Guru Vashishtha's favourite cow, Nandini, fell in a chasm and was rescued by Arbuda, the snake son of Himalaya. In recognition of Arbuda's virtuous deed, the place came to be called after him — Arbuda or Abu. Mount Abu is a picturesque hill-station.

Getting there
The nearest airport is Udaipur, 185 kilometres (115 miles) overland. From there one has to travel by bus to Mount Abu, an eight-hour journey. The nearest railway station is Abu Road, on the Delhi to Ahmedabad line. Mount Abu is 29 kilometres (18 miles) from the station with regular bus and jeep services. A more direct way is by bus from Udaipur or Ranakpur.

When to go
Being a hill-station, Mount Abu is pleasant all the year round.

Where to stay
Hotel Connaught House, Palace Hotel, Hotel Hilltone, Hotel Savera Palace, Hotel Madhuban, Mount Hotel and the Rajasthan Tourism Development Corporation-run Hotel Shikhara provide accommodation to suit every budget. See listings for 'Hotels'.

Sightseeing
Nakki Lake, believed to have been excavated with the fingernails of gods, is the social hub of this town, watched over by a curious toad-shaped rock on a hill. The small market with its countless shops selling coffee and *bric-à-brac* appears never to rest. Abu has always been the abode of saints and sages. The most famous —

Vashishtha Ashram — lies in a glen, deeply forested with flame-of-the-forest, *gulmohur*, jacaranda, *amaltas* and oleander.

The silence of this botanist's paradise is shattered only by screeching black-faced langurs, parrots and birds of myriad hues. At the foot of the *ashram* (**hermitage**) is the **Gomukh**, a perennial spring flowing out of a cow's head carved in marble.

The *agnikund* (ritualistic fire) at the hermitage, from which emerged the four warrior Rajput races of Parmara, Pratihara, Solanki and Chauhanas, is still maintained by priests.

Excursions from Mount Abu
Achalgarh, 11 kilometres (seven miles) from Mount Abu, has a concentration of temples built amid unspoilt sylvan surroundings.

The **Shrine of Achalesvara Mahadev**, Abu's presiding deity, is guarded by a colossal brass *nandi* (Shiva's bull-vehicle).

The **Laxmi Narayana Temple**, the **Mandakini Tank** with its famous statue of Dharavarshadeva, a valiant Parmar ruler, and the **Kumbhaswami, Saranesvara Mahadev Temples** and **Rana Kumbha's Palace** are also part of this complex, though the palace is now an interesting ruin.

The **Achalgarh Fort** crowns a steep hill, shared by two large tanks, a **temple** to Chamunda Devi and two **Jain shrines**.

The 15-kilometre (nine-mile) road from Achalgarh to **Gurushikhara**, the Mount Everest of Rajasthan, runs through some spectacular Rajasthan countryside.

Footprints of the fourth-century Vaishnava preacher Ramananda are preserved atop this 1,723-metre-high (5,653-feet) mountain.

And, as always, the view of the valleys and undulating hills below is captivating. A bell carrying an inscription dated 1411 is also of interest.

The most memorable aspect of a Mount Abu visit is a trip to the **Dilwara Temples,** architectural wonders in translucent white marble of unrivalled excellence. These fine temples are not conspicuous externally — a deliberate attempt to escape the notice of marauding invaders — but enclose within them magnificent sculptural wealth, the pride of Indian artisans.

Vimal Vasahi, dedicated to the Jain Tirthankara, Adinatha, was built in 1031 at the staggering cost of 185 million rupees. Over 14 years, 1,200 artisans worked to accomplish this masterpiece.

Divine mediation inspired a black stone image on this spot — perhaps the image housed in Cell No 20.

The *pièce de résistance* is the ceiling of the **Sabhamandapa** (1150), raised on eleven concentric rings and a circular arcade of ornate dwarf pillars joined by serpentine scalloped arches, a grouping of elegant pendants over a ring formed by 16 figures of Vidyadevis.

James Todd regarded Vimal Vasahi as 'the most superb of all the temples of India and there is not an edifice besides the Taj that can approach it'.

Perhaps the only rival to the Vimal Vasahi is the smaller **Luna Vasahi** (1231) which stands within the same complex. It is a replica of the earlier temples on pillars, except that its ceiling is hung with a fantastic lotus carved with what appears to be amazing weightlessness. Its extraordinary finesse and unbelievable artistry has won many admirers.

The other shrines there — **Chaumukha, Pittalhara, Adinatha** — are excellent but mostly ignored amid such grandeur. Visitors to the Dilwara Temples are allowed in only in the afternoon.

The other attractions of Abu include visits to **Honeymoon** and **Sunset Points**, places, as their names suggest, that attract those who wish to steal away for a few quiet hours undisturbed.

Opposite: Somnath Temple.

Gujarat: from the Desert to the Sea

Gujarat lies on the west coast. It has extreme variations both in terrain and in climate. Guarded in the north-west by the Rann of Kutch, an almost rainless desert with a huge salt marsh and edged in the south and west by the Western Ghats, with their cool forests and gentle hills and the Saputara resort, a 1,650-kilometre-long (1,023-mile) coast marks its eastern extent.

The state is a repository of cultural expression, with historic temples, stone and wood architecture, crafts and skilfully worked decorative textiles. It is also a centre of industrial development, trade and enterprise. The people know how to preserve their fine heritage while adopting the most modern approach to commerce.

Famed archaeological finds, at Lothal near Dhandhuka in Ahmedabad district and Razdi in Saurashtra, show Gujarat's links with the civilization of Harappa and Mohenjodaro. It derives its name from the Gurjaras who ruled there during the eighth and ninth centuries. An immigrant tribe, who entered India through the northern passes, finally settled in this region.

Mythological and religious epics tell of how Lord Krishna and his brother Balarama settled at Dwarka on Gujarat's western coast over 5,000 years ago. Near the Somnath Temple, another small temple marks the spot where Lord Krishna was supposedly killed by a hunter's arrow.

Gujarat was under the rule of the Solanki dynasty and then the Vaghelas, who were defeated by the Sultan of Delhi, and finally the Mughals in the 16th century. In the mid-18th century, the Marathas took over the state and finally, in 1818, it came under the British. At independence, Gujarat — except Kutch and Saurashtra — were included in Mumbai State. Only in 1960 was Mumbai State divided into the present-day Maharashtra and Gujarat.

When to go

Winter temperatures in some parts of Gujarat drop to almost freezing point. In the desert areas, they soar in summer to 48ºC (118ºF). The best season for travel is between September and March, but year-round most areas of tourist interest enjoy warm to hot weather in the day, with tolerably cool nights. The most exciting time to be in urban Gujarat is during Navaratri, in September-October. The **Tarnetar Fair** is held in **Sundernagar** during the same period. Various fairs and festivals are held in different parts of the state throughout the year, except in May and June. Makara Sankranti marks the official end of winter on January 14 and is celebrated in Gujarat as **Kite Flying Day**.

The Tourism Department organizes a **Kite Festival** with food and craft stalls and competitions — a colourful and exciting way to banish winter chills. December and January are crisp, sunny and clear, just perfect for a leisurely exploratory tour of Kutch, where the desert night skies can be stunning. In midsummer, the state's only hill resort at **Saputara** presents tribal dances, drama and music in a socio-religious atmosphere.

Ahmedabad

Ahmedabad was known as Karnavatti, the capital of Gujarat, until 1411. Founded by Ahmed Shah I, it blends the culture of both Hindus and Muslims, most visible in its Indo-Saracenic architecture. The city is immense fun once you learn to tolerate the noise, fumes and pace.

Getting there

Ahmedabad is well connected by air, rail and road to the rest of the country. From Mumbai the flight takes less than an hour. By rail it is an overnight journey. The flight from Delhi takes a little over an hour, and fast trains take about 18 hours.

From Vadodara (Baroda), Ahmedabad is only four hours away by road. By bus, Ahmedabad is 510 kilometres (316 miles) from Mumbai and 625 kilometres (388 miles) from the city of Jaipur.

Above: The arched triple gateway or *Teen Darwaza*, Ahmedabad.

When to go

As the commercial and industrial capital of Gujarat, Ahmedabad has streams of visitors throughout the year. Avoid April-June.

Where to stay

Hotels and guest-houses provide good fare at reasonable prices. Toran Guest House, opposite Gandhi Ashram, has affordable air-conditioned double rooms, or rooms with fans only.

Cama, Karnavatti, Natrak and Riviera have tariffs and facilities likely to please a range of tourists. See listings for 'Hotels'.

Sightseeing

Sidi Saiyad's Mosque near **Relief Road** is known for its classic architecture. Its two carved and latticed sandstone windows display a timelessness that stands apart from the hubbub all around. The **shaking minarets** at **Gomtipur** and **Sidi Bashir's Mosque** at **Kalipur**, demonstrate a whimsy of the architect by vibrating when pressure is exerted on the inner walls.

Muslim architecture is discernible by its floral and geometric figures, while the exquisitely carved wooden façades, with their windows, balconies and doorways in **Doshiwada-ni-Pol**, demonstrate the Hindu style. Most wood sculpture in Gujarat forms part of temples or private buildings or *havelis* (mansions with inner courtyards) and the figures depict deities, flowers, birds and animals.

For an idea of what modern Ahmedabad offers, the **ashram** or hermitage built on the banks of the **Sabarmati River** by Mahatma Gandhi, who led the country to freedom, is well worth a visit, particularly in the evening when a tour of the exhibition section of Gandhi memorabilia and literature can set the mood for an hour's *son-et-lumière* experience. This is a landscape of Gandhi's life and India's Freedom Movement, and highlights various sections of the original, older ashram. Following a tradition set by Mahatma Gandhi, Ahmedabad has a number of institutions of imposing intellectual and physical stature.

The **Indian Institute of Management Building** was designed by Louis Kahn and the **National Institute of Design** does high

Above: The 15th-century Jami Masjid in Ahmedabad.

style work. The fountains near it are created out of large, traditional metal pots. The **Gandhi Labour Institute** does important work on labour relations, and the **Gujarat Vidyapeeth**, a university founded by Mahatma Gandhi, has an excellent library, museum, printing press and research centre. For scholars and travellers alike, time spent in these institutions will not be wasted.

For the more artistically inclined, the best known textile museum in India, the **Calico Museum**, is located at Shahibag. Visiting hours are short but the spread of brocades, embroidered, printed and handwoven Indian textiles is a fitting tribute to Ahmedabad from a family of textile magnates. Gujarati folk crafts are selected lovingly and displayed at the **Shreyas Folk Museum** in **Ambavadi** and the **Tribal Museum** on **Ashram Road**. They contain a representative collection of hand-made rural artefacts for use in the daily lives of the many varied communities that make up the heterogenous character of Gujarat.

Gujarat Tourism organizes a half-day city tour which covers **Adalaj Vav**, the Gandhi Ashram, Calico Museum, **Sundarvan Snake Park**, **Sarkhej Roza** and the **Vishala Restaurant Complex** with its **Vechar Utensil Museum**.

Excursions from Ahmedabad

Gujarat presents its culture on a platter. The beautifully laid-out **Vishala Restaurant**, 13 kilometres (eight miles) outside Ahmedabad, towards **Vadodara**, serves wonderful vegetarian delicacies in a rural ambience. Swings, *charpoys*, pottery, music, puppet shows and the fine **Vechar Utensil Museum,** displaying a collection of metal vessels of all shapes and sizes, is entertainment and food in true Gujarati style, fine-tuned for the tourist.

Lothal, 87 kilometres (54 miles) southwest of Ahmedabad, is an important archaeological site dating back to the second millennium BC. An ancient port and settlement of the Harappa era, excavations have uncovered a planned city with intricate underground drainage systems, wells, houses and baths. A **museum** on the site

Opposite: The Sun Temple at Modhera.

displays many of the excavated objects. An ideal day trip by rail or road. **Modhera** has a thousand-year-old **Sun Temple**, 106 kilometres (66 miles) away. Its supporting pillars are profusely carved with figures of animals and gods, while the interior is austere. Only the rays of the sun reflect the spot where the Sun God once stood before invaders destroyed it.

Palitana is 215 kilometres (133 miles) south of Ahmedabad. It has 863 **Jain temples**, all on the summit of the **Shatrunjay Hill**. Some date back 1,000 years. The sky-scraping temple spires are a fascinating sight. **Shri Adishwar Temple** has a most fabulous collection of jewels viewable with special permission.

Patan, 130 kilometres (81 miles) north of Ahmedabad, is little known as a tourist spot. It has over 100 superbly carved Jain temples, a beautiful stepwell and houses with ornately carved wooden façades. The famous *patola* saree, woven with pre-dyed silk threads in traditional patterns, is an example of India's finest handloom skills.

The 15th-century stepwell called the **Adalaj Vav**, is 17 kilometres (11 miles) north of Ahmedabad by bus or taxi. A prime example of Indo-Saracenic architecture, elaborately carved stone pillars and lintels line the steps leading down to a rectangular-shaped well. Adalaj is the best of the many artistic wells found in Gujarat.

Kutch and Bhuj

Kutch, as a magical world, was discovered only in the past two decades, and is located in the north-west of Gujarat, bordering Pakistan in the north and lapped by the Gulf of Kutch and the Indian Ocean in the south. Hard, dry and flat, it becomes marshy during the rains. The semi-arid desert area of **Banni** is full of scrub, mud huts, camels, buffaloes and a number of communities producing intricate mirror-work embroidery, beadwork, decorative leather-work, lathe-turned wooden lacquer-ware, animal bells in copper alloys, hand-painted fabrics and patchwork quilts in a variety of designs identifiable with the community. The entire area is often cut off

from the main road during the monsoon months of June to October. Water is scarce except in Bhuj and along the south-west coast, so carry your own.

The communities living in Kutch are nomadic herdsmen, pastoralists or settled farmers. They are mostly immigrants from various parts of the vast subcontinent. Its trading towns are **Bhuj**, the capital and district headquarters, Mandvi and Mundra.

The population speaks the Kutchi language which is an amalgam of Gujarati and Sindhi, but the Muslims also speak Urdu. The locals understand Hindi, though only the men communicate in Gujarati.

Getting there

By bus or car from Ahmedabad, you will see a good cross-section of Gujarat, including small industrial towns like Limdi and Morvi, and the salt flats which extend from the Little Rann of Kutch. A good road makes the 10-hour journey pleasant. The overnight Gandhidham or Kutch Express from Vadodara arrives at Bhuj the next morning. By air from Mumbai takes less than an hour, while from Jamnagar in western Gujarat, it is a 13-minute hop.

When to go

October to March is the best time to visit.

Where to stay

A few simple hotels in Bhuj provide clean rooms and traditional food.

Sightseeing

Bhuj town reflects Kutch's openness to ancient maritime influences. Near the Hamirsar water tank is the **Kutch Museum**, the oldest in Gujarat, opened over 100 years ago. It has an impressive collection of woodwork, textiles, costumes, maritime coins, silver jewellery and Indo-Scythian inscriptions dating back to AD 89. The **Bhuj bazaar** is full of tie-dyed and embroidered fabrics made in the villages of Kutch — cushion covers, skirts, bed-spreads, blankets and shawls, wall hangings and doorway decorations.

The tourist influx has at times resulted in a flood of mediocre stuff, so the quality-conscious and discerning should visit the

Top: Mahatma Gandhi's Sabarmati Ashram, Ahmedabad.
Above: Mahatma Gandhi's birthplace, Porbandar.

Above: Milkmen, Saurashtra.

villages where they are produced and ask to see the originals. Bhuj town is partly protected by walls built in 1723. Entrance to the main bazaar is through one of its gateways, facing the **Aina Mahal**, a beautiful multi-balconied palace built in 1865. The inside is unforgettable as its inner walls are covered with gilded decorations and tiny mirrors. It has gold and silver ornaments of past rulers, even their silver shoes which jingled as they walked.

European and Indian paintings and intricate, inlaid, ivory doors made in 1708 are some of the more spectacular items in this fairyland-like palace. The quieter areas near **Umed Bhavan**, the government guesthouse, and the alley-ways leading off the main bazaar still afford a whiff of history.

Excursions from Bhuj
Bhujodi is a small village 10 kilometres (six miles) short of Bhuj, which has a number of handloom weavers. A wellstocked cooperative shop, and the piles of shawls, blankets, bedspreads and floor rugs in weavers' homes provide an interesting product range. A long, straight road

to **Khavda** leads to a cluster of villages where all women above the age of 10 are always engaged in embroidering. Turn into **Banni** for scrub desert with its fine dust and rough roads. Villages like **Hodka, Dhordo** and **Gerorewali** provide a wide array of locally made crafts. The circular mud huts with verandahs and a large community courtyard hum with life, especially embroidering, which is both a pastime and an economic activity. The interiors are beautifully decorated with mud-work relief designs embedded with mirrors.

The Sodha community at **Jhura Village** and **Camp** are the most recent settlers. Their distinctive embroidery is available in a small shop. If you love wide dusty expanses and enjoy the spirit of adventure, explore other villages in the Banni tract. **Mandvi**, a charming old port town about 70 kilometres (43 miles) south-west of Bhuj, has a narrow winding bazaar famed for its tie-dyed fabrics.

An underdeveloped beach, still close to its pristine state, is tucked away behind the local **Travellers' Bungalow** over which an **old palace** still stands sentinel.

Maharashtra: the Great State

Maharashtra, which literally means 'the Great State', is one of India's largest states both in terms of area and population. Situated on the west coast, it stretches from the Arabian Sea, over the hilly region of the Western Ghats, to the Deccan Plateau and into central India. Diversity marks not only its physical features and geography but also its range of religion and culture.

Mumbai, Maharashtra's capital city, is the financial centre of the country and home to a wide cross-section of people, who call themselves 'Bombayites'. Unique in character, the city seems to absorb people, instilling the essential traits of a 'Bombayite', while letting them retain their individuality. Everyone is welcome — or, at least, accepted.

Historically, the long-running struggle for control between the British and the Marathas, who also showed great resistance to the Mughals, ended in 1803. It was under the rule of Shivaji (1646-80) that the Marathas rose to power. A hero to the Maharashtrians, Shivaji and his exploits are the stuff of legend to this day in villages and towns across the state.

Pune, the place where Shivaji was born and raised, essentially Maharashtrian in outlook, is the cradle of Marathi culture. His deification is pronounced, though Pune has recently acquired a more cosmopolitan outlook. Maharashtra's history has left behind the ingredients for an exciting journey through this land.

Besides Pune, other major towns are Kolhapur, Aurangabad, Nagpur and Nasik; all hold varying degrees of interest for the visitor and provide a good base for trips elsewhere. Maharashtra's rock-cut caves are outstanding, with this art form reaching its aesthetic and creative peak in the caves of Ajanta and Ellora. The Western Ghats have a scattering of hill-stations.

Matheran, where motor traffic is not permitted, is reached by a tiny narrow-gauge railway. Mahabaleshwar has fine walks and good viewpoints for scenic mountains, and is a wonderful place for a relaxed holiday. Neighbouring Panchgani is quieter. On the other hand, the coast is less developed, with few popular resorts. Of the national parks, Borivili National Park, just outside Mumbai, is one of the most frequented in Asia, probably more as a bolt-hole from the stress of Mumbai life than for its relatively unremarkable wildlife. However, a large variety of birds visit the sanctuary. Other parks include Kinwat, Nazira, Nawegaon, Taroba and Pench, the last attractively located with rest-houses along the river. Maharashtra is also home to the Melghat Tiger Reserve, one of the first in the Project Tiger conservation programme.

Mumbai (Bombay)

The port of Mumbai is perhaps the most exciting introduction to Maharashtra or, for that matter, India. Geographically a western extremity, Mumbai, over the years, in many ways has become India's nerve centre. The region's transformation from seven swampy islands to India's financial, industrial, commercial, trading and entertainment capital is a story of excitement, energy, triumph and exploitation. This bustling city, where almost every culture in the country is represented, has a unique flavour. Mumbai's size and cosmopolitan character impose a distinctive stamp on its inhabitants, cuisine, culture and language.

Originally a group of isolated fishing villages, Mumbai was first home to the Koli fisherfolk from whose patron goddess, Mumbadevi, the name Mumbai was taken. In 1534, the region came under Portuguese rule and was renamed Bombaim.

Passing into British hands as dowry at the time of Catherine of Braganza's marriage to Charles II, the islands were leased in 1668 by the British Government to the East India Company. Profit-hungry British traders transformed the swampland into an excellent port. Trade changed the face of Mumbai and it grew and prospered, developing into one of the major centres of British administration. Encouraged by the British, skilled immigrants flooded in. Today, Mumbai bears the imprint of successive cultures, from the original Koli islanders to British empire-builders, and from Portuguese seafarers to Parsi entrepreneurs.

Like all other large cities, Mumbai has its problems. About 50 per cent of the people live in slums, many without electricity and running water. At the other end of the real estate spectrum, prices of residential and office space vie with those of Manhattan and down-town Tokyo. Pollution is high, the transportation system strains at the seams and the monsoons wreak annual havoc. Yet people continue to pour into the city and, though the infrastructure groans in response, somehow they and their ever-increasing needs are accommodated.

Getting there
Mumbai is among the most accessible cities in India, with international flights arriving at Sahar Airport, and domestic services operating out of Santa Cruz Airport. There are several flights a day from major cities, and services of varying frequency from others. Mumbai is equally well connected by rail and road with the rest of India.

When to go
The weather is best in December. November and January are generally pleasant. By March the heat and humidity have risen, with May and October the hottest, muggiest months when the monsoon reigns with occasional dry spells. For the city tourist, the rains are a deterrent, but the monsoon gives Mumbai a splendour all its own. Festivals are full of colour and celebration, but increasingly tainted by unbearable noise.

The Ganesh (or Ganapati) festival, one of the most important in Maharashtra, stretches over 10 days in September, when hundreds of processions literally dance their way through the streets, bearing aloft elaborately clothed and bejewelled clay images of the benign, elephant-headed deity before their immersion in the sea.

Dusshera, usually celebrated in October, is preceded by another spurt of music, dance and people in the streets, this time for nine nights. Diwali, the Hindu New Year, follows soon afterwards, though this festival of light has also become one of sound, with the snap, crackle and pop of fireworks more in focus than the visual. A festive air is discernible in the city all the way through to Christmas and New Year.

Where to stay
One should stay in south — down-town — Mumbai. The upper end is either the 'Taj' (the red-domed Taj Mahal Hotel built in the early 1900s or its contemporary high-rise annexe, the Taj Mahal Inter-Continental) or the Oberoi (Oberoi Towers and its newer, even more state-of-the-art hotel, the Oberoi). The old Taj, with its grand staircase, its wide marbled corridors and spacious rooms, has a following among those for whom ambience is a major consideration. There are several centrally located hotels with medium-range tariffs, including the Ambassador, the Natraj and the Ritz. The President, run by an affiliate of the Taj group, falls in between.

There is also the Royal Mumbai Yacht Club, with enormous if slightly down-at-heel rooms, some even overlooking the Gateway of India. The tariff includes all meals and the services of a personal attendant. There are several budget hotels on the Gateway sea-front in Colaba, and along Marine Drive. Top of the line choice for transit visitors will be the Leela Kempinski near Sahar Airport or the less luxurious government-run Centaur Hotel at Santa Cruz Airport. See listings for 'Hotels'.

Sightseeing
Mumbai's sights do not draw on the usual amalgam of history and architecture. Of course, there are several old and rather fine buildings in the Fort area, which refers to the locality dotted with scattered remnants of **St George's Fort**, built by the East India Company to protect the southern tip of their precious harbour. This region runs north to south from the Gothic **Victoria Railway Terminus (VT)** to the pale-domed **Prince of Wales Museum**, and includes the **University Buildings** (with the **Rajabai Clock Tower**), **Town Hall**, **Mint**, the **High Court**, and the **General Post Office**. Built

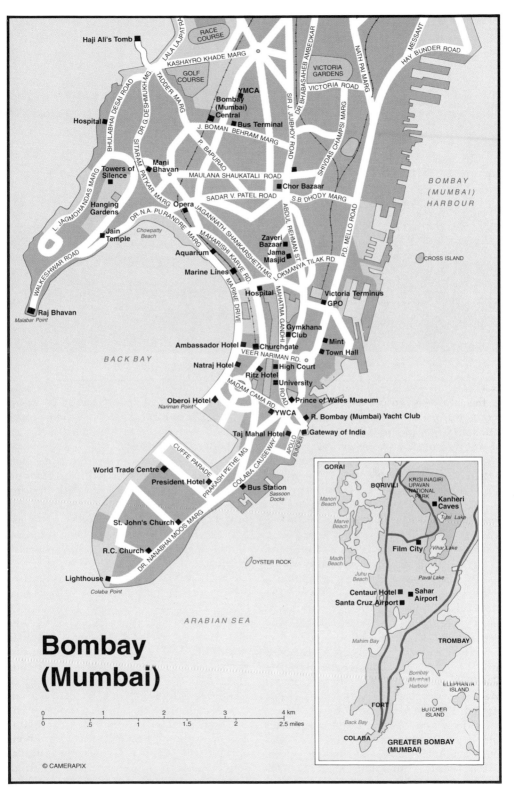

Bombay
(Mumbai)

Haji Ali's Tomb

RACE COURSE

KASHAYRO KHADE MARG

LALA LAJPATRA

GOLF COURSE

YMCA

Bombay (Mumbai) Central

Hospital

BHULABHAI DESAI ROAD

DR. G. DESHMUKH MG.

TADDER MARG

SITARAM PATKAR MARG

J. BOMAN BEHRAM MARG

P. BAPURAO

Bus Terminal

SIR J. JIJIBHOY ROAD

DR. BHABASAHEB AMBEDKAR

VICTORIA GARDENS

VICTORIA ROAD

NATH PAI MARG

HAY MESSANT

HAY BUNDER ROAD

Towers of Silence

Mani Bhavan

MAULANA SHAUKATALI ROAD

Chor Bazaar

SHIVDAS CHAMPSI MARG

BOMBAY (MUMBAI) HARBOUR

Hanging Gardens

L. JAGMOHANDAS MARG

Opera

SADAR V. PATEL ROAD

DR. N.A. PURANDRE MARG

S.B. DHODY MARG

P.D. MELLO ROAD

Jain Temple

Chowpatty Beach

Aquarium

MAHARISHI KARVE RD.

MAHARISHI SHANKARSHETH MG.

JAGANNATH SHANKARSHETH MG.

Zaveri Bazaar

Jama Masjid

ABDUL REHMAN ST.

LOKMANYA TILAK RD.

CROSS ISLAND

WALKESHWAR ROAD

Marine Lines

MARINE DRIVE

Hospital

MAHATMA GANDHI ROAD

Victoria Terminus

GPO

Raj Bhavan

Malabar Point

BACK BAY

Gymkhana Club

Mint

Ambassador Hotel

Churchgate

VEER NARIMAN RD.

Town Hall

Natraj Hotel

High Court

Ritz Hotel

University

MADAM CAMA RD.

Prince of Wales Museum

Oberoi Hotel

Nariman Point

YWCA

R. Bombay (Mumbai) Yacht Club

Taj Mahal Hotel

APOLLO BUNDER

Gateway of India

World Trade Centre

CUFFE PARADE

President Hotel

PRAKASH PETHE MG.

COLABA CAUSEWAY

Bus Station

Sassoon Docks

St. John's Church

DR. NANABHAI MOOS MARG

R.C. Church

OYSTER ROCK

Lighthouse

Colaba Point

ARABIAN SEA

GORAI

BORIVILI

KRIGI INAGIRI UPAVAN NATIONAL PARK

Manori Beach

Kanheri Caves

Marve Beach

Tulsi Lake

Madh Beach

Film City

Vihar Lake

Juhu Beach

Paval Lake

Centaur Hotel

Sahar Airport

Santa Cruz Airport

Mahim Bay

TROMBAY

Bombay (Mumbai) Harbour

ELEPHANTA ISLAND

FORT

BUTCHER ISLAND

Back Bay

COLABA

GREATER BOMBAY (MUMBAI)

| 0 | 1 | 2 | 3 | 4 km |
| 0 | .5 | 1 | 1.5 | 2 | 2.5 miles |

© CAMERAPIX

135

Above: On the streets of Mumbai (Bombay) outside Victoria Station.

in the late 19th century to give the city a more 'European' look, the buildings are still fairly well maintained. The **Gateway of India**, built to commemorate George V's visit to India in 1911, stands right by the sea at **Apollo Bunder**. It is perhaps Mumbai's most distinctive monument.

The **Prince of Wales Museum** nearby, built between 1905 and the late 1930s, was used as a hospital in the First World War, and was opened to the public as a museum in 1923. One of the finest museums in the country, it houses interesting collections in art, archaeology and natural history. The miniature paintings are particularly good, and the natural history section is extremely popular with children.

Sightseeing tours take in a scattered mix. A couple of temples, the **Hanging Gardens,** with their view of the city and **Mani Bhavan**, where Mahatma Gandhi stayed and some important buildings provide a good basic orientation, after which you should opt for the black and yellow metered taxis and walking shoes. Life in Mumbai unfolds on the city streets — hordes of hurrying commuters, vociferous street vendors, and *dabbawallas* carrying thousands of lunch pails between home and office every day, in a system that defies both logic and logistics.

Moving north from the crowded Fort area, **Marine Drive** and the famous **Chowpatty Beach**, with great junk food for those with stomachs of steel, **Teenbatti**, the **Jain Temple**, the **Parsi Towers of Silence** and the **Hanging Gardens** near the residential **Malabar Hill**, all follow in sequence. Further north, the **Haji Ali Mosque,** set in the middle of the sea, and the **Race Course**, are other places of interest.

Shopping

Like everything else in Mumbai, shopping draws on variety. Clothes run the entire gamut from production overruns, samples and rejects of the export rag trade, to designer garments, drawing both on traditional and contemporary styles.

The first may be found in a concentration of street stalls dubbed **'Fashion Street'** opposite the **Mumbai Gymkhana Club**, en route to **Metro Cinema**. Stores such as **Ensemble**, not far from the Prince of Wales

Above: The Gateway of India, Colaba, Mumbai.

Museum, stock the more pricey goods. In between is the **Khadi Emporium** in the Fort area, whose rows of cool shift-like *kurtas* make for ideal wear while travelling in India. **Cotton World**, behind the Taj, is well stocked with reasonably priced Western-style casual wear.

Silk fabric can be bought at **Indian Textiles** at the Taj Hotel shopping arcade, at **Kala Niketan** on Marine Lines, and at **Cottage Industries Emporium** near the Gateway of India. This large store is well stocked with a variety of hand-crafted items from all over India. Other outlets with a range of interesting gift possibilities are the **Mumbai Swadeshi Stores** in the Fort area and **Contemporary Arts and Crafts**, off Nepean Sea Road.

Mumbai is well known for its leather accessories. **Rasulbhai Adamji**, on Colaba Causeway near the Taj Hotel, specializes in well-made, brand-name fakes, and **Csango**, a couple of shops away from Cottage Industries is also worth a visit — no fakes, though. **Christina** at the Oberoi combines silk and leather in its range. Accessories in hand-tooled hide are also available in the

Oberoi shopping arcade. Kolhapuri *chappals*, the slippers in hand-tooled hide that are special to Maharashtra, are best bought in the little, hole-in-the-wall, stall outside **Metro Shoes** on Colaba Causeway.

Chimanlals (fort area) offers a selection of handmade paper and related products, and **Shyam Ahuja** — in the Oberoi arcade and a large basement store in **Worli** — is an international name in handwoven floor coverings and home furnishings. For shopping that borders on sightseeing, make the trip to **Chor Bazaar** (Thieves' Market) for antiques, not-quite-antiques and much *bric-à-brac*, as well as to **Zaveri Bazaar**, the gold and diamond jewellery market of the city.

Excursions from Mumbai (Bombay)

An hour-long launch ride takes you to **Elephanta Island**, 10 kilometres (six miles) from the Gateway of India, and its rock-cut **Hindu temples** from the seventh and eighth centuries AD.

A hillside stairway leads to the **caves**. The sculptures are in poor condition, having been considerably damaged by the

Portuguese. The caves are sometimes very crowded. Tours, some of which are guided, leave regularly from alongside the Gateway. A trip to **Film City**, the entertainment centre frequently dubbed Bollywood, can also be arranged. Mumbai is the centre of India's movie industry, the largest in the world. Hindi films are a mix of action, romance and family drama, usually all in one, and watching a scene being shot can also be fun.

The **Borivili National Park**, about 35 kilometres (22 miles) north of south Mumbai, is the only remaining natural forest in the region. A morning hike through the nature trails is invigorating for many city dwellers. It is also India's only national park that lies within a city. The **Kanheri Caves** in the park boast 109 rock-cut Buddhist temples dating from 200 BC to AD 600.

Many beaches along the Konkan Coast are a short drive from Mumbai. The heavily peopled **Juhu Beach** is shunned for the more peaceful **Marve Beach**, 40 kilometres (25 miles) away. Marve has cottages and bungalows, and its palm-filled skyline is now broken by the high-rise Raheja hotels, the Resort and the Retreat.

Manori, a short ferry ride across the creek, is even more tranquil, with the cottages of the family-run Manoribel offering an accommodation option.

A few kilometres down the road is **Gorai**, where it is possible to rent a shack for a sun-and-sea-filled holiday.

Pune and the Western Ghats

An interesting blend of fast-paced Mumbai life and a relatively relaxed small-town ambience, Pune provides an entirely different flavour of Maharashtra. While overpopulation and industrialization seem to pull at the city's seams, the city is distinctly Maharashtrian and is the cultural capital of the state. Pune, situated on the Deccan Plateau at the foot of the Parvati Hills of the Sahyadri Range, is 549 metres (1,800 feet) above sea-level. The city was the capital of the Maratha empire, once ruled by the great Maratha King Shivaji and, later, by the Peshwas. Pune eventually fell to the British in 1818. First favoured as the 'monsoon capital', Pune ultimately became an army base, and was renamed Poona. Years later, Pune became the centre of many Hindu social reforms and an important centre for the independence movement.

Getting there

Pune is easily accessible by air, road or rail from Mumbai and is en route to Goa or Aurangabad. The flight from Mumbai is a 20-minute hop. It makes the most sense, however, to take the train. Most southbound trains pass through there, but the Deccan Queen and the Indrayani are the fastest. Each covers the 192 kilometres (119 miles) of beautiful countryside in three-and-a-half hours, with the train weaving in and out of the Western Ghats, all lush green and silver waterfalls in the monsoon. Pune is also accessible by rail from Delhi, Chennai, Hyderabad, Jammu and the other major cities. The road journey from Mumbai is 170 kilometres (105 miles) of adventure, lasting up to five hours.

Taxis as well as the state transport and Asiad bus services ply between Dadar (in Mumbai) and Pune. Pune is also connected by bus to Shirdi, 195 kilometres (121 miles), Nasik, 202 kilometres (125 miles), Nagpur, 730 kilometres (453 miles), Aurangabad, 226 kilometres (140 miles), and Bangalore, 835 kilometres (518 miles).

When to go

Its geographical location makes Pune one of the few Indian cities to have a somewhat dry, comfortably cool climate for most of the year. Pune is much drier than Mumbai and less affected by the monsoons. April can be oppressively hot. The Ganesh festival in September sees a flurry of religious and social activity. Now the Pune Festival adds to the celebration with a variety of events: bullock cart races, folk dances, arts and crafts exhibitions and performances by renowned musicians and performers.

Opposite: Colonial architecture in Mumbai (Bombay) dates from the mid-19th century.

Where to stay

There are two five-star hotels: the Blue Diamond Hotel (Koregaon Road) and the Hotel Executive Ashok (University Road). Cheaper accommodation is available at Hotel Aurora Towers (Moledina Road), Hotel Regency (Dhole Patil Road) and Hotel Sagar Plaza. Hotel Amir, near the station on Connaught Road, is convenient and reasonable. See listings for 'Hotels'.

Sightseeing

Visitors to Pune have much to see and do. The **Rajneesh Ashram** once attracted a number of Westerners. Today the spirit of Rajneesh, or *Osho*, is still kept alive at **Koregaon Park** through his *ashram* (hermitage) and teachings, a mix of spirituality and pop psychology. An AIDS test is mandatory for entry to the *ashram*, though the short conducted tour held in the afternoons is free of this stipulation. The **German Bakery** outside the ashram has good coffee and is a great place to watch people, while the recently transformed **Nallah Garden**, with its lush greenery and occasional statuary, is marvellous for an early evening stroll. The charming, Rajasthani-style **Raja Kelkar Museum** houses the personal collection of a spry old man called Shri Dinkar Kelkar.

The entire collection cannot be on show simultaneously, so the exhibits are rotated. For a nominal fee, the visitor is invited to enjoy a variety of Indian artefacts and antiques, including nutcrackers, musical instruments, lamps and carved doors. Another place to visit is the **Palace of Shanwarwada**. Burnt down in 1736, the ramparts of this Peshwa palace now house a pleasant garden, a reminder of bygone grandeur. The **Aga Khan Palace**, where Kasturba Gandhi died when incarcerated with her husband Mahatma Gandhi, was a British prison. Several **gardens** and remnants of the Maratha empire also deserve a visit.

Shopping

Shopping in Pune centres upon indigenous items — the typical Pune saree in both its six- and nine-yard variations — and

Opposite: Ajanta Caves — a most popular excursion from Aurangabad.

Kolhapuri-style gold jewellery. Biscuits and baked goods, especially Shrewsbury biscuits, are oven-fresh and so popular at **Kyani's**, on East Street, that hordes queue up for them. At the junction of Main Street and Moledina Road, **Manneys** is an excellent bookshop in the new Clover Centre.

Excursions from Pune

Pune is surrounded by the remains of the Maratha kingdom. Forts like **Pratapgarh, Rajgarh, Torna** and **Simhagad** are within driving distance from the city. **Simhagad** lies south-west of Pune, a 25-kilometre (16-mile) drive through the Western Ghats. In the battle that won the Marathas this fort, Shivaji lost his favourite General Tanaji. On hearing the news, Shivaji remarked, *'Ad aala pan singh gela'* — 'the fort has come to us but the lion is gone'. Hence the fort was named Simhagad. There are spectacular views from the top.

The more modern **Panshet Lake Resort,** run by the Maharashtra Tourism Development Corporation, is 50 kilometres (31 miles) from Pune, and offers both accommodation and watersports. Pune is also a convenient departure point for several hill stations and wildlife sanctuaries in the Western Ghats.

One of the most popular hill-stations is **Mahabaleshwar**, 120 kilometres (74 miles) by road. **Panchgani, Lonavala** and **Khandala**, still well forested hill-stations, provide respite from the heat and dust of the plains. Ironically, the tourist demand for hot water is leading to the destruction of precious tree cover. Conservationists, therefore, suggest that visitors should stay at only those hotels which have installed solar heaters, or which use kerosene or electricity for heating water.

Aurangabad

Aurangabad sits 500 metres (1,640 feet) above sea level atop the Deccan Plateau, less than 400 kilometres (250 miles) north-east of Mumbai. Originally christened Khadke, Aurangabad derived its present name when it became the viceregal capital in the Deccan of the Mughal emperor

Aurangzeb. The distinct Muslim flavour and the remains of the fort wall that surround the city serve as reminders of the city's past. Without doubt, Aurangabad's major claim to fame is its unique position as the gateway to the incredible Ajanta and Ellora caves. But those whose senses are tuned to more than the imperatives of 'guide-book travel' will find the city interesting. As with almost every Indian urban centre, Aurangabad's daily life unfolds at several levels. Outside your hotel, under a large banyan tree, a barber will probably be plying his trade, oblivious to the dust clouds and ear-shattering hoots of the windhorns of passing trucks.

Getting there
The 40-minute flight from Mumbai or the 200-minute one from Delhi are two options. The Mumbai-Aurangabad-Udaipur-Jodhpur-Jaipur-New Delhi flight is usually heavily booked. The airport at Aurangabad is 10 kilometres (six miles) from the main city and visitors have to choose between hiring a private taxi or an autorickshaw. The latter is slower and is accompanied by the heat, dust, smells and sounds of India.

For the hands-on traveller, the nine-hour journey by train, with a change at Manmad, is a less expensive and infinitely more interesting way to get to Aurangabad from Mumbai. From New Delhi the 1,395-kilometre-long (865-mile) train journey passes through Agra, Gwalior, Jhansi, Bhusawal and Manmad. An inexpensive option is to make the trip by road. Regular state transport buses run from Mumbai, Pune, Nasik and other local cities. The Maharashtra Tourist Development Corporation (MTDC) operates daily bus services and conducted tours from Mumbai to Aurangabad by luxury coach. The 420-kilometre (260-mile) journey from Mumbai takes about nine hours depending on road conditions. If you travel by train or bus, an overnight one-way trip is recommended.

When to go
As with most of Maharashtra, the best time to visit Aurangabad is between October and March when the temperature varies between 10ºC (50ºF) and 33ºC (91ºF). April through June is hot, with temperatures often hovering around 40ºC (104ºF). The monsoons, from June to September, though beautiful, can hamper sightseeing.

Where to stay
Aurangabad has a couple of luxury hotels located a few kilometres outside the city near the airport. The Ajanta Ambassador and Welcomgroup Rama International are five-star hotels. The Aurangabad Ashok is more centrally located, as is the slightly less expensive Hotel Amarpreet.

The conveniently located Youth Hostel has dormitory-style accommodation, but reservations have to be made well in advance. In the city's southern section, near the railway station and the Tourist Office, is the MTDC Holiday Resort, with rooms ranging from dormitory-style to some with air-conditioning and attached bathrooms. Several other inexpensive hotels are nearby. See listings for 'Hotels'.

Sightseeing
A day spent wandering around the old northern part of the city is worthwhile, since Aurangabad has quite an assortment of interesting sights. **Panchakki**, an ancient water mill, bears testimony to the abilities of 17th-century engineers. Built by Malik Amber, the mill brought water from a spring on a hill which turned huge grinding stones that pounded flour for pilgrims.

The quiet garden of the mill is a good place to relax in before moving on towards **Bibihka-Maqbara**, the mausoleum of Rabia-ud-Darani, Aurangzeb's wife. A poor replica of the Taj Mahal, the tomb was built in 1679 by an adoring son.

A short car ride or a good uphill walk further north sweeps you into yet another religion, time and culture. The 10 **Buddhist Aurangabad Caves** from the sixth or seventh century are often overshadowed by those at Ajanta and Ellora. **Cave Seven** is interesting, with well executed figures. A particularly good figure is a large Bodhisattva praying for deliverance. **Cave Six** has riveting and well preserved sculptures of women. Other places that should not be missed are the **Sunher Mahal** and the **Nehru Udyan**.

Above: Bibi-ka-Maqbara, a poor replica of Agra's Taj Mahal.

Shopping

Aurangabad is particularly well known for intricately worked, brocaded or *zari*-bordered silk sarees from the nearby town of Paithan. *Himroo* shawls (of silk and cotton weave), *mashru* and *kimkhab* weaves, and *bidriware* are also good buys.

Excursions from Aurangabad

The **Pithalkora Caves**, about 78 kilometres (48 miles) from Aurangabad, provide picturesque views of ravines from their hilltop setting. These 13 elaborately carved cave sanctuaries, of the same period as Ajanta, attract less attention.

An interesting stop, 13 kilometres (eight miles) on the road to Ellora is **Daulatabad**, a fort with a fascinating history. This apparently impregnable hilltop fort was chosen for a new capital by Mohammed bin Tughluq in 1327. The eccentric king moved his entire kingdom from Delhi to Daulatabad, forcing the entire population to make the arduous trek.

Some 17 years later, another trek was made — back to Delhi. A few kilometres from Daulatabad is **Khuldabad** — or Rauza — where Aurangzeb's austere tomb lies in stark contrast to the mausoleum of his wife.

Less than half a kilometre (a third of a mile) from Ellora is the **Grishneshwar Temple**, one of the 12 Shiva *jyotirlingas* in India (five of them in Maharashtra).

The most popular excursions from Aurangabad are to either the **Ajanta** or **Ellora caves**. The caves at **Ellora**, about 30 kilometres (19 miles) from Aurangabad, are over 10 centuries old and among the most important historical monuments in India. The 34 rock-cut caves (12 Buddhist, 17 Hindu and five Jain) are carved in a curve on the slope of a large, low, sickle-shaped hill.

There seems to be no religious animosity to disturb the region's tranquillity, and externally the structures exhibit some structural similarity. On the inside, however, the caves display marvellous variety.

The **Buddhist Caves** — except Cave Ten — are all *viharas* (monasteries) rather than *chaityas* (prayer halls). **Cave Ten**, the two-storeyed **Vishvakarma Cave**, has a finely carved, trefoil window in the façade of the upper level. This structure, that is both vihara and chaitya, has a giant seated Buddha in the centre and pillars with friezes.

The Hindu caves are of far more complex and dramatic designs. **Cave Fifteen (Das Avatar)** is one of the finest at Ellora, and **Cave Twenty-nine (Dumar Lena)** is similar in plan and style to the cave shrine at Elephanta (Mumbai).

The **Kailasanatha Temple (Cave Sixteen)**, the centre-piece of Ellora, epitomizes India's rock-cut temple architecture, with a variety of beautifully carved panels. Dedicated to Shiva, this temple has a huge courtyard, a bridge connecting the outer enclosure with the inner and surrounding galleries.

A frieze of elephants and lions along the base of a carved podium seemingly carries the whole main shrine on the animals' backs. Transcending the earlier concept of a cave-temple hollowed out of rock, the entire structure is a monolithic rock-carving in architectural form, the largest of its kind in the world. It was carved by hand with hammer and chisel, working from top to bottom to avoid scaffolding.

Of the Jain caves, the most interesting is the double-storeyed **Cave Thirty-two**, where the upper level is ornately carved.

The closest airport and railhead to Ellora is Aurangabad. MTDC operates daily bus services and conducted tours to the caves. It is also possible to take a bus to Ellora from Mumbai.

Although most people who visit Ellora make day trips from Aurangabad, there are a few places to stay closer to the caves. The Kailash Hotel, with cottages facing the caves, is the most expensive. Three kilometres (two miles) away in Khuldabad, there are less costly options. The Traveller's Bungalow and the Khuldabad Guest House, both require advance reservation.

Ajanta is 100 kilometres (62 miles) from Aurangabad, and the 30 caves are cut into the side of a cliff. The all-Buddhist **Ajanta Caves** are renowned for their beautiful paintings and predate Ellora.

Discovered quite by chance in the early 19th century by a group of British officers, the caves are spread in a giant horseshoe along an inner fold of the Sahyadri Hills. Painstakingly excavated by monks, these caves span a period of about 800 years, and the first is said to date from the second century BC. Many caves at Ajanta are unfinished. A few of the caves are chaityas, but most are viharas.

While the older caves belong to the Hinayana school of Buddhism, the later ones belong to the Mahayana school. **Cave One** has awe-inspiring sculpture and vibrant paintings, whereas some of the murals and important paintings on the ceiling of **Cave Two** are damaged.

The many-pillared **Cave Four**, with some fine sculptures, is the largest vihara cave. **Cave Nine** with an arched window set in its simple façade is an early chaitya cave. **Cave Ten**, thought to be the oldest, is the largest of its kind and similar in design to Cave Nine.

Cave Sixteen is an elegant vihara. Beside it, **Cave Seventeen** has the best paintings in Ajanta in terms of number, variety and condition. Beautiful nymph-like *apsaras*, or celestial beauties, fly overhead; carved dwarfs support the pillars; and detailed scenes decorate the walls.

Chaitya **Cave Nineteen** displays both fine painting and sculptures, particularly the sculpture of a seated Nagaraja, with his female attendant and consort.

Aurangabad is the nearest airport. The nearest railhead, Jalgaon, is about 55 kilometres (34 miles) away. However, Aurangabad is a more convenient starting point.

There are frequent buses to Ajanta from both Aurangabad (travel time in excess of two hours) and Jalgaon (90-minutes). Private taxis may also be hired.

It is preferable to stay in Aurangabad and make a day trip to Ajanta, but the Ajanta Traveller's Lodge and the MTDC Holiday Resort at the caves are other options. The MTDC Holiday Resort at Fardarpur, one-and-a-half kilometres (one mile) from Ajanta, offers a medium-priced and comfortable stay.

Opposite: Kailasanatha Temple, Ellora.

Goa: Churches and Beaches

No other place in India excites the sun-and-sand-seeking holidaymaker more than Goa, with the possible exception of Kovalam.

This tiny state on the Arabian Sea was an object of interest for many centuries even before Vasco da Gama came to India in 1498 and noticed that the fertile land, natural harbour and mineral wealth, notably iron and manganese, would make a perfect base for Portuguese rule in the East.

However, at that time, Goa was an important port of the Vijayanagara kingdom and Arab merchants were actively engaged in the spice trade. Before long it was discovered the sea route from Goa to Europe was shorter and allowed a quicker turnover and, consequently, more profit than the longer and more arduous land and sea route travelled by the Arabs. Moreover, Goa was safer than Kochi and Cannanore, which were being constantly invaded by neighbouring dynasties.

The Portuguese attempts to secure Goa met with stiff resistance from the Sultans of Bijapur and Golconda, who controlled the spice trade in the early 16th century. Yusuf Adil Shah, the Sultan of Bijapur, went so far as to establish a shipbuilding industry there to keep the Portuguese out of Goa's coastal waters.

However, these Muslim rulers were not quite prepared for a Portuguese nobleman called Alfonso de Albuquerque who, having captured the forts in Kochi and Cannanore, was determined to secure the more peaceful port of Goa for his homeland. What followed was a fierce battle that left the Portuguese victorious on the feast of St Catherine, 25 November 1510.

Following this victory, an invasion of another sort took place. First missionaries of the Francisan Order and then in 1542, St Francis Xavier, a Jesuit priest, arrived on the shores of Goa. By a process of coercion, subterfuge, persuasion and concession, mass conversion to Roman Catholicism was the order of the day. In 1567, a decree

allowed the destruction of all places of worship alien to the Christian faith. And for the next 450 years, of more or less uninterrupted rule, the Portuguese occupied Goa and conducted its affairs even while the rest of India bowed to the sovereignty of Britain. Goa was absorbed into the Indian Union in December 1961, as a union territory along with Daman and Diu, two lesser Portuguese territories. In 1987, Goa was granted statehood, a status it long sought, becoming India's 25th state.

Since the Portuguese would not bring their womenfolk to India, they were allotted Muslim women captured from the harems of the sultans or wives of those killed in battle. As a result, generations descended from these marriages, and names such as De Souza, Pereira and Gonsalves became common. Such miscegenation created a lively, warm and fun-loving culture.

Strangely, the Hindus who were converted clung to their caste system, and even today, though their cultural tilt is basically Portuguese, they are inclined to refer to their castes particularly at times of marriage. Many older Goans still speak Portuguese, though Konkani is the state language and English the lingua franca.

Getting there

Daily flights between Mumbai, Delhi, Ahmedabad, Bangalore, Chennai, Kochi and Thiruvananthapuram arriving at Dabolim Airport, 30 minutes from Panaji, are the most convenient means of getting to Goa. Flights from Hyderabad and Pune are also available. Less convenient, though cheaper and more adventurous, is the 24-hour ferry trip from Bhaucha Dhakka in Mumbai. By train, the nearest railhead is Londa Junction, on the Miraj-Bangalore metre-gauge. By road, daily buses leave for Goa opposite Cross Maidan in Mumbai. The Kadamba Transport Corporation runs an interstate bus service between Bangalore, Mumbai, Mangalore and Pune.

Opposite: Goan fisherman with a prize swordfish.

Above: Altar, Bom Jesus, Velha Goa. Previous pages: Goa's lush coastline.

Baga is the inter-city bus stand. Local transport takes the form of buses and taxis and, curiously, motorcycles. Some travellers hire these motorcycles for a week or more. The Goa Tourist Development Corporation organizes luxury cruises on the Mandovi River.

When to go
The best time to visit is between October and March. However, those who wish to experience the famed romance of the monsoon should arrive between June and September. Another enjoyable time is during the pre-Lenten carnival in February or March. Three days of uninhibited merry-making bring happy Goans out into the streets in fancy dress, to dance in processions complete with colourful floats.

Where to stay
For de luxe accommodation, the Fort Aguada Beach Resort, Goa Renaissance Resort, the Leela Beach Resort and Majorda Beach Resort are perfect for a pleasure-filled holiday. Cidade de Goa, and the Oberoi Bogmalo Beach are five-star hotels. Others

lower down the spectrum are Hotel Fidalgo, Keni's Hotel, Hotel La Paz Gardens, Namu Resort, Hotel Baia Do Sol, Hotel Golden Goa, Hotel Zuari, Goa Woodlands Hotel and Vagator Beach Resort. Some families open their homes to travellers which could be cheaper if a longer stay is planned. Goan food, in particular seafood, is both authentic and incredibly cheap at the tiny restaurants bordering the beach. See listings for 'Hotels'.

Sightseeing
Goa's biggest draw are its churches and beaches. **Old (Velha) Goa,** 10 kilometres (six miles) from the capital Panaji (or Panjim), is a 16th-century city that was known as Goa Doraido or Golden Goa. Lying within the estuary of the Mandovi River, this was the heart of Portuguese Goa, plainly reflected in its monasteries, churches, convents and wide boulevards. Sadly, since the great plague made the city uninhabitable, many of the fine old monuments are in ruins or have vanished.

However, those that remain still take your breath away. The largest church in

Asia, the **Cathedral of St Catherine da Se,** is the finest expression in India of baroque architecture. It took 57 years to build and has intricate floral frescos, a fusion of Indian and European styles, and a magnificent gilt altar. In spite of its imposing Renaissance presence, it is dwarfed in importance by the **Basilica de Bom Jesus**, a small chapel that houses the remains of **St Francis Xavier**, returned to Goa two years after his death in China in 1552. The glass coffin within a locally crafted silver casket used to be opened at regular intervals to allow crowds to seek the blessings of the patron saint of the people. However, since the body began to shrivel, the last exposition was in December 1974, and the devout now have to be content with viewing the saint through a window in the coffin. The tomb itself was a gift from the Grand Duke of Tuscany.

Other places to see in Old Goa are the **Monastery of St Francis of Assisi**, which has a gilded interior and a museum displaying Hindu sculpture, relics from 10th- to 12th-century temples destroyed by the Portuguese, and a bronze statue of Albuquerque. The **Church of St Cajetan,** modelled after St Peter's Basilica in Rome, has seven baroque altars, all gilded in gold. Beside the church stands a recently restored **monastery**. The **Viceroy's Arch**, built of local, reddish laterite stone, was first one of the gates of Adil Shah's fort before a grandson of Vasco da Gama made it the ceremonial entry to the city, on the way to Panaji, where the viceroy made his home.

There is also the **Nunnery and Church of Santa Monica**, one of the largest in Goa. The walls of the convent are fortress-like, and the **Augustine Tower,** nearby, is one of four which survive in the Augustine Church.

Despite the prominence churches occupy in Goa's landscape, a number of noteworthy temples cannot be ignored. Though Christian and Hindu customs have mingled into a seamless Indian tradition today, this was hardly the case under Portuguese rule, when all the temples were systematically destroyed. Subsequently, when they were resurrected in the 18th-

century, many of the builders, who were forced to build only churches following the Portuguese occupation, incorporated domes into temple design, since they built as they imagined a structure should be without the guidance of an architect.

Ponda is the area for temples. **Shri Mangesh Temple**, eight kilometres (five miles) from Ponda, dedicated to Lord Shiva, and the **Mahalasa Temple**, a kilometre (less than a mile) from the Mangesh Temple, were both removed to their present locations between the 16th and 17th centuries by devotees who wished to protect them from the marauding Portuguese. **Shri Bhagavati Temple** in Pernem is 500 years old, and two lifelike, black, stone elephants at the entrance guard an imposing deity, the goddess Bhagavati Ashtabhuja, inside. The Dusshera festival in October, draws large crowds there. **Nagesh Temple** shares with the rest of Goa's temples the distinctive *deepmal* or free-standing, many-storeyed lamp tower, which is probably the result of a fusion of Portuguese and Islamic influences. It also has a Marathi inscription dating from the 15th century and intricate wood carvings depicting scenes from the *Ramayana* in the main gallery.

Other temples of interest are the **Shri Shantadurga Temple** dedicated to the goddess Parvati, the **Shri Mahadeva Temple** (in Panaji) built between the 11th- and 13th-century Kadamba rulers, and **Shri Mahalaxmi Temple** dedicated to the goddess Mahalakshmi, which has a main gallery with idols of Vishnu depicting 18 of the 24 forms he is believed to assume. The two mosques of historical importance are **Safa Masjid** on the road from **Banastarim**, just short of Ponda, built by Ibrahim Adil Shah of Bijapur in 1560 — which suffered destruction under the Portuguese — and the 17th-century **Namazgah Mosque** in Bicholim district. The only other mosque of interest is the 19th-century **Jama Masjid** at Sanquem, 26 kilometres (16 miles) from **Margao**. But Goa's main tourist attraction is undoubtedly its 130-kilometre (80-mile) coastline, and a variety of splendid beaches. To the north, are the **Arambol, Vagator** and

Anjuna beaches. Vagator is sheltered by the **Chapora Fort** built in 1717, while Anjuna, haven to hippies and voyeurs, is also well known for its Wednesday flea market.

A low hill, easily climbed, separates Anjuna and **Candolim** across the **Mandovi River**. It has a crystal clear stream which broadens into a natural pool and is surrounded by lush vegetation. Candolim also known as Baga, and **Calangute**, seven kilometres (four miles) long, form a stretch of five beaches north of **Aguada Fort**, the best preserved fort in Goa, not far from Panaji. It is believed to have 79 guns, but as a prison in use, visitors are not allowed.

From the Taj hotel group's resort of the same name, the fort's outlying bastion can be seen jutting into the sea. It also has a citadel and a lighthouse. **Miramar**, the capital's beach, and **Dona Paula**, the cosy bay formed by the mouths of Goa's two major rivers, the **Mandovi** and the **Zuari**, create a contrast of blue sea and dark sand.

South of the **Zuari River**, more out of the way, but no less beautiful, beaches stretch from **Bogmalo** to **Palolem**. In between, **Velsao, Cansaulim, Colva**, one of the loveliest, eight kilometres (five miles) from Margao, **Benaulim** and **Betul**, remain relatively undisturbed by tourism. **Siridao**, near the estuary of the Zuari, is a paradise for the shell enthusiast.

Beside the Chapora Fort and the Aguada Fort, Goa has a scattering of other forts of interest. **Maratha Fort** bordering Maharashtra, **Reis Magos Fort** and **Cabo Fort,** to name a few. While little remains of the original Cabo Fort, **Cabo Raj Bhavan**, the lieutenant-governor's residence, occupies its place and bears its name.

Churches of interest include the **Reis Magos Church,** built in 1555 beside the fort of the same name. It is dedicated to the three kings of the Magi. There are also the **Gothic Church of Mae de Deus** (1873) at Saligao in Bardez, the **Church of St Alex** at Curtorim dating back to 1597 and the 17th-century **Church of St Ana** at Talaulim, in Ilhas, on the bank of the River Siridao — a tributary of the Zuari — which

has, interestingly, hollow walls that made it possible for people to walk in unseen for confession.

There is also a church at **Verna** between Margao and the Zuari River, and another at **Santa Cruz** on the way from the ferry at Panaji.

Goa's two main towns are **Panaji**, the capital, and **Margao**. Panaji on the southern bank of the Mandovi River — the ferry is a popular means of crossing the Mandovi, and is shared by people, bicycles and scooters — grew in importance only when the governor's residence was moved there from Old Goa. It came to be known as Nova Goa in 1843, and became the capital of Portuguese India in 1853 after plague swept through the old city. The atmosphere in Panaji is distinctly Portuguese. It is, needless to say, dominated by a church, the **Church of the Immaculate Conception**, one of Goa's oldest. Its baroque façade and tall towers dominate **Church Square**. Built in 1541, it has undergone many alterations. On the riverside boulevard stand a

DEDICATED
TO THE MEMORY OF THOSE
KNOWN AND UNKNOWN,
DEAD OR ALIVE,
WHO HAVE GIVEN THEIR ALL
IN THE CAUSE OF FREEDOM
FROM FOREIGN DOMINATION.

Opposite: The tranquil Harambol Beach, Goa. Above: Memorial to the freedom fighters.

Above: Mortal remains of St Francis Xavier lie at the Basilica, Bom Jesus.

number of important buildings, including the **Secretariat** dating back to 1615. It was built on the site of the palace of the Sultan of Bijapur, Ismail Adil Shah. It is thus also called Largo di Palacio (Palace Square). The odd **statue** of a man hypnotizing a woman stands beside the Secretariat. The man honoured is Abbé Faria (1755-1819), who is credited with developing hypnotism through suggestion.

Azad Maidan, another square, has the **police headquarters**, and the well preserved **Menezes Braganza Institute**, with its impressive library and historic wall panels clustered around it.

Other places of interest in Panaji are the **High Court** (1878), the **Main Post Office** (Tobacco Trading House) and **Mint House** (Casa Moeda).

In Margao, farther south, life revolves around the bustling port of Marmagao, Jorge Barreto Park, the hub of the main square, and its bazaar. The **Damodar Temple** was destroyed by the Portuguese and what remains is insignificant compared with the church built in its place in Church Square. Built in 1564 and rebuilt in 1675, it is a marvellous example of Indian baroque architecture.

Services are still conducted there, so those who wish to worship in historical ambience may do so.

The town also boasts some exquisite old houses reflecting 18th- and 19th-century Goan architecture. Only three towers remain of the seven of the magnificent **Silva House** or Casa Grande, an 18th-century house built by the secretary to the viceroy. On a hill above Margao is the **Chapel of Nossa Senhora de Piedade,** rebuilt in 1820.

Despite its many attractions, Goa is best appreciated away from the tourists and towns. Paddy fields, coconut palms and red-tiled, airy houses with broad verandahs, are typical of life in the village where the true spirit of Goa resides.

The people are laid back and the *soucegad* feeling, Goa's chief lure, tends to take over after a few days of sea, siesta and *feni*, the local brew.

Madhya Pradesh: Forests, Valleys and Rivers

Madhya Pradesh, in the heart of India, is the country's largest state. Much of it is covered with thick forests of teak, ebony, sal and rosewood, replete with deep valleys, ravines and rain-fed rivers.

Rich in natural resources, chiefly coal, iron ore and manganese, Madhya Pradesh is the only state that has diamond mines — at Panna, near Khajuraho.

The Satpura Range is known for the Mahadeo Hills, which are sanctuary to a bewildering variety of wildlife, including tiger, panther, Indian bison and many rare species of birds and other fauna and flora. The life-giving waters of the Chambal, Betwa, Narmada, Tapti, Mahanadi and Indravati rivers also flow through the state.

Compared with the other states, Madhya Pradesh, by and large, has remained untouched by industrial progress. There are only a few big cities and the population has the largest chunk of *adivasis* (tribals). The earliest inhabitants — the Bhils in the western sector and the Gonds in the central area — are the two most prominent tribes, predating the advent of the Indo-Aryans.

Sequestered within dense forests in far-flung areas, these communities were the first to introduce cultural refinement, evident in the cave frescos at Bhimbetka near Bhopal. This aboriginal heritage is the pride of contemporary India.

Though cities like Ujjain are of ancient origin, it is with Emperor Ashoka that the state's known history began. He built the core of the great stupa at Sanchi, already a prosperous city, in the third century BC.

When Hsuan Tsang visited the state in the seventh century AD, Harsha ruled and Buddhism was on the decline. Later, the Chandellas, builders of the Khajuraho temples, ruled the northern region. The south-western Malwa region was governed by the Parmars, Raja Bhoj (1018-60) being the best remembered among them. With the advent of the Delhi Sultanate, both the Gwalior and the Malwa regions showed the effects of change. The Mughals completed the rout of the Hindu kingdoms. Only those cities and temples which lay off the beaten track, hidden by forests, survived. **Gwalior**, near Delhi, bore the brunt of the Muslim invasion. Neighbouring **Shivpuri** and **Orchha** — now in Uttar Pradesh — were built much later under the more stable rule of the Mughals.

Sightseeing

Today visitors can trek the rarely frequented eastern sector with its amazing wealth of forests. **Pachmari**, 210 kilometres (130 miles) south-east of **Bhopal**, is a lovely hill-station in the **Satpura Hills**, seldom explored. Fantastic waterfalls and vistas of natural splendour surprise trekkers in the Maikala Range.

Jabalpur, 334 kilometres (207 miles) east of Bhopal, is famous for its **Marble Rocks**, also called the Bhera Ghat, on the **Narmada River**. **Madan Mahal**, a Gond fortress, and an ancient **Chausath Yogini Temple** are worth visiting.

Rafting along the turbulent **Narmada**, which rushes through a two-kilometre-long (one-mile) gorge, is an exhilarating experience. The **Kanha National Park**, one of the most prestigious wildlife sanctuaries in the world, is a Project Tiger conservation park. The park has India's densest population of tigers. Kanha is also haven to swamp deer, another endangered species, and nearly 100 varieties of birds. North-west of Kanha the **Bandhavagarh Sanctuary** lies below the historic fort of the same name. The cliffs of the fort are 244 metres (800 feet) high. The **Bandhavagarh Fort** is allegedly more than 2,000 years old. **Rock caves** with Sanskrit inscriptions are all around the fort.

Amarkantak, which is the source of the rivers Narmada and **Sone**, is a holy place. Two great fairs are held on **Shivaratri** and **Nag Panchami** in February and July, respectively. The Narmada stirs the simple rustic people to devotional fervour. It is the largest westward flowing river in India and passes through the Marble Rocks at Jabalpur. **Bastar** lies in the remote south-

eastern region of the state, in the densely forested **Jagdalpur** area, home to many colourful tribes. **Teerathgarh Falls** have a spectacular height of 250 metres (820 feet). The remote **Kotamser Caves** are known for their amazing stalactites and stalagmites.

Western Madhya Pradesh has better known tourist places. **Indore**, south-west of Bhopal, is an ideal base. On the banks of the **Saraswati** and **Khan** rivers, this modern city is known for its **Kanch Mandir**, a Jain temple, the interior of which is inlaid with mother-of-pearl, glass and multi-coloured mirrors. **Dhar**, the capital of the Parmar rulers, has a fort built by Muhammad Tughluq.

Mandu, pleasure resort of the Malwa rulers, is 36 kilometres (22 miles) southwest of Dhar. From Dhar, the **Bagh Caves**, 158 kilometres (98 miles) west of Indore, can be reached by bus. Rare seventh- to eighth-century frescos, comparable to the best in Europe, though much restored now, are the main attraction. Two temple towns, **Omkareshwar** and **Maheshwar,** are nearby.

Omkareshwar, 77 kilometres (48 miles) from Indore, is a pilgrimage centre for the *jyotirlinga* (Shiva's image of great importance) at the shrine of **Sri Omkar Mandhata**. Big fairs are held in February and March during Maha Shivaratri, and in November on *Kartika Purnima* (full moon) day.

Maheshwar, 90 kilometres (56 miles) from Indore, on the Narmada River, figures in the *Ramayana* and *Mahabharata* epics, and is famous for its bathing ghats. It was a glorious city at the dawn of civilization, when it was Mahishmati, capital of King Kartaviyarjuna.

Gwalior, to the north of the state, is at the centre of a cluster of gems. **Shivpuri** is known for its *chattris* or canopies.

Ujjain, 55 kilometres (34 miles) northeast of Indore, is one of the holiest cities in India. Built on the banks of the **Kshipra River**, Ujjain is as sacred as Varanasi to the Hindus, Shiva's abode.

Ujjain is the site of a mammoth fair held every 12 years, the **Kumbha Mela**. India's greatest poet-dramatist, Kalidasa, served as a poet in the court of Vikramaditya

of Ujjain. The **Mahakal Temple** has a jyotirlinga in the sanctum. Jaipur's Sawai Jai Singh built an **observatory** of gigantic masonry instruments there.

Chanderi, with its Mughal fort and many Jain shrines; **Datia,** where fine specimens of Bundela architecture include a magnificent fort and palace; **Narwar**, recently discovered as a tourist spot because of the romantic ruins of Rajput palaces, all have something to offer.

Shopping

The arts and crafts of the people belong typically to a region: **Chanderi** is known for its textiles and brocades; Chanderi sarees are the delight of connoisseurs; **Maheshwari** cotton sarees are equally famous; blankets are a speciality of **Mandsaur**.

Gwalior is a centre for carpet weaving and pottery with a large market abroad. **Bhopal** is famous for its traditional gold and silver embroidered handbags, much sought after as gifts.

The brasswork of **Chindwara** and **Belaghat,** and the lacquer-work of **Seoni** are also craft industries passed down from father to son.

The handicrafts of Madhya Pradesh have a certain originality and simplicity to them since they are unaffected by commercialism and mass production.

Bhopal

Bhopal, the state capital of Madhya Pradesh, was founded by Raja Bhoj in the 11th century, but it was only after Dost Mohammad, the Afghan soldier, made it his political centre in the 18th century that it acquired a countenance of its own. It was called Islamnagar at that time.

Between 1819 and 1926, the powerful Bhopal begums built splendid mosques and palaces, laid out lush gardens and created a city of medieval luxury.

Although modern architecture has made inroads into this setting, the pace of life is still unhurried.

Opposite: The dramatic Marble Rocks in Jabalpur.

Above: Taj-ul-Masjid, Bhopal.

Getting there
Air links from Bhopal to Delhi, Gwalior, Indore and Mumbai are available. Bhopal is on the main Delhi-Chennai rail route, and trains running between Mumbai and Delhi via Itarsi and Jhansi pass through Bhopal.

When to go
September to March is the best time to visit Bhopal. Avoid the summer months of May, June and July.

Where to stay
The Madhya Pradesh Tourism (MPT) bureau runs Hotel Palash and Hotel Pancham. Ashok Lake View is run by the Indian Tourist Development Corporation (ITDC). There are many mid-range hotels, like Hotel Raj Tilak, Jehan Numa Palace, Youth Hostel, Ramsons International, Hotel Mayur and a Youth Hostel, to name a few. See listings for 'Hotels'.

Sightseeing
The **Taj-ul-Masjid** monument dominates the city of Bhopal. Believed to be among India's largest mosques, it was completed only recently, though work began in the late 19th century.

The two splendid minarets, dominating the city and the main prayer hall, are very impressive. **Jami Masjid** and **Moti Masjid** were built in 1837 and 1860, respectively. The latter follows the architectural design of Delhi's Shahjahan's Jama Masjid. **Shaukat Mahal** and **Sadar Manzil**, located in the **Chowk** area in the heart of the city, display curious architectural styles. This area also houses many small, old mosques, *havelis* (mansions with inner courtyards) and family workshops, where the traditional crafts of silver jewellery, beadwork and embroidery on purses and cushions are still carried on.

Bharat Bhawan, a modern building designed by Charles Correa, does not detract from the surrounding landscape. The open courtyards and exhibition areas are congenial to the performing arts.

The **Upper** and **Lower lakes** are divided by an overbridge. The Madhya Pradesh Tourism Department provides boating facilities on the Upper Lake.

Excursions from Bhopal
Islamnagar, 11 kilometres (seven miles) out of Bhopal, has Mughal-style palaces and pavilions built amid formal Islamic gardens with fountains and pools. The **Chaman Mahal** and the **Rani Mahal** are also worth a visit. **Bhojpur**, 28 kilometres (17 miles) from Bhopal, is known for the stupendous ruins of the **Bhojeshwar Shiva Temple** by the lake.

In all likelihood, this temple was never completed. Outstanding features include two massive columns, 12.2 metres (40 feet) high, surmounted by capitals with huge stone blocks for door jambs, with figures of attendant deities and the rivers Ganga and Yamuna. The *Shivalingam* (phallic symbol) in the sanctum is 2.5 metres (eight feet) high and 5.5 metres (18 feet) in circumference. A plan of the temple can be seen on one of the rocky plinth slabs.

Bhojpur's **Cyclopean Dam**, even in its ruined state, is another attraction. The scale of this rare hydraulic project is amazing and testifies to the remarkable engineering skills of the artisans of those times. The gigantic earth dams resisted the enormous water pressure, with unmortared stones.

In the neighbourhood of the Bhojpur ruins rises the huge ruined **Jain Temple** with three massive monolithic statues of the Jain *Tirthankaras*. The Mahavira statue is seven metres (22 feet) high.

Forty kilometres (25 miles) south of Bhopal, the picturesque countryside leads to **Bhimbetka**. Bhimbetka means 'the Sitting Place of Bhima', one of the five Pandava heroes in the *Mahabharata*.

Seven hundred **rock shelters** lay sheltered by the Vindhya Ranges until discovered in 1958 by Dr Wakankar. They represent the largest concentration of ancient rock shelters in the world, and are older and more varied than those of southwestern Europe. An uninterrupted record of the history and growth of human social habits are revealed in the motifs engraved there, which have remained unchanged for centuries. The Bhimbetka rock shelters show continuous habitation from the early Stone Age, 10,000 years ago. In places, these paintings reveal some superimposition, which suggests habitation by a different group of dwellers. The **Zoo Rock** is covered with animal figures, while the **Bull Rock** depicts a large animal with flared nostrils, chasing a frightened human being. While a visit to the shelters can be memorable do not go alone. The place is lonely and deserted, and a guide is a must.

Sanchi

Situated 46 kilometres (29 miles) north of Bhopal, Sanchi cradles the ruins of several Buddhist monasteries. Early inscriptions refer to Sanchi as Kakanadabota. *Chaityas* or prayer halls, temples and magnificent stupas sit on top of a hill covered with thick vegetation. These are the greatest Buddhist monuments in India, and the earliest specimens of sculptural ornamentation of the Satavahana period between 30 BC and 11 BC. Emperor Ashoka was responsible for much of this work.

When Aurangzeb's armies conducted their marauding raids on all work unrelated to Islam, these structures remained unharmed as they were hidden by the undergrowth. But after General Taylor of the British army discovered them in 1818, they were plundered by treasure hunters.

This was halted by Sir John Marshall in 1912, who cleared the jungles and began restoration work which resulted in some alterations. What remains today are relics that have been preserved from that time.

Getting there
The nearest airport is in Bhopal, with regular flights to Delhi, Gwalior, Mumbai, Indore, Jabalpur and Raipur. Sanchi lies on the Jhansi-Itarsi section of the Central Railway. First-class passengers on express trains may ask for a halt at Sanchi by prior arrangement. Only passenger trains stop at Sanchi. There is an excellent bus service from Bhopal and Vidisha to Sanchi.

When to go
Avoid May, June and July.

Sightseeing
Stupa I, India's oldest surviving stone structure, is unsurpassed in beauty. The

Above: A view of the main stupa at Sanchi.

original stupa, built by Ashoka, was damaged in the second century BC. The structure is 36.5 metres (120 feet) in diameter and 16.5 metres (54 feet) high. Its immense hemispherical dome, paved processional path, stone balustrades enclosing the stupa and three-tiered umbrella enclosed by a railing on top of the dome, were added later.

During the Satavahana period (128-10 BC), the four splendid gateways covered with bas-relief sculpture symbolising scenes from the Buddha's life — lotus for birth, tree for enlightenment, wheel for his first sermon, footprints and throne — were installed.

Around AD 400, during the Gupta period, the four images at the entrances were set up.

The Eastern Gateway, with the figure of *Yakshi* (female tree nymph) projecting from the architraves, is one of the best known pieces of sculptures.

Depicted on the **Western Gateway** are the seven incarnations of Buddha.

The Wheel of Law, which crowns the **Southern Gateway**, depicts the miracles associated with the Buddha as told in the **Jataka Tales**.

The three lions which once crowned the polished Chunar stone **Ashokan Pillar**, an excellent example of Indo-Bactrian art, have been adopted as the state emblem, as every Indian currency note will justify.

Stupa II, built by Ashoka's wife Devi, is notable for the flowers, animals and people carved on the balustrades and the giant-sized stone food bowl for disciples.

Stupa III, beside Stupa I, is small, with only one gateway. The stone casket containing relics of two disciples of the Buddha was removed to London in 1853 but was subsequently returned to a nearby modern *vihara* (monastery) in Sanchi.

The stone **Gupta Temple**, built in the fourth century AD, has a roof of flat slabs and a porch in front of the sanctum, uncommon to Buddhist architecture. The 17th-century Greek-columned **Chaitya Hall** shows traces of earlier wooden structures, which confirm its ancient character.

Mandu

Mandu, the most beautiful place in central India, is perched 610 metres (2,000 feet) in the Vindhya Mountains. Mandu was the capital of various ruling dynasties until it was overrun by the Delhi Sultanate in the 13th century, and came to be renamed Shadiabad, or 'City of Joy'. The Khakra Koh Hills, which surround the fort and palaces at Mandu, preserved it from wanton destruction. 'There is no place so pleasant in climate and so pretty in scenery as Mandu in the rainy season,' the Mughal emperor Jahangir wrote in his memoirs.

Getting there
Indore is the nearest airport, 100 kilometres (62 miles) away and is linked by air with Delhi, Gwalior and Bhopal. Indore and Ratlam are also the nearest railheads to Mandu. Regular bus services are available from both Indore and Ratlam but a change at Dhar may be necessary. Tourist taxis can be engaged from Indore but are rather undependable.

When to go
July to March, when the rains do wonders to the Mandu landscape is the time to visit.

Where to stay
The Tourist Bungalow, Tourist Cottages and Travellers' Lodge run by the Madhya Pradesh Tourist Department (MPTD) are reliable. Smaller rest houses are dingy and unhygienic. See listings for 'Hotels'.

Sightseeing
Mandu is at its romantic best during the rainy season. You enter the magic circle through the **Alamgiri Gate** and **Bhangi Darwaza**. **Jahaz Mahal** is the most spacious and magnificent of the royal palaces. The 120-metre-long (394-feet) palace is located between two lakes — **Kapur** (Camphor) **Talao** and the **Munj Talao**.

Besides its three huge halls, the palace has antechambers and subterranean chambers kept cool by water from two lovely tanks. There, Ghiyas-ud-din Khalji kept his 15,000 strong harem. The whole palace was once lit with candles, which created the image of a ship at anchor. In the centre of the Munj Talao, stands the double-storeyed **Jal Mahal**, or 'Water Palace', with its lotus-shaped pools and water tanks, where Jahangir and Nur Jahan whiled away many a happy hour.

Hindola Mahal, or 'Palace of Swings', is a misnomer for a palace which was used as an audience hall. The structure is ponderous and the battered walls speak of a foreign influence.

West of Hindola Mahal lie **Dilawar Khan's Mosque, Nahar Jharokha** (Tiger Balcony) and the **Open-Air Theatre**, an unusual structure in the middle of a predominantly Muslim architectural style.

Towards the **Delhi Gate**, on the eastern side, stands a grand audience hall called **House and Shop of Gada Shah** and a deep *baoli* (stepped-well). The royal enclave is best viewed from the **Taveli Mahal** (stables) terrace, where a museum displays sculptures first discovered in the ruins of Mandu. A rest house of the Archaeological Society of India is also located there. There is a group of monuments at the village end, too. Be prepared for some long walks in Mandu since there are no taxis or tongas. Some tempos operate from point-to-point.

Built in 1454, the **Jami Masjid** is among the finest and largest mosques in India, modelled after the Great Mosque at Damascus. The huge domed porch raised on a high plinth, so much like the Tughluq mosques in Delhi, is very impressive. In front of the mosque stands **Ashrafi Mahal**, built to house a school for religious instruction. A truncated tower of victory is part of the ruins. The high terrace offers a panoramic view of the Jami Masjid and the market area.

Hoshang Shah's Tomb, fitted with exquisite lattice screens, is built entirely in white marble. It stands behind the Jami Masjid. Shah Jahan sent his architects to study the tomb's finer points before finalising the details of the Taj Mahal. **Rewa Kund**, a reservoir built by the famous lover-prince of Mandu, Baz Bahadur, for his paramour

Overleaf: The imposing ramparts of Gwalior Fort.

Above: Inside Gwalior Fort.

Roopmati, is a long journey from the village group. The **Roopmati Pavilion**, except for the two pavilions on the high terrace, is rather disappointing, much more so since you frequently hear of the romantic couple.

The view of the **Narmada** from this windswept pavilion is devastating. The **Baz Bahadur Palace**, a splendid example of Afghan architecture, is built around a central pool. Close by, **Nilkanth**, a rest house overlooking an awesome gorge, was built for Akbar.

Visitors take a break at **Echo Point,** where the hoots and whistles of tourists ring off the hills.

Gwalior

The Fort of Gwalior, built on a 90-metre (300-foot) hill, is a magnificent sight. It is believed that Suraj Sen, the sixth-century Rajput chieftain, was cured of leprosy there by Gwalipa, a hermit.

In gratitude, Suraj Sen promised to build a fort atop the hill. His descendants were promised unbroken rule so long as they called themselves Pal. Tej Karan, 84th in line, changed this and lost the kingdom.

Since then Gwalior has seen many battles. The present former rulers, the Scindias, were given Gwalior in 1885 by the British. Man Singh Tomar (1486-1517) was the greatest ruler and built splendid palaces within the fort.

Getting there

There are regular flights to Gwalior from Delhi, Bhopal, Indore and Mumbai.

Gwalior lies on the main Delhi-Mumbai and Delhi-Chennai railway line. The fastest trains from Delhi are the Taj Express and the Shatabdi Express. Buses from all major north Indian cities converge on Gwalior.

When to go

Avoid May, June and July.

Where to stay

Hotel Usha Kiran Palace, Hotel Tansen, run by the Madhya Pradesh Tourism Development Corporation, Hotel President, Hotel Safari, Hotel Regal, Hotel Gujari Mahal and Hotel India. See listings for 'Hotels'.

Sightseeing

There are two roads to the top of the hill. The south-eastern side reveals the much restored and towering **Jain monoliths** carved on the cliff-face, which Babur found offensive and defaced. Autorickshaws and taxis stop short of the uphill climb. The **fort** is girdled by a high wall with frowning ramparts and six gates up to the last, **Hathiya Pol**.

Man Singh's most magnificent palace, **Man Mandir**, is decorated with motifs in coloured tiles, exquisite carvings, *jali* (lattice) screens, sculptured columns, peacock brackets and grand arches. Akbar's palaces in Agra and Fatehpur Sikri were in imitation of Man Mandir. The later Mughals used the basement chambers to detain troublesome princes until they died.

Gujari Mahal was built by Man Singh for his gazelle-eyed beloved, Mrignayani. It now houses the **Archaeological Museum**, which is open from 1000 to 1700 every day, except Mondays. The *salabhanjika*, a tree-goddess sculpture from Gyraspur, is a perfect specimen of female charm.

Teli ka Mandir is a ninth-century AD Vishnu temple built in Dravidian style. The Jain **Saas-Bahu** (mother-in-law and daughter-in-law) **temples**, built between the ninth and 11th centuries, have rich sculptural wealth. Long distances have to be traversed on foot to reach the **Jahangir** and **Shah Jahan Palaces**. **Surajkund**, where the founder of the fort was cured of his affliction, is a pond beside the Teli ka Mandir.

The **Cenotaphs of Rani Lakshmi Bai** of Jhansi, the splendid jali screens of the **Tomb of Muhammad Ghaus**, a 16th-century saint, and the simple marble **Tomb of Tansen**, the legendary musician and creator of various *ragas* (musical notes) and one of the nine gems at Akbar's court, beg mention. The annual **Tansen Sangeet Samaroh** held there in December is a cultural event of national importance.

At **Lashkar**, the city centre, stands **Jai Vilas Palace** built in just three years (1872 to 74). The present royal family of the Scindias lives in a big portion of the palace. Some 35 rooms house a unique museum of Persian carpets, antique furniture and curios, notably, a silver toy train with cut glass wagons used for serving guests at table, swords worn by Shah Jahan and Aurangzeb, miniature paintings and manuscripts and two huge chandeliers weighing several tonnes, with 248 candles each.

Three elephants had to be hoisted onto the roof to test its strength before the chandeliers were installed. Open from 1000 to 1700, except Mondays. **Surya Mandir**, a replica of the Konarak Sun Temple, and the **Baiji Cultural Complex**, opposite **Moti Mahal**, are worth a visit.

The Tourist Office in Motel Tansen is near the railway station.

Orchha

Situated in a deeply forested area fed by the turbulent River Betwa, Orchha, 19 kilometres (12 miles) from Jhansi, is rich in cultural wealth from medieval times.

Built by the Bundela chief Rudra Pratap, it was Sohan Pal who founded the small kingdom in 1292. Orchha was abandoned in favour of Tikamgarh in 1780. The royal palaces lie behind the forbidding crenellated fortifications.

Above: Indigenous girls from Madhya Pradesh.

Getting there
The nearest airport is Gwalior, 120 kilometres (74 miles) away. Jhansi, the nearest railhead, is on the Delhi-Mumbai, Delhi-Chennai line. All major trains stop there. Bus services connect Orchha to Jhansi.

When to go
Avoid May, June and July.

Where to stay
The Madhya Pradesh Tourism Development Corporation-run Hotel Sheesh Mahal, within the fort, is the only place to stay.

Sightseeing
The two main palaces are within the **fort**. **Jahangir Mahal**, where the Mughal emperor stayed for only three days, is a grand palace, built in a pastiche of architectural styles, predominantly Hindu and Islamic.

The upper balconies offer spectacular views of temples, ruins and the fast-flowing **Betwa River** below. **Sheesh Mahal**, decorated with mirror insets, is now a luxury hotel. **Raj Mahal**, residence of the Orchha rulers, has spacious rooms built around a vast quadrangle, long winding stairs, exquisite pavilions and some original frescos of lissome dancing girls and deities. The temples are magnificent.

At the **Raja Ram Temple**, with its silver doors, Lord Rama is worshipped as a king. The palace's wealth is immeasurable. The **Chaturbhuj Temple** with tall spires, high-domed ceilings, pine-cone steeples, which are typical of Bundela architecture, and an austere exterior, first housed the image of Rama of the Raja Ram Temple.

The hilltop **Lakshmi Narayana Temple**, a fortified structure, is famous for its glorious murals in brown, red and black. The **Hardaul Palace** should be visited for its fine garden and a gigantic stone bowl.

The 14 cenotaphs on the Betwa River present a spectacular sight. Remains of many massive structures, uprooted by the river's currents, lie half sunken in the sand.

Thankfully, today Orchha is still untouched by rampant commercialism.

Opposite: Spectacular Orchha.

Khajuraho

Long before visitors to India arrive, they have heard of the Khajuraho temples because their erotic sculptures have earned them a reputation far and wide. In reality, these sculptures form but a small per cent of the total. Khajuraho, or Kharjuravahaka as it was known in its heyday, lies 172 kilometres (107 miles) north-east of Jhansi, in a remote and deeply forested area.

The Chandella rulers built some 85 of these magnificent temples between AD 850 and 1100 in homage to their gods, of which only 20 survive today.

They remained hidden in a little-frequented jungle till Captain T C Burt discovered them by accident in July 1838. Since then, the sculptural wealth of the Khajuraho temples has attracted art lovers and critics from all over the world.

Getting there
A daily Boeing 737 service links Khajuraho with Delhi, Agra and Varanasi. The nearest railheads are Harpalpur, 93 kilometres (58 miles), and Mahoba, 63 kilometres (39 miles), away. From the railway station, state buses will take you to Khajuraho. The Shatabdi Express from Delhi to Bhopal stops over at Jhansi. Most other trains stop over at Jhansi where buses and tourist cars transport visitors to Khajuraho. Satna, 117 kilometres (73 miles) from Khajuraho, is convenient for visitors from Mumbai, Calcutta and Varanasi. Taxis and buses are also available from there. Other direct bus services connect Khajuraho to Panna, Chattarpur, Bhopal, Indore and Varanasi.

When to go
Avoid May, June and July.

Where to stay
The Hotels Payal and Rahil, run by the Madhya Pradesh Tourism Development Corporation (MPTDC), Hotel Chandela, Hotel Khajuraho Ashok and Hotel Jass Oberoi offer a comfortable sojourn. The most convenient and informal eatery is Raja's Café, in front of the Western Group of Temples. See listings for 'Hotels'.

Sightseeing

The Khajuraho temples are divided into groups — western, eastern and southern. The **Western Group of Temples**, in the middle of the village, is closest to the hotels. Guides explain the finer points of the architecture and sculpture. Among a cluster of temples to the left is the bigger **Lakshmana Temple**, dedicated to Vishnu.

The soaring *shikhara*, or tower of the temple built by Lakshmanavarman alias Yashovarman after his conquest of the formidable Kalinjar Fort, was meant to rival the snow-clad peaks of the Himalayas. All the four-corner shrines on the high platform are well preserved. The curved *torana* (ornate arch) has lace-like carving and the oriel windows, where one can sit, light up the interior. The sanctum is enclosed within a perambulatory passage.

The sculptures on the outside are elegant and sensuous in detail. The *nayikas* (heroines) are graceful and uninhibited in form. An elephant-head frieze adorns the lower horizontal bands. The plinth of the temple carries the most explicit of erotic sculptures. At its simplest, the erotica celebrates life and acknowledges the duality of the self, the *purush* and *prakriti*, immanent in all living beings.

This long frieze also includes superbly executed scenes of royal hunts, wars and domestic felicity. The animals, too, have been depicted with meticulous detail.

The **Matangeshwar** is a Shiva shrine, still in use centuries after its construction. The granite *Shivalingam* (phallic symbol) is 2.5 metres high (eight feet) and the *gauripatta* (receptacle) is two-and-a-half times larger in diameter. The smaller **Varaha** and **Devi Temples** are also worth a visit.

Within the huge enclosure around the Western Group, the **Kandariya Mahadeva Temple** (Shiva of the Cave), standing on a high platform at the south-western corner of the gardens, is the most magnificent. Its 35.5 metre-high (117-feet) shikhara, the five-looped torana at the porch, oriel windows, exquisitely sculptured pillars, concentric rings of the ceiling and perfectly proportioned *apsaras* (celestial beauties) display an unparalleled sophistication.

The triple bands of sculpture on the outside include musicians, ascetics, nymphs, *surasundaris* (celestial nymphs), nayikas, gods and goddesses, mythical animals and groups of erotic couples in orgiastic scenes, all celebrating the exuberance of life. The crescendo of peaks clustered around the main body of the shikhara is a striking feature of the Kandariya Mahadeva Temple.

The small **Mahadeva Shrine**, next to the Kandariya Mahadeva, contains the famous leogriff sculpture of a young man (perhaps the founder of the Chandella dynasty) fighting a lion, closely resembling the Hoysala sculpture at Belur (Karnataka), of a man killing a tiger. The **Devi Jagadamba Temple**, originally a Vishnu shrine, now houses a Kali image and contains a wealth of sensuous sculpture. The **Chitragupta Temple**, last in the series, is dedicated to Surya (Sun). The **Vishwanatha Temple** (1002-03) is dedicated to Shiva. The original emerald *lingam* was replaced by one in granite, which is what is seen today. A huge *nandi* (Shiva's bull-vehicle) stands in a pavilion facing the Vishwanatha Temple. There is also a small shrine to Parvati.

A cycle-rickshaw is the easiest way to get to the **Eastern Group** on the village outskirts. The **Brahma**, **Vamana** and **Javari** are small shrines, with exquisite nayikas. The **Jain Group** includes the small **Adinatha Temple**. **Parsvanatha Temple** is the most magnificent, large and profusely sculptured. There are no oriel windows to interrupt the long rows of sculptures.

Again, the nayikas steal the show. Some famous postcards of Khajuraho feature nayikas from the **Parsvanatha:** a curvaceous beauty applying kohl to her eyes, a stunner removing a thorn from her foot, or a lovelorn damsel writing a letter. Even the divine couple, Lakshmi-Narayana, are unmistakably sensuous. The **Shantinatha Temple** has some rare sculptures in a small museum. There, the Jain *dharamshala* (rest house) provides facilities for washing and refreshing yourself. A soft drink and souvenir stall is close by. The unfinished

Opposite: Visitors at the Eastern Group of temples at Khajuraho.

Above: Kandariya Mahadeva Temple, Khajuraho's most magnificent edifice.

Ghantai Temple has exquisitely sculptured pillars supporting a flat roof but no shikhara.

The **Southern Group** consists of two temples, both in the country, which afford a fine view of villagers at work. The **Duladeo** is known for its *apsara, gandharvas* (celestial musicians), *vidyadhara* (angels) and *gana* (cherubs) sculptures. Though much ruined and restored, the Duladeo is a beautiful temple.

It is a rough ride to the **Chaturbhuj Shrine** but worth the effort. In the sanctum stands a most magificent image of Vishnu, three metres (10 feet) high, four-armed and wearing fine jewellery and a benign smile.

Time, patience and energy permitting, visit the ruins of the **Chausath Yogini Temple**, the oldest at Khajuraho. Of the 65 original cells housing deities, only 32 have been preserved. On your way back, pause to catch a reflection of Kandariya Mahadeva Temple in a lake.

Shopping

Khajuraho is a small town with tourism its only industry. The market in front of the Western Group has a few shops which cater to souvenir hunters.

Excursions from Khajuraho

If you decide to stay in Khajuraho for a day or two, visit the **Rajgarh Palace**, 25 kilometres (16 miles) north-east of Khajuraho.

Built by Raja Chatrasal at the foot of the Maniyagarh Hills, this magnificent edifice is 150 years old.

Pandav Falls, 30 kilometres (19 miles) from Khajuraho, is a grand sight after the monsoon.

Panna National Park, one of the biggest in India spread over 546 square kilometres (211 square miles), is home to tigers, panthers, bears, sambhars, spotted deer and langurs.

Between November and June the Ken River Lodge, Village Mandla, Panna, organizes jeep, pony and elephant rides, boating, rafting, fishing and nature walks.

Accommodation is in a scenically located lodge. The gorge of the **Raneh Waterfalls**, 20 kilometres (12 miles) from Khajuraho, is famous for rock formations.

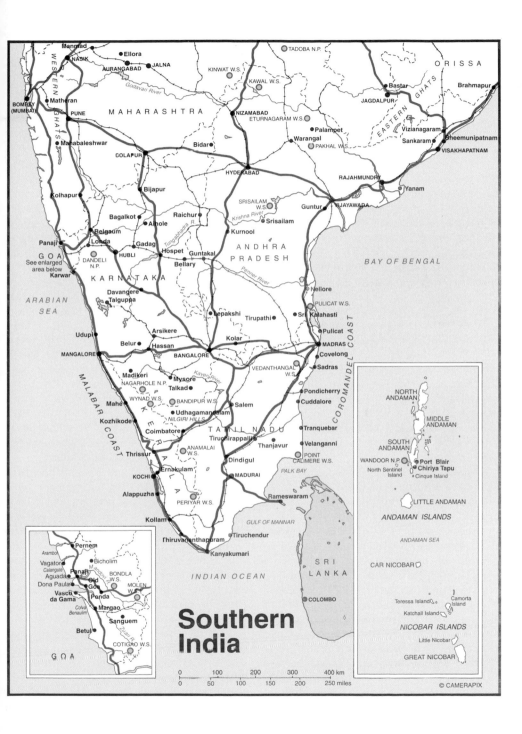

Southern India

Andhra Pradesh: Land of Legend

The State of Hyderabad was founded in 1725 by the Nizams after years of turbulent rule by the Kakatiyas, the first owners of the Golconda Fort and the Mughals. The present state of Andhra Pradesh was the result of a merger with the Telugu-speaking regions of the Chennai and Hyderabad States after the Independence of India in 1947.

Sightseeing

Known earlier as Orukallu or Ekasila-nagaram ('Town of the Single Stone'), **Warangal,** as it is known today, lies 157 kilometres (97 miles) north-east of Hyderabad. Lying between the mighty Krishna and Godavari rivers, **Warangal's fort** lies mostly in ruins today. However, the **temple** area in the centre of the town, with its elaborately carved and free-standing granite gateways, sometimes crowned with beautiful *hansa* (swan) sculptures, bears testimony to the might and splendour of the 12th- and 13th-century Kakatiya dynasty. The famous thousand-pillared **hall** with lattice screens and lavish ornamentation was built in 1162. Its cruciform platform has Shiva, Vishnu and Surya shrines guarded by pairs of rock-hewn elephants.

Outside the shrine, the monolithic, two-metre (seven-foot) polished black *nandi,* or Shiva's bull-vehicle, stands guard, untouched by time or the elements.

At **Palampet**, 74 kilometres (46 miles) from Warangal, stands the Ramappa Temple, described as the 'brightest gem in the galaxy of medieval Deccan architecture'. Created by Ganapati Deva in 1213, it is enclosed within a spacious courtyard and raised on a high star-shaped platform. Of particular beauty are the 12 sculptured *apsaras* (celestial beauties) on pillar brackets and scenes from the *Ramayana* and *Mahabharata* carved in low relief on panels.

Tirupati, 'The Shrine of Seven Hills', is most accessible by bus from Chennai (Tamil Nadu), 150 kilometres (93 miles) away. It is India's richest and most frequented shrine.

This ancient shrine is dedicated to Lord Venkateswara, with attributes of both Shiva and Vishnu. Krishnadevaraya of the Vijayanagara dynasty adorned the temple images with priceless jewels. He also took part in the *Kanakabhishekam,* or 'ritual bathing of the image of Lord Venkateswara with 30,000 gold coins'. The *vimana* (tower) over the sanctum was also gilded with 30,000 gold coins, a gift from the same ruler. The main *gopuram* (gate tower) is in the typical Vijayanagara style.

The **seven hills** of Tirupati are believed to represent the seven coils of the eternal serpent, Adishesha, on which Lord Venkatapati dances, and the winding track to the top is strewn with the ruins of forgotten kingdoms. A trek uphill or a bus journey offers a breathtaking view, but the ride can be unnerving unless you are keen to attain *moksha* (salvation). A quick trip to the **Papavinasam Shrine** is well worth the visit. Ancient rock formations and the shrine of Lord Varahswami are major attractions.

Srikalahasti, 35 kilometres (22 miles) away from Tirupati, is the sacred shrine of the wind god Vayu. Built in the 12th century by the Chola king Raja Rajendra, it was named after the first three devotees of the *Shivalingam* (phallic symbol), a *sri* (spider), *kala* (snake) and *hasti* (elephant).

The **Chandragiri Fort** and **palaces**, on a 56-metre (185-foot) rock prominence, 11 kilometres (seven miles) from Tirupati, were a stronghold of the Vijayanagara rulers.

Lepakshi (Anantpur District) is an Eldorado for Indian painting and sculpture and lends its name to state emporia all over the country. The **Virbhadra Temple** complex, uses the rocky terrain to its advantage. It was elaborately developed by Virupanna, a high-ranking Vijayanagara official, who, fearing punishment for his reckless pursuit of channelling state funds to build the temple, plucked out his eyes and dashed them against the temple wall. Two blood stains stand testimony to this legend and the village acquired the name *Lepa-Akshi,* which means 'blinded eyes'. Besides, the

Above: Gold-plated temple towers at Tirupati.

exquisitely sculptured columns, the two-metre (seven-foot) Ganesha, a *lingam* under a seven-hooded cobra, and a colossal nandi, eight metres (26 feet) long and five metres (16 feet) high, with the insignia of the double-headed eagle, Gandabherunda, on one of its chains, justify a trip there. Moreover, the hanging tower is a marvel of architectural design.

Perched on a hill, **Srisailam** — also called Sriparvata or Srigiri (Kurnool District) — has a group of **Shaivite temples** dedicated to Lord Mallikarjuna and his consort Bhramarambha. Srisailam has one of the 12 *Jyotirlingams* (Shiva's image of great importance) in India believed to have been placed there by the gods.

A stately gopuram at Srisailam is attributed to Shivaji, who, overwhelmed by what he saw, left behind a contingent of soldiers to defend the temple against invaders.

Alampur, one of the gateways to Srisailam, is known as the *Kashi* of the south. It stands on the left bank of the Tungabhadra River. The seventh-century **Nava Brahma Temples**, though named after Brahma, are dedicated to Shiva. (The only Brahma temple in the country is in Pushkar, Rajasthan.) Called Vishakha after the god of Valour, the port of **Visakhapatnam** is now a thriving harbour on the Bay of Bengal.

Popularly known as Vizag, its unspoilt and uncrowded beaches at **Rishikonda** and **Ramakrishna** are perfect for a secluded holiday. There is a chapel at **Rose Hill**, a mosque and shrine at **Dargakonda** and a temple built at Sri Venkatesvarakonda by a Christian. A gigantic rock close by the harbour is known as **Dolphin's Nose**.

At **Simhachalam** a **temple** to Lord Narasimha, 16 kilometres (10 miles) from Vizag, has some 500 inscriptions dating back to 1098. Other attractions are a temple at **Bheemunipatnam**, 24 kilometres (15 miles) from Vizag. **Sankaram**, a cluster of ancient **Buddhist ruins** dating back to the period between 300 and 700 BC, is 41 kilometres (25 miles) from Vizag. Nature has also contributed immense charm to **Araku Valley,** with its Jilda and Dudina **water-falls**. The **Borra Caves**, 90 kilometres (56 miles) from Vizag, some one million years old, are noted for their lovely stalagmites

and stalactites. **Amaravati**, 26 kilometres (16 miles) from Guntur, on the southern bank of the River Krishna, was a great Buddhist centre where a missionary of Ashoka built a stupa around 200 BC. Today, except for a mound, little is left of the great stupa, which fell victim to marauding adventurers and treasure hunters. A few pieces are on display at the museum in Chennai. Known earlier as Vijaipuri, **Nagarjunakonda** was one of the most important Buddhist centres during the second and third centuries BC. It was so named after the Buddhist teacher, Nagarjuna.

When work began on Nagarjunasagar dam, the world's tallest masonry dam, the splendid stupas, monasteries and sculptures depicting the life of Buddha, besides tools of Palaeolithic and Neolithic ages excavated from this area, were transported stone by stone to the top of **Nagarjunakonda Hill** to save them. Today, a huge statue of the Buddha dominates the hill. For a little peace and quiet, 11 kilometres (seven miles) downstream, the **Ethipothala Waterfalls** offer a splendid sight.

Hyderabad

A love story is told of the founding of Hyderabad. Mohammad Quli, as a young prince, fell passionately in love with a maiden from the Chichlam Village, across the River Musi. Even when the river was in spate he would venture to cross it to keep his tryst with his beloved.

Ibrahim Qutb Shah, his father, unhappy that the crown prince should endanger his life in this manner, built a bridge across the river. When Mohammad Quli ascended the throne, he built the Charminar on the site of his love tryst, in the village. The city was called Bhagnagar, or 'City of Good Fortune', after his beloved, Bhagmati.

Later it was renamed Hyderabad, fashioned after the Isfahan in Iran and built under the supervision of the Prime Minister, Mir Momin, a poet, architect and aesthete who shared his master's love for the fine things in life.

Opposite: Colourfully attired Lambadi woman.

Getting there
Regular flights connect Hyderabad to Delhi, Bangalore, Mumbai, Calcutta and Chennai. Hyderabad-Secunderabad is a major railway junction. Fast express trains from different parts of the country, like the A P Express from Delhi, the Charminar Express from Chennai, the Hyderabad Express from Bangalore and numerous other trains, reach the city every day.

When to go
Between October and March is the best time of the year to travel.

Where to stay
Hotel Krishna Oberoi, Gateway Hotel, Bhaskar Palace Hotel, Ritz, Hotel Dwarka, Taj Mahal Hotel, Hotel Brindavan, Hotel Kakatiya, Hotel President, Hotel Golconda, Hotel Krystal, Hotel Sampurna, Hotel Deccan Inter-Continental, Andhra Pradesh Tourism Development Corporation-run Yatri Niwas, and Asrani International Hotel offer food and stay to suit every budget.

Sightseeing
Today Hyderabad, with the twin city of **Secunderabad** (formerly cantonment), is a sprawling, crowded city. Hyderabad has a grid plan of two broad intersecting streets, with the **Charminar** as a kind of triumphal arch at the centre.

The Charminar has a square structure, each side measuring 30 metres (98 feet) and ending in a central arch. The whole edifice of stucco plaster contains numerous small decorative arches arranged vertically and horizontally. The cornice on the first floor upholds a series of six arches and capitals on each façade, rising to the double-storey gallery of the four minarets.

The domed finials of the minarets rise from their lotus-calyx base to a height of 54 metres (177 feet) from the ground. On top a terrace that serves as a roof is decorated with a balcony made of intricately worked screens. A thriving market, spread around the Charminar, attracts people and merchandise of every description. Beside the Charminar stand four arches called **Char Kaman**, each 18 metres (59 feet) high and 11 metres (36 feet) wide at the base, which

175

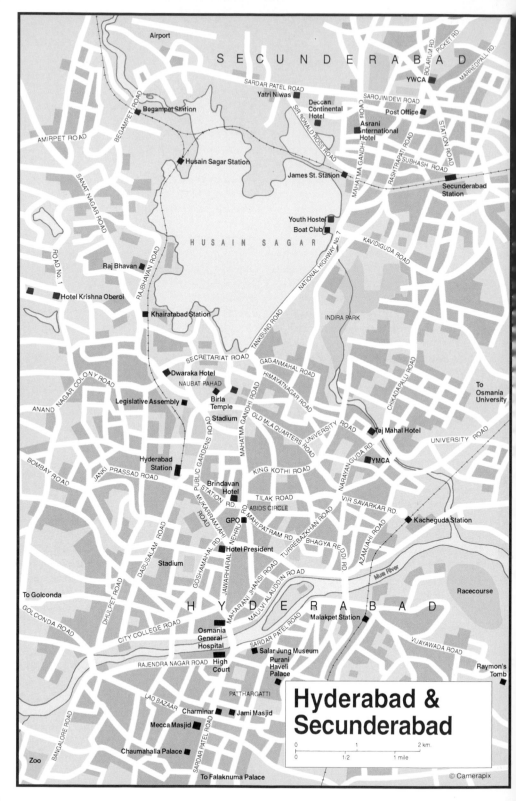

Hyderabad & Secunderabad

0   1   2 km.
0   1/2   1 mile

© Camerapix

serve as a gateway to the *zilu khana* (ante-chambers) of the royal palace. Individually, they are named **Machli Kaman, Kali Kaman, Sher Gil ki Kaman** and **Charminar ki Kaman**.

The **Charsu-ka-Hauz**, a cistern with a fountain in the centre of these arches, is now called Gulzar Hauz. None of the royal residential palaces that once stood around the Charminar remain.

Near the Charminar stands the massive 17th-century **Mecca Masjid,** built of sandstone and mammoth boulders, which can accommodate as many as 10,000 men at prayer. The other two mosques, the **Jami Masjid** and the **Toli Masjid,** are small and modest in comparison. Mohammad Quli Qutb Shah built the Jami Masjid in 1518 after founding Hyderabad.

Musa Khan, a supervisor of works at the Mecca Masjid, levied a *damri* (a coin of little worth) for every rupee spent on its construction with which he built the Toli Masjid, near the **Purana Pul**. Two other buildings, the **Badshahi Ashur Khana** and **Darul Shifa**, built in 1594, are in need of large-scale repair.

The Nizams, who ruled Hyderabad after the Mughal Empire, were fabulously rich. Before Hyderabad joined the Union of Indian States, Mir Osman Ali Khan, the last Nizam, ranked among the world's wealthiest. Though the Nizams were not known for their mosques or palaces, he built the **Falaknuma Palace,** which housed the most exquisite and most expensive *objets d'art*, tapestries and carpets and owned the largest single-man collection of diamonds. It was there the Nizam received England's King George V and King Edward VIII.

Monsieur Raymond, a French adventurer and commander of the Nizam's troops, earned the Nizam's respect and a **granite obelisk** inscribed 'JR' was erected in his honour on a hill in **Sarurnagar.** The **Regency Mansion,** built in 1803 by James Kirkpatrick, is also well worth a visit. Kirkpatrick married a Hyderabadi girl and built the **Rang Mahal** for her, a suite of rooms in the native style. The acquisitions of Mir Yusuf Ali Salar Jung III, displayed in the **Salar Jung Museum,** include jewels, ivory, manuscripts, clocks and thrones from the famed Mughal courts and Europe.

Of much interest to visitors is **Husain Sagar**, a large artificial lake lying between Hyderabad and Secunderabad. It was created by Ibrahim Qutb Shah around 1550 in gratitude to Husain Shah Wali who cured him of a disease.

The white marble **Birla Temple** crowns the **Naubat Pahad,** a hill that offers a spectacular view of the city's **State Legislative Assembly Building, Osmania University,** the **High Court** and **Osmania General Hospital**. When the city was flooded by the Musi River in 1908, the large **Osman Sagar** and **Himayat Sagar Reservoirs** were constructed. They have saved the city from devastation ever since.

Hyderabad is also well-known for its bustling markets, which crowd the Charminar, **Abid Road** and **Patherghatty**.

The city has become a legend for its wealth in pearls and diamonds.

The Qutb Shahi rulers and the Nizams of Hyderabad wore ropes of pearls studded with diamonds around their necks and ate a paste of crushed pearls as a beauty aid.

When the last Nizam was offered an egg-sized diamond, he did not know what to do with it. So, he demanded six more to use as buttons. It is believed that he used a 280-carat diamond as a paperweight.

Golconda has a legendary reputation for diamonds and diamond mines. It is believed that the Koh-i-Noor originally belonged to Golconda, as did the Darya-i-Noor, the Orloff, the Pitt and the Great Table. Little wonder, then, that a market for prized jewels still flourishes there.

Shopping

The market around the Charminar draws avid customers for pearls. Currently Japan has replaced **Basra** as the major supplier of raw pearls, which are manually drilled, cleaned and whitened before they are soaked in bottles of hydrogen peroxide and left to dry in the sun, which brings out their characteristic pearly lustre. **Hyderabad** is also famous for its exquisite *bidri*-ware. One metal is inlaid or overlaid on another,

achieving a vivid contrast of dull black and lustrous white. Originating from **Bidar** in Karnataka, the bidri design is inlaid by hammering strands of wire into engraved linear designs or patterns in the metal.

Later the alloy is permanently blackened by a chemical process which leaves the inlaid designs brilliant and unaffected. After it is washed and dried, it is finished with a coating of oil. Bidri-ware enjoys pride of place in many reputed museums abroad.

Another good buy in Hyderabad is the irresistible three-dimensional *ikat* weave from **Pochampalli**, a village 40 kilometres (25 miles) outside the state capital. Entire families work over 5,000 pit-looms. The patterns are prepared by resist-dyeing or tie-dyeing the yarn before it is put on the loom. Birds, animals or diamond motifs are typical of Andhra Pradesh.

Sarees from **Siddipet, Dharmavaram, Narayanapet** and **Gadwal** have also charmed women from all over the world. Also typical of the state is *kalamkari*, the hand-painted fabric with animal and floral motifs which traditionally adorns temple walls. First block-printed, then coloured in ochre, pale pink, indigo, madder red and dull black, the quality of workmanship and colours make authentic kalamkari work a collector's item. However, an expert's eye is essential.

The other equally famous fabric-art characteristic of the state is *nirmal*, with origins in the **Adilabad** district.

The best, however, is available in Hyderabad. Nirmal recreates scenes from the great Indian epics, the *Mahabharata* and *Ramayana*. Wooden nirmal toys and animals painted in brilliant colours are also sold in Hyderabad.

Probably the most fascinating is the dazzling array of glass and lacquer bangles at **Laad Market** in the Charminar area.

Excursions from Hyderabad

Golconda Fort, 11.5 kilometres (seven miles) on a 128-metre (420-feet) hill, was declared an independent kingdom in 1510 by Quli Qutb Shah. He improved on the nucleus of the fort established by the Kakatiya and Gulbarga rulers, and included new palaces, mosques, baths and gardens, and strengthened the meandering, six-kilometre-long (four-mile), crenellated fort walls with 87 semi-circular bastions, eight gateways, four drawbridges and forbidding cannons on the ramparts.

The present entry to the fort is by the **Fateh Darwaza** gate, which affords a view of the buildings within the high walls.

The acoustical effects of this fort are such that a clap of the hands from the portico to warn against intruders can be heard in the citadel above. This engineering marvel is put to the test by hordes of raucous tourists.

Picking your way through the fort, you will chance upon the **Baroodkhana** ruins (gunpowder store), the **armoury**, **Taramati's mosque**, the **stables** and the **Hall of Justice**.

Your guide is sure to point out the clay pipes fitted in the walls. A 16th-century service of Persian Wheels lifted water to reservoirs, from where it was piped to provide running water for the residents of the fort.

The complex also has a mosque and a temple, which was originally a small jail where a prisoner had carved stone images of his gods, Rama and Hanumana.

The only structure still well preserved is the **Bala Hisar Baradari,** or 'Darbar Hall', 12-arched and triple-storeyed, with a stone throne.

An amazing feature is the double air-conditioning system, which sucks air into a gap between two walls and forces it into the hall.

Seven royal tombs of the Qutb Shahi rulers, guarded by the **Banjara Gate** in the landscaped gardens, have typical onion-shaped, high domes rising from a lotus calyx set upon a square base and surrounded by an arcade of pointed arches. Small minarets at each corner add the only note of ornamentation. **Mosques**, appended to the tombs, are also found there.

Opposite: Gleaming domes of Hyderabad's High Court.

Karnataka: Land of Dramatic Contrasts

Karnataka, one of the four southern states, is a land of dramatic contrasts. Divided into the two districts of North and South Kanara, its 320-kilometre (200-mile) coastal strip between Mangalore and Karwar on the Arabian Sea is dotted with some spectacular beaches. Elsewhere, the hilly tracts of the Western Ghats are covered with thick rainforests. Beyond the Ghats, on the eastern side, lies the Gondwana Plate, a plateau which is one of the oldest and most bizarre land formations in the world. The state is served by the Tungabhadra River in the north and the Kaveri in the south.

Karnataka is rich in its cultural and architectural heritage of past dynasties. From the second century BC to the second century AD, the Satavahana dynasty ruled. Then followed the Kadambas, the Gangas, the Chalukyas (of Badami) and the Rashtrakutas. The Hoysalas and the Vijayanagara Rayas built magnificent temples. In 1565, when the Vijayanagara kingdom at Hampi was destroyed, the state became open to Muslim, Maratha and British influences.

The land is known for its black soil yielding the finest cotton in the country. But it becomes immediately apparent that rock contributes immensely to the charm of the state; from the free-standing, monolithic statue of Bahubali at Sravanabelagola to the solid rock temples at Badami and Aihole, and the lavishly carved sculptures at Belur and Halebid. In Karnataka, great symbols of splendour have emerged from rock, a tribute to the sculptor's consummate craftsmanship and patience.

Sightseeing

Eastern Karnataka is robed in natural splendour. **Karwar** is an enchanting beach resort, 520 kilometres (322 miles) from Bangalore. At **Maravanthe**, 110 kilometres (68 miles) north of Mangalore, sundown is reflected in both the River Sauparnika and the sea. The almost inaccessible **Jog Falls** are perhaps the prettiest falls in the world. The Sharavati River plunges 253 metres (830 feet) down a yawning chasm in four spectacular cascades called Raja, Rani, Rocket and Roarer. Rainbows play on the thick curtain of foam and mist, and in winter, the surrounding landscape is splashed with the rich red of silk cotton blossoms.

Accommodation is available at the Jog Falls Guest House and Hotel Woodlands, but bookings have to be done well in advance. The nearest railhead is **Talguppa**, a few kilometres from the falls. Extremely slow trains connect Jog Falls to Hassan, Arsikere and Bangalore, and the seven-hour bus journey to Karwar, although tedious, is enlivened by bewitching scenery.

Farther south, **Mangalore**, an ancient port on the Arabian Sea, despite its increasing modernization, retains a quaint charm with coconut groves, lovely beaches, and the exotic fragrance of jasmine, the Mangalore Maligee. The **Mangaladevi Temple** and **Kadri Hill** are two places worth a visit. **St Aloysius College chapel** is famous for its frescos done by an Italian artist, Jesuit Antonio Moschemi. **Udipi**, 60 kilometres (37 miles) from Mangalore, has the famous **Krishna Temple**.

Uncrowded **Malpe**, 10 kilometres (six miles) from Udipi, has silver sands and boating facilities. Noteworthy are high basalt columns on **St Mary's Island,** an ideal picnic spot. **Ullal**, five kilometres (three miles) from Mangalore, has a quiet beach with 42 cottages.

Madikeri (Mercara), 120 kilometres (74 miles) south-west of Mysore, in the Coorg area of South Kanara, is known for its coffee plantations and oranges, magnificent forested slopes, streams and emerald-green landscape. A big temple dedicated to Onkareshwar and a small fort were built by the Coorg rajas. **Talakaveri**, 25 kilometres (16 miles) from Madikeri, is the

Opposite: Buddha image in Nagarjunakonda.

source of the River Kaveri and is sacred to the Coorg people. Karnataka is the only state in India with gold mines. Visits to the **Kolar Gold Mines**, 100 kilometres (62 miles) from Bangalore, can be arranged by the Karnataka State Tourism Development Corporation. The artisans of Karnataka excel in sandalwood and ivory carving, and their artistry finds expression in jewel boxes, fans, florid scroll work and miniature animal figures. Karnataka is also known for a unique folk entertainment, called **Kambala**. Pairs of buffaloes are raced through paddy fields by muscle-men in keeping with an ancient show of valour.

Bangalore

Kempe Gowda, a Yalahanka Prabhu chieftain, was gifted a large tract of land near what is known as Bangalore today by the Vijayanagara King Achyuta Raya. Little did he realize that his dream of a small fiefdom might one day become reality. In 1537, he laid the foundations of the city by building a mudbrick fort in the centre and towers at Bellary Road (north), Lal Bagh (south), Ulsoor (east), and Kempambudhi Tank (west) in present-day Bangalore. The city was first called Bengaluru ('City of Boiled Beans') in honour of a poor woman who offered the chief shelter and a simple meal of boiled beans when he lost his way one night. In addition, he gave her a piece of land which now lies under Majestic Circle.

Kempe Gowda's city grew quickly and became an important trade centre. In 1638, Bangalore came under the Bijapur Sultans and later, in 1687, was ruled by the Mughals.

The Mysore rulers persuaded the Mughal governor Kasim Khan to sell the city to the Wadiyars for 500,000 rupees. In 1759, Haider Ali claimed it. After the fall of Srirangapatnam in 1799, the British established their cantonment there. In 1881, the city was restored to the Wadiyars.

Now the nation's fifth largest, and the world's seventh fastest-growing city, with avenues lined with gulmohur, jacaranda and laburnum, Bangalore is India's greatest scientific and technological centre.

Getting there
There are daily flights from Delhi, Mumbai, Chennai, Hyderabad, Kochi and Madurai. Chennai is the nearest international airport. There are three railway stations — Cantonment, Bangalore East and Bangalore City. City station is a major junction, connected by fast trains to different parts of the country. Bangalore has a good road network and de luxe coaches ply to important destinations in the south.

When to go
Year round: October to March is the best.

Where to stay
Hotel Ashok, Bangalore International, West End, Holiday Inn, Taj Residency, Windsor Manor, Woodlands Hotel, Brindavan, Broadway, Nandi Hotels, Hotel Ajantha, Airlines Hotel, Ashraya International and Gateway Hotel offer wide range. See listings for 'Hotels'.

Sightseeing
Housing the State Legislature and Secretariat, the newly built granite **Vidhan Soudha** is Bangalore's most spectacular building. Located in the heart of **Cubbon Park**, the massive sandalwood doors of the cabinet room (not open to visitors) are its chief attraction. The dome, raised on concentric circles, and the columned portico are magnificent. Its neo-Dravidian style of architecture is a fitting foil to the colonial architecture of the British-built **Gothic High Court**, also in Cubbon Park.

Built in 1887 by the Maharaja of Mysore, the royal **Bangalore Palace**, amid sprawling lawns and neat flower beds, is a copy of Windsor Castle in Great Britain.

The lawns and greenery of **Cubbon Park** cover 300 acres (121 hectares) in the centre of the city. Cubbon Park was laid out in 1864. Many Greco-colonial style buildings, like the **Public Library** and the Attara Katchery (Eighteen Courts), now the **High Court**, are located there. The **Fairy**

Opposite: Gold-plated temple chariot at Udipi Math.

Fountain is illuminated in the evenings. The **Government Museum**, near Cubbon Park, is among the oldest museums in the country, housing specimens of sculpture, paintings, coins and some Harappan finds dating back 5,000 years. Open from 0930 to 1630, the park is closed on Wednesdays.

In 1740, Haider Ali laid the foundation for **Lal Bagh**. Tipu Sultan imported rare varieties of trees for this extensive garden. It has the largest collection of tropical and sub-tropical plants in Asia. The huge garden covering 240 acres (97 hectares), is Bangalore's most prestigious, with over 1,800 species and 890 varieties of trees, shrubs, creepers and medicinal plants. The British brought a supervisor from Kew Gardens to look after Lal Bagh. Albert Victor, Prince of Wales, laid the foundation for the Glass House, which turns into a magnificent display of dazzling blossoms during the annual flower shows in February and August. One of the four towers built by Kempe Gowda stands in Lal Bagh. The floral clock is a big attraction.

Haider Ali replaced Kempe Gowda's original mud-brick **fort** with stone walls. Since it was rebuilt in granite, not much remains within except a **Ganesh Temple** and the **Delhi Gate,** one of eight gateways.

Part of a bigger palace which has since disappeared, **Tipu Sultan's Palace**, built mostly of wood in 1791, has exquisite arches, slender pillars and a painted interior, much of which has faded away. It was called *Rashke Jannat* (Envy of the Heavens) for its splendour. Some portions retain traces of grandeur. It was modelled after Srirangapatnam's Daria Daulat Bagh. The British used the building as the Commissioner's office.

The **Venkataramaswamy Temple**, built by the Wadiyars, remains a spiritual centre for the people. Built by Kempe Gowda towards the south of the city, near one of his watch-towers in Basavanagudi, the **Nandi Temple,** dedicated to *nandi,* Shiva's bull-vehicle, is visited by thousands every year. The monolithic nandi is five metres (16 feet) high and resembles the nandi in the Chamundi Hills, near Mysore. It is said that the nandi started growing and that the temple had to be built to contain it. A

Groundnut Fair is held there and offerings of jaggery and groundnut are made to the nandi, profusely decorated for the occasion. The **Kempambudhi Tank** on which stands another Kempe Gowda temple is also worth a visit. The temple of **Gavi Gangadheshwar** is dedicated to Shiva and Parvati. It has been so designed that on **Makara Sankranti**, a festival in January, the last rays of the sun fall on the *lingam*.

When the British chose Bangalore as their summer resort, they built a number of gardens and public parks which still act as the city's lungs. They built big bungalows hidden behind thick curtains of foliage and creepers, some of which can still be seen in the cantonment area. Some streets bear names nostalgic of England — Richmond Town, Kensington, Cunningham Road, Edward Road, Cook's Town, Fraser Town and Langford Gardens.

Russel Market was built to stop the undesirable hobnobbing of British ladies with the local *seths* (merchants). Bangalore retains its love for golf and horse racing. Bandstands in the parks invoke nostalgia for typically British habits.

Shopping

A dazzling array of handicrafts, sandalwood and ivory carvings, inlaid items, lacquerware, *bidri*-ware, and its famous silk make Bangalore a shopper's paradise. **M G Road** is the centre for sophisticated shopping. Also visit **Commercial Street**, **Chickpet**, **Kempe Gowda Road** and **Krishnarajasagar Market**.

Excursions from Bangalore

Bannerghatta National Park, a wildlife reserve 16 kilometres (10 miles) from Bangalore, is fast emerging as a lion safari park. It covers an area of 104 square kilometres (40 square miles). There is also a crocodile and snake farm there.

Nandi Hills, a popular hill resort 68 kilometres (42 miles) north of Bangalore, has an exquisite garden and two temples, each about 1,000 years old. **Tipu's Drop**, a 600-metre (1,970-feet) cliff, is believed to have been used during Tipu's rule to push prisoners down to their deaths. **Karnataka Folk Museum** is well worth a visit for its

Above: High-rise in Bangalore.

collection of masks, costumes and artefacts relating to the folk arts. The **Visvesaraya Industrial and Technological Museum** and the **Venkatappa Art Gallery** need a leisurely inspection. For cultural shows — dance, music and drama — the Corinthian-pillared **Town Hall**, or the violin-shaped **Chowdaiyya Memorial Hall**, or the **Rabindra Kalakshetra,** guarantee good performances.

Hampi

In 1336, Hakka and Bukka, two Telegu princes, founded the Vijayanagara kingdom of Hampi by the River Tungabhadra.

Vijayanagara soon became the most magnificent city of the Deccan with seven concentric rings of defence fortifications. Incomparable for its ruins, Hampi is spread over 26 square kilometres (10 square miles). Set aside a whole day to see as many ruins as possible.

Getting there
The nearest airport is Bellary, 74 kilometres (46 miles) away, connected to Bangalore by Vayudoot flights. Hospet, 13 kilometres (eight miles) away, is the nearest rail-head, connected to Bangalore, Hubli and Guntakal. Bus services from Bangalore, Bidar, Bijapur, Gadag and Hospet are frequent and convenient.

When to go
October to March is the best season to visit.

Where to stay
Hotel Mayura Vijaynagara, run by the Karnataka State Tourism Development Corporation (KSTDC), and Lokare Lodge, Malligai Tourist Home, Mayura Lodge, Hotel Sandarshan, Pampa Lodge and the Inspection Bungalow at Hospet provide modest accommodation. The KSTDC-run Hotel Mayura Vijaynagara is at the dam of Tungabhadra. See listings for 'Hotels'.

Sightseeing
Dedicated to Shiva, the **Virupaksha Temple** in the heart of the city, is dominated by its 52-metre (171-feet) *gopuram*. Two grand courtyards and smaller gopurams lead to the sanctum. Every February-March, the

185

Car Festival draws large crowds from the neighbouring villages, as does the celebration of Virupaksha's marriage to Pampa in December.

Further down the street, within a ruined pavilion, stands a gigantic, unfinished, monolithic *nandi,* Shiva's bull-vehicle.

The unfinished **Vithala Temple** (1513-21), dedicated to Vishnu, is the pride of Vijayanagara architecture. Modest in height, the shrine has 56 richly sculptured columns. When struck lightly, these slender pillars reverberate with the notes of different percussion instruments. The **stone chariot**, the wheels of which once rotated, is an imaginative sculpture.

The **King's Balance**, with its five-metre (16-feet) granite pillars and four-metre (12-feet) crossbeam, was used to weigh kings against gold and silver on auspicious occasions.

The **Kodanda Rama Temple**, mentioned in the *Ramayana*, stands across the river. Stone pylons of a **bridge** across the River Tungabhadra are extant.

South of the Virupaksha Temple is the seven-metre (23-feet) statue of **Narasimha**. Carved in 1528, this stupendous sculpture is shaded by a seven-hooded cobra canopy. Other sculptures include one of **Lakshmi**, two colossal sculptures of **Ganesh** and a three-metre (10-feet) *Shivalingam* submerged in a pool.

The elegant, double-storeyed **Lotus Mahal**, residence of the royal women, is noteworthy for its stucco ornamentation and exquisite arches. A row of 11 variously shaped domes over high arched chambers were once the **elephant stables**.

The walled, octagonal **queen's bath** in Islamic style, noted for its decorative balconies and vaulted corridor and the recently excavated 11-metre (36-feet) **Mahanavmi Bibba**, a high, sculptured, platform tank of great architectural splendour.

The superbly ornamented **Hazara Rama Temple**, south of the *zenana* enclosure, was once the king's private chapel. The various incarnations of Vishnu are depicted in highly polished basalt pillars.

The market in front of the Virupaksha Temple sells temple trinkets, tawdry gift items and refreshments.

Bijapur

Bijapur or Vijaipura was founded by the Chalukyan rulers of Kalyani. Ala-ud-din Khalji and then the Bidar Sultans acquired Bijapur in the 14th century. In 1490, Yusuf Adil Shah, a runaway prince from Turkey, founded the illustrious Adil Shahi dynasty of Bijapur and built the city's magnificent palaces and tombs.

Getting there
The nearest airport, Belgaum, 205 kilometres (127 miles) away, is connected to Mumbai by regular flights. Bijapur enjoys direct rail links with Bangalore, Mumbai, Hospet and Vasco da Gama. Excellent bus connections from Bangalore via Hubli and Badami and Mumbai are available.

When to go
Visit between October and March.

Where to stay
Hotel Mayura Adil Shahi Annexe, Hotel Lalitha Mahal, Hotel Prashanta, Hotel Sanman, Hotel Tourist and the Karnataka State Road Transport Corporation Guest House are all budget accommodation.

Sightseeing
Standing in a well maintained garden, **Gol Gumbaz**, the tomb of Muhammad Ali Shah (1627-56), is famous for its magnificent dome, 40 metres (131 feet) in diameter, second only to St Peter's Basilica in Rome.

The dome stands unsupported by pillars. The acoustics of the whispering gallery are astounding, echoing every utterance seven times, over a distance of 37 metres (121 feet). The whole structure has a distinctly Mongol appearance.

The great **Jami Masjid** mosque was built in 1565. The huge onion-shaped dome towers over a grand hall divided into 45 compartments. The mosque is notable for its lack of minarets. Nearby, the unfinished **Mihtar Mahal** is an extremely ornate double-storeyed mosque.

The garden tomb, or **Ibrahim Roza** of Ibrahim Adil Shah II (1580-1627), also has a grand mosque. Its remarkable symmetry,

Above: Stone chariot, Vitthala Temple, Hampi.

slender minarets, cupolas, cornices and lavish ornamentation in marble, are believed to have been the inspiration for the Taj Mahal. **Taj Baoli**, **Jodi Gumbad** and the magnificent cannon **Malik-i-Maidan**, one of the largest in the world, weighing 55,000 kilos (55 tonnes) and mounted on one of the bastions of the city wall, are worth a visit.

Asar Mahal, a grand structure, houses two hairs of the Prophet Muhammad. Its five-arched façade is majestic. The much ruined **Gagan Mahal**, built by Adil Shah I (1557-80), is an impressive palace-cum-audience hall. Its central arch, 21 metres (70 feet) wide, is the highest in Bijapur. A seven-storeyed tower and water pavilion are among the citadel's ruins.

The incomplete, 12-arched **Bara Kaman**, the tomb of Ali Adil Shah II, is also splendid.

Mysore

Mysore derives its name from 'Mahisa', the demon killed by Chamunda Devi, the goddess whose temple stands on the hill.

Mysore was ruled by the dynasties of the illustrious Chola, Hoysala, Vijayanagara and Wadiyar before the state merged with the Indian Union.

The city has a quiet air and its pace is unhurried despite increasing modernization. It has its own recognizable aroma, a fusion of sandalwood and jasmine.

Getting there

Mysore is connected with Bangalore and Hyderabad by Vayudoot flights, but flight schedules must be checked in advance.

Several express trains run between Bangalore and Mysore daily. Mysore is also served by trains from Bijapur and Mangalore. The Karnataka Road Transport Corporation buses run between Bangalore and Mysore at half-hour intervals, beside other private tourist coaches.

There are excellent road connections with Belur, Bijapur, Hampi, Mangalore and Madikeri. Karnataka State Tourism Development Corporation (KSTDC) offers guided tours to Bangalore, Halebid, Belur and Sravanabelagola. Book at the KSTDC office on Irwin Road or at Hotel Mayura.

Above: Mysore Palace illuminated for the Dusshera celebrations.

When to go

The best season to visit Mysore is between October and February. For the Dusshera festival in October the city and palace are gaily decorated.

Where to stay

Ashoka Radisson Lalitha Palace, Rajendra Vilas Palace (Chamundi Hills), Dasaprakash Paradise, Hotel Metropole, Hotel Highway, Hotel Dasaprakash, Airlines Hotel and Krishnasagar Hotel, 19 kilometres (12 miles) at the Brindavan Gardens cater to all kinds of travellers. See listings for 'Hotels'.

Sightseeing

The **Amber Vilas City Palace** is the most prestigious of Mysore's monuments. Built after fire destroyed the original palace in 1897, it combines attractive architectural features of Hindu and Islamic styles, with elegant domes, turrets, archways, colonnades and sculptures. The **Darbar Hall** is particularly magnificent. During the **Dusshera celebrations**, the legendary throne of the Pandavas is displayed. Weighing more than 250 kilos (550lbs) in solid gold, ivory

and silver, the ancient throne is exquisitely carved with an imposing umbrella to lend it the royal touch. The original splendour of the City Palace is well preserved — painted columns, silver doors, gorgeous ceilings, palanquins, numerous thrones and a set of crystal chairs. During the Dusshera festival, the City Palace is transformed into a fairyland with millions of lighted bulbs and floodlights.

Sri Jay Chamrajandra Art Gallery contains a large selection of paintings by Raja Ravi Varma, ceramics, sandalwood, ivory and stone antiques, teak furniture, and ancient musical instruments. Gold leaf paintings and the works of Russian painter Svetoslav Roerich are also on display. Open 0830 to 1730 every day.

St Philomena's Church, built in the neo-Gothic style, is one of the largest and most beautiful churches in India. The crypt contains the statue of St Philomena. The stained glass windows are extremely lovely.

The **Chamundi Hills**, 13 kilometres (eight miles) from Mysore, are topped with a 2,000-year-old temple dedicated to the goddess Chamundi, who killed the demon

Mahisa and saved the town. An awesome sight is the gigantic, magnificently carved, monolithic *nandi* or Shiva's bull-vehicle, five metres (16 feet) high and 7.6 metres (25 feet) long. To get to the top, either take a jeep or bus, or trek up the arduous 1,000 steps. A garishly painted statue of the vanquished demon stands outside the temple.

Shopping

The city markets have the most congenial atmosphere for leisurely souvenir hunting. Salesmanship is unaggressive and cheating seldom practised, except when expensive sandalwood artefacts are being sold. Frequently, ordinary wood is sprayed with sandalwood perfume and passed off for the real stuff. The **Kaveri Government Arts and Crafts Emporium** is the best place for local handicrafts, rosewood furniture and exquisite table tops with inlaid work. Ivory is never sold. The KSTDC helps in arranging visits to the **Government Silk Weaving Factory,** where Mysore's sensuous pure silks are woven. Prices are reasonable and give immense value for money. Sandalwood *agarbattis* (joss sticks) make popular gifts which are eminently affordable.

Excursions from Mysore

South India's magnificent terraced **Brindavan Gardens**, 19 kilometres (12 miles) south of Mysore, has sparkling fountains and colourful lighting. The lights, which are a major tourist attraction, are turned on for only an hour, so check with the garden authorities or tour operators before making the trip.

The **Krishnasagar Dam** is one of the most impressive dams in India, built entirely of stone without any cement. Sir M Visveswaraya, India's greatest architect, created this engineering marvel across the Kaveri River.

Somnathpur, 35 kilometres (22 miles) away, has a perfect Hoysala temple Completed in AD 1268 and dedicated to Vishnu as Keshav, this triple-celled, triple-spired, shrine has lavish decoration with friezes of Hindu deities, panels of geese, elephants, horses, mythical beasts and floral scrolls. The **Sivasamudram Waterfalls**, 85 kilometres (53 miles) south-east of

Mysore, are spectacular during the rainy season in July-August. Asia's first hydro-electric power station was set up there in 1902. **Talakad**, an ancient temple town, 45 kilometres (28 miles) south-east of Mysore, remained buried under the Kaveri River sands for centuries until excavated, revealing some Hoysala-style temples of astounding sculptural wealth.

Once every 12 years, during the **Panchalinga Darshan**, this sleepy town resonates with the sounds of festivities and fairs.

Sravanabelagola, Belur and Halebid

Hassan, 157 kilometres (97 miles) northwest of Mysore, is the point of entry to the enchanting towns of Sravanabelagola, Belur and Halebid.

Getting there

Hire a taxi from Hassan and spend the day at Sravanabelagola, and visit the other two another day. One-day conducted bus tours from Bangalore or Mysore are another option worth considering.

When to go

Between October and March is the best season to visit.

Where to stay

In Hassan: Hotel Hassan Ashoka, Hotel Amblee Palika, Hotel Dwarka, Prasantha Tourist Home and Hotel Satyaprakash. In Sravanabelagola: the Tourist Canteen and Rest House of the Karnataka State Tourism Development Corporation, Sriyans Prasad Guest House and the government-run Tourist Bungalow. The KSTDC-run Hotel Mayura Velapuri at Belur is comfortable. Tourist Cottages and Bungalow offer accommodation at Halebid. See listings for 'Hotels'.

Sightseeing

Sravanabelagola, otherwise known as 'Monk-on-Top-of-the-Hill', lies on the approach to this holy town of the Digambara Jains, 52 kilometres (32 miles)

Above: Temple complex at Belur.

from Hassan. It is marked with excitement as everyone tries to catch a glimpse of the **Gomateshwara statue** standing atop the Vindhyagiri Hill. Carved out of monolithic rock in AD 981 by the Gangas of Talakad, it represents Bahubali, a Jain prince, who fought a bitter battle with his brother over possession of the kingdom, only to renounce it shortly afterwards, when he retired to the forest to start a 1,000 year penance.

The 58.8-metre-high (193-feet) statue, in the *Pratimayoga* posture, is the tallest freestanding statue in the world. To get to the top, one has to confront the 140-metre (459-feet) sheer rock-face and 614 daunting steps that lead to the summit. The Vindhyagiri Hill is also embellished with eight temples, five gateways, four pavilions and two ponds.

Every 12 years, the Jains observe a **Mahamastakabhishekha** ceremony. A giant scaffolding is built behind the statue and priests and devotees bathe the image with thousands of gallons of milk, ghee, saffron, vermilion, coconut water, gold and silver coins and millions of rose petals

in a ceremony of consecration. The Jain *bastis* or settlements on the Chandragiri Hill are interesting. Most notable among them is the **Chandragupta Basti**, built by Emperor Ashoka, to honour Chandragupta Maurya, the emperor turned monk, in the fourth century BC.

Belur, 40 kilometres (25 miles) from Hassan, boasts the **Chennakeshava Temple**, built by Vishnuvardhana, after he won a battle against the Cholas in 1611.

The Hoysala dynasty has its origins in legend. A Jain ascetic was attacked by a tiger in the forest and when he cried 'Hoy sala', he was rescued by a brave tribal youth. In return, the youth was blessed with a kingdom. Nripkama, the founding ruler, adopted 'Hoy Sala' as the name of the dynasty. This legend of the youth slaying the tiger is immortalized in all Hoysala sculpture. The Hoysala temples are squat, modest in height and cruciform in ground plan with multi-pillared *navaranga* (dance) halls. Other typical features are perforated windows and exquisite sculptural embellishment. The entrance to the temple is by the **eastern** gateway, which is elaborately sculptured with panels depicting court scenes, mythical beasts and deities and bracket figures of celestial maidens or *apsaras*.

The pillars in the **Navaranga Hall** are all hand-lathe-turned and most ingeniously crafted. It is believed that the Nrarsimha Pillar could even be rotated at one time. A small place is left uncarved for anyone wishing to challenge the artistry of the Hoysalas.

The **main shrine** stands in a vast courtyard and its entrance is flanked by two miniature *vimana* (towers).

Horizontal friezes are sculptured with unending rows of elephants, horses, lions, birds and warriors. The interior remains semi-dark, but a lighted torch will pick out the images of four superb apsaras on the pillar brackets, modelled after Shantaladevi, Vishnuvardhana's queen. She used to dance on the small circular platform in front of the deity. The hourly *puja,* or devotional prayer, allows visitors to make their offerings.

The larger panels on the exterior walls, between *jali* (lattice) screens, depict the various incarnations of Vishnu, scenes from the *Ramayana* and *Mahabharata* epics, and other gods.

The other temples in the enclosure include the temples of **Channigaraya**, **Soumyanayaki**, **Veeranarayana** and **Andal**. The grand **Vijayanagara Gopuram** on the eastern wall was built in 1397 to replace the original Hoysala gateway, which was destroyed in 1310.

Known earlier as Dwarsamudra, or 'Gateway on the Ocean', **Halebid**, 32 kilometres (20 miles) from Hassan, has the twin-shrined **Hoysaleshwara Temple**, dedicated to Shiva.

Though work began in 1121, the temple was still incomplete when the Hoysalas were destroyed in 1325. Every feature of the temple at Belur is duplicated there with added ornamentation. On the five-metre (16-feet) star-shaped platform, the larger panels with divine couples (Vishnu-Lakshmi, Shiva-Parvati), celestial beauties, scenes from the *Ramayana* and *Mahabharata* and the elephant-headed god Ganesh stand in stylized postures under a canopy of rich foliage. The *dwarapalas* or gatekeepers epitomize the Hoysala eye for detail and fine craftsmanship.

To amaze you with the creative genius of the time, your guide will insert a thread into the pupil of an eye and it will emerge from the nose.

The lower horizontal friezes are carved with some 2,000 elephants with riders and trappings, horses, mythical beasts and miles of floral scrolls.

On the outskirts of the village stands the small **Kedareswara Temple**, rich in architectural and sculptural wealth. The Jain temples are well preserved and the silk-smooth granite pillars are noteworthy.

Aihole, Badami and Pattadakal

These three cities and the Malaprabha River in northern Karnataka formed the nucleus of the Chalukyan kingdom, which flourished from the fifth century until vanquished by the Rashtrakutas in AD 757. Aihole, or Arya-Hole ('City of the Aryans'), the earliest, was founded in AD 450.

Badami was founded by Pulakeshin I in AD 550 and Pattadakal, the last of the Chalukyan capitals, was founded early in the eighth century.

Getting there
Badami is the most convenient base to visit them all. The nearest airport is Belgaum, 192 kilometres (119 miles) away. Badami, on the Hubli-Sholapur route, is served well by rail and road. The nearest railway station is Badami, five kilometres (three miles) from town. Badami is 128 kilometres (79 miles) from Hubli and 163 kilometres (101 miles) from Bijapur.

Badami and Bagalkot, both 46 kilometres (29 miles) from Aihole, are the nearest railheads. Karnataka State Road Transport Corporation buses ply between Badami and Bangalore, Bagalkot, Belgaum, Bijapur, Gadag, Hospet and Hubli.

When to go
The best season is from October to March. Summer is far too hot.

Where to stay

Hotel Mayura Chalukya, run by the Karnataka State Tourism Development Corporation (KSTDC), the Inspection Bungalow and Public Works Department (PWD) Guest House at Badami are good places to stay. Accommodation is unavailable at Pattadakal which is reached by bus between Badami and Aihole. Run by the Department of Tourism, the Tourist Home Aihole, is comfortable. See listings for 'Hotels'.

Sightseeing

Many of **Aihole's** 125 or so temples lie scattered across fields or within ruined fortifications. Within the village, the **Durga Temple** is unique in its apsidal form in true Buddhist *chaitya* (prayer hall) style. The unfinished *shikhara,* or tower, is the first of its kind there. The temple is a veritable treasure trove of splendid sculpture with scenes from the Ramayana and Mahabharata and some erotica.

Lad Khan (AD 450), near the bus stand, shows an early experimentation with temple structure modelled after the wooden assembly halls of the village. The **Ravana Phadi Cave Temple** is particularly impressive for its triple entrance and rhythmic sculptures of Shiva as Ardhanarishwara and Nataraja, Mahisasuramardini and the Saptamatrikas. Pulakeshin II built the **Meguti Jain Temple** in AD 634 when the Chalukyas moved to Badami. The temples of **Kont Gudi** and the **Hucchimalli** are also noteworthy. Built by Pulakeshin I, **Badami** was earlier known as Vatapi, and Ptolemy called it Badamoi in AD 150.

Its attractions are four magnificent monolithic cave shrines, gouged out of solid rock. These *mandapams* or pavilions have an open porch, central pillared hall and a squarish cell for the deity. The sculptures are extremely refined and sensuous.

Cave One has a superb Nataraja with sixteen hands, exhibiting 81 classical Indian dance poses. Shiva and Parvati and Hari and Hara are also very impressive. Vishnu, in his many *avatars,* or incarnations, appears in the other caves. **Cave Two** has two gigantic panels. Among the incarnations represented in **Cave Three**, Vishnu,

sitting under the canopy of a five-hooded cobra, is the pride of Badami sculpture. **Cave Four** is rather austere in ornamentation. The golden sandstone cliffs are crowned with the ruins of a fort.

Gun Point, crowning the rocky summit, is a treacherous climb up uneven steps. On the hill opposite the caves and across the **Agastyamuni Tank**, stand the **Upper Shivalaya** and three curious structures called **Tipu's Treasury**. On the slopes towards the bus stand, there are **Melegitti Shivalaya** (Shiva as a garland-maker) and a fine Dravidian tower. Huge tamarind trees lower their branches into the sacred tank.

At sunset, the **Bhutanatha Temple** acquires a distinctive glow. Its southwest rock-face has splendid images of many Hindu gods in relief. At the end of a thrilling crawl through a tunnel is the image of Koshtaraya, the king who was cured of leprosy at Badami.

The **Archaeological Museum** displays rare sculptures excavated from sites around Badami, where every stone is stamped with the mark of the Chalukyas.

Pattadakal, 29 kilometres (18 miles) from Badami, came into prominence when the Chalukyas moved there. Now only a small village with a complex of magnificent temples, the pride of Chalukyan architecture is the **Virupaksha Temple**, dedicated to Shiva.

Built in AD 740 by the senior queen of Vikramaditya II in celebration of the Chalukyan victory over the Pallavas, its hall of 16 monolithic columns is superbly sculptured, and the ornamental doorkeepers in the porch and Ravana shaking Mount Kailash are exquisite.

A magnificent *nandi*, Shiva's bull-vehicle, sits in the courtyard. The **Temple of Mallikarjuna** was built by another queen of Vikramaditya II, Trailokyamahadevi. The ceiling panels showing Gajalakshmi and Nataraja with Parvati are sculptural masterpieces. Within the enclosure are smaller temples — **Galagnatha**, with a north-Indian shikhara, **Jambulinga**, and **Sanghameshwara**, and, outside, the unfinished **Papanatha Temple**. The Dravidian or Pallava style was favoured by architects and sculptors imported by the two queens of Vikramaditya II. The eloquence of carved stone speaks of an era of unparalleled art.

Srirangapatnam

This small island on the Kaveri River, near Mysore, has immense importance. In AD 894, a temple was built for Vishnu and later the fort came up around it. Named after Vishnu as Ranganatha, the town was strengthened by successive rulers.

Getting there
The nearest airport is at Bangalore, 140 kilometres (87 miles) away. Convenient fast trains travel to Bangalore daily from Srirangapatnam. Srirangapatnam, on the Bangalore-Mysore highway, is well linked with both cities by bus services.

When to go
Throughout the year. Avoid the summer months of May and June.

Where to stay
Hotel Mayura Riverview, run by the Karnataka State Tourism Development Corporation (KSTDC), Harris Bungalow and two economy class lodges offer accommodation. See listings for 'Hotels'.

Sightseeing
Built in 1454, the double-walled fortifications of **Srirangapatnam Fort** are protected by the river and deep moats filled with river water. The **Elephant Gate** leads to **Lal Mahal,** the ruined residence of Tipu Sultan.

Sri Ranganath Temple, the biggest of the three island temples, over the centuries has received various architectural alterations.

The grand wooden chariot outside the temple gateway was a gift from Haider Ali.

Non-Hindus are prohibited from entering the sanctum, where a colossal image of Vishnu reclines on his eternal, seven-hooded serpent.

Built in 1787 by Tipu Sultan, the grand **Jami Masjid** mosque has two tall minarets, each adorned with cornices and crowned with a brass *kalash* or finial. The inside is decorated with the 99 names of Allah. Only

a small stone tablet marks the spot where Tipu Sultan, the hero of many a war, died. However, in **Lal Bagh**, the graves of Sultan Haider Ali, his wife and Tipu Sultan lie under a splendid dome known as **Gumbaz.**

The decorations are in stucco but the black marble pillar lends an air of stately splendour. The three fine rosewood doors inlaid with ivory were gifts from **Lord Dalhousie.**

Built in 1784, the severe exterior of **Darya Daulat Bagh**, summer palace of Tipu Sultan on the banks of the Kaveri River, belies the extravagance within. The walls are covered with fabulous murals depicting both Haider Ali and Tipu Sultan victorious in battle. The teak pillars supporting the trefoil arches are decorated with floral arabesques. The palace houses Tipu's personal collection of coins, paintings and arms.

Other places of interest are **Colonel Baille's Tomb**, the **Garrison Cemetery**, **Harris Bungalow** and a **church** built by Abbé Dubois, a French missionary.

Excursions from Srirangapatnam
Thirty-five kilometres (22 miles) upstream, **Ranganathittu Bird Sanctuary**, is the breeding ground for thousands of birds and waterfowl including cormorant, shag, white ibis, egret, open-billed stork, spot-billed duck, kingfisher, river tern and even whistling teal.

Kerala: Rice, Coconuts and Spices

Kerala occupies about one per cent of India's total land area. A narrow strip on the south-west coast, it is one of the smallest states of the Republic. It has a dense population and scenery so lush, green and sparkling it warms the hearts of ecologists and holiday-makers alike. The majestic Western Ghats undulate further westwards through dense velvety forests until they give way to brilliant green rice fields, coconut palms, a network of rivers and 1,771 kilometres (1,098 miles) of inland waterways flowing into the Arabian Sea.

Among the many rivers, the most important are the Pampa, Periyar and Bharatapuzha, which provide much of the state's hydroelectric power. The state has a wondrous coastline dotted with sand dunes, lagoons and backwaters. It is bounded in the north by Karnataka, to the east and south by Tamil Nadu, and boasts the highest peak in peninsular India, Anai Mudi 2,695 metres (8,842 feet).

Kerala maintains an equitable climate ranging from 27ºC to 32ºC (81ºF to 90ºF) in the plains, which drops to 21ºC (70ºF) in the hilly regions. Kerala's foliage flourishes in the ample annual rainfall, which averages 300 centimetres (118 inches). Kerala gets both the south-west and north-east monsoons. The heaviest rainfall is between mid-May and end of August, with pleasant occasional showers October to December.

Kerala's economy is agro-based, with rice and coconut occupying most of the cultivated area. It is also a major producer of rubber, pepper, cardamom, cocoa, cashew, arecanut, sugarcane, coffee, tea and ginger. Aromatic spices like nutmeg, clove and cinnamon are also cultivated. The forests have yielded some of the world's best teak, black wood, ebony and rosewood, while its sea coast yields an abundance of prawns, sardines, mackerel and shrimp. Kerala has been fortunate in its development of human resources too. Both politically unusual and culturally

Opposite: Kerala's tranquil backwaters.

mixed, its population is 60 per cent Hindu and 20 per cent both Muslim and Christian. It even has a tiny community of about 20 Jews.

Literacy and education were high priority for a series of rulers, whether kings or communists. By the turn of the century, Kerala's literacy rate was double that of the rest of India. Today, the state has over 400 newspapers and journals in the state's language — Malayalam — and a literacy rate which, at 87 per cent for females and 94 per cent for males, is higher than any low-income country. It was the first state in the world to elect a communist government democratically.

Kerala became a single, unified state only in November 1956, but the ancient epics of the *Ramayana* and *Mahabharata* (1500-1000 BC) mention Kerala as a political entity. References in the Old Testament date back to 1500 BC, and a rock inscription referring to Kerala was left by Emperor Ashoka in AD 200. Legend, of course, has it that Kerala emerged frothing and foaming out of the depths of the mighty ocean, when the sage Parasurama, an incarnation of Vishnu, heaved his axe into it in a fit of remorse for waging a vengeful war on the *Kshatriyas*, causing devastation all around.

The coast was familiar to the Arabs, Phoenicians, Romans and the Chinese. The original inhabitants were perhaps related to the forest nomads of Sri Lanka and are largely of Dravidian stock. Aryan immigration from the north probably began around 1,000 BC. The Apostle St Thomas reached Kerala in AD 52, and Vasco da Gama established a direct sea route from Europe to India through Portugal in 1498.

The Dutch ousted the Portuguese in the 17th century, after which Tipu Sultan marched up to Alwaye from Mysore. In the late 18th century, Kerala came under British suzerainty. Famous personages associated with Kerala's history include Adi Shankaracharya, the religious philosopher

(AD 788-820), Swati Tirunal (1813-46), an enlightened ruler and composer of music, Dr Herman Gundert, who enriched the literature on Kerala by writing 21 books in 20 years on its language and history, and Raja Ravi Varma (1848-1906), an outstanding painter in the classical style.

From the far-away mists of tales of long ago until today, Kerala is a unique example of diverse cultural and religious streams integrating into a harmonious and enlightened whole.

Many place names have reverted to their older spellings and pronunciations. Quilon is now Kollam, Cochin is Kochi and Alleppey is Allapuzha. Trivandrum has been replaced by Thiruvananthapuram, Trichur is now Thrissur and Calicut is Kozhikode.

Furthermore the 'zh' sound is more like the American way of saying 'r' than a 'z'.

Thiruvananthapuram (Trivandrum)

Kerala's capital is Thiruvananthapuram now much harder to pronounce but, nevertheless, a sophisticated city which blends the old and the new with grace. It was a princely state ruled by maharajas until it was merged with the state of Kerala in November 1956, under the State Reorganization Act. One of its earlier rulers, Swathi Tirunal Rama Varma (1813-46), was a musician and gifted composer of Carnatic music. His 355 compositions were written in Sanskrit, Malayalam, Hindi, Telugu, Kannada and Tamil.

Getting there

Thiruvananthapuram is well connected by air, including Sri Lanka and the Maldives. Local flights go to Mumbai, Goa, Delhi, Chennai and Kochi. The Kerala Express from Delhi takes 52 hours. Other trains are the Island Express to Mangalore, besides trains to Mumbai, Delhi, Chennai and Kochi. Buses connect with Chennai, Madurai, Coimbatore and Pondicherry.

Opposite: Facial painting for Kathakali.

When to go

Avoid the monsoon, May to September.

Where to stay

For luxury with reasonable tariffs there are the Mascot, South Park, Luciya Continental and Fort Manor. For reasonable rates, opt for the Horizon, Chaitram, Regency and Residency. Paramount Park and plenty more like it at Thampanoor give you a choice. For the student, junior employee or shoe-string budget tourist, Silver Sand, near the railway station, Sangaman, Jacob's and Poorna (near the Secretariat) are centrally located. See listings for 'Hotels'.

Sightseeing

Temples are the best examples of classical Kerala architecture. Near the city bus station, in East Fort, is the famous **Padmanabha Swamy Temple** dedicated to Lord Vishnu.

Travellers with children can visit **Lake Akkulam**, three kilometres (two miles) from the city. It has a huge **children's park**, **boating facilities** and the scenic **zoo**. Open from 0900 to 1700, except Mondays.

Thiruvananthapuram has both temple and tourist festivals where the state culture can be studied and enjoyed. The **Amman Kudam Festivals** at Attingal Muthuraman Temple are held in February, and the **festivals** at the **Janardanaswamy Temple** in Varkata in March. Tourism fairs include Food Festivals and the Tourism Week, in September usually so that it coincides with the local festive season of **Onam**, after the harvest season.

Kathakali is the popular, extraordinary and invigorating classical dance form of Kerala. Elaborate make-up, costumes, and traditionally, all night performances draw locals and tourists alike. The **Vijnanan Kala Vedi Centre** is an arts training centre with performances of Kathakali, Mohiniattam and Bharatnatyam in the evenings. The **Nishagandhi Dance Festival** is held from October to March and the **Surya Festival** in early October. Dates of festivals, particularly the religious ones, change according to the lunar calendar.

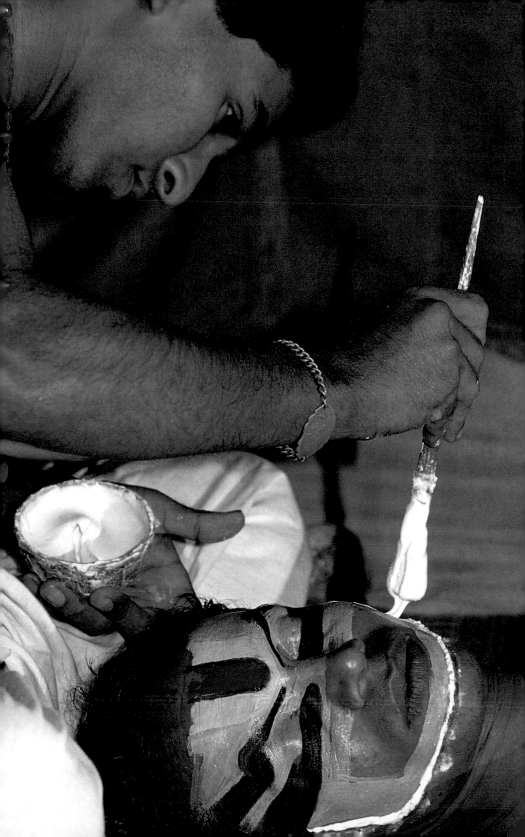

Excursions from Thiruvananthapuram

Trips out of Thiruvananthapuram are fun because of the variety of options. You can choose between a hill-station or a stunning beach resort, or even manage both since distances are not too great and the roads are fairly good.

Ponmudi is 65 kilometres (40 miles) away, at an altitude of 1,000 metres (3,281 feet). In an hour you travel up a narrow winding path through dense green forest into the fresh mountain air. Dotted with tiny picturesque cottages, abounding in picnic spots, full of orchards and trekking paths, Ponmudi is a small magical world.

Kovalam is quite the opposite. Sixteen kilometres (10 miles) south of the capital city, it has wonderful beaches, boat rides in local catamarans, sunbathing and luxurious amenities expected of all high-profile tourist spots.

There are plenty of hotels but tariffs are relatively steep compared with the other towns.

The most distinctive elements of Kerala are its lush greenery, its waterways and its architecture. About 56 kilometres (35 miles) from Thiruvananthapuram, towards Cape Comorin, is the finest example of Kerala's architectural genius, the **Padmanabhapuram Palace**. The oldest section was built *circa* 16th century, with subsequent sections added by various maharajas until the 18th century, when the capital of Travancore moved from Padmanabhapuram. There is a nominal entry fee for tourists, which assures a wonderful visit into the area enclosing five temples, two large bathing ponds, two schools, several shops and houses, and the fabulous palace.

Mahogany and teak pillars, lattice carvings and sculptures, roofs sloping inwards into sunken stone courtyards called *nalukettu*, carved wooden ceilings and fine murals provide a rich ambience. The king's bedchamber has a magnificient bed made of 64 different kinds of medicinal woods.

Most distinctive about Kerala architecture is its smooth highly polished black (or deep red) floors. While today only poor imitations are available, earlier recipes for glossy black flooring included the mixing of egg white, coconut shells and a black or red oxide to make floors shine without further maintenance. The roof of the oldest section of the palace, the *thaikottaram*, is supported by four corner pillars. In the south-west corner is a pillar two metres (seven feet) high and one metre (three feet) thick, made of a single block of wood.

The worship chamber of the palace is called the *upparikamalika*. The walls are one-metre (three-feet) thick and are covered with exquisite murals, depicting religious and mythical themes. The painting of Shri Padmanabha (Lord Mahavishnu) reclining on a serpent couch, the lotus from his navel holding Brahma, the Lord of Creation, is notable. Scenes from the daily life of the 18th-century people of Kerala are among the illustrations in the chamber in which the ceremonial sword of the rulers of Travancore is placed. Swathi Thirunal, the famous composer-king, built the *natakasala* as a theatre. Sculptured pillars and a gleaming floor provide the perfect setting for dance and dramatic performances.

The shrine of the goddess Saraswati, the clock tower, and a separate, exquisitely carved building called the *nerapura*, old paintings, weapons and sculptures are additional delights that make Padmanabhapuram a delightful experience.

Kollam (Quilon) and Alappuzha (Alleppey)

The backwaters for which Kerala is best known, after its coconuts, are spread between three coastal towns and carry the bulk of freight to and from the three main ports of Kochi, Alappuzha and Kozhikode. People live among the canals and lagoons and transport food, coconuts, building materials and fish.

A visit is incomplete without a boat trip starting at Kollam, an old seaport on the banks of the Ashtamudi Lake in the south of the state, moving through Alappuzha to Kottayam.

Suspended fishing nets, Chinese in origin, hark back to Kerala's importance on the Europe-China trade route.

Above: Kerala's unique fishing nets.

Getting there

Bus travel from Thiruvananthapuram to Kollam, 71 kilometres (44 miles), takes about two hours. Several daily trains cover this distance in less time.

When to go

In September-October, during the Onam Festival, the backwaters host the famous boat race *vallumkalis*. Experience the excitement and vigour as more than 100 men, singing in unison and pitting themselves against one another, row giant snake boats, each 30.5 metres (100 feet) in length.

Where to stay

Alappuzha has a few reasonably priced hotels. Narasimhapuram, Komala and Raiban have rates in the same range — with only Prince Hotel charging a 'princely sum' — for a double room affordable even by the budget traveller. See listings for 'Hotels'.

Sightseeing

Five kilometres (three miles) from the town of Kollam is the ancient **Thangasseri Fort**.

Alappuzha is 64 kilometres (40 miles) south of Kochi. It is the centre for backwater cruises, and holds the famous **Nehru Boat Race** on the second Saturday of August. Other boat races are held in June, July, August, September and December every year. Forty-seven kilometres (29 miles) from Alappuzha is the **Palace of Krishnapuram**, which has a large collection of wall murals.

Famous temple festivals in and near Alappuzha are held at the **Mannarasala Nagaraja Temple,** 32 kilometres (20 miles) from Alappuzha. It is an important centre for serpent worship. The **Ambalapuzha Krishna Temple Festival**, between March and April, is famous for its *payasam* (sweet milk porridge).

Festival dates change according to the local calendar and the moon's position.

Catch a boat from **Kumarakom** or **Muhamma** to visit the small yet beautiful **Pathiramanal Island** in the **Vembanad Lake. Karumadikkuttan**, only three kilometres (two miles) east of Ambalapuzha, is also the name of the 11th-century statue of Buddha found there.

Above: Kalarayipattu, Kerala's traditional martial arts.

Kottayam

Kottayam, the last halt of a backwater cruise, is 76 kilometres (47 miles) south-east of Kochi, with the lofty Western Ghats rich in cardamom, coffee, tea and pepper to the east, and the beautiful Vembanad Lake and paddy fields of Kuttanad to the west. It has vast rubber, coffee, tea and coconut plantations, which form a panoramic backdrop to the glistening blue-green waters. Kottayam made history by becoming the first Indian district to achieve 100 per cent literacy.

Getting there

Kottayam town is easily accessible by road, rail or boat from Kochi and Alappuzha. It is 160 kilometres (99 miles) north of Thiruvananthapuram, the state capital, on the railway line from Kanyakumari in the south to Kochi in the north and beyond.

When to go

October to April, unless you want to enjoy the sheer pleasure of sharp bouts of monsoon rain that drench the countryside.

Where to stay

All hotels assure spartan cleanliness even if they are decidedly cheap compared with elsewhere, among them the Aiswarya, Prince, Shakthi, Ambassador and the Venad Tourist Complex. If you pay more attention to decor and style, there is the Anjali, Green Park, Adia, Taj Garden Retreat, Vembanad Lake Resort and the Nisha Continental. Typical of Kerala, courteous service and cleanliness take priority over frills. See listings for 'Hotels'.

Sightseeing

The best temple architecture in Kerala can be seen in Kottayam district. Just 40 kilometres (25 miles) north of Kottayam the **Vaikom Siva Temple**, is linked with the legendary sage Parasurama and dedicated to Lord Shiva. The temple festival is in November-December.

The **Thirunakkara Siva Temple** in Kottayam town has one of the best *koothambalams* — performance halls for religious epics in traditional dance-theatre styles — in the state. St Mary's Church at **Valliapally** and **Cheriyapally** are fine examples of old architecture; the latter has some exquisite murals.

St Mary's Church in Kuruvilanad, built in AD 355, has an old bell with an undeciphered inscription.

Excursions from Kottayam

The **Kumarakom Bird Sanctuary**, 12 kilometres (seven miles) from Kottayam, is spread across 14 acres (six hectares) on the Vembanad Lake. Siberian storks visit every year. Take a chance any time between 1000 and 1800. Due east of Kottayam is the **Periyar Wildlife Sanctuary** at **Thekkady**. A gentle cruise at sunset on the **Periyar Lake**, may give you a glimpse of elephants, spotted deer, wild pig, bison and perhaps even a tiger or a leopard coming to the water for an evening drink.

Kochi (Cochin)

Until 1956, Kochi was a princely state run by maharajas, who, unlike their counterparts elsewhere in the world, accorded welfare activities high priority. Kochi now consists of mainland Ernakulam, the islands of Willingdon, Bolghatty and Gundu in the harbour, Fort Cochin and Mattanchery on the southern peninsula, and Vypeen Island, north of Fort Cochin, thought to be the most densely populated piece of land in Asia. Kochi has one of the finest natural harbours in the world. The picturesque Chinese fishing nets are permanent eye-catchers.

Getting there

Kochi can be reached by air from Mumbai, Thiruvananthapuram, Bangalore, Goa, Delhi and Chennai. There are two railway stations, Ernakulam Junction and Ernakulam South. The Himsagar Express connects Ernakulam with New Delhi; the Netravati Express leaves for Mumbai three days a week; and there is a daily Kochi-Chennai Express. Buses link Kochi to Alappuzha, Kollam, Kottayam, Thiruvananthapuram, Thrissur in Kerala; Madurai, Coimbatore and Chennai in Tamil Nadu; Bangalore and Mumbai. The government runs the Kerala State Roadways Transport Corporation (KSRTC), while private bus operators, run services out of the state as well.

When to go

A fast growing commercial centre with cosmopolitan shopping complexes, restaurants and entertainment centres, Kochi is very wet between June and September, but always bustling and welcoming.

Where to stay

Plush fare at Malabar Hotel with its colonial atmosphere, and the Casino, a new enterprise, both on Willingdon Island, offer the best at high tariffs. Sea Lord, Grand, Presidency, Bolghatty Palace — on the island — Bharat Tourist Home, Abad and many others. For the budget traveller, the Blue Diamond, Biju's, Sangeetha or Airlines. See listings for 'Hotels'.

Sightseeing

You would do well to start with a visit to the mini sound and light show highlighting important milestones in the history of Kerala. Portrayed through sculptures, the **Museum of Kerala History** at **Edapally**, on the Ernakulam-Alwaye route, has a one-hour presentation in Malayalam or English. Open from 1000 to 1200 and 1400 to 1600, except Mondays and holidays. A fascinating panorama, well executed to the smallest detail, it also encapsulates details of Kerala's cultural traditions, social movements and secular polity.

An **Art Gallery** and **Centre for Visual Arts** are on the same campus.

Fort Cochin has a pace of its own. Stroll along its streets to savour the old colonial bungalows or visit **St Francis' Church** built in 1503. Vasco da Gama's remains were buried there for 14 years before they were transferred to Lisbon, Portugal.

The **Jewish Synagogue** at Mattanchery, built in 1568, is sure to delight. The oldest synagogue in the Commonwealth, it is full of art treasures. The hand-painted, willow-patterned floor tiles are from China. Belgian chandeliers and scrolls of the Old Testament are on view.

Open from 1000-1200 and 1500-1700, except Saturday and Jewish holidays.

Also at Mattanchery is the **Dutch**

Palace, built by the Portuguese in 1557, and renovated in 1663 by the Dutch — hence its name.

It was presented to the Raja of Kochi, Verra Kerala Varman. It houses outstanding murals showing scenes from the *Ramayana, Mahabharata* and *Puranas*.

The contrast between these old pockets of Kochi and the new art deco styles of department stores in downtown Kochi, demonstrate the changes that have taken place in just two or three decades.

A boat ride around the **harbour** from Malabar Hotel to Bolghatty Island, where the **Bolghatty Palace,** built by the Dutch in 1744, now a well-preserved period-hotel, is a wonderful experience.

A ferry ride to **Vypeen Island** can be fun, especially when you have to travel cheek by jowl with fish, goats, motorcycles and Maruti cars on comfortable old boats.

Standing room only on the car ferry, but seats are available exclusively for two-legged passengers from the jetty at Ernakulam.

A stroll along a fascinating market-place at **Broadway** takes you to traditional bell-metal vessels in shops where Gujarati women sell pyramids of spices on the pavement.

The museums of **Parikshith Thampuran**, Ernakulam, and **Hill Palace**, Thripunithara, have fine collections.

Thrissur (Trichur)

Situated almost in the middle of Kerala, Thrissur is fast developing into a commercial and intellectual centre, with museums, libraries and fine educational institutions.

Getting there
Most buses and trains travelling the length of Kerala will stop at Thrissur.

When to go
The best time to visit would be during the Pooram Festival in April or in September during the Onam Festival, which is celebrated in various traditional ways in every household in Thrissur.

Where to stay
The tariff range in most hotels and tourist hostels is easily affordable, among them Casino, Elite International, Luciya Palace, Alukka's near the railway station, Surya International, Bini and Yatri Niwas. See listings for 'Hotels'.

Sightseeing
The impressive **Vadakumnatha Temple** is one of the oldest in Kerala. It holds the famous **Pooram Festival** on its grounds in April every year. This spectacular event is full of gorgeously caparisoned elephants, frenzied percussion from temple drums and a fabulous fireworks display that brings the whole town out to witness it.

Two kilometres (one mile) from the heart of the town is Museum Road, which has the **Art Museum** and **Zoo** in the same compound.

The collection of metal sculptures, wood carvings and ancient jewellery, apart from old manuscripts and costumes, is a pleasant complement to the lions, tigers, birds and a vast collection of snakes in the zoo section.

Bell-metal, an alloy of five metals, is used to make traditional vessels used for lamps and household containers. They are manufactured in **Irinjalakuda**, 24 kilometres (15 miles) from Thrissur, and sold in the gleaming utensil shops around the Vadakumnatha Temple.

Irinjalakuda also has a famous training and performing centre for Kathakali. Shows are held every second Saturday.

Excursions from Thrissur
If you are based in Thrissur and want to make forays out of town just for the day, you have a choice between temples, waterfalls, a cultural centre and a picnic spot near a reservoir.

About 30 kilometres (19 miles) northwest is **Guruvayur**, one of Kerala's most sacred pilgrim centres.

Its stone carvings, performance hall, elephants and huge bell-metal vessels are indicative of its religious importance.

Opposite: Inside the Jewish Synagogue.

The **Waterfalls** of **Athirappally** and **Vazhachal** are 63 kilometres (39 miles) away, at the Sholayar Ranges entrance.

Peechi Dam is only 20 kilometres (12 miles) from Thrissur. It is quiet, peaceful and pleasant, and the drive is through rubber plantations on simple roads.

Kerala's most famous modern poet, the late Vallathole Narayana Menon, founded Kathakali's prestigious training centre and other classical arts of Kerala, called **Kalamandalam**.

Located 32 kilometres (20 miles) north of Thrissur, its surroundings, architecture and ambience, and the talent of its outstanding faculty and students, make it a cultural experience not to be missed.

Top: Dutch and Portuguese tombstones.
Above: One of the centuries old churches at Kochi.

Opposite: Pennants adorn the forecourt of what is believed to be one of the oldest mosques in India.

Lakshadweep: Unspoilt Beaches and Lagoons

The union territory of Lakshadweep, in the south-west of India on the Arabian Sea, is off the coast of Kerala. It is composed of a scattered bunch of 36 islands, of which only 10 are inhabited.

Covering a total area of 32 square kilometres (12 square miles), the Lakshadweep Islands offer some of the most unspoilt beaches and natural lagoons in the world. The predominantly Muslim population trades in copra from coconuts.

Given the islands' strategic location in the Arabian Sea, bona fide foreign tourists are permitted visits only to the uninhabited Bangaram Island. Indian tourists can visit the populated islands, too, but because of the population density, the government regulates the tourist inflow.

The Administrator, Union Territory of Lakshadweep, Indira Gandhi Road, Willingdon Island, Kochi, Kerala, issues entry permits. Applications should be presented with four passport-sized photographs. For tourists, it is easier to contact Casino Hotel, Willingdon Island, Kochi, for permits and transport as they arrange package tours to the islands. See listings for 'Hotels'.

Getting there

Flights by the Vayudoot Service connect Agatti in Lakshadweep with Chennai and Kochi on the mainland. Tourists are also taken to Bangaram Island by speedboat. The other islands are connected to Agatti by a helicopter service. Kochi is the nearest railhead.

It takes 12 to 16 hours to reach the Lakshadweep Islands. M V *Tipu Sultan* and M V *Bharatseema*, of the Shipping Corporation of India, make round trips to the islands five to six times a month. Sailing time is between 16 and 18 hours.

Where to stay

Kavaratti, Kalpeni and Minicoy have tourist cottages, while Casino Hotel in Kochi runs a private resort on Bangaram Island.

Sightseeing

Kavaratti is the administrative capital of Lakshadweep and is the most developed island of the group. **Kalpeni** and **Minicoy islands** boast the finest lagoons and offer a number of water sports. On Minicoy Island an old **lighthouse** built by the British is a major attraction.

The warm, peace-loving islanders offer a distinct flavour of Indian culture and beauty. **Bangaram Island** is ideal for deep-sea diving, fishing and windsurfing.

For details of package tours, restaurants and travel, contact the Assistant General Manager (Sports), Lakshadweep Office, Kochi. See listings for 'Hotels'.

Opposite and above: Serene Lakshadweep, remote and little-known island beauty.

Tamil Nadu: Land of the Arts

Geographically and culturally, Tamil Nadu is different from the north Indian states. Tamil Nadu, the seat of an ancient Dravidian civilization, is rich in religious, literary, artistic and philosophical accomplishments traceable to a pre-Christian era.

Generally, Tamilians are swarthy in complexion, their foreheads marked with stripes of *chandan* (sandalwood paste) and *vibhuti* (sacred ash), marks of faith.

The Tamilian womenfolk wear rich silk sarees in striking colours, decorate their glistening black hair with long ropes of jasmine and orange *kanakambaram* blossoms, and adorn themselves with fabulous gold and diamond jewellery.

The leafy shade trees typical of the north are replaced by endless rows of coconut palms fringing the lush paddy fields, where gaily-dressed women provide a splash of vibrant colour.

Sightseeing

The only big city is **Madras**, now called **Chennai,** the state capital. Tamil Nadu has witnessed the rise and fall of many illustrious dynasties — Pallava, Pandya, Chola and Vijayanagara.

Their capitals survive as great temple towns — **Mamallapuram**, **Kanchipuram**, **Madurai**, **Thanjavur** and **Tiruchirapalli**, where some of the most magnificent temples may be found. Along the Coromandel coast, lying between **Pulicat**, north of Chennai, and **Kanyakumari** and **Padmanabhapuram**, at the extreme tip of the state, some grand churches and ruins of forts and forgotten empires, built by the Dutch, Portuguese, French and British, who came first to trade and later established themselves there, dot the coastline.

As far back as the second century AD, the Tamilians travelled to the Malayan Peninsula, Sumatra, Java, Bali, Borneo and Sri Lanka. Monuments in Indonesia and Thailand show strong Pallava influence. On the lake banks at Pulicat, ruins of British settlements, a cemetery and a decaying, early 17th-century Dutch fort lie scattered. Boating and picnics are well provided for.

At **Sadras**, south of Mamallapuram, stands a ruined 18th-century Dutch fort. Bird-watchers are assured of many engrossing hours at the **Vedanthangal Sanctuary**, where more than 100,000 winged Siberian visitors flock.

Yet another natural wonder, albeit of a rare kind, is **Thiruvakkarai Fossil Park**, where metal-hard, 20 million-year-old, wood fossils are displayed. This is an ancient region where prehistoric burial sites have been found.

The **Fort St David** at **Cuddalore**, south of Pondicherry, the magnificent shore temple at **Tirumullaivasal**, and **Poompuhar**, south of Chennai, the ancient port of the Chola kingdom, originally called *Kaveripoompattinam*, 'the Flower of the Kaveri', make visits there rewarding. Poompuhar has a lovely little beach and a modest rest house. The Tamil Nadu state emporium derives its name from this village.

Tranquebar, also called Tarangambadi, or 'the Village of the Dancing Waves', stands on the coast, south of Poompuhar. The Dutch East India Company built charming Dutch houses along King and Queen streets. The **Danesborg Fort** stands guard on the coast. The church and cemetery speak of the country's first Protestant mission. An old, well maintained, Catholic church at **Koraikkal**, and the Roman Catholic Church of Our Lady of Good Health at **Velanganni**, where many offerings of gold and silver are made, speak of a strong Christian presence. At Velanganni, a major festival is held annually in September, drawing people of diverse faiths.

At **Vedaranyam**, Rama's footprints are preserved in rock. It is believed Rama stopped there on his way back to Ayodhya. Marshy Point Calimere is a natural haven for 50,000 migratory flamingos. From there

Opposite: An ancient temple on Vivekananda Rock, Kanyakumari.

the inward curve of Palk Bay has some quiet fishing villages and still quieter virgin beaches, where the morning and evening silence is broken only by fishermen shouting to one another as they push their catamarans into the sea.

Rameshwaram is hallowed as the point where Rama rescued Sita from the clutches of the demon king Ravana in the epic *Ramayana*. **Kanyakumari**, **Suchindran** and **Padmanabhapuram** are the last points in Tamil Nadu on the Coromandel coast.

Throughout Tamil Nadu, the similarity of architecture is striking — mostly of native genius. Tamil Nadu shows a distinctive continuation of building traditions because all its rulers built in their own styles without destroying the existing work.

The temples were built as village centres. Grand temple *gopurams* (gate towers) rise over a landscape of paddy fields, and serve as landmarks. The temples made another contribution to the cultural heritage of the country — **Bharatnatyam**, a temple dance in which the costume, jewellery and music are essentially classical. It is a dance of devotion in the presence of the Lord.

Known all over the world, the great Pallava and Chola bronzes were created as temple deities. The Nataraja image in bronze is synonymous with Tanjore art. These bronzes, made by the lost wax method, reached unparalleled excellence under the Cholas.

Other traditional arts include *repoussé* (metalwork in relief) and copperwork inlaid with brass and silver. These Tanjore bronzes and plates are the most typical of Tamil Nadu art.

Pongal, the harvest festival in January, reveals Tamilians at their joyous best. This four-day festival involves the decorating of homes and cattle in celebration of plenty. *Kolams* (decorative geometric patterns), auspicious symbols of prosperity and good luck, appear on every doorstep.

Gigantic cinema hoardings are yet another distinctive feature with larger-than-life cut-outs of popular film stars. If gods rule the temples, film stars dominate every other place. Cinema halls are packed. In Tamil Nadu many a popular film hero has made it to the world of politics.

Elected governments tend to change the names of towns, landmarks and streets at whim. Though this is commonplace, the locals frequently stick to what is old and familiar and go to great lengths to help the confused traveller.

Chennai (Madras)

Chennai or Madras, 'the Gateway to South India', presents a kaleidoscope of moods. Founded in 1631, Chennai is not ancient.

The Raja of Chandragiri gave Francis Day, a trader of the East India Company, a grant of land to build a factory and a warehouse in the village of Madraspatnam. The British walled this in on April 23 — St George's Day — and called it Fort St George, the centre for British trade. Outside the fort the village Chennapatnam grew up.

In 1683, Madras became independent of its Java overlords, and five years later James II of England granted Madras a municipal charter, making it the oldest municipality in India. Ten years later, Elihu Yale, who founded the famed university in America, secured Egmore and other areas from Aurangzeb.

In 1793, Calcutta became the administrative centre of the East India Company and Madras was therefore allowed to continue as a trading centre.

There are no ancient monuments there. However, it is the gateway to some great cultural and religious centres, such as Mamallapuram, Kanchipuram, Thanjavur and Madurai.

Getting there

The Meenambakkam International Airport receives flights by Air India, Air Lanka, British Airways, Singapore Airlines and Malayasian Airlines, in addition to domestic flights from Delhi, Bangalore, Mumbai and Calcutta. Chennai is well connected to all parts of India. The best trains are the Tamil Nadu Express, from Delhi, the Dadar-Chennai Express from Mumbai, the West Coast Express from Ernakulam and the Brindavan Express and Bangalore Express from Bangalore. Interstate bus

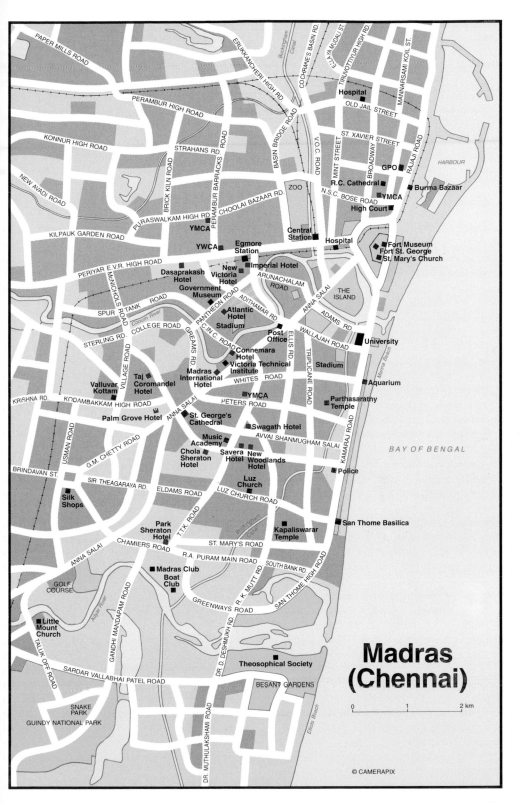

Madras (Chennai)

0   1   2 km

211

services, and travel within the state, to almost all destinations, are excellent.

When to go
Chennai is usually hot and humid. Visit between December-February. The Pongal festival in mid-January is a grand affair.

Where to stay
Luxury hotels include Chola Sheraton, Taj Coromandel, Park Sheraton, Connemara, The Trident, and Hotel Savera. Middle-range hotels include New Woodlands, Dasaprakash, Hotel Palmgrove, Hotel Swagath, Hotel Ramprasad, Hotel Atlantic, New Victoria Hotel, Chennai International Hotel, Imperial Hotel, Hotel Srilekha Inter-Continental and Hotel Pandian. See listings for 'Hotels'.

Sightseeing
Today, Chennai is the fourth largest city in India. Site of the original British settlement, **Fort St George** was built in 1640. Most of the present structures date from 1711. **Factory House**, to the north, houses the Tamil Nadu State Legislative Assembly and Secretariat. The **Fort Museum** contains some Raj memorabilia. Open from 0900 to 1700 every day, except Fridays. There are 10 galleries housing treasures in French porcelain and glass, clocks and early 19th-century prints of Daniells.

Within the fort, **St Mary's Church**, the oldest Anglican Church in India, was built in 1680 from voluntary donations. The roof is bomb-proof — built only of stone without any wood. Both Robert Clive and Elihu Yale were married there. **Clive's House** is now the office of the Archaeological Survey of India. Only one room — **Clive's Corner** — is open to visitors. A small, interesting structure close by is **Cornwallis Cupola**.

The second oldest museum in the country, the **Government Museum and Art Gallery** on Pantheon Road, near Egmore Station, has the finest collection of eighth to 12th-century Pallava and Chola bronze sculptures. There are also ivory carvings, miniature paintings from the Chola,

Vijayanagara, Chalukya and Hoysala periods and a Modern Art section. Free entry 0900-1700; closed Fridays.

'Doubting' St Thomas arrived in AD 52, secured some conversions and offended the authorities. He took refuge and was eventually martyred on **St Thomas Mount**, near the present airport. It is believed that Armenian Christians built a church over his grave in the sixth century. This neo-Gothic structure was converted into the **Basilica of San Thomas** in 1956.

North of the fort, the **Lighthouse,** built in 1844, offers a fine view of the grand Indo-Saracenic edifice of the **High Court Buildings**, built on the site of the Chennapatnam village in 1892.

Valluvar Kottam is a quite impressive memorial to the great Tamil saint and poet Thiruvalluvar. The massive stone chariot, 31 metres (102 feet) tall, is drawn by two stone elephants, each two metres (seven feet) high. All 1,330 verses of his *magnum opus*, the *Thirrukural*, are carved on 67 granite pillars.

Marina Beach, the second largest in the world, is always full of people. The **Aquarium** draws huge crowds. Farther down from Marina Beach is the more secluded and sophisticated **Elliot's Beach**. On Elliot's Beach Road, **Guindy Park** includes a **Deer and Snake Park**, open daily from 0803-1700.

The peaceful **Theosophical Society** on the south bank of the Adyar River estuary has beautiful gardens and lawns and a grand banyan tree covering an area of 3,716 square metres (40,000 square feet). The library contains nearly 17,000 volumes and is open from Monday to Friday, 0800-1100, and 1400-1700. Saturday timings are from 0800-1100. It is closed on Sundays.

The **Kapaleeshwar Temple**, built in 1566 by the Vijayanagara rulers, is the grandest temple in Chennai. Dedicated to Shiva, its 37-metre (121-feet) *gopuram* (gate tower) is covered with a riot of sculptures.

Non-Hindus are excluded from the sanctum. The **Parthasarthy Temple**, originally built in the eighth century by the Pallavas,

Opposite: The towering steeple of the cathedral in Chennai.

is dedicated to Vishnu and is the oldest temple in Chennai. The Tamil Nadu Tourism Development Corporation organizes city tours conducted mornings and evenings. The Indian Tourism Development Corporation (ITDC) runs similar tours.

Shopping

Chennai is the best place to purchase south Indian silks. Available at the **India Silk House** and the government-owned **Co-optex**, the prices are fixed and the quality excellent. **Khadi Gramodyog Bhawan** and the **Indian Art Museum** offer handicrafts and handwoven material at reasonable prices. Most Indian states have their emporia on **Anna Salai**, better known as Mount Road. **Poompuhar** is the Tamil Nadu emporium. **Victoria Technical Institute**, also on Anna Salai, has a wide range of handicrafts.

Daily newspapers like *The Hindu* carry shopping guides. **Burma Bazaar's** spurious and smuggled foreign goods are a craze among the locals and the market itself is a delightful place to hang about. The **Madras Music Academy** on Mowbray's Road holds excellent cultural shows in Bharatnatyam and folk dances, Carnatic music and puppet theatre.

Excursions from Chennai

Cholamandal Artist's Village, 15 kilometres (nine miles) en route to Mamallapuram, is home to talented artists, painters and sculptors, who will sell you their work.

Covelong, 38 kilometres (24 miles) from Chennai, down the same road, is a fishing village and good picnic spot in unspoilt natural surroundings.

About two kilometres (one mile) north of Mamallapuram on the Covelong Road, **Silversands**, the largest resort, offers accommodation over a wide range.

Udhagamandalam (Ootacamund), better known as Ooty in the Nilgiri Hills (Blue Mountains), lies between the Eastern and Western Ghats, where the three states of Tamil Nadu, Karnataka and Kerala meet.

Ooty has lush green hills covered with tea, pine and eucalyptus. The township revolves around the **Lake** and the **Botanical Gardens**. Ooty is ideal for a long, leisurely vacation. The area around Ooty is home to the buffalo-worshipping Toda tribes and the Irulas who farm snakes to extract venom. **Dodabetta**, 2,623 metres (8,606 feet), the highest peak in Tamil Nadu, is only 10 kilometres (six miles) from Ooty.

The 46-kilometre (29-mile) hill railway between Ooty and Mettupalyam, featured in David Lean's *Passage to India*.

The most convenient way to get there is by the Blue Mountain Express, overnight from Chennai. There are direct buses between Ooty and Chennai, Coimbatore, Mettupalyam, Mysore and Bangalore.

From Ooty, visit **Coonoor,** where **Sim's Park** is a major attraction, and **Kotagiri**, the fruit-growing region of this district. Today, silver jewellery and embroidery are much valued local crafts.

Mamallapuram (Mahabalipuram)

Forty-five kilometres (28 miles) south of Chennai lies Mamallapuram, the ancient port of the Pallavas, who ruled from the seventh to the eighth century AD.

Getting there

It is best reached by jeep from Chennai or bus tours, conducted by the Indian Tourism Development Corporation (ITDC) and the Tamil Nadu Tourism Development Corporation (TTDC).

When to go

Throughout the year, though May and June can be unbearably hot.

Where to stay

Day trips from Chennai are best. Silversands, Temple Bay Ashok and Golden Sun Hotel, luxury beach resorts along the coast, are also options worth considering.

Sightseeing

The Pallavas were famous for their masterpieces in rock. **Arjuna's Penance,** the gigantic rock face, nine metres (30 feet) high and 27 metres (89 feet) wide, carved in basrelief, is perhaps the world's largest. It was executed under the patronage of

Top: Descent of the Ganga, Mahabalipuram.
Above: Rockcut *mandap* or pillared pavilion, Mahabalipuram.

Narasimhavarman I (AD 630-670), after whom the town is called Mamallapuram or 'City of Mamalla'. Some regard the penurious central figure to be Arjuna, the hero of the *Mahabharata*, seeking Shiva's blessings for victory. Others believe it is Bhagiratha, the sage who beseeched Shiva to release the Ganga from his locks.

The scene largely depicts all of creation out to witness the descent of the Ganga. The Naga and Nagi, in the natural cleft, emphasize the river image.

The seven- or eight-pillared *mandapam* (pavilion) temples, cut out of gigantic boulders around Arjuna's Penance, contain some fascinating sculptured wall panels. **Krishna Mandap** shows a cowherd milking a cow, and the child Krishna lifting the Govardhan Mountain to save his people from torrential rain caused by Indra.

A piece of unrivalled splendour is that of Durga killing the demon in the **Mahisasuramardini** panel, facing which **Vishnu,** in all his supine grace, reclines upon the thousand-headed Sheshnag. Elsewhere in the **Varaha Mandapam**, Vishnu appears as a mighty boar.

The five seventh-century monolithic *rathas* (chariots) named after the Pandavas — **Bhima, Arjuna, Dharmaraja, Sahdeva** and **Draupadi** — have stood sphinx-like for centuries but are not shrines. These rathas served as prototypes for the elaborately sculptured *vimanas* or towers, pillared halls and façades that were created centuries later. The **Valayankuttai** and **Pidari Rathas** to the north-west and the **Ganesh Ratha** to the north are not as important.

Against the background of the lashing waves, rise the twin towers of the **Shore Temple**, enfolding the shrines of Shiva and Vishnu within them. The creation of King Narasimhavarman II (AD 690-715), it represents the culmination of excellence in Pallava architecture. For more than 1200 years, these temples have resisted the ravages of time. Six other pagodas are feared destroyed by the sea. A very special kind of pilaster decoration, fashioned as a rampant lion, is a daring experiment in a new form of architecture. The temple complex also includes a king on his throne, the sculptured representation of King Narasimhavarman, the creator of most of the beautiful rock sculptures, and a monolithic lion with a female rider perched on its left shoulder. A square on the lion's chest bears the carved image of Durga.

Excursions from Mamallapuram

At **Thirukkalikundaram**, a hill 14 kilometres (nine miles) from Mamallapuram, a pair of sacred Brahmani kites regularly appear to partake of food from a brass tray. The 406 steps to the summit are tiring but rarely do the birds disappoint. A visit is usually included in the bus tour.

Kanchipuram, 65 kilometres (40 miles) from Mamallapuram, is an ancient temple town, one of the Seven Sacred Cities of India. Its 1,000 or so temples, of which only about 125 remain, were built by the Pallavas, who were patrons of temple architecture. The Chola, Pandya and then Vijayanagara rulers added to the architectural wealth of Kanchipuram.

The **Kailashnatha Temple** (AD 725), dedicated to Shiva, is a masterpiece of Pallava architecture. It has the most splendid sculptural decoration. The carved *yali* (hippogriffs) columns are typical of south Indian temples.

The **Vaikunthperumal Temple**, also built by the Pallavas, is dedicated to Vishnu. It has three sanctums, one on top of the other, and the vimana over the sanctum is larger than the one at the Kailashnatha Temple. The marvellously sculptured, 1,000-pillared, **Ekambaresvara Temple**, built in the 16th century, is the largest of these temples, with a 10-storeyed *gopuram* (gate tower) rising 186 metres (610 feet) from the ground.

The **Kamakshiamma Temple** is dedicated to Parvati, Shiva's consort. The high gopuram and 100-pillared hall of the **Varadarajaswami Temple** is grand, but the *pièce de résistance* is a massive stone chain.

The name Kanchipuram is synonymous with fabulous silk sarees, a must in every Indian woman's trousseau. The weaving of these sarees is a craft many centuries old.

Opposite: Weaving silk in Kanchipuram.

Madurai

Madurai vies with Varanasi in antiquity. When Emperor Augustus ruled Rome in about 25 BC, he established trade links with this city, a fact proved by Roman coins found in excavations along the Vaigai River.

Getting there

There are regular flights to Madurai from Chennai and Bangalore. Direct train and bus services from Chennai and other major cities are the most convenient for visitors. Madurai is 447 kilometres (277 miles) and Tiruchirapalli 128 kilometres (79 miles) from Chennai.

When to go

Avoid May and June.

Where to stay

The Madurai Ashok, Taj Garden Retreat and Pandyan Hotel offer first class accommodation. Hotel Prem Niwas, Hotel Aarathy, Hotel Supreme, Hotel Tamil Nadu and Tamil Nadu Star Hotel are budget hotels.

Sightseeing

While numerous dynasties ruled Madurai, it was the Nayaks of the 16th and 17th centuries who were responsible for its gigantic *gopurams* (gate towers) and splendid pillared *mandapams* (pavilions).

The soaring **gopurams** of Madurai are the most distinctive landmarks of the city. Ranging from 43 to 49 metres (140 to 160 feet) in height, these gopurams are crowded with gods, goddesses, demons and beasts, painted in numerous garish colours.

The **Southern Gopuram**, the most magnificent, is also the tallest, nearly 49 metres (160 feet) high, which you can climb for a small fee. The view it affords takes in other gopurams, the Yanai Malai and Naga Malai — Elephant and Snake hills — and the slow-moving Vaigai River.

The **Meenakshi Temple**, Madurai's most famous attraction, is dedicated to Shiva's consort, the fish-eyed goddess Parvati. During the **Chitra Festival**, in April-May every year, the wedding of the divine couple is celebrated with great pomp.

The dimly lit Parvati sanctum is not accessible to non-Hindus. Its sunless interior is musty, and the smell of coconut and milk offerings, jasmine and joss sticks, is overpowering. The devotional fervour is further heightened by the temple music picked out on the *mridangam* and *nadesvaram*, with temple priests scurrying about with glowing brass lamps, ringing temple bells. For a small fee, the priests will willingly arrange a special *darshan* (homage) of the goddess.

The **Sundaresvara Shrine**, next to the sanctum is no less grand. Pilgrims first take a ritualistic bath in the pool outside, usually nothing more than a symbolic sprinkling of a few drops of water over their heads while chanting a mantra or two.

Numerous mandapams surround the sanctum. Entry into the temple is by way of the **Meenakshi Nayakkar Mandapam**, the temple elephant stable built in 1707. It is dominated by a 7.6-metre-high (24-feet) brass *tiruvatchi* (lampstand) that can hold 1,008 lamps. The mythical *yali* (hippogriff) is carved on each of the 110 mammoth monolithic columns.

The **Padumandapam** has 124 magnificently carved pillars built by Tirumallai Nayak (1626-33). Within the temple, the **Pontamaraikulam** or 'Tank of the Golden Lotuses', offers the best view of the gopurams.

The colonnades on the eastern and southern sides still bear traces of faded murals depicting the Lord's divine sporting pursuits. The **Kalikkoondu Mandapam** is filled with screeching caged parrots and magnificent pillars. Farther on, lies the **Kambatti Mandapam**, with its grand pillars carved with different manifestations of Shiva. The 1,000-pillared hall (997, to be exact) or **Ayirakkal Mandapam**, built by the Nayaks in 1560, is famous for its fascinating musical pillars. The pillars are sculptured with Shiva in his various forms and other gods and goddesses depicting every conceivable human emotion, and symbolize the *kadamba* forest where the *Shivalingam* (phallic symbol) was first

Above: The soaring *gopurams* or gate towers of Madurai.

found. The hall is now a museum of exquisite bronzes with a magnificent *nataraja* as its showpiece.

Thirumalai Nayak's Palace in Indo-Saracenic style is the only other attraction. Though much of it is ruined, the tall Roman columns, ornamentation in stucco and spectacular dome over the Swarga Vilasam (Celestial Pavilion), which has neither supporting girder nor rafter, are of immense architectural interest.

Madurai is well known for its cotton textiles, especially its colourful and immensely comfortable *lungis*.

Excursions from Madurai

Thiruparankundram, 10 kilometres (six miles) away, is a 350-year-old temple dedicated to Subramanya. The original sanctum is an excavated cave with the superstructures added subsequently by generations of rulers and devotees.

Alagarkovil, 20 kilometres (12 miles) from Madurai, has a **Vishnu Temple** and some marvellously sculptured pillars. Alagar (as Vishnu) was the brother of Meenakshi, who gave his sister in marriage

to Lord Sundaresvara. The ruins of a fortified town lie forgotten amid green hills. **Kodaikanal** or Kodi, 120 kilometres (74 miles) from Madurai, is a hill-station in the Palani Hills reached by bus from Madurai. Boating on the **lake**, horse-riding and walking through unspoilt country are some of the pleasures this place offers. **Coaker's Walk** takes you to a hilltop observatory from where one might see Madurai on a clear day. **Pillar Rocks**, three stupendous granite rocks each 120 metres (394 feet) high, command the landscape for miles.

Pondicherry

Pondicherry, 160 kilometres (100 miles) south of Chennai, is a bustling town on the sea coast, where spiritual pursuits coexist with business. Founded by the French in 1673, the village of Pulichery soon became a fast growing trading centre. That was the beginning of a constant power struggle between the French and the British.

The oval-shaped city of Pondicherry has a peripheral boulevard surrounding the French residential area, mainly facing the sea front. The Ville Blanche (for the white settlers) and the Ville Noir (for the natives) is divided by a canal.

The old French street names are being replaced by Indian names. Pondicherry became part of the Indian Union in 1954. The Union Territory includes Mahe in Kerala, Yanam in Andhra Pradesh and Karaikal in Tamil Nadu.

Pondicherry has an ancient heritage which goes back to 1500 BC, when, as Vedapuri, it was a famous centre of Vedic scholarship. The sage Agastya had an *ashram* (hermitage) there.

The Romans, navigating between the Red Sea and the East Indies, developed a trading point at Arikamedu in the first century AD.

A Sanskrit university flourished there in the ninth century AD. Little is known about Pondicherry thereafter, until the French arrived. Today, it is known for its Aurobindo Ashram, and an international community at peace with itself.

Getting there

Pondicherry can only be reached by train or bus. The Pondicherry Express is the only direct train from Chennai.

Other trains go as far as Villipuram, 60 kilometres (37 miles) from Pondicherry, and the rest of the journey has to be covered by bus. Other regular and efficient bus services link Pondicherry to Chennai, Chidambaram, Mamallapuram, Bangalore, Udhagamandalam and Madurai. The Thiruvalluvar bus stand in Pondicherry is well organized and efficient. The Mofussil bus stand for state and private buses is chaotic, with no signs in English.

When to go

November-March is the best season.

Where to stay

There are no luxury hotels in Pondicherry. Pondicherry Ashoka Beach Resort is in the medium-range, while the Grand Hotel d'Europe, Aristo Guest House, Ellora Lodge, Yatri Niwas, Hotel Bristol, and the Ajantha Guest House offer cheap accommodation. See listings for 'Hotels'.

Sightseeing

Raj Niwas, a 200-year-old mansion, belonged to Marquis Joseph François Dupleix, who built the French settlement there even as Clive set up the British settlement in Madras (Chennai). It is now the residence of the lieutenant-governor. A statue of Vishnu as a boar (*Varaharupa*) stands in the garden. Visitors are allowed only a distant view of the Raj Niwas.

The **Romain Rolland Library,** established in 1827, has some 60,000 volumes in French and English, but it is the **Pondicherry Museum** which is worth visiting. A room with paintings, mirrors, clocks and furniture is maintained in typical French style. Besides, there are Pallava and Chola bronzes, and Roman artefacts excavated at Arikamedu nearby. Open from 1000-1700. Closed on Mondays, entrance free.

The **House of Subramanyam Bharathi,** Tamil poet and patriot, has been preserved as a monument. **The Church of the Sacred Heart of Jesus** is a Gothic structure with some exquisite stained glass windows. **The Church of Notre Dame des Anges** (1856) has a rare oil painting of 'Our Lady of the Assumption', a gift from Napoleon III. The original ambience of the house in which **Anand Ranga Pillai**, an Indian nobleman of the 18th century, lived is maintained. Anand Ranga was a confidant and trusted trade agent of Dupleix. His diaries pertaining to the period between 1736-60 contain interesting details of French rule in India.

The **beach** at Pondicherry is lovely, an ideal place to swim, and **Goubert Salai**, the main promenade, perfect for a morning jog. The old lighthouse and new pier to the south, and the statue of Dupleix, are attractions along the beach.

Aurobindo Ashram was founded by Aurobindo Ghose, a first-class graduate from Cambridge, who joined the freedom movement, was jailed by the British and relinquished his political dreams to retire to Pondicherry in 1910. When 'the Mother' (born Mira Alfassa in Paris) joined him, the ashram grew into an international centre for yoga, the study of spiritual resurgence and philosophy. Aurobindo died in 1950,

Opposite: French memorial at Pondicherry.

and 'the Mother' in 1973. The *samadhi* (memorial) to them in marble is the focus of the ashram. A guided tour starts from the main gate at 0845 each day.

Excursions from Pondicherry

Auroville, the 'City of Dawn', designed by the French architect Roger Anger, is a futuristic town envisioned for a society where men and women from all over the world would discard their human differences. Auroville, lies seven kilometres (four miles) north of Pondicherry, along the Tamil Nadu border. The settlements there are called **Promise**, **Hope**, **Aspiration** and **Peace**. The city is divided into five zones representing work, dwelling, education, society and the world.

Matri Mandir, the Sanctuary of Truth, stands in the centre of this mini-city. The **Hall of Meditation** is shaped like a sphere.

Soil from 124 countries and all the Indian states is kept in an urn — a symbol of international harmony. There are three guided tours of Auroville each week. Inquire at the **Auroville Information Centre**, Nehru Street, Pondicherry.

At **Chidambaram**, 60 kilometres (37 miles) north-west of Pondicherry, one of the greatest Chola temples of the same name, is spread over a 32-acre (13-hectare) complex with four magnificent *gopurams* (gate towers).

The northern gopuram, built by Krishna Deva Raya, King of Vijayanagara (1509-30), is the tallest, 45 metres (148 feet) high. The original temple dates back to AD 500. In the 12th century Vikram Chola built much of the core structure.

Chidambaram celebrates Shiva as the cosmic dancer. According to legend, Shiva defeated Kali (Parvati) in a dance contest. The *Anand Tandava* (Dance of Bliss) was beyond Kali, who took up residence outside the city. **Thillai Kali Amman**, the Kali shrine, stands outside the village.

The temple is decorated with 108 sculptures, illustrating classic Bharatnatyam poses, based on the classical work *Natya Shastra*. The famous sculpture of Nataraja — Shiva as the cosmic dancer — stands in the **Kanak Sabha**, the golden hall. The large Shivaganga Tank lies behind the main shrine, which also has a 1,000-pillared hall, the **Raja Sabha**. The dance hall has 56 pillars carved with dancing figures. The daily devotional prayer, or *puja*, is at 1800. A dance festival is held there in February-March, a prestigious event attracting dancers from all over India.

To get to Chidambaram, either take the metre-gauge train from Cuddalore or the bus from Pondicherry to Thanjavur, which stops over at Chidambaram. Buses are a better mode of transport. Visit between November and March and stay at the Hotel Tamil Nadu, which is modest and comfortable, or the Star Lodge or Hotel Raja Rajan.

Thanjavur (Tanjore)

Thanjavur rose to great prominence as capital of the Cholas between the 10th and 12th centuries AD. Thanjavur is named after a demon, Tanjan, who was killed by Sri Anandvalli Amman and Vishnu — who granted the last wish of the demon by naming the city Thanjavur after it. Today, Thanjavur is known for the magnificent **Brihadeshvara Temple**.

Getting there

There are flights from Chennai and Madurai only. Alternatively, fly to Tiruchirapalli (Trichy), 60 kilometres (37 miles) away, and take a train or bus to Thanjavur which is on the metre-gauge coastal railway between Chennai and Tiruchirapalli. Excellent bus services connect Thanjavur with Chennai, Madurai, Pondicherry, Tirupati, Tiruchirapalli and Kumbakonam. There are two bus stations on Hospital Road, between the Anicut Canal and the old city walls. The bus stand at Thiruvalluvar handles long-distance buses. The bus for Tiruchirapalli leaves from the chaotic municipal bus stand.

When to go

Visit between September and February.

A music festival is organized every year at Thiravayaru, 11 kilometres (seven miles) away, in honour of Thyagaraja, the renowned saint-composer. It is a great event for lovers of classical Carnatic music.

Above: A view from Gingee Fort, Tamil Nadu.

Where to stay
There are no luxury hotels. Good comfortable stay is available at the Hotel Tamil Nadu, managed by the Tamil Nadu Tourism Development Corporation (TTDC) Units I & II, the Indian Tourism Development Corporation-run (ITDC) Traveller's Lodge, Hotel Parisutham and Ashoka Lodge.

Sightseeing
Built by the greatest Chola king, Rajaraja I (AD 985-1014), the **Brihadeshvara Temple** is the main attraction of Thanjavur.

Dedicated to Shiva, the *Shivalingam* in the sanctum is believed to have increased in size after it was pulled out of the Narmada River. *Brihadeshvara* comes from *brihad* meaning huge.

A majestic 13-storeyed tower rises 58 metres (190 feet) above the city. The spherical *stupika* (loadstone), which is a mammoth, monolithic block weighing nearly 80,000 kilos (80 tonnes), was moved to its present height by means of an inclined plane starting at Sara Pallam village, six kilometres (four miles) to the south.

The *vimana,* or tower, is called *Dakshinameru* as it depicts Shiva and Parvati. The grand *shikhara* (tower) and the *stupika* do not ever cast their shadows on the ground.

At the temple entrance, a huge *nandi* (Shiva's bull-vehicle) rising six metres (20 feet) long and four metres (13 feet) high, watches over the shrine. The two huge statues of *dwarapalas* (doorkeepers) and the *gopuram* (gate tower) are remarkable pieces of sculpture. Recently, the original Chola frescos were discovered under frescos of the later Nayak period. You need permission from the office of the Archaeological Survey of India (ASI) in Fort St George, Chennai, to see these frescos. Brihadeshvara Temple is now a World Heritage Site.

Other places worth a visit are the **Saraswati Mahal Library**, where a collection of 30,000 palm-leaf manuscripts and rare books in Tamil, Telugu, Sanskrit, Marathi and some European languages are stored, and the **Art Gallery** where some 10th- to 12th-century Chola sculptures are displayed. Open daily from 0900-1330 and 1500-1800, except Fridays. The Art Gallery

223

also has some rare specimens of Chola bronzes and Tanjore paintings, 16th- to 18th-century masterpieces executed on large wooden panels, which once adorned temple walls. Devotional in character, Lord Krishna is a favoured subject. Gold leaf and precious stones were used for ornamentation.

The **Schwartz Church** was built in 1779 by Raja Serfoji. The **Rajaraja Museum** has an excellent collection of Chola artefacts.

Shopping

Thanjavur has always been known for its exquisite **bronze icons**, in particular the Chola Nataraja. Its repoussé and copperwork **Thanjavur plates**, with brass and silver motifs, are much sought after.

With **Tanjore paintings** setting the tone for period paintings, this new rage has virtually rendered genuine antiques unavailable. Replicas of this rare art with semi-precious stones and glass are good buys.

Excursions from Thanjavur

Kumbakonam, 40 kilometres (25 miles) from Thanjavur, has roughly 18 temples, notably the **Kumbheshwara Swamy**, **Sarangapani**, **Chakrapani** and **Rama-**

Above: An icon from Madurai.

swamy temples. The *gopuram* of the Sarangapani Temple is the tallest, rising to 45 metres (148 feet). **Darasuram**, four kilometres (three miles) west of Kumbakonam, is known for the **Airavatesvara Temple**, built by Rajaraja II (1142-63). A chariot with wheels and horses serves as the entrance hall. The 26-metre (85-feet) tower is covered with a profusion of sculptures.

Gangaikondacholapuram, 71 kilometres (44 miles) north-east of Thanjavur, is yet another great Shiva temple. The sculptures decorating the exterior of the temple are fascinating, particularly the Lingodbhava, depicting Shiva within the flaming *lingam*, and Chandresanugrahamurti, showing Shiva blessing Chandres, who chopped off his father's legs because he interfered with his worship of the Lord. The *navagriha* (nine planets) panel, hidden in darkness over the sanctum, reflects the artistry of the period. The gigantic 55-metre (180-feet) tower has been kept lower than the 58-metre (90-feet) tower of the Brihadeshvara Temple out of sheer filial deference.

Rameshwaram

Rameshwaram, an island in the Gulf of Mannar, at the very tip of the Indian peninsula, is an important pilgrim centre for Hindus. It is believed Rama, hero of the epic *Ramayana*, built a bridge across the sea from there to rescue his wife from her abductor, Ravana. The temple sanctum has two *lingams*, the **Rameshwar Lingam** made from sand which Rama, it is said, worshipped, and the **Vishwanath Lingam**, brought by Hanumana, the monkey god.

Getting there

Madurai, the nearest airport, is 173 kilometres (107 miles) away. Trains between Mandapam and Pamban on the Rameshwaram Island over the Indira Gandhi Bridge, and frequent buses from Madurai, Chennai, Kanyakumari, Tiruchirapalli and Thanjavur in Tamil Nadu, make travelling there convenient and dependable.

When to go

Avoid May and June, the hottest months.

Where to stay

Hotel Maharaja, Alankar Tourist Home, Sanathana Lodge, Hotel Tamil Nadu and Devasthanam Lodges and Cottages offer budget accommodation. See listings.

Sightseeing

The **Ramanathaswamy Temple** was built between the ninth and 16th centuries. The stupendous 54-metre (177-feet) *gopuram* (gate tower), 1,220 metres (4,000 feet) of magnificent corridors, the longest measuring 195 metres (640 feet), and 1,200 gigantic granite columns, have made this temple famous.

A festival in June-July celebrates the installation of Rama's *Shivalingam*. Named after Rama's bow, the bridge to Sri Lanka stands at **Dhanushkodi**.

Excursions from Rameshwaram

Tiruchendur, known for its profusely sculptured **Murga Temple** (non-Hindus are not allowed into the sanctum) and magnificent stretch of golden beach, is a stop not to be missed on the way to Kanyakumari from Rameshwaram.

Kanyakumari

Located at the southern-most tip of India at the confluence of three seas — Arabian Sea, Bay of Bengal and Indian Ocean — Kanyakumari is visited for the spectacle of the merging of these three waters with their different textures and tones.

Getting there

Trivandrum, the nearest airport, is 80 kilometres (50 miles) away. Some long-distance trains from Mumbai and Delhi, besides the services within Tamil Nadu, terminate there. Buses connect major south Indian cities and the Kerala Tourism Development Corporation (KTDC) conducts one-day tours to Kanyakumari.

When to go

May-June are very sultry.

Where to stay

Only budget accommodation is available, at Hotel Sangam, Hotel Tamil Nadu, Kerala House, Manickhan Tourist Home and DVK Lodge. See listings for 'Hotels'.

Sightseeing

The **beach** there is a good place to spend the day, bargain-hunting among the handicraft stalls. The **Kanyakumari Temple** on the shore is dedicated to a manifestation of Parvati, Shiva's consort, as a virgin. The diamonds adorning the goddess are awesome.

The modern **Gandhi Mandapam** houses a memorial to India's greatest freedom fighter. The height of the memorial in feet coincides with Gandhi's age — 79 — when he died. The urn with his ashes enjoys the curious phenomenon of being warmed by the sun's rays at noon on the second of October, the slain leader's birthday.

The **Vivekananda Rock Memorial**, built in memory of the great philosopher, stands on a rocky outcrop in the ocean. Its main attractions include a grand statue in the meditation hall and footprints of the virgin goddess Kanyakumari at **Shri Padaparai**. A steamer to the memorial operates between 0700-1100 and 1400-1700.

Sunrise over the Bay of Bengal and the equally thrilling sunset over the Arabian Sea, with the moon rising in the east, are unforgettable.

The market around the beach is filled with children selling coloured sand gathered from the beach and other trinkets. Be cautious when approaching the slippery rocks, and remember swimming is forbidden.

Excursions from Kanyakumari

Suchindran, 13 kilometres (eight miles) away, has a grand **Shiva Temple** with a lavishly sculptured *gopuram* (gate tower).

The pagoda-shaped **Padmanabhapuram Palace** of the former Maharaja of Travancore has great natural splendour and is only 45 kilometres (28 miles) away.

Overleaf: Kanyakumari, where three oceans meet.

A Necklace of Ocean Pearls

The Andaman and Nicobar islands are a string of thickly forested tropical islands, stretching across eastern Bay of Bengal, between India and Sumatra. The Andamans comprise 293 islands. Only 26 are inhabited and occupy a total area of 8,293 square kilometres (3,202 square miles).

Likewise, only 12 of the 19 Nicobar islands are populated. The islands are home to six of the most ancient tribes in the world which form 20 per cent of the population and broadly fall into two main groups. The first, Negroid in origin, includes the Onges, Sentinelese, Andamanese and Jarawas, who inhabit the Andaman Islands. The second, of Mongoloid descent, includes the Nicobarese and Shompens. Each group has its own distinct physiognomy, language and lifestyle, of which very little is known. Most actively resist outside contact, barring the Sentinelese and the Jarawas.

The Onges, said to be the oldest inhabitants, are concentrated on Little Andaman. They are small, dark-complexioned, wear no clothes other than tasselled genital decoration, and are fond of colourful makeup. Their main source of livelihood is hunting and gathering. The Sentinelese, who live on North Sentinel Island, fiercely resist any attempts to integrate them, hence very little is known about their habits and lifestyle. The Jarawas, the largest group, live on the Middle and South Andaman islands. Recently, contact has been established with this tribe. The Andamanese tribe, the smallest group, live on tiny Strait Island.

The Nicobarese, who inhabit Car Nicobar Island, are a fair-complexioned people who were the first to adapt to contemporary Indian society. They are the largest tribe found in these parts and lead settled lives in organized villages, controlled by a village headman. Their main source of living is from fishing, coconuts and rearing cattle and pigs. The last group,

the Shompens who inhabit Great Nicobar, have so far resisted attempts to integrate and prefer to keep to themselves.

Since independence, the Indian government has adopted a two-pronged strategy with regard to the inhabitants of the Andaman Islands. On the one hand, the government is committed to protecting their natural rights, culture and customs, along with protecting the flora, fauna and other natural resources.

On the other hand, it has made several attempts at integrating the people into the 'social mainstream' through development programmes — such as education, health care and modern communication — but with little success on both fronts. Massive transmigration from the mainland, especially expelled Tamil refugees from Sri Lanka, has pushed up the population in the last 15 years, almost swamping the culture of the natives.

The most interesting thing about the Andamans is their relative seclusion from the 'modern' world. For a long time, the islands were considered uninhabitable by succeeding batches of foreign invaders. The existence of the islands were first reported in the ninth century AD by Arab merchants sailing past them to enter the Strait of Sumatra.

Danish explorers and merchants were, perhaps, the first Westerners to set foot on them, in the 18th century. The Danes left in 1768 due to poor health conditions. In 1789, Lieutenant Reginald Blair surveyed the islands and established a penal settlement on the South Andaman Island.

After the Sepoy Rebellion of 1857, many of the rebels were sent to this penal settlement to serve life terms, and this earned the island the name *Kala Pani* meaning 'Black Water'.

In 1872, the British-Indian government built a huge jail infamously known as Cellular Jail, and during World War II the island was annexed by the Japanese army.

Opposite: A woman from Port Blair.

Above: An unspoilt beach in the Andamans.

It is said that Subhash Chandra Bose landed on the islands in 1943 and established India's sovereignty by unfurling the national tricolour.

Unfortunately, the turbulent history of the islands, in which the natives suffered the most, has caused them to remain suspicious of all outsiders.

Getting there
Indian nationals can visit any part of the Andaman and Nicobar islands. Foreigners need entry permits to land on the Andamans and cannot visit the Nicobars. Permits can be acquired from Indian missions outside India and the Foreigners' Regional Registration Offices in Delhi, Mumbai, Chennai and Calcutta.

It normally takes 48 hours to issue a permit, valid for 15 days which can usually be extended another 15 days without any problem.

Port Blair is the entry point to the Andaman Islands. Indian Airlines connects Port Blair with Calcutta, Chennai and Car-Nicobar. A three-day voyage from Calcutta or Chennai is another way of travelling.

Once on the Andamans, local transport is by taxis with fixed point-to-point fares. Motor launches and ferries ply between Port Blair and the other islands.

When to go
The Andamans are blessed by both the south-west and north-east monsoons. The south-west monsoon comes to the islands between mid-May and October, and the north-east monsoon between November and January. Throughout the year there is very little seasonal climatic variation. Proximity to the Equator and continuous sea breezes keep the temperature between 23°C and 31°C (73°F and 88°F) and humidity at around 80 per cent throughout the year. The best time to visit is between mid-November and April.

Where to stay
Since the islands are geared to tourism, government guest houses, circuit houses, and tourist homes provide accommodation and facilities.

In addition there are other resorts, hotels and cottages run privately.

Sightseeing

Port Blair, the administrative capital of the Andaman and Nicobar islands, is a small, hilly town, quite beautiful in itself. It has a post and telegraph office and a bank with foreign exchange facilities. The population is largely migrant with a Bengali and Burmese predominance.

The **Cellular Jail**, completed in 1906, once housed 400 or so political prisoners. Today, part of it is a national monument. Originally, it had six wings extending from a main central tower but only three remain today. It still gives a fair impression of the atrocious conditions under which detainees were kept. Remarkably, it is still a functioning jail.

While the tribal islands are strictly protected, the small **Anthropological Museum** has an interesting collection of old photographs, models and tools which portray the islanders' way of life. The museum is closed on Saturdays. The **Herbarium** has interesting collections of the Botanical Survey and the Zoological Survey of India.

Other places of interest include the **Marine Museum**, a **Burmese Temple** at Phoenix Bay, the **Ghol Ghar Spice Stores** and the **Cottage Industries Emporium**.

Excursions from Port Blair

At **Haddo**, two kilometres (just over one mile) out of Port Blair, there is a small zoo, with hornbills and crab-eating monkeys, where estuarine crocodiles are bred.

Corbyn's Cave, the nearest beach, is about six kilometres (four miles) away. The easiest way to get there is by taxi. Or hire a bicycle in **Aberdeen Bazaar** and cycle out for the day. A hotel there offers wind-surfing and water-skiing facilities.

Ferries and excursion trips are available to such beaches as **Wandoor**, 25 kilometres (16 miles) away which is ideal for snorkelling and diving. The Marine Department runs boats to the smaller outlying islands from Wandoor Beach. A visit to **Jolly Bay** is a day-long excursion.

There is no accommodation so it is advisable to take food. The reefs around the island are a sight to behold. The **Chiriya Tapu**, or **Bird Island**, with dense mangroves at the southern tip of the island, is noted for its butterflies. Most hotels and tour operators in Port Blair offer picnics, scuba-diving and snorkelling trips to **Redskin**, **Grub**, Jolly Bay and **Snob islands** only for the day.

Above all, an overnight excursion to **Cinque Island**, including a small trek through the forest with its exotic birdlife, is offered by tour operators in Port Blair.

Top: A local fisherman.
Above: Fish is a food staple.

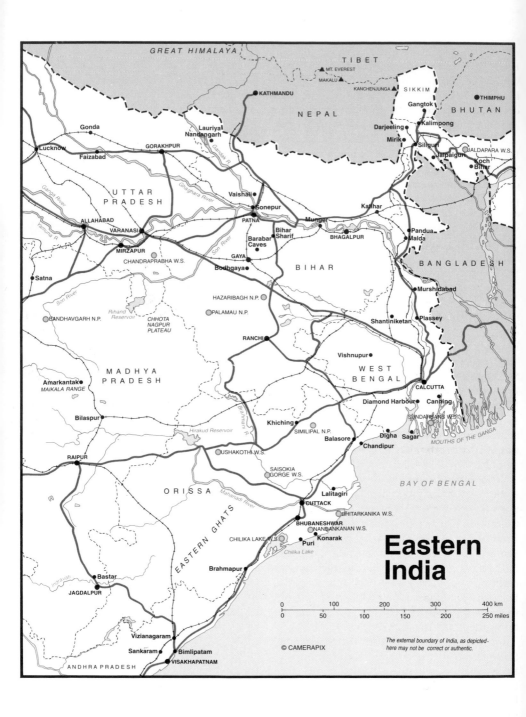

Eastern India

Bihar: Land of the Buddha

A land of pilgrimage and religion, its very name is proof of its antiquity. The name Bihar is derived from *vihara* or monastery, which befits a state where the major attractions are the Buddhist monasteries and edicts on polished pillars of the great king Ashoka.

It was in Bihar, 25 centuries ago, that Prince Siddhartha gave up his royal comforts to wander in search of wisdom and attain enlightenment. As Lord Buddha, all the places he travelled to and stayed in, many of them in Bihar, became sacred. No wonder, then, that Bihar is also known as 'The Land of Buddha'.

Where to stay
Though this eastern state was the cradle of some powerful and glorious empires, travel in Bihar today is not for the comfort conscious. Most towns have cheap, private hotels which offer only the bare essentials.

Sightseeing
Patna is the capital city, and **Bodhgaya, Nalanda** and **Rajgir** places of religious significance. Bihar is dotted with a few indifferently managed wildlife resorts — **Palamu, Bhimband, Dalma, Hazaribagh** — but few other popular tourist spots.

The **Chhota Nagpur** region, a long sweep of undulating hills, is inhabited by the *adivasi* tribes of Santhals, Hos, Mundai, Orans, Bhuny, Kols, Cheros, Khariars and Phariars, who have distinct lifestyles. **Sonepur**, at the confluence of the Ganga and the Gandak rivers, hosts the largest cattle fair in India — including elephants. Dozens of elephants, large and small, frolic in the Ganga with crowds of pilgrims taking a dip in the sacred river

Shopping
Ethnic handicrafts are best picked up in the villages around **Bodhgaya**. Articles of bamboo, leather, wooden toys, delicate white metal statues and cane and grass baskets are easily available. Jute wall hangings are very popular all over Bihar.

The extraordinary, intricate art of **Madhubani painting** originates from the old houses of the Maithali Brahmins. The women use vegetable dyes to etch needle-thin lines, which are transformed into lively scenes of everyday life and cameos from the life of Lord Krishna under their artistic fingers. This art form now finds expression on paper as well as on cloth.

Patna

Patna, the capital of Bihar, is an ancient metropolis earlier called Patliputra. It has been witness to the rise and fall of India's first important empires from the sixth century BC to the fifth century AD under the Magadh, Maurya and Gupta kings.

Today, amid the chaotic traffic and crowds, only a few vestiges of the old city can be seen.

Getting there
There are regular flights from Delhi, Calcutta, Lucknow, Ahmedabad, Ranchi and Kathmandu (Nepal). Patna is an important junction on the main line of the Eastern Railway and is also easily accessible by the State National Highway.

When to go
Bihar may be visited all the year round, but October to April is the best time, since the summers are harsh. These months also coincide with the various fairs and festivals celebrated in the state, notably, Holi, Buddha Jayanti and Mahavira Jayanti at the beginning of the year. Dusshera, Diwali, Chat Puja and the Sonepur Mela are celebrated later in the year.

Where to stay
Hotel Maurya, Patliputra Ashoka, Hotel Chanakya, Tourist Bhawan, Samrat and Hotel President are top-of-the-line hotels with comfortable accommodation. A large number of middle-class rest houses and hotels are also available.

Above: Golgarh, the beehive-shaped state granary. Opposite: Wares at a local market in Patna.

Sightseeing

A 16th-century **mosque** built by Sher Shah Suri is an exemplary specimen of Afghan architecture in India — and the nearby **Harminder Gurudwara** is one of the holiest Sikh shrines. The 10th guru (spiritual guide) of the Sikhs, Guru Gobind Singh, was born there. Patna is also called Patna Sahib in reverence to his memory. The 18th-century beehive-shaped structure is **Golgarh,** built to serve as a state granary. Steps lead up to the 29-metre (95-foot) building to give a view of the River Ganga and the city. The **museum** has interesting stone and terracotta figurines from different excavation sites in Bihar. Another attraction is the **Khuda Baksh Oriental Library,** which has a collection of rare Arabic and Persian manuscripts, and Rajput and Mughal art.

Excursions from Patna

Maner, 22 kilometres (14 miles) north of Patna, is the burial site of a Sufi saint, Mukhdoon Yahiya Maneri. It is the most important Muslim shrine in Bihar.

Vaishali, 55 kilometres (34 miles) north, is a small village with banana and mango groves and paddy fields, the place where the Jain saint, or *Tirthankara*, Mahavira, was born. It is also believed that Buddha spent the last years of his life there. A stupa stands over Buddha's relic. **Lauria Areraj**, 150 kilometres (93 miles) away, has a smooth, polished lofty column with six of Emperor Ashoka's edicts.

Lauria Nandangarh, 100 kilometres (62 miles) further on, has remains of Buddhist stupas scattered over two sites. It also has a **lion pillar** erected by Emperor Ashoka. State transport buses and taxis can be hired to reach these sites but make Patna your base because good hotels are few.

Bodhgaya

Bodhgaya, 181 kilometres (112 miles) south of Patna, is where Gautama Buddha attained enlightenment under a *pipal* tree.

Getting there

Bodhgaya is 15 kilometres (nine miles) from Gaya, an important railway junction,

234

well connected with Calcutta, Patna and Delhi. There are motorable roads and bus services from most towns in the state. Taxis, rickshaws and tongas are available. Patna is the nearest airport.

When to go
Between October and April or to witness a particular festival.

Where to stay
Hotel Bodhgaya Ashoka, Public Works Department (PWD) Inspection Bungalow and Tourist Bungalows, Maha Bodhi Rest House, Birla Dharamshala and guest-houses attached to the Japanese, Thai, Burmese and Tibetan monasteries.

Special permission from the monk-in-charge is needed to stay at the monasteries.

Sightseeing
Bodhgaya, situated on the banks of the **Falgu River**, with a row of hills as its back-drop, is perhaps the most peaceful and calmest of Bihar's towns.

The pipal tree which stands on the holy spot today is said to have grown from the original Bodhi tree. The **Mahabodhi Temple** which enshrines a gilded image of the Buddha in an earth-touching posture, and the **Bodhi Tree**, are prime pilgrim attractions.

Also, architectural remains of the Maurya, Gupta, Shunga and Pala periods lie scattered over the town. Not as ancient are the gracefully built Burmese, Tibetan, Chinese, Japanese and Thai Buddhist **monasteries** in their native styles. A kilo-metre (less than a mile) from the temple is the **International Magadh University**.

Excursions from Bodhgaya
En route to Bodhgaya you pass **Gaya,** an important pilgrimage site for Hindus who assemble along the banks of the Falgu River on auspicious days to pray for the souls of their ancestors.

It is believed that Lord Vishnu blessed Gaya, and that those whose last rites are performed there go straight to heaven.

Dungeshwar, 12 kilometres (seven miles) from Bodhgaya is a natural cave where, it is said, the Buddha meditated. **Barabar Caves**, 39 kilometres (24 miles) from Bodhgaya — the setting for the enigmatic encounter in E M Forster's *Passage to India* — are rock-cut caves from the Mauryan period. The surrounding hillside is verdant and calm.

Nalanda

Nalanda is the site of the world-famous International University of the fifth century.

Getting there
It is most convenient to reach Nalanda by road, 90 kilometres (56 miles) from Patna, and 15 kilometres (nine miles) from Rajgir. There are regular bus services from Patna and Gaya to Rajgir. Nalanda is on the way.

When to go
A particularly attractive time to visit is during the Chat Puja festival in November and December.

Where to stay
There is a Public Works Department Rest House in Nalanda but Rajgir, with better hotel facilities is close by. The Tourist Bungalow, Centaur Hokke Hotel, PWD Rest House and Inspection Bungalow are the places to look for.

Sightseeing
The ancient travellers Hsuan Tsang and Fa-Hsein gave vivid descriptions of the **International University** in their accounts. The carefully excavated remains of the stupas, lecture halls, dormitories and meditation rooms take you back to a long forgotten era of scholarly pursuit, when 10,000 students studied under 2,000 teachers. The rulers of the land were among the many patrons who financed the building of *chaityas* (prayer halls), *viharas* (monasteries) and temples, within the 35-acre (14-hectare) campus. In Nalanda,

Opposite: Monks perform the ritual circumambulation around the main temple at Bodhgaya.

Above: Sher Shah Suri's mausoleum at Sasaram.

the **Archaeological Museum** and the **Nav Nalanda Mahavir Institute** are worth a visit for more details about that period. The **Sun Temple** and lake at **Bargaon** attract Hindu devotees twice a year during the Chat Puja festival. During this time, women chant prayers and sing devotional songs before floating thousands of earthen lamps, or *diyas,* on cane winnows on the lake, lighting it up with a thousand flickering flames.

Excursions from Nalanda

Meaning 'Home of Royalty', **Rajgir** is only 15 kilometres (nine miles) from Nalanda. It is a valley surrounded by the lush green forests of five small mountains.

The Buddha spent many rainy seasons there and delivered sermons too. The site where Emperor Bimbisara converted to Buddhism is also at Rajgir. He later built the **Venuvan Vihar**, a residence for the Buddha.

The **Jivakamravan Monastery** has since been excavated. Rajgir was the venue for the First Buddhist Council where the unwritten teachings of the Buddha were first penned. It is a popular winter health resort with a number of hot water springs. **Biharsharif** is 25 kilometres (16 miles) from Rajgir. It has the **Tomb of Makhdum Shah Sharif-ud-Din** and was a centre of Islamic learning from the 13th to the 15th centuries.

Pawapuri, 38 kilometres (24 miles) from Rajgir, is a Jain pilgrimage centre. Mahavira, the last of the Jain *Tirthankaras,* attained salvation there. The last rites of the saint were performed in the middle of a lotus pond, where a beautiful **marble temple** has since been constructed.

Opposite: A Madhubani painter. Originally, these paintings decorated the walls of village huts.

Orissa: Reserves, Temples and Beaches

Orissa presents a kaleidoscope of ancient splendour and contemporary expression with its old monuments built by Buddhist, Jain, Hindu and Muslim rulers and new universities, gigantic irrigational projects and modern industry.

Besides, Orissa has provided state protection to *adivasis* (tribals) of the Bonda, Juang, Santhal, Paraja and Koya, who live in vast tracts in the hilly areas, to preserve their cultures which are fast disappearing. Bhubaneswar (the capital), Konarak and Puri make up the tourist triangle in Orissa.

Sightseeing

Chandipore, in the northern part of the state, is a quiet beach which stretches six kilometres (four miles) into the sea at low tide. **Balasore** was an important trading centre where the Dutch, French and British established their factories, beginning with the British in 1634.

The **Simlipal National Park** is the largest chunk of forest in Orissa, with a rich tribal culture. Its rich wildlife includes the royal Bengal tiger, leopard, elephant, four-horned antelope and deer. It is one of the reserves under the conservation programme, Project Tiger .

The **Bhitarkanika Sanctuary** on the mouth of the Mahanadi River has saltwater crocodiles and water-monitor lizards.

The white crocodile at **Dangamala** is the second of its kind in the world; the first is at the Thailand Crocodile Research Corridor.

The **Gahirmatha**, 130 kilometres (81 miles) from Bhubaneswar, is a breeding ground for Pacific Ridley turtles. From September onwards more than seven million turtles swim the seas from South America to reach this coast, where they lay over 60 million eggs.

The **Nandankanan Biological Park**, near the capital city, is worth a visit for its white tiger safari.

If the wildlife reserves display the natural wonders of the state, the Buddhist monuments in Orissa open a page from the land's ancient history. After his victory at the Kalinga battle near **Dhauli**, eight kilometres (five miles) from Bhubaneswar, Emperor Ashoka, overwhelmed by the massacre, turned to Buddhism.

The Dhauli rock edict evokes memories of the Kalinga war. The **rock-cut elephant** above the edict is the earliest Buddhist sculpture in Orissa. The hill is crowned by a **modern stupa** built by Japanese Buddhists.

The twin hills of **Udaigiri** and **Khandagiri**, eight kilometres (five miles) north of the capital, carved out as abodes for Jain monks in the pre-Christian era, were later improved to house the royalty.

Rani Gumpha is a double-storeyed cave complex with remarkable architecture.

Hathi Gumpha, another cave, chronicles the life of the Jain King Kharabela, who ruled in the second century BC. Take along a guide who can explain the historical aspects of these caves, and enjoy a picnic.

Lalitagiri and **Ratnagiri**, near **Cuttack**, were ancient seats of Buddhist learning. **Pushpagiri** had a flourishing university when the Chinese traveller Hsuan Tsang visited the place in the seventh century AD.

Recent excavations at **Lalitagiri** have yielded relics of Buddha and some rare images of Bodhisattva. The Padmapani image at **Jaipur,** near Cuttack, is the largest Buddhist image in Orissa. **Khitching**, in the northern part of the state, also has exquisite Buddhist images.

Cuttack, 32 kilometres (20 miles) from Bhubaneswar was the state capital before they built the new city, the present Oriyan capital. Cuttack is virtually an island surrounded by the river, except for a narrow strip of land. A stone embankment on the **Kathajuri River** was built in the 11th century by the Kesari rulers. An engineering marvel, the embarkment still protects the city from seasonal floods. The ancient **Barabati Fort** ruins are quite interesting.

Opposite: Colourful canopies cover the massive juggernauts for Puri's Rath Yatra.

Shopping

Orissa is known not only for its temples and beaches but also for its wealth of appliqué work, terracotta toys, bold papier mâché masks (originally used for epic dramas), bell-metal bowls and plates from Pipli, *dhokra* work (cast by the lost wax technique) from Mayurbhanj and Barapali, *patachitra* (paper or cloth paintings on religious themes), and gold and silver filigree work, the speciality of **Cuttack** and **Puri**.

Oriyan silk, particularly the double *ikat*, is splendid material for sarees or sophisticated dresses.

The state-owned **Utkalika Showroom, Orissa Cooperative Handicrafts Corporation** in Hall One of East Market Building, **Handloom Weavers Cooperative** in Hall Two of West Market Building and **Gauri Handicrafts** in Bhubaneswar's old town are reliable outlets for these handicrafts and textiles.

Bhubaneswar

Bhubaneswar, the capital of Orissa, is known as 'The Cathedral City of India' for the largest cluster of temples in one place in the country. Bhubaneswar as part of the Kalinga and Ganga kingdom had about 7,000 temples in its heyday. Muslim invaders destroyed most, leaving only 400 or so around the sacred tank, the legendary Bindusarovar at the centre of Ekamrakshetra, as Bhubaneswar was then known. Regarded among the holiest cities in India, it is revered as the abode of Lord Shiva.

Getting there

Bhubaneswar is linked by regular flights from Delhi, Mumbai, Hyderabad, Calcutta and Nagpur. The superfast Konarak Express from Hyderabad, the Coromandel Express from Calcutta, the Kalinga Express and the New Delhi-Puri Express from Delhi, besides many other trains, facilitate travel there. The bus service in the state is efficient, reaching even distant cities, as is the interstate bus service to Calcutta.

When to go

September to March is the best season to visit Bhubaneswar.

Where to stay

In Bhubaneswar there are no luxury hotels. First class hotels include the Oberoi Bhubaneswar, Hotel Kenilworth and Hotel Kalinga Ashok. Modest and budget accommodation is available at Panthaniwas Tourist Bungalow run by Orissa Tourism Development Corporation, Hotel Anarkali, Hotel Pushpak, Hotel Swosti, Safari International and Hotel Meghadoot. See listings for 'Hotels'.

Sightseeing

The most convenient way to visit the important temples is to take a cycle-rickshaw, hired taxi or a conducted tour organized by the OTDC. Most of the famous temples are situated at the southern end of

Above: Mukteshvara Temple. Opposite: Lingaraja Temple.

Above: Jagamohan at the Temple of the Sun.

Bhubaneswar and are all within walking distance from one another. **Parushramesvara** is Bhubaneswar's oldest temple. Built in the seventh century AD, and dedicated to Shiva, it has an elaborately carved exterior, countless celestial beauties, hunting scenes, deities and devotional scenes, and exquisite latticed windows with musicians.

Mukteshvara is a ninth-century AD temple, with carvings that show strong Buddhist influence. Scenes from the Panchatantra are carved on the exterior, beside depictions of Jain and Buddhist images. The *gajasimha* — half-elephant, half-lion — and the lotus ceiling seem inspired by the Kalinga period. It has been called a 'dream realized in sandstone'. The *torana* (ornate arch) is the *pièce de résistance*, crowned by a pair of indolent maidens on either side.

The **Vaital Deul**, a small shrine, is noteworthy for its unusual barrel-shaped roof, imitating Buddhist rock architecture.

The famous **Lingaraja Temple** has the *Svayambhu lingam* (half-Shiva, half-Vishnu) as the presiding deity in the sanctum. Built in the 10th century AD within a high-walled enclosure, the Lingaraja has the most impressive 52-metre (170-foot) curvilinear tower. The lion statues appear inspired by the Kesari dynasty. Non-Hindus are not allowed into the sanctum but can view the temple from a terrace built for Lord Curzon within the temple's precincts.

The tower is covered with delicate carvings of maidens, nymphs, dryads and erotica. The large compound also contains numerous smaller shrines. An important structural feature is the tower, hollow from inside save for a staircase hewn out of the two-metre-thick (seven-foot) walls. **Bindusarovar,** the sacred central tank, is fed by waters from India's holy rivers. A **sacred island** stands in the lake.

If the Lingaraja impresses by its stupendous structure, the **Rajarani Temple** charms everyone by its modest size. Its golden sandstone, called Rajrania, makes the sculptures appear alive and three-dimensional. The temple celebrates feminine beauty and is admired for the languid charm of its *alaskanyas* (indolent maidens) and *salabhanjikas* (maiden holding a tree branch). Standing in a well-maintained

Above: One of the wheels of the Sun Temple.

garden, the temple has no image in the sanctum. Clinging to the main body of the tower is a cluster of miniature shrines, reminiscent of Khajuraho. Forlorn amid green fields, off the beaten track, is the small 10th-century **Brahmeshwar Temple**. It has a lingam in the sanctum and the exterior is covered with some exquisite sculpture — beauties and lovers, warriors, elephants, monkeys and birds. It is the only Brahma shrine in Bhubaneswar allegedly, though it has a *Shivalingam* in the sanctum.

The **Orissa State Museum** in the **old town** is a must for those who never tire of looking at ancient art treasures. Exquisite sculpture, coins, palm-leaf manuscripts, tribal and traditional artefacts and musical instruments can be viewed every day between 1000 and 1700, except Mondays.

Konarak

Konarak is famous for its Sun Temple. The greatest showpiece of Oriyan art, a trip to see just this one temple is worthwhile.

Getting there
A conducted tour to Konarak and Puri from Bhubaneswar, or taxi, is the best way to visit Konarak. State transport buses are crowded and uncomfortable.

When to go
September to March is the best time to visit the Sun Temple in Konarak.

Where to stay
There are only three modest places to stay overnight — Panthanivas, Travellers' Lodge and the Inspection Bungalow.

Sightseeing
No Indian temple can match King Narasimha Deva's fantastic architectural achievement. It was he who built the **Konarak Sun Temple** in the 13th century. Fashioned as a chariot driven by seven pairs of caparisoned horses, this temple remains the crowning glory of Oriyan architecture. It stands beside the sea, 66 kilometres (41 miles) south-east of Bhubaneswar. Much devastated by nature and people, the main edifice remains as

245

Above: Gopalpur-on-Sea. Opposite: A local shrine.

evidence of past human ingenuity and skill. The main tower over the sanctum collapsed soon after completion, Muslim invaders removed the metal finial, the Raja of Khurda plundered carved panels and stone for work at the Puri Temple and sand dunes engulfed three-quarters of the structure.

Yet whatever has been salvaged after restoration is of unparalleled splendour. What remains today are the ruins of the dance hall, *jagamohan* (assembly hall) and fragments of the *deul* (sanctum).

The pair of massive *gajasimhas* (half-elephant, half-lion) flanking the huge flight of steps to the floor of the **dance hall** are impressive. The pillars are exquisitely chiselled with dancers and musicians.

The celestial chariot of the sun is drawn by 14 galloping horses. The 24 elaborately sculptured chariot wheels have a diameter of 2.5 metres (eight feet) and portray the passage of time. Each wheel has eight thick and eight thin spokes, symbolizing the eight parts of a day. The wheels have been ornamented with fastidious and lavish attention to detail. The pyramidal

structure of the jagamohan is magnificently sculptured — court and hunting scenes, dance, music, mythical animals, explicit erotica and floral arabesques. The temple base is decorated with nearly 1,052 small elephant figures. On the south side of the jagamohan stands the masterpiece of Oriyan sculpture, a fully caparisoned, enraged war horse trampling a fallen warrior beneath its hooves. On the other side, sculpted on two masonry platforms, colossal elephants crush unfortunate men to death.

The tower, now completely collapsed, once rose 70 metres (230 feet). However, three life-sized chlorite **images of Surya**, strategically positioned to catch the light of the sun in the morning, noon and evening, remain. The sanctum stands bereft of the main image. In the background, crowned by an *amalak* (circular ridged cushion resembling the Indian gooseberry) and triple rows of sculpted musicians, dancers and *nayikas* (heroines) beside frowning beasts, the pyramidal jagamohan is filled with stone and sand to prevent the collapse of the roof. The annual dance festival in

February adds another dimension to the temple's ethos. Indian classical dancers perform within the temple precincts. The **Archaeological Museum** at Konarak, with sculptures from the ruins, is open from 1000 to 1700, except Fridays.

Puri

One of India's four holiest cities, Puri is known for its Jagannatha Temple dedicated to Vishnu, and some lovely stretches of beach along the Bay of Bengal.

Getting there
Thirty-five kilometres (22 miles) from Konarak and 60 kilometres (37 miles) from Bhubaneswar, Puri completes the golden tourist triangle of Orissa formed of these three places. Domestic flights leave for Puri from Delhi, Calcutta, Mumbai, Hyderabad and Nagpur. The Howrah-Coromandel Express, Hyderabad-Karnataka Express, Delhi-Kalinga Express and New Delhi-Puri Express are superfast trains to Puri. Interstate bus services link Calcutta and Puri.

When to go
Between September-March is the time to go. The *rath yatra* (chariot procession) in June-July, attracts more than a million pilgrims and tourists.

Where to stay
Mid-range hotels include Nilachal Ashok and Toshali Sands. The Orissa Tourism Development Corporation-run Panthanivas Tourist Bungalow, Hotel Holiday Resort, Vijoya International, South Eastern Railway Hotel, Sea Side Inn, Puri Hotel and Subhadra Hotel offer budget accommodation.

Sightseeing
Built by King Chodaganga Deva in the 12th century, the **Jagannatha Temple,** with its majestic tower topped with a wheel and flag, can be seen for miles around. All four structural components — **Bhoga Mandap** (Hall of Offerings), **Nat Mandap** (Dance Hall), **Jagamohan** (Assembly Hall) and **Bada Deul** (Sanctum) — are intact and well maintained. Non-Hindus are not allowed inside, but can view the temple from the terrace of the **Raghunandan Library**. The 11-metre (36-feet), 16-sided monolithic **Aruna Stambha** (pillar), removed from the Konarak Sun Temple, can be seen from the entrance. The sculptural wealth of the temple comes a poor second to the Lingaraja in Bhubaneswar. A colourful market borders the road.

During the **Rath Yatra Festival**, the images of Jagannatha, Balbhadra and Subhadra are placed in mammoth juggernauts, the largest of which is 14 metres (46 feet) high and has 16 wheels, each more than two metres (seven feet) in circumference. This journey commemorates that of Lord Krishna from Gokul to Mathura. At the end of the procession the images are housed in the **Gundicha Mandir** for a week and are then returned by another *rath yatra.*

Millions of pilgrims and tourists form part of the surging sea of humanity. The law has stopped devotees throwing themselves under the giant wheels to be crushed to death in the hope of salvation. At the end of the return journey, the cars are broken up and used to make religious relics.

The beach at Puri is one of the loveliest and those who cannot swim can avail themselves of the services of the tall, dark-skinned lifeguards or *nuliyas* from Andhra Pradesh, who wear conical wicker hats.

Excursions from Puri
Pipli village, 20 kilometres (12 miles) from Bhubaneshwar on the road to Puri, is famous for its wall hangings, umbrellas and lampshades in vibrant appliqué work. **Raghurajpur**, an artists' village 12 kilometres (seven miles) away, is a treasure trove of local crafts such as wood carving and appliqué. In the heart of coastal Orissa is fauna-rich **Chilika Lake**, 30 kilometres (19 miles) south of Puri. Between October and February, the cluster of islands in the lake is home to wintering migratory birds from Siberia. Accommodation is available at the small Panthanivas Guest House at **Barkul**, on the lake itself.

Opposite: Chilika Lake.

West Bengal: Tigers, Poets and Politics

West Bengal, with Calcutta as its capital, stretches from the Himalayan foothills to the Bay of Bengal. On the east, it shares a long, blurred boundary with Bangladesh in the Ganga-Brahmaputra river system, the largest delta in the world, as well as the world's largest estuarine forest, the Sundarbans, domain of the royal Bengal tiger.

Bengal is intricately linked with the history of the British Raj. The British defeated Nawab Siraj-ud-Daulah there at the decisive Battle of Plassey in 1757, the key to their conquest of India. The first rudiments of Western education, technology and thought, the first shot of the Great Mutiny of 1857 in Barrackpur, and the Indian National Conference of 1885, in which lay the seeds of the Freedom Movement, were among many historic moments that Bengal witnessed. At Independence, Bengal was one of two provinces carved up to create Pakistan.

In medieval times, the kingdom of Gaur, near present-day Malda, was renowned as a seat of learning and art. Vishnupur, an ancient capital, was another centre of culture. After the Muslim conquest in the 13th century, the centre of power gradually shifted to Murshidabad, 219 kilometres (136 miles) north of Calcutta. It was the nawabs of Murshidabad who capitulated to the British. Bengalis are known for their love of poetry, politics and *adda* (informal group discussion). Bengal's immense contribution to modern Indian culture is best symbolized by poet — and Nobel Laureate — Rabindranath Tagore and film-maker Satyajit Ray.

Getting there

Calcutta and **Siliguri** (Bagdogra Airport) are the entry points to the state.

Sightseeing

The beach resort of **Digha** is 187 kilometres (116 miles) south-east of Calcutta by road. It is well served by a number of private hotels. **Sagar**, at the mouth of the Bay, is the site of the religious fair, **Gangasagar Mela**, in January. It is a long haul to Sagar — by bus from Calcutta to Namkhana, 105 kilometres (65 miles), then a launch to Chemaguri and another 10-kilometre (six-mile) bus ride. Accommodation is in a 50-bed Youth Hostel.

Vishnupur, 152 kilometres (94 miles) west of Calcutta and connected by rail and road, is unique for its terracotta temples, toys, jewellery and curios, the best known of which is the Bankura horse, and the exquisite Baluchari saree.

Excursions can be made to the scenically enchanting **Mukutmanipur**, 80 kilometres (50 miles) away, and the **Ayodhya Hills**, 200 kilometres (125 miles), for natural sights and a taste of tribal culture.

Shantiniketan, Tagore's famous open-air university and the seat of contemporary Bengali art and culture, 210 kilometres (130 miles) north-west of Calcutta, is linked by road and rail.

Murshidabad, accessible by both road and rail, soaks in the grandeur of the *nawabs*. Highlights, apart from its silk and bell-metal work, are **Hazarduari** (Mansion of a Thousand Doors). **Plassey**, site of the battle that changed the history of the sub-continent, is 40 kilometres (25 miles) away.

Malda, 340 kilometres (211 miles) north of Calcutta and on the road and rail route to Siliguri, is the site of the archaeological ruins of the kingdom of Gaur. It is also famous for its mangoes and sericulture. **Pandua** 18 kilometres (11 miles) away, has a concentration of Muslim monuments, including the gigantic Adina Masjid.

Besides the tiger, the **Sundarbans marshes** are home to a variety of boar, big cats, crocodiles, deer and turtles. Strategically located watch-towers are perfect for viewing wildlife.

To get there, first take the road to **Canning** or **Sonakhali** from where a launch will take you into the interior.

Opposite: Calcutta's high-rise buildings.

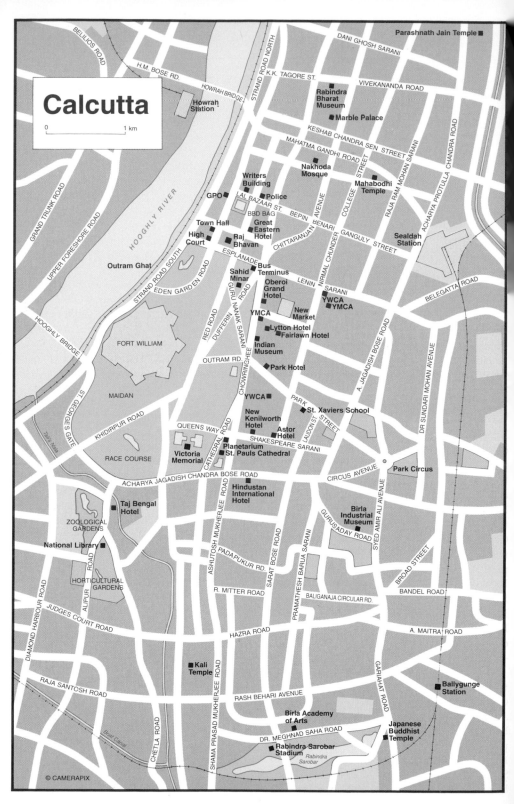

Calcutta

0   1 km

Parashnath Jain Temple ■

BELILIOS ROAD
H.M. BOSE RD.
HOWRAH BRIDGE
STRAND ROAD NORTH
K.K. TAGORE ST.
DANI GHOSH SARANI
VIVEKANANDA ROAD
ACHARYA PROTULLA CHANDRA ROAD

Howrah Station

Rabindra Bharat Museum ■
Marble Palace ■

KESHAB CHANDRA SEN STREET
MAHATMA GANDHI ROAD
Nakhoda Mosque ■
COLLEGE STREET
Mahabodhi Temple ■
RAJA RAM MOHAN SARANI

HOOGHLY RIVER
GRAND TRUNK ROAD
UPPER FORESHORE ROAD

Writers Building ■
GPO ■
LAL BAZAAR ST.
BBD BAG
Police ■
BEPIN BENARI GANGULY STREET
CHITTARANJAN AVENUE
NIRMAL CHUNDER STREET

Sealdah Station ■

Town Hall ■
High Court ■
Raj Bhavan ■
Great Eastern Hotel ■
ESPLANADE

BELEGATTA ROAD

Outram Ghat
STRAND ROAD SOUTH
EDEN GARDEN ROAD
RED ROAD
DUFFERIN ROAD
GURU NANAK SARANI

Bus Terminus ■
Sahid Minar ■
Oberoi Grand Hotel ■
YMCA ■
LENIN SARANI
YMCA ■
YMCA ■

New Market ■
YMCA ■
Lytton Hotel ■
Fairlawn Hotel ■
Indian Museum ■
Park Hotel ◆

FORT WILLIAM

MAIDAN

OUTRAM RD.
CHOWRINGHEE ROAD

YWCA ■
PARK STREET
St. Xaviers School ■
LAUDON ST.
A. JAGADISH BOSE ROAD
DR SUNDARI MOHAN AVENUE

ST. GEORGES GATE
KHIDIRPUR ROAD
Tally's Nala

RACE COURSE

QUEENS WAY
CATHEDRAL ROAD
New Kenilworth Hotel ■
Astor Hotel ■
SHAKESPEARE SARANI

Planetarium ■
St. Pauls Cathedral ■
Victoria Memorial ■

ACHARYA JAGADISH CHANDRA BOSE ROAD
CIRCUS AVENUE
Park Circus ◉

Taj Bengal Hotel ■

Hindustan International Hotel ■

Birla Industrial Museum ■
GURUSADAY ROAD
SYED AMIR ALI AVENUE

ZOOLOGICAL GARDENS
National Library ■
ALIPUR ROAD
HORTICULTURAL GARDENS

ASHUTOSH MUKHERJEE ROAD
PADA PUKUR RD.
SARAT BOSE ROAD
PRAMATHESH BARUA SARANI
BALIGANJA CIRCULAR RD.
BROAD STREET
BANDEL ROAD

DIAMOND HARBOUR ROAD
JUDGES COURT ROAD
R. MITTER ROAD

HAZRA ROAD
GARIAHAT ROAD
A. MAITRA ROAD

RAJA SANTOSH ROAD
CHETLA ROAD
SHAMA PRASAD MUKHERJEE ROAD

Kali Temple ■

RASH BEHARI AVENUE

Ballygunge Station ■

Boat Canal

Birla Academy of Arts ■

DR. MEGHNAD SAHA ROAD
Rabindra Sarobar Stadium ■
Rabindra Sarobar

Japanese Buddhist Temple ■

© CAMERAPIX

Above: The Maidan, one of Calcutta's many green areas.

Calcutta

Calcutta stands on the right bank of the River Hooghly, 193 kilometres (120 miles) before it meets the Bay of Bengal. Once the capital of British India and now of West Bengal, Calcutta has been the gateway to the eastern states since 1690, when Job Charnock, an English merchant, got the trading rights of the villages of Gobindapur, Sutanati and Kalikata for the East India Company. The city that has given us Robert Clive and Rabindranath Tagore, Netaji and Swami Vivekananda, Satyajit Ray and Mother Teresa, has an ambience of grandeur, grime, culture — and charm — without parallel.

Getting there

Calcutta is well connected by rail, road and air with all the major points in India, and by air with most international cities. Its airport is at **Dum Dum**; its two stations are at **Howrah** and **Sealdah**. Besides Calcutta State Transport Corporation and private buses, metered taxis, suburban trains, ferry services and the circular rail, travel within the city is also possible by autorickshaws, hand-pulled rickshaws or even horse-drawn carriages. The two features unique to this city are the old tramways and the modern underground Metro railway, between Esplanade and Tollygunge. The latter is well maintained, and the murals at the Rabindra Sadan and Kalighat stations are truly enchanting.

When to go

October to March is the best time to visit.

Numerous package tours are available from the city to places such as Digha; Shanti-niketan-Bakreswar-Tarapith-Kenduli; Antpur-Vishnupur-Mukutmanipur-Kankrajhore-Jhargra Murshidabad-Malda-Gour; Jairambati-Tarakeshwar-Dakshineshwar-Belur; Bandel Church-Hooghly Imambara; and the Sunderbans.

Where to stay

The Oberoi Grand on Chowringhee and the Taj Bengal in Alipore are the two de luxe five-star hotels. Other hotels with five-star facilities are the Airport Ashok Hotel

Above: The gardens around Victoria Memorial are a popular picnic spot.

in Dum Dum, the centrally located Park Hotel on Park Street and Hotel Hindustan International. The other star-rated hotels include the traditional Great Eastern Hotel, the more recent Astor Hotel, Kenilworth Hotel, Hotel Rutt Deen, Lytton Hotel, Fairlawn Hotel and Lindsay Guest House. The YWCA, YMCA, Rail Yatri Niwas and other government-approved facilities offer low-budget accommodation. See listings for 'Hotels'.

Sightseeing

On a busy day, more than 10,000 platform tickets are sold at **Howrah Station**, the commodious Eastern Railway terminus, built in 1906, which serves as the city's main gateway. The huge cantilevered **Howrah Bridge**, or Rabindra Setu, opened in 1943, is an engineering miracle that accommodates eight lines of vehicular traffic, including two tramway tracks and two wide, pedestrian footpaths.

Beside the main Howrah Bridge, there is the second **Hooghly Bridge,** or Ishwarchandra Vidyasagar Setu, completed in 1991. The **Botanical Gardens** created in

1787 at Shibpore, the outskirts of Calcutta, have a 1.7 kilometre (more than a mile) frontage on the west bank of the river. Of the many varieties of plants and trees, the ancient banyan is the most famous. The herbarium has 40,000 species. There are picnic spots and boating facilities.

Residence of viceroys till 1912, and later of the governors of Bengal, the **Raj Bhavan** or Government House (1799) was opened by the Marquess of Wellesley with a grand ball in 1803 to celebrate the signing of the Treaty of Amiens. It is a silvery dome with four-corner blocks. The national coat of arms hangs over each of the four columns which lead up from the portico. Its six-acre (two-hectare) **park** is ringed by six gates, four of which are surmounted by a stone lion holding a globe in its forepaw. The **Throne Room,** so called because it contains curios like the throne of Tipu Sultan and the **Grand Marble Hall,** is on the first floor. The **Ball Room** is on the floor above.

The **Writers Buildings**, the **Town Hall**, the **West Bengal Legislative Assembly** and other majestic buildings and commercial establishments are all around the city's

Above: The cantilevered Howrah Bridge.

hub at **BBD Bag**, once Dalhousie Square. The old **Statesman House**, the Newspaper Office and **Victoria House** (1897), now the Calcutta Electric Supply Office, with an illuminated globe on its dome, are along the way towards Chittaranjan Avenue from Esplanade.

The Gothic style **Calcutta High Court** (1872), towards Eden Gardens, has a tower 55 metres (181 feet) high and sculptured colonnades. It is famous for Zoffany's portrait of Sir Elijah Impey.

The sprawling **Eden Gardens,** with a Burmese pagoda, were named after the Misses Eden, sisters of Lord Auckland, who helped design them in 1840. Today, they enclose the **Akashvani Bhavan** (All India Radio), **Ranji Cricket Stadium** and **Netaji Indoor Stadium**.

The **Calcutta Maidan**, the lungs of the city, stretches from the **Strand** (west) to **Chowringhee** (east), and from **Esplanade** (north) to the **Race Course** (south). Many sports clubs, vendors and joggers are part of the scene. Besides, it is the venue for many *melas* (fairs), notably the **Annual Book Fair**. Erected in memory of martyrs,

the **Shahid Minar**, 48 metres (158 feet) high, is also called the Octherlony Monument after the Nepalese war hero Major-General David Octherlony. A fluted column of brickwork with 198 steps, its base is Egyptian, the column Syrian and the dome, with its metal cupola, Turkish. It faces the **Esplanade Bus and Tram Depot**.

Fort William (1773) stands opposite the Gwalior Monument. It has an impressive arsenal and six gates. **Victoria Memorial**, resembling the Taj Mahal with its white marble grandeur, has an **art gallery** and a **museum** with interesting portraits, documents and statues of the Victorian era. Artefacts like Hastings' snuff box and Haider Ali's sword are also on display.

Built in 1922 under the patronage of Lord Curzon, its foundation stone was laid by King George V. Some of the figures around the entrance, and the 56-metre (184-feet) dome with the revolving Sphere of Victory, were crafted in Italy.

Chowringhee is just a stroll away, and there are many cemeteries of distinguished persons on **Park Street**, beside the **Scottish** and **Armenian cemeteries** and the old

Above: Fishing near Calcutta. Opposite: A boatman repairs his fishing net.

residence of the **Roman Catholic Archbishop**. The pretty Rose Aylmer, to whom poet W S Landor dedicated his elegy, lies buried there.

St Xavier's and **Loretto House** in the vicinity are two old and renowned schools. Park Street also boasts the **Royal Asiatic Society of Bengal**, built in 1784 by Warren Hastings and Sir William Jones for Oriental research, which contains many rare manuscripts. Along Chowringhee, the **Indian Museum** (1875) exhibits a breathtaking collection including relics from Mohenjodaro and Harappa, an Egyptian mummy and the largest dinosaur shoulder blade ever unearthed. The nearby **Government College of Art and Crafts**, opened in 1864 by Havell and Abanindranath Tagore, is alma mater to many famous painters.

The Anglican **St Paul's Cathedral** of Calcutta and the **Metropolitan Church of India,** built by Bishop Wilson in 1847, are other landmarks on Chowringhee.

The **Academy of Fine Arts,** beside it, has permanent galleries of Rag Ragini miniature paintings, old textiles and engravings, and the works of Tagore, Jamini Roy and British painters in India. Regular art exhibitions are also held here. The **Birla Planetarium**, near Shakespeare Sarani, has daily shows on astronomy. The **Nehru Children's Museum** is also on Chowringhee. Further down, the fine auditoriums **Rabindra Sadan, Nandan** and **Shishir Mancha**, all within the same complex, hold cultural programmes throughout the year.

The triangular **Calcutta Racecourse** (behind the Maidan and Victoria Memorial), managed by the Royal Calcutta Turf Club, attracts great crowds in the racing season.

The **Calcutta Zoological Gardens** at Alipore is close by. Built in 1876, with its rustic benches and shady arbours, it is India's largest, and is home to many exotic animals and birds. The **National Library**, across the street, was formerly Belvedere House, the residence of the governors-general.

And 100 metres down the road, the **Agri-horticultural Gardens**, founded in 1820 by William Carey, comprise a 30-acre (12 hectares) paradise of lakes, trees, nurseries, ferneries and hothouses, and the

celebrated annual flower show is a big draw for nature lovers. Across the Hooghly River at **Khidderpore**, are the **docks** with their jetties, warehouses and transit sheds.

Built in 1809 on a 350-year-old structure, the **Kali Temple** at **Kalighat** in south Calcutta is a single, curvilinear building of masonry and green mosaic covered by a double canopy-shaped roof. Insignificant architecturally, it is said to contain the severed relics of the living deity. Its perpetual crowds, dark ceilings, dim windows and fretted pillars set the ambience for the encounter with the terrifying image of the Goddess Kali, consort of Shiva, a black goddess with tongue hanging out and wearing a necklace of bloody scalps.

Further south are the lakes at **Rabindra Sarovar** which offer swimming and boating facilities. Regularly the Rowing Club holds regattas there. Near Rabindra Sarovar stand the **Japanese Buddha Temple** and an open-air auditorium, **Nazrul Manch**.

Across the road on Southern Avenue, the **Birla Academy of Art and Culture** holds regular exhibitions and classes. The **Ramakrishna Mission Institute of Culture**, farther down in Gol Park, organizes lectures and meditation sessions, and has a well-stocked library and art gallery.

A visit to the **Birla Industrial and Technological Museum** on Gurusaday Road in the Ballygunge area is recommended. Deep into the south is 'Tollywood' or **Indrapuri Studios**, Bengal's Hollywood. Close by, and also in Tollygunge, **Mysore House**, the palace built by Tipu Sultan's son, is now the **Sangeet Research Academy**.

North Calcutta has many places of interest. Founded by Raja Rajendra Mullick Bahadur, the **Marble Palace** on Muktaram Babu Street off Chittaranjan Avenue, with its fountains, palm trees, Greek statuettes and even two Rubens' masterpieces, used to have orang-utans and peacocks and a roof of gold. The **Nakhoda Mosque**, a gift by the Cutchi Memon sect, is an imposing structure where as many as 10,000 Muslims pray at one time. Built in 1926, the Saracenic structure has been modelled on Akbar's tomb in Sikandara. Its two lofty minarets and 25 smaller ones topped by cupolas prettify an otherwise congested area in **Rabindra Sarani**. The strongholds of ancient academia — **Calcutta Medical College**, the **Hindu School, Presidency College, Sanskrit College** and **David Hare School** — are all located in and around College Street. The **Ashutosh Museum** in the Centenary Hall of Calcutta University has a collection of the art of Bengal dating back to the third century BC.

The famous **Star Theatre** is on Bidhan Sarani. The **Pareshnath Jain Temple** on Belgachia Road, near the Shyambazaar five-point crossing, was built in 1867 by Rai Badri Doss Bahadur. Its four temples are dedicated to Shree Shree Sheetalnathji, the 10th of the 24 Jain *tirthankaras*. Its shimmering kaleidoscopic lights, playing on crystal chandeliers and mirrors, are a fascinating sight.

Rabindra Bharati, the birthplace of Rabindranath Tagore, is now a museum and a university. In the north-east lies the **Salt Lake Stadium**, the largest in Asia, pandering to soccer, Bengal's sporting passion. Calcutta is a city that offers retrospectives, balls, *jatras* (dance-dramas), festivals, *melas* (fairs) and parades throughout the year. Areas like **Diamond Harbour** and **Outram Ghat** are ideal for picnics.

Shopping

Lindsay Street's **New Market**, or Sir Stuart's **Hogg Market** built in 1874, and its New Market extension is the one-stop shopper's paradise, where everything, from pins to pork, is on offer. Off Park Street are dainty shops like **Women's Friendly Society** and **Good Companions** which sell embroidered linen and other gift items.

For local handicrafts and textiles, **Bengal Home Industries, Refugee Handicrafts, Khadi Gramodyog Bhavan, Cottage Industries** and state government emporia — like **Manjusha** for West Bengal — are also represented at **Dakshinapan** in Dhakuria.

West Bengal is known for Murshidabad silks, Kalighat *pats*, Bankura horses, Krishnagar dolls, Malda brass-ware, Kumartuli clay images, Antpur temple terracotta, Darjeeling silver and Shantiniketan leather.

Darjeeling

Darjeeling is the jewel in West Bengal's crown. Facing the mighty Himalayas and surrounded by coniferous-covered hills, Darjeeling is perched at a height of 2,134 metres (7,000 feet) in the shadow of the world's third-highest peak, Kanchenjunga.

A maze of steps and terraces, studded with exotic little bazaars, villas, forests and gardens, the town stands in the middle of the evergreen gardens that produce the world-famous Darjeeling tea.

Getting there

Darjeeling is 90 kilometres (56 miles) from Bagdogra airport and 80 kilometres (50 miles) from the railhead of Siliguri.

When to go

Mid-April to mid-June is the greenest, most beautiful time to visit Darjeeling. Autumn — September to November — provides the best mountain view.

Where to stay

Among the many hotels, the more prominent are the Windamere Hotel, Bellevue Hotel, Pineridge Hotel and New Elgin Hotel. See listings for 'Hotels'.

Sightseeing

The mini-train from **New Jalpaiguri** offers an exciting journey through deep jungles, rice fields, tea gardens and pine forests. **Observatory Hill** offers an unforgettable view of the Kanchenjunga, while **Tiger Hill** affords the awe-inspiring spectacle of the sun's play on the world's highest mountain, Everest.

Excursions from Darjeeling

Excursions from Darjeeling can be made to the quiet hill retreats of **Kalimpong**, 51 kilometres (32 miles) away, famous for its cheese, and **Kurseong**, which is 36 kilometres (22 miles) away. A new resort, **Mirik,** boasts a lake nestled in the hills. These places are accessible by road from Darjeeling and Siliguri, with Kurseong falling on the route of the toy train as well. Each has a number of quality lodges. For those in search of adventure, **Sandakphu**, 59 kilometres (37 miles) from Darjeeling, is a two-day trek through fields of alpine flowers, interrupted by stately magnolia and rhododendron. On a clear day, the view from Sandakphu is spectacular, with four of the world's highest peaks — Everest, Kanchenjunga, Makalu and Lhotse — clearly visible.

Further afield is **Phalut**, situated at a height of 3,600 metres (11,812 feet) at the junction of West Bengal, Sikkim and Nepal. The road from Sandakphu remains fairly level for about 21 kilometres (13 miles) with the snow peaks to the right. However, the last stretch is a series of hairpin bends up to Phalut, where the view is similar to that at Sandakphu. The best months for these treks are April-May and October-November.

Wildlife buffs can drive to **Jaldapara**, 121 kilometres (75 miles) east of Siliguri, home of the one-horned great Indian rhino. The sanctuary stretches 65 kilometres (40 miles) from the River Malangi in the east to the River Torsa in the west. It has a number of perennial streams and acres of grassland. Stay at the Hollong Forest Lodge within the sanctuary.

Above: The tranquil waters of a pool.

Above: A view of Gangtok. Opposite: An orchid in bloom.

Sikkim: A Green and Gentle State

Tucked away in the lap of the Kanchen-junga and surrounded by Nepal, Tibet, Bhutan and India, the tiny kingdom of Sikkim, 'the New House', had its own independence until 1975. Under a treaty, the Government of India was allowed to control its foreign affairs and defence. India annexed the state in 1975 as the 22nd state of the Indian Republic.

Sikkim covers 7,214 square kilometres (2,785 square miles). Nepalese form 75 per cent of Sikkim's total population, the Lepches 18 per cent and the Bhutias and others make up the remaining seven per cent. The main language is Nepali. About 60 per cent of the population is Hindu and 28 per cent are Buddhist. The two religions exist, as in many parts of Nepal, in a synergetic form.

Getting there
There are flights to Bagdogra from Calcutta. From there you make the 124-kilometre journey (77-mile) to the capital, Gangtok, either by helicopter, a trip that lasts about half-an-hour, taxi (about three-and-a-half to four hours) or bus (five hours).

The two closest railway stations to Gangtok are Siliguri, 114 kilometres (71 miles) away, and New Jalpaiguri, 125 kilometres (78 miles) away, in West Bengal. Main roads connect Gangtok with Siliguri, Calcutta, 725 kilometres (450 miles), Darjeeling, 139 kilometres (86 miles), and Guwahati, 589 kilometres (365 miles).

When to go
The best season to visit this green and gentle mountain state is between February and May and from October to December.

Where to stay
Modest to expensive accommodation is available in Gangtok at Hotel Tibet, Central Hotel, the Public Works Department

Above: Inside Rumtek Monastery. Opposite: Floating islands on Manipur's Logtak Lake.

(PWD) Bungalow, Norkuhill Hotel, Hotel Tashi, Hotel Swagat and Hotel Himachal. See listings for 'Hotels'.

Sightseeing

The ancient Buddhist monasteries and the view of the eastern Himalayas are the most important attractions of Sikkim.

The Royal Chapel, **Tsuk-La-Khang**, is the main place of Buddhist worship. It is the repository of a large collection of scriptures. The interior is covered with murals, decorated altars holding Buddha's images, Bodhisattvas and Tantric deities, and the finest wood carvings.

A most beautiful and impressive piece of architecture, it is not always open to visitors, particularly in the off-season, from November to February. Photography is not allowed inside.

Established in 1958, and built in traditional style, the **Namgyalk Institute of Tibetology** promotes research on the language and traditions of Tibet and Mahayana Buddhism.

It has an astonishing collection of finely executed silk-embroidered *thangkas*, rare manuscripts on Mahayana Buddhism, and one of the world's largest collections of books.

The institute is open from 1000 to 1600 daily, except Sundays. Entry is free.

Surrounding the institute, the **Orchid Sanctuary** boasts 600-odd species of orchid found in Sikkim. The sanctuary is at its best in April-May, July-August and October-November.

The **Institute of Cottage Industries**, on the main road above the town, produces wonderful handwoven carpets, blankets, shawls, masks, bright *choktse* tables, carved furniture and thangkas hangings. It is open from 0900 to 1430 and from 1300 to 1530, except Sundays and the second Saturday in the month.

On the edge of the ridge, next to the Secretariat Building, the **Deer Park** is home to hundreds of deer. A replica of the Buddha image at Sarnath in Uttar Pradesh also finds a place there.

The 200-year-old **Enchey Monastery**, next to the **Tourist Lodge**, about three kilometres (two miles) from the centre of the town, is well worth a visit.

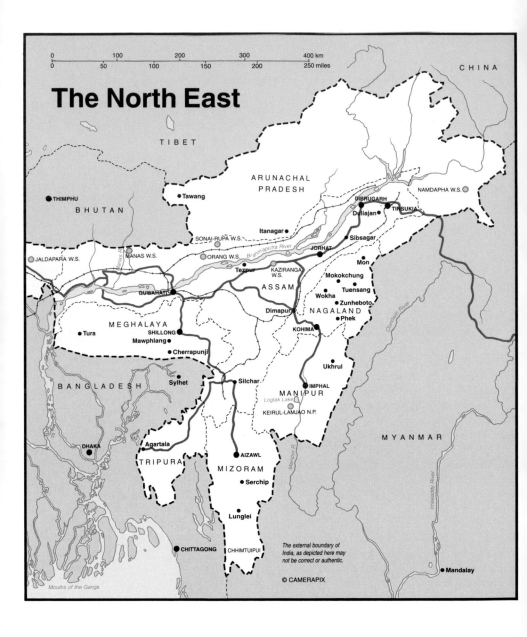

The North East

CHINA

TIBET

ARUNACHAL PRADESH

● Tawang

● THIMPHU

NAMDAPHA W.S.

BHUTAN

DIBRUGARH ●
Duliajan ● ● TINSUKIA

SONAI-RUPA W.S.
Itanagar ●
Sibsagar ●

JALDAPARA W.S.
MANAS W.S.
Manas R.
Brahmaputra River
ORANG W.S.
JORHAT ●
Mon ●

Tezpur ●
KAZIRANGA W.S.
Mokokchung ●
Tuensang ●

GUWAHATI ●
ASSAM
Wokha ●
Zunheboto ●
Chindwin River

Dimapur ●
NAGALAND
● Phek

MEGHALAYA
SHILLONG ●
KOHIMA ●

● Tura
Mawphlang ●
● Cherrapunji

Ukhrul ●

BANGLADESH
Sylhet ●
Silchar ●
MANIPUR
● IMPHAL

Logtak Lake
KEIRUL-LAMJAO N.P.

MYANMAR

DHAKA ●
Agartala ●

TRIPURA
● AIZAWL
MIZORAM
● Serchip

Manipur R.
Irrawaddy River

● Lunglei

● CHITTAGONG
CHHIMTUIPUI

The external boundary of
India, as depicted here may
not be correct or authentic.

© CAMERAPIX

● Mandalay

Mouths of the Ganga

0   100   200   300   400 km
0   50   100   150   200   250 miles

The North-Eastern Region: Seven Tiny States

The north-east region of India is a border area. The 'region' arose from the creation of seven tiny states three decades after independence. Originally the area was made up of Assam and the states of Manipur and Tripura. In medieval times the area was ruled by various indigenous dynasties, such as Chatuja, Koch, Kachari or Bodo. Later the Ahoms from Burma ruled this far-flung region for about 600 years. The British annexed the area in 1826 and were more emphatic about calling it 'Assam'. Historians think that the word is a Sanskrit derivative for 'Ahom'. Today, Assam alone no longer comprises the north-east region. The other states are Meghalaya, Tripura, Arunachal Pradesh, Manipur, Nagaland and Mizoram. Geographically, no other region is as vulnerable to outside powers for it shares borders with four countries — Bhutan, China, Myanmar and Bangladesh.

The region covers 236,401 square kilometres (91,274 square miles) and has a population of over 20 million. The people are polyglot, a large percentage of them tribes whose links with the rest of India during the British Raj were virtually non-existent. The British deliberately barred all contact between the plains people and the highlanders of Assam and the neighbouring areas.

They introduced the Inner-Line System, ostensibly an economic measure to protect the way of life of the people of the hills against interference; but really to create an impenetrable barrier between the hillmen and the rest of the region and, by extension, the rest of the country.

The seven states of this region have another common feature, local bazaars where visitors are provided with the choice of a feast of local produce — wild game and dried fish and an idea of local cuisine.

Getting there
For convenience, getting to the states within this region has been dealt with as a single entity. Indian Airlines' connections are available to Delhi, Calcutta, Patna and all the north-eastern state capitals. Vayudoot flights, though scheduled, are often cancelled for various reasons. Several broad and metre-gauge trains link the region to the rest of the country.

Roads lead to Manas and the Kaziranga wildlife sanctuaries, the towns of Dimapur (Nagaland), Kohima (Nagaland), Itanagar (Arunachal Pradesh), Imphal (Manipur), Shillong in Meghalaya (three-and-a-half hours drive from Guwahati, Assam), Agartala (Tripura) and Aizawl (Mizoram). Besides state transport buses, sometimes de luxe and video coaches are available. Modes of local transport are taxis, autorickshaws, jeeps and cycle-rickshaws. Though the Indian Government recognizes that the natural wealth can be a source of much tourist revenue, permits are necessary to visit the north-eastern region.

Tourists visiting Nagaland require an Inner-Line permit issued by the Resident Commissioner, Nagaland House, New Delhi. Foreigners have to obtain a Restricted Area permit from the Secretary, Foreigners' Division, Ministry of Home Affairs, Government of India, Lok Nayak Bhawan, Khan Market, New Delhi, at least six weeks in advance.

When to go
All the states within this region are best visited between October and May. The north-eastern region is known for its rare silks, woven textiles and wicker artefacts.

Assam

Perhaps one of the richest states in India, Assam, known for its tea and oil, sprawls across the Brahmaputra, south of Arunachal Pradesh and the kingdom of Bhutan.

The immense Brahmaputra brings both grave devastation and prosperity to the state. The river's silt, distributed by its 120 tributaries, has made Assam extremely fertile. The Assamese, a gentle people, whose interesting philosophy on life is *laahe laahe*,

Above: The mighty Brahmaputra.

or 'slowly slowly', possess a laid-back attitude, no doubt greatly influenced by this fertile land full of tea plantations and rice fields. Indeed farmers boast of rice seedlings sprouting of their own accord filling the valleys with a good harvest.

In ancient times, Assam was known as Pragijyostishpura, 'Light of the East'. Ruled by the Kamrupas, the kingdom was taken over by the Ahoms, Buddhists from Myanmar — originally Burma — who established themselves in Sibsagar.

After the 17th century, Assam was involved in political manoeuvres between the Burmese and the British. The British annexed Assam in 1874.

In 1980, the contented Assamese people suddenly woke up to an alarming influx of foreigners, particularly from Bangladesh. The agitation led by students resulted in the state being governed by possibly the youngest political leaders in the world in the mid-1980s.

Where to stay
Accommodation in Guwahati is available at Hotel Ashok Brahmaputra, Hotel Nandan, Belle Vue Hotel, Khyber International, Tourist Bungalow and the YMCA Hostel. Kaziranga Forest Lodge and the Tourist Lodge are for wildlife enthusiasts keen to visit this sanctuary. See listings.

Sightseeing
Guwahati, capital of Assam, is also the gateway to the rest of the north-east. This city is famous for the **Khamakhya Temple** on the Nilanchal Hill, an important centre for tantric and Shakti cult worship in India.

Guwahati, situated on the banks of the **Brahmaputra**, offers excellent views of the river. The **Umananda Temple** on the river, accessible only by boat, is cut off from the city for most of the year. Visitors give generously to help the Hindu priests stranded there during the long monsoon spells. Other temples are **Navagraha** (Temple of Nine Planets) and the **Sulkeswar Janardhan**.

The town's **State Museum** is a showcase of the region's cultural heritage with exhibits on textiles, sculptures and anthropology. Assam produces half of India's total tea output and 10 per cent of India's oil. The main town around the tea plantations

Above: A view of Tawang Monastery.

is **Jorhat**. The centre for oil is **Duliajan**, at the eastern end of the state. Ancient monuments and other remnants of the Ahom kingdom can be seen at **Sibsagar**, 83 kilometres (52 miles) north-east of **Jorhat**.

Assam is famous for the **Kaziranga National Park**, home to the Indian rhinoceros. **Manas Wildlife Sanctuary** is one of the more popular tiger reserves in the country.

Shopping
Three types of valued silk, namely, *muga* (rare and pale gold), *endi* and *pat*, are produced in Assam. A silk weavers' village called **Lualkuchi**, two hours' drive from Guwahati, encourages almost every family to continue the weaving tradition.

Arunachal Pradesh

Entry to this state, on the frontier between India and China, is difficult because of its location.

The largest state of the north-east, its tribal population was never influenced by missionaries. The capital is a planned town called Itanagar, built in 1982.

Where to stay
The Inspection Bungalow and Field Hostel, run by the government, Ashok Hotel and Subansari Hotel ensure comfort.

Sightseeing
The state has some 60,000 square kilometres (23,166 square miles) of luxuriant, **tropical rainforests**, untouched and untrodden. It also has a wide variety of orchid species in an **orchid sanctuary**.

The main tribes are the Miris, Padams, Khamptis, Wangchos and Apatanis. Most of these tribes have a lifestyle closely linked with nature and have been self-sufficient, little influenced by modernization.

The main river is **Brahmakund**, which joins the **Brahmaputra**. At the confluence, thousands of Hindus converge in January on Makar Sankranti day to bathe in the waters, which they believe cleanse them of their sins. At 3,050 metres (10,000 feet), **Tawang**, the country's largest Buddhist monastery, is 350 years old and the birthplace of the sixth Dalai Lama. It is the centre of the spiritual life of the Gelupa, one of the four sects that emerged during the growth of Buddhism in Tibet. Another Buddhist sect, the Dhukpas, used to attack the monastery in the past, which may explain the protective fort-like structure of the monastery, which has a huge library containing Buddhist scripts dipped in gold.

Nagaland

About fifteen major tribes inhabit this state south-east of Assam, bordering Myanmar. The word *naga,* which includes all the tribes, is generic. The tribes make their unlikeness obvious through such symbols as hairstyles, language and, most noticeably, their large and colourful tribal shawls.

Each tribe boasts its own unique pattern and colour variations. The tribes are Angami, Ao, Sema, Lotha Rengma, Chakhesang, Sangtam, Konyak, Phom, Chang, Yimchunger, Khiamungan, Zeliang, Kuki and Pochury.

Getting there
Dimapur is the only airport in Nagaland, connected to Calcutta and Delhi.

Where to stay
Japfu Ashok, the government-run Circuit House, and low-budget private lodges in the market, offer board and lodging.

Sightseeing
Kohima, the capital, has an extremely well maintained war cemetery dating to World War II. Kohima, Mokokchung, Mon, Phek, Tuensang, Woka and Zunheboto are the districts that make up the state.

The Tourism Department organizes package and conducted tours within and outside the state and make trekking and camping equipment available. Lovers of nature can enjoy the most breathtaking views of this mountainous area studded with a large variety of flowers, valleys, deep gorges and rivers. Before the missionaries came, the Nagas were fierce head-hunters,

believing that the soul of the slain person would enrich the one who had taken the head. Remnants of these customs, which were always accompanied by ritualistic ceremonies, can still be witnessed through spectacular **war dances** performed on special occasions. The Naga warrior-dancer, with huge spears decorated with tufts of dyed goat hair, can be dramatic and terrifying.

The Nagas have fiercely protected their rich and varied traditional customs. In a few places the traditional institution of chieftainship still exists. These proud dynastic rulers are still greatly revered and live in **huge palaces**, complete with **opium gardens**.

Meghalaya

Once the favourite summer retreat of the British, Meghalaya is perhaps the most beautiful hill area of India. It is also known for its unique matrilineal system, where women inherit wealth and are extremely powerful. It is perhaps one of the very few places in the world where the men talk of liberation.

Dubbed by the British as the 'Scotland of the East', this title was due to its climate, green rolling mountains and rivers.

Three major tribes inhabit the state — Garos, Khasis and Jaintias. They, too, were governed by traditional rulers, called 'Sieyams', until annexation in the 19th-century. Though now a practising doctor, one such ruler still occupies a thatched palace, built entirely without the use of any material made of iron, including nails. Every April, after a careful selection, young virgins dressed in gold and silk dance for the king.

Where to stay
Hotel Pinewood Ashok and Shillong Tourist Hotel are open to visitors in Shillong.

Sightseeing
All over **Shillong**, the capital, the British built beautiful summer bungalows. They

Opposite: Virgin forests of the north-east. Following pages: The war cemetery at Kohima.

Above: Logtak Lake, one of the region's largest freshwater lakes.

also prepared a polo ground and golf course. About 40 kilometres (25 miles) east of this capital is **Mawphlang**, the site of giant stone **monoliths**, believed to be remnants of an ancient practice of ancestor worship. Traditionally, the population practised unique forest conservation methods as part of its animistic worship.

Seven mountains of the Laitkor, which surround Shillong, were held in reverence because the people believed their ancestors came down from heaven to dwell in these forests. When Christianity came, this attitude changed, resulting in poor forest cover and even a shortage of water.

Cherrapunji, in the south of Shillong, once recorded the highest annual rainfall in the world at 1,150 centimetres (453 inches).

Manipur

Approximately 60 per cent of the population are the Meiteis, who occupy Imphal Valley, the beautiful capital. The rulers of Manipur, under the influences of neighbouring kingdoms, converted to Hinduism as did their Meitei subjects, who were orginally Tibeto-Burmese tribals. It is the Meiteis who dominate the culture, having established many cultural institutions.

They are known for their excellence in martial arts and sword fights, and for their famed drummer-dance called *chhung-phulong* — bare-chested drummers clad in crisp, white cotton appear to fly while beating their magnificent elongated drums.

Where to stay
Hotel Imphal Ashok, Hotel Deesh de Luxe, Hotel White Palace and Hotel Diplomat offer accommodation to suit every pocket.

Sightseeing
Manipur, once a princely state, is famous for its **Logtak Lake**, the last remnant of a once extensive wetland ecosystem in south Asia. In this **Logtak Keibut Lamjao** complex lives a well-known tribal fishing community called Thanga-Karang. The lake is also home to a rare brown-antlered deer, the sangai of Manipur.

The town is famous for its great **market**, a traditional commercial and social place

Above: Weaving cloth on a loin loom.

where the day's business is run exclusively by approximately 1,800 women.

Any government plans to make the market available to men or to modernize it meets with stiff opposition, with the women strongly united in defending their right and monopoly of the market. There they sell everything from mushrooms, dried fish, vegetables and textiles to silver and gold jewellery.

The most famous celebration, which brings the gentle valley alive with customs, songs and vibrant dances is the famous **Lai Haroaba Festival**, between spring and the monsoon. The festival makes offerings to deities who existed long before Hinduism came to Manipur. Besides the dances, such sports as wrestling and a quaint philosophical game called *kang* — supposed to teach the player that the course of life is balanced by both luck and skill and accompanied by happiness and sorrow — are part of the festivities.

Excursions from Manipur

If the Imphal Valley reflects Hinduism, the original tribal culture still abounds outside the valley in the mountains, three hours by road into **Ukhrul district**. There, many of the tribes belong to those in Nagaland and retain a strong tribal culture.

Tripura

Claiming to be the most ancient of the princely states of India, this tiny state borders Bangladesh. Tripura acceded to the British when the British gave it protection.

Where to stay

Broadway Guest House, Hotel Meenakshi and Royal Guest House offer accommodation in the capital, Agartala.

Sightseeing

Maharaja Bikram, the most remembered king, built the **Tripura Palace** in Agartala, the capital. Part of the palace is now a government office. The palace, made of marble and set amid **Mughal gardens**, was architecturally greatly influenced by Calcutta's Victoria Memorial.

King Maharaja Bikram was close to

Rabindranath Tagore and helped him establish Shantiniketan. The inhabitants of Tripura came from several tribes — the Reangs, Tamata, Tripuri, Lusei, Halam and Kukis. But an influx of Bangladeshi refugees has not only displaced the tribal population but reduced them to a minority group in their own homeland.

An interesting place of pilgrimage in the state is **Unaikoti**, crowded with sacred rock figures and stone images dating from the 12th century. The **Pushmela Festival** is held there yearly, during Dusshera elsewhere.

As in other tribal areas of north-east India, bamboo is greatly valued. The local customs, music, dance and other facets of culture are based on the slash-and-burn system. So precious is bamboo that it is worshipped as a symbol of different gods.

Mizoram

Originally from Burma, the Mizos believe that half their population is still in Burma. 'Mizo' is a generic term covering half-a-dozen tribes, of which the Lussei are the most dominant. Because Mizoram occupies extremely difficult mountainous terrain, the British left it alone until the Mizos descended on their Assam tea plantations on raiding sprees.

It was annexed in 1872 and the Inner-Line System introduced, which allowed only foreign missionaries entry. This resulted in mass conversions, and today 95 per cent of the population is Christian.

Mizoram's traditional rulers were the Sailos, who ruled dynastically and whose power was disrupted due to the modern-day politics of the 1950s. Soon afterwards, the state was rocked by 25 years of political turbulence, when a famine broke out and the people felt the central government was not paying enough attention to their plight. A peace accord was signed in 1986.

The Mizos nurture a unique philosophy, which, in the past, striving with hostile forces of nature, helped them to survive. This is termed *tlawmngaihna*, best translated as 'selflessness'.

Where to stay

The Tourist Bungalow, Hotel Chaulhna, Hotel Shangrila and the Embassy Hotel offer accommodation in Aizawl, the capital.

Sightseeing

Busy and bustling, **Aizawl** has the dubious tag of being the fastest developing town of the north-east. Other towns worth visiting are **Serchhip** and the second town of **Lunglei**.

South of Mizoram is the **Chhimtuipui** area, which has the highest eminence, called **Blue Mountain**.

The Mizos perform a vibrant, colourful, geometric bamboo dance called *cheraw*, in which lithe men and women in equal numbers display intricate and nimble footwork to great acclaim.

Above and opposite: At the local market.

PART THREE: SPECIAL FEATURES

Above: Parasailing in the Himalayas.
Opposite: Folk Music in the Punjab.

Wildlife of India: Fascinating Diversity

Like everything else in India, the diversity of wildlife is immense. There are two kings of the Indian jungle — the **tiger** and the **elephant.** Both are endangered and both can be dangerous. But they are also immensely beautiful and their survival ensures the survival of animals further down the food chain, and of forests, which ensure better quality of life as well.

The Indian tiger

The **Indian tiger,** one of six surviving tiger sub-species, is at home in habitats varying from Himalayan forests to the swamp grasslands of the Terai, the arid hills of the peninsula and the mangrove swamps of the Sunderbans in West Bengal. It has been saved for the time being, thanks to Project Tiger. When the project started in 1972, there were 268 tigers in nine reserves.

By 1993, there were 19 Project Tiger reserves covering nearly 30,000 square kilometres (11,583 square miles) of forest, containing 1,330 tigers out of a population of some 4,000. In these reserves, and others not specifically for tiger, the visitor has the best chance to see the animal in the wild.

Some of the most notable national parks are the Corbett and Dudhwa in Uttar Pradesh, Ranthambore and Sariska in Rajasthan, Kanha and Bandhavgarh in Madhya Pradesh, Bandipur in south India, Manas in Assam and the Sunderbans in West Bengal. Although the climate for plains parks is most comfortable in the winter months, game viewing is generally best in the hot weather, when the grass and the undergrowth dies back, and tigers, like other animals, are found near waterholes. Many parks are closed during the monsoon.

The Asian elephant

A project to save the **Asian elephant** has also been started by the government. The elephant is threatened by poachers and the destruction of its environment. Elephants require huge quantities of fodder — some 200 kilos (440 lbs) a day — and cannot exist in degraded forests. Due to human expansion its populations are isolated and fragmented into four widely separate areas: the terai area of Uttar Pradesh, the north-eastern states and part of West Bengal, a central area comprising Orissa, Bihar and the southern part of West Bengal, and southern India, principally Kerala, Karnataka and Tamil Nadu.

Elephants generally move in family groups led by a female, as elephant society is matriarchal. The rest of a typical family group consists of two or three mature cows and some half-grown animals. The males lead an independent existence, joining a group when a female comes into oestrus, and leaving once the mating period is over.

Only male Asian elephants have tusks, and sometimes many males do not. On occasion, elephants can be seen in large numbers, especially when they make seasonal migrations from one area to another. A famous herd in Manas, Assam, has numbered nearly 150 animals.

Long-lived, an elephant's average life span is between 70 and 80 years. Females produce young from about the age of 15 up until they reach 60. Despite their size, they move silently and are often difficult to spot in a forest. In grasslands they stand out, looking rather like great grey boulders. In Periyar, south India, you can observe elephants on the edge of a reservoir from boats, while in other parks you have to be content with motor vehicles.

In such parks as Bandhavgarh, Bandipur and Corbett, you can watch wild elephants from the backs of tame elephants. The Asian elephant is exceptionally intelligent and trainable, and can follow 40 or more spoken commands.

Primates

Though the elephant and the tiger have become endangered, some primates seem to have profited from their association with humans. All over the lower Himalayas, Assam and northern, central and southern India, one cannot fail to notice the **rhesus macaque.** These monkeys are common in

Top: Elephants at Periyar.
Above: Tiger in the forests of central India.

Above: Rhino at Kaziranga.

towns and villages, and often play havoc, steal food and generally make a nuisance of themselves. In places where they are most respected, they are often less aggressive — for example, at the Hanumangarhi in the temple town of Ayodhya and the Sankat Mochan Temple in Varanasi. Both places are centres of worship for Hanuman, the monkey god, and the macaques there receive food regularly and do not have to grab. The other common macaque is the bonnet macaque of the peninsula, with its pale face and spiky head of hair.

The **lion-tailed macaque,** much shyer and rarer, inhabits the evergreen tropical forests of the Western Ghats and south India at altitudes between 610 and 1,070 metres (2,000-3,500 feet). Still, like other macaques, this one, too, is gregarious — living in groups of 12 to 20 or more.

An impressive primate, found practically throughout India, is the **common langur** or **Hanumana monkey,** with its black face and coat of silver-grey hair. There are over 10 races of this long-limbed monkey, which is 60 to 75 centimetres (two to 2.5 feet) high when seated, and again travels in troops. It acts as a lookout for spotted deer in the forest, warning the deer of predators.

The **Nilgiri langur,** a native to south India, is, by contrast, glossy black or blackish with a yellowish-brown head. By far the rarest of the langurs, shy and highly arboreal, is the golden langur found in the north-east, in the evergreen forests of north-western Assam. Despite its name, its colouring is predominantly cream.

The **hoolock,** a type of gibbon, is the only ape to be found in India, and is best looked for in the Namdapha Tiger Reserve in Arunachal Pradesh. Two kinds of **loris,** the slow and the slender, are found in India, the first in Assam and the second in the forests of south India. Being nocturnal, they are difficult to spot.

Other wild cats

Although India's most famous cat is the tiger, the other members of the cat family should not be forgotten. The largest is the **Indian** or **Asiatic lion,** now found in the wild only in the forests of the Gir National

Above: Sambar at Ranthambhore.

Park in Gujarat — all that remains of the vast forests which once covered Saurashtra. Although shaggier than the African lion, in many respects the Indian lion is similar. Its tolerance of the proximity of humans has also helped its survival in Gir.

Most widespread of the big cats is the **leopard.** Unlike tigers, leopards are not restricted to forests or heavy cover, and do as well in open country as among scrub. They usually hunt by day, although they are most often spotted in the evenings or early mornings. The leopard takes a wide variety of prey, from birds to cattle and deer, its main enemy (apart from humans) being the tiger. In areas like the Western Ghats, where there is a very high rainfall, black leopards (or panthers) are not unusual.

The **snow leopard** is a high altitude animal, rarely descending below 2,130 metres (7,000 feet), while the **clouded leopard** is found in the forests of Sikkim and Assam. Smaller cats include the **golden, marbled leopard** and the **fishing** and **desert cats.**

There are also varieties of **civet** and **mongoose.** In parts of India it is considered very lucky if a mongoose crosses the road in front of you, and the common mongoose is ubiquitous and likely to do so. This particular species is found all over India, from the Himalayan foothills to Kanyakumari, the southernmost tip of the country.

Other mammals

Like the European fox, the **jackal** has learnt well how to live around humans. However, the **Indian wild dog** is perhaps the most widely distributed of this family, making his home in regions as remote as Ladakh to southern India. **Wolves** are now rare, although their range extends from Ladakh to peninsular India. A relative of the cat is the **striped hyena,** which prefers open country to forest, and often lives in an enlarged porcupine hole.

Three species of **bear** — the **sloth, brown** and **Himalayan black** — are resident in India. They are all shy. Sloth bears can be spotted from the base of the Himalayas to Sri Lanka, while the brown bear lives above the treeline in the Himalayas. The Himalayan black bear is restricted to habitats in Assam and Kashmir.

The deserts of the Rann of Kutch, in

Above: Most widespread of the big cats is the leopard. Unlike tigers, leopards are not restricted to forests or heavy cover.

eastern India, are home to the **Indian wild ass,** which grazes between dusk and sunrise on flat areas of grass known as *bets.*

The **Indian rhinoceros,** found on the opposite side of the country, is most easily seen in Kaziranga, Assam, although poaching has become a serious problem there. The rhino habitat is grassland with marshy areas, lakes and forests nearby.

By far the rarest of India's deer is the **Manipur brow-antlered deer,** which is restricted in the wild to a tiny area of floating matted grass in the swamps of Manipur. The **Kashmir stag** or **hangul** also survives in small numbers. The barasingha — literally twelve-horned — is another deer which has suffered due to humans. It is a specialized feeder, dependent on grasslands which too often have been converted into fields. **Barasingha** can still be seen in parks like Dudhwa.

The **sambar** is India's largest deer, with a shaggy coat and fine antlers. It is common and widely distributed, as is the **chital** or **spotted deer,** found throughout India, often in large herds.

The **hog deer** is closely related to the chital, while the **barking deer** is another common deer. Like the **mouse deer,** or **chevrotain,** and the **musk deer** of the Himalayas, the barking deer has tushes as its main form of defence, rather than antlers. The most elegant of Indian animals is the **blackbuck,** a species of antelope. The best places to see blackbuck today is the Velavadar National Park in Gujarat, parts of Rajasthan and the Kanha National Park. This is one of the world's swiftest species. India's largest antelope, the **nilgai** or **blue bull,** wanders largely unmolested even through fields, thanks to the respect Hindus have for it, while the **chousingha** is the only animal in the world to have four horns and is also the smallest Asian antelope. It has a large range, but is wary of human beings.

The dainty **chinkara gazelle** can be found in good numbers in the Desert National Park, south-west of Jaisalmer in Rajasthan.

The **gaur** or **Indian bison** is the most impressive of wild oxen. A bull stands as high as 195 centimetres (6.5 feet) at the shoulder. Mature bulls are jet black with an ashy forehead and white-stockinged feet. Among the places where herds of gaur are found are Nagarahole, Bandipur, Mudumalai and Annamalai, Periyar and Parambikulam in south India, and Kanha in Madhya Pradesh. The **Asiatic wild buffalo** numbers less than 2,000 and is found in various scattered areas, the purest in bloodline probably concentrated in central India.

Among other fascinating mammals is the **red panda,** with its long tail and rufous- and white-patterned face, found in the Eastern Himalayas and Sikkim. Of the pig family, the **pigmy hog,** 25 centimetres (10 inches) high, lives in savannahs and forests where there are few people, while the omnivorous **wild boar** is much more common and a regular crop raider.

There are many species of **martens, weasels, ferrets, hog, honey badgers, hedgehogs, hares** and small rodents. Flying and giant squirrels are a spectacular sight in the forests, while palm squirrels are in abundance in towns, parks and villages. The nocturnal Indian **porcupine** is found throughout the country, while the Indian **pangolin** is restricted to the north-east and the peninsula. Among the many species of bat found in India, the **flying fox** with a wingspan of 120 centimetres (four feet) is most spectacular.

Reptiles

India's reptile population is also large. **Geckos, lizards** and even **monitor lizards**

are found in and around human habitation and in fields — as are some snakes, especially during the monsoon. There are 236 snake species in India, of which only 50 are venomous. The most common among the poisonous snakes are the **cobra,** the **krait** and **Russell's** and **saw-scaled vipers,** while others include the **king cobra, pit vipers** and **coral** and **sea snakes.** Non-venomous snakes include the **reticulated python,** which grows up to 10 metres (33 feet), and the **worm snake** which grows to just 10 centimetres (four inches).

In national parks, and at various breeding centres, you can see crocodilians. The **gharial,** with its narrow snout, is probably the most remarkable and lives in fast-flowing rivers. The other two crocodilians found in India are the marsh and salt-water **crocodiles.**

The black pond and flap-shell **turtle** are common fresh-water turtles, while four species of marine turtles nest on the country's beaches.

Insects

The insect life of India is spectactulary diverse. There are some 15,000 species of butterfly alone, ranging from the southern birdwing, which has a wingspan of up to 19 centimetres (7.5 inches), to the grass jewel, whose wings measure only 1.5 centimetres (0.5 inch) across.

Above: Sambar stag.

Birdlife of India: Spectacular Species

The Indian subregion has some of the most spectacular birds in the world. Of some 8,650 species worldwide, almost 2,000 species and subspecies find a home there. This subregion is part of the Oriental Realm, one of the six bio-geographic zones into which the world is divided. One of the reasons that the Indian region is so rich in birdlife is the great variety of habitat.

The Himalayan zone

The country is divided into seven different zones, each having its own special characteristics. The first is the Himalayas, with the great mountain chain dividing the Oriental realm and the Paleartic to the north. In ornithological terms, the Himalayan zone begins from an altitude of 1,000 metres (3,281 feet). With the increasing altitude the climate changes from subtropical to warm, cool, temperate, alpine and finally arctic. So, within a short distance, there is a marked change in the flora and avifauna. For example, on ascent into the western Himalayas the white-cheeked **bulbul** replaces the red-vented bulbul of the plains, the blossom-headed, slaty-headed and Alexandrine **parakeets** replace the rose-ringed parakeet, and the smaller, grey-hooded house **crow** is replaced by the larger, shiny, black jungle crow. Altitude also affects size. Higher-altitude animals are generally larger than their plains counterparts. Instead of the plains **tree pie,** the Himalayan tree pie or, more commonly, the red-billed Himalayan blue **magpie,** one of the most spectacular of hill birds, which is often seen in flocks of five or six, become common at high altitudes.

The oak, pine and cedar forests around the hill-stations are traversed by hunting parties of typical hill birds. In the company of **nuthatches,** Himalayan **treecreepers** and a variety of **woodpeckers** can be seen the red-headed, green-backed, yellow-cheeked Shimla **black tits,** plus the brightly coloured yellow-bellied **flycatcher warbler.** The Himalayan **whistling thrush,** known for its fluting song, is a common sight, foraging or flying low through the forest. Kasauli is a hill-station where the Pekin **robin** or red-billed **leiothrix** is often spotted. Skulking in the undergrowth and chattering incessantly, are streaked laughing **thrushes,** which overshadow the shyer and more spectacular white-crested laughing thrush.

Chats, like the dark-grey bush chat, perch on exposed positions waiting to spot prey, while **flycatchers,** like the **verditer,** choose even higher perches from which to make aerial sorties after insects. **Finches** and **buntings** are found in small flocks, perching on trees or feeding on the ground.

The most plentiful of the hill pheasants is the **kaleej.** This, compared with the iridescent **monal** and crimson-patterned blood **pheasant,** is a low-altitude bird. The blood pheasant is found only in the eastern Himalayas. It is worth noting that there is a considerable difference between birdlife in the eastern and western Himalayas.

Other birds specific to the eastern Himalayas are the rufous-necked, ashy, grey-sided, black-faced and crimson-winged laughing **thrushes,** and various species of **parrotbills.** However, other high-altitude birds like the golden **eagle, lammergeier** and Himalayan **griffon vulture** are found from the western Himalayas to Bhutan. Lammergeiers, in particular, have been spotted at altitudes of 7,300 to 7,600 metres (23,951 to 24,936 feet) and **choughs** at 8,300 metres (27,232 feet) high.

The snowline in the Himalayas varies between 4,500 and 5,500 metres (14,800 and 18,000 feet) in summer, and from 2,500 to 2,700 metres (8,200 to 8,850 feet) in winter. This naturally causes movements in bird population. The black and red-winged **wallcreeper,** with its most striking flight pattern, is one such bird. In summer it is found up to 4,900 metres (16,000 feet) and

Opposite: Top left: Golden oriole. Top right: Rufous-backed shrike. Bottom left: Black-capped kingfisher. Bottom right: Black-necked stork.

Above: Greater spotted eagle.

in winter it migrates virtually down to the plains. Other birds travel from the Himalayas to a similar height in the Nilgiri Hills of the south.

North-west and north India zones
South of the Himalayas are the zones of north-west and north India — the first covers the plains of Punjab, and the arid and semi-arid areas of Rajasthan and Gujarat, the second, the terai forests at the foot of the Himalayas and the Gangetic plain.

The greatest of the desert birds is the great Indian **bustard,** which weighs between eight and 14 kilograms (18 to 31 pounds) and measures 120 centimetres (four feet). This rare bird is generally seen in family flocks of about half-a-dozen in places like the Desert National Park in Rajasthan. The various types of **sandgrouse** are examples of how desert birds adapt their colouring as camouflage. India's painted and spotted species of sandgrouse are best seen at a waterhole where they often gather in flocks. The grey **partridge,** another bird found in small parties, is well adapted to desert living because of its

minimal dependence on drinking water. **Peafowl, quails, bee-eaters, rollers, larks, finch-larks, pipits, shrikes, drongos, babblers, flycatchers, bulbuls** and **warblers** can be found in abundance in semi-arid zones.

Urban birds
It is also worth noting that Indian cities can be very interesting birding sites. Travelling between Delhi, Agra and Jaipur, pariah **kites** can be seen in their hundreds, besides several species of **vulture,** red-vented and red-whiskered **bulbuls,** red and white-backed **munias,** lesser golden-backed **woodpeckers,** common, bank, brahminy and pied **mynas,** hoopoes and a host of other small birds: **warblers,** wren warblers, purple **sunbirds,** jungle and common **babblers.**

In summer, the calls of two **cuckoos** — the koel and the brainfever bird — are unmistakable. The koel has a call rather like its name 'ko-el', while the brainfever bird, or common hawk cuckoo, is reputed to say, 'It's getting hotter, getting hotter, getting hotter . . . I can't STAND it, can't STAND it, can't STAND it!'

Another species, endemic throughout India, is the Indian **robin,** slightly larger than a sparrow with a white patch on the shoulder and red under the tail. It is found in dry, open and lightly wooded country. The black-winged **kite,** a common roadside sight, is a very attractive raptor in shades of pale grey with black wing patches.

Birds of the forest
However, it cannot be denied that the terai area of India is a much bigger attraction for the birdwatcher than urban India. Much of the original terai forest has been destroyed to make way for farming, but the Jim Corbett and Dudhwa National Parks in Uttar Pradesh have preserved large tracts of the original landscape. In Corbett, for example, you can see grassland birds like **munias** and collared bush **chats.** By the Ramganga River, plumbeous and white-capped **redstarts, kingfishers** (including the Himalayan pied), **wagtails** and, on perches over the stream or flying up and down the river, Himalayan grey-headed **fishing eagles** are common. In the

forest are blue-throated and other **barbets,** fairy **bluebirds,** golden, black-headed and maroon **orioles,** to name but a few. Perhaps the most impressive of forest birds, the great pied **hornbill,** keeps to the treetops or flaps noisily overhead. The river flows into a reservoir where **osprey,** Pallas **fishing eagles,** marsh and other **harriers** can be seen, plus flocks of **cormorants** and **egrets.** Wintering birds, waterfowl and waders are numerous wherever there is water.

Winter visitors

Migratory birds add a great deal to India's attraction for birdwatchers. Even in the capital, Delhi, tens of thousands of **ducks** and **coots** congregate in winter on the River Jamuna, while **avocets, redshanks, godwits, snipe** and other waders pick their way around the banks, and purple **gallinules** pluck at weeds where lotus and water hyacinth grow. With the waterfowl come the raptors — eagles and harriers.

Shallow lakes or *jheels* are common all over India, but the most celebrated wetland is Keoladeo Ghana National Park, a small sanctuary on the outskirts of the Rajasthan town of Bharatpur. Bharatpur was once a princely state, and the raja dammed canals to create this wetland, the only home in India of the extremely rare eastern strain of the Siberian **crane.** This snowy white and black crane, with its distinctive red face and bill, is one of many species which travel here from the former Soviet Union every winter.

Among the **ducks** which arrive are the widgeon, the teal, the mallard, the pintail and the gadwall. Not all ducks are visitors — the spotbill and lesser whistling teal are residents. Birds like the brahminy duck and bar-headed **goose** are winter visitors but only locally migrant. Bharatpur also has a good variety of **lapwings,** the white-tailed being one of the most common.

Keoladeo is remarkable for its heronries as well. Water-birds like **egrets, storks, ibis, cormorants** and **spoonbills** nest in colonies during the monsoon when the food they rely on is in abundance. Several species share the same colonies. The monsoon is also the time when **weaver birds,** with

Above: Shikra, a resident bird of prey.

their penduline nests constructed of grass, and **munias** breed. Large birds of prey breed between October and March, while most other common birds breed between February and May. Among the most remarkable of courtships is that of the sarus **crane,** a resident bird often seen standing in fields. They are rarely found alone and, therefore, to Indians, they have come to symbolize fidelity.

Avifauna of the peninsular

Peninsular India lies south of the Aravalli and Vindhya Hills and is bordered on the west by the Arabian Sea and the east by the Bay of Bengal. In the heart of this region is the Kanha National Park, with a wide spectrum of forest and water-birds. The city of Mumbai also falls in this zone and a visit to the Borivili National Park on the outskirts of the city can bring many rewards — racket-tailed **drongos, minivets,** jungle **owlets, ioras, bulbuls, hornbills** and **paradise flycatchers.** Also within the peninsular region lies the south-west zone, composed principally of the high hills of the Nilgiris and Annamalais, and

Above: Greylag geese, Bharatpur. Opposite: Shivalik Hills, Uttar Pradesh.

the forests of the Wynad, where Kerala, Karnataka and Tamil Nadu meet.

The south-west is a different region because of its particular birdlife. Among the birds of the southern hills are the yellow-browed **bulbul,** Nilgiri rufous-breasted laughing **thrush,** the spotted and quaker **babblers,** slaty-headed scimitar babblers, Nilgiri wood **pigeon** and orange-headed **ground thrush.**

There is remarkable birding to be had in the Wynad forest and in the three adjoining the national parks of Nagarahole, Bandipur and Mudumalai. Among the species which can be seen are the Malabar **trogon,** the Malabar pied **hornbill,** the great black **woodpecker,** green imperial **pigeon,** blue-winged **parakeet** and hill **myna.** Game birds include the red **spurfowl** and grey **jungle fowl,** while there are also many species of raptors, vultures and owls. The peninsula also enjoys the honour of being the location where a bird, long thought to have been extinct, was rediscovered. Last recorded in 1900, Jerdon's **courser** was found again in 1986 in the Lankamalai Hills of Andhra Pradesh. The area, which

this exceedingly shy, nocturnal and crepuscular bird inhabits, has now been declared the Sri Lankamaleswara Wildlife Sanctuary. Unfortunately, other Indian species, like the pink-headed **duck,** the Himalayan mountain **quail** and the forest spotted **owlet,** appear to have disappeared.

The southern coasts of India are also a birdwatcher's paradise. A trip down the backwaters of Kerala showcases the region's wealth of **cormorants, egrets,** golden **plovers,** whiskered **terns,** reef and night **herons, bitterns** and **gulls.**

It is also a point of crossing for the colourful **pitta,** which summers in India from Sri Lanka, returning in November and December. In the salt lagoons, **pelicans, storks, spoonbills** and a variety of waders and flocks of **flamingo** provide a visual feast.

The north-east region starts at the deltas of the Ganga and the Brahmaputra and extends northwards to include all the forests of Arunachal Pradesh, Mizoram, Meghalaya and Nagaland.

As the birdwatcher progresses east-wards the birdlife reveals that it has strong affinities with the Indo-Chinese sub-region.

Indian Flora: from Alpine to Desert

The variety of climate, rainfall and soil type is reflected in the immense variety of Indian flora. It is estimated that in the western Himalayas and Nepal alone there are 9,000 different species.

The bio-diversity of vegetation is typical of various geographical zones. The western Himalaya has considerably less rainfall than the eastern. Therefore, much of its flora has a close relationship to the flora of West Asia. The lower and temperate part of these mountains, up to about 2,400 metres (7,900 feet), is to a large extent under cultivation, while higher up there are still dense forests of birch, conifers and evergreen oaks. The abundance of shrubs is especially clear in the varieties of rhododendrons. A ride up to Shimla shows how quickly flora changes with altitude. The plains vegetation gradually gives way to the pine and cultivation in terraced fields, and then to the forests where there are trees of a single species — either the stately deodar (literally 'door of the gods'), cedar or silver oak. In these forests you can find wild strawberries, balsams and many other small flowering plants which resemble those of western Europe.

The treeline stands at about 3,700 metres (12,140 feet). Beyond this is the alpine zone, whose lower levels have luxuriant summer grazing grounds and meadows. The upper area has high altitude flora. The alpine flowers are at their best in July and the first half of August.

The Valley of the Flowers, approachable from Joshimath in Garhwal, is one obvious destination, while parts of Kulu district, near Manali, are also easily accessible. By contrast, in Ladakh, which falls in the rain shadow of the Himalayas, there are deserts practically devoid of plant life. However, areas with slightly less rainfall, such as Zanskar, are worth a visit.

The eastern Himalaya, in contrast, is more humid with greater rainfall. As these ranges lie at a lower latitude than the westerns, they are relatively warmer and the timberline and alpine flora are at slightly higher altitudes than in the west region. About 4,000 species of flowering plants are estimated to grow here, of which twenty are palms. The temperate zone has a large number of broad-leaved trees — oak, magnolia, laurel, maple, alder and birch. Conifers grow above 2,700 metres (8,859 feet). Numerous rhododendrons, beside dwarf willows, are common here, and bamboo forms dense thickets. Some rhododendrons and junipers extend from the temperate into the alpine zone.

The hill forests of the north-east are similar to those of the eastern Himalaya, except that there is no alpine zone. Hence, there are evergreen, broad-leaved and pine forests. South and west of the Himalayas are the plains of Punjab, Rajasthan, Kutch and northern Gujarat. Most of this area is arid or semi-arid, and, in the desert, the annual rainfall can be less than 12.5 centimetres (five inches) a year. The extremes of temperature allow only those plants to grow which can adapt themselves — for example, the trees of the desert thorn forests like acacia.

Below the Himalayas — edged in the foothills with the remains of the thick terai forests — is the area of the Gangetic plain, stretching from the Aravalli Hills to Orissa and West Bengal. Most of this area has been under cultivation from very early times, but there remain what must have once been large sal forests.

The sacred, spectacular and medicinal

Many of the trees and plants of this region are found in other parts of the country, too. They are of use to humans in many ways, and have a wealth of legends about them.

Some are even worshipped. Outstanding among these is the holy basil or *tulsi*, enshrined in millions of Hindu homes and venerated as the god Vishnu in plant form. It also has many medicinal properties. Some members of the fig family are particularly noteworthy — the *pipal* or *bodhi* tree, with its heart-shaped leaves, is sacred to Hindus. Buddhists believe that it

Top: Valley of the Flowers.
Above: Hibiscus in bloom.

was under this tree that the Buddha found enlightenment. The banyan is also sacred to Hindus and deserves mention for its immense aerial roots. The twigs of *neem* or margosa are traditionally used as toothbrushes, while scientists use its extract for purposes as varied as pest control and human contraception. Among the spectacular flowering trees are the silk cotton, with its large waxy blooms appearing in February and March; the coral tree with its spikes of red flowers; the *amaltas* or Indian laburnum with cascades of yellow flowers; the *kachnar* or bauhinia; and introduced species like the *gulmohur* and jacaranda. These trees flower in hot weather.

The autumn festival of Dusshera is associated with the flowering of the *harsingar* or coral jasmine trees, the scent of whose small white and orange blossoms carries far, and was praised by the celebrated Sanskrit poet Kalidasa as far back as two thousand years ago. The onset of winter is seen in the flowering of tall grasses which grow in clumps near the Ganga River and are used for making mats, thatches and reed stools. The lower Gangetic plain, consisting of Bihar and Bengal, is much more humid than the upper regions. Areca palms, which produce betel-nut, coconut and bananas, are commonly cultivated.

The Sunderbans, bordering the Bay of Bengal, have many plants which differ from those of the rest of the region, especially several species of mangroves.

Down the west coast of India runs a range of mountains which, on its western escarpments, takes the full force of the monsoon. The last remaining tropical evergreen forests there have a great number of trees, shrubs, climbers and other plants. These forests contain valuable sandalwood trees, as well as ebony and *toon*. In areas with a lower rainfall, there are deciduous trees like teak, lagerstroemia, grewia and dalbergia. Commercial crops like coconut, pepper, coffee and tea, cashew nuts and eucalyptus occupy much of this area.

The remaining part of peninsular India, known as the Deccan Plateau, covers Tamil Nadu, Andhra Pradesh, most of Karnataka, Madhya Pradesh and parts of Maharashtra and Gujarat. In the northern areas stand single-species forests of tall sal trees, while in the south, large trees like teak, mahogany, Indian rosewood and sandalwood grow.

One of the most spectacular flowering trees is the flame of the forest, whose blooms have been praised since ancient times.

Top: Plumeria or frangipani.
Above: 'Queen of the Night' or *harsingar*.
Opposite: Calcutta's flower market.

Tastes of India: Regional, Seasonal and Spicy

Indian cooking defies definition. A portrayal of the many tastes and flavours it represents would be much like the six blind men in the story trying to describe an elephant.

To begin with, given India's cultural, religious, ethnic, geographic and climatic diversity, it is hard to describe Indian food under a single catch-all title. The British, in an overly simplified attempt, called all Indian food 'curry'. It is much like saying that all Western food is roast beef and potatoes.

Basically, Indian food is the inspired use of ingredients meant to bring out in every meal the six main flavours or *rasas* — sweet, sour, salty, bitter, pungent and astringent.

The inherent heating and cooling properties of foods also determine when in the year they will be served — *dahi*-based (curds/yoghurt) preparations are recommended in summer, while dried fruits and nuts feature in winter meals, particularly in north India.

Indian food is not so much hot as it is spicy. Of course, no two cooks agree on the balance of spices to be used. In all, some 25 spices, herbs and condiments, always added in a specific sequence, produce wonderfully aromatic and excitingly flavoured Indian cuisine.

Very loosely, the food habits of Indians revolve around the wheat-eating north and the rice eaters of the south and east. Western India draws a mix of both.

Divine breads

Accordingly, whole wheat, unleavened fat-free *rotis* (*chappatis*/*phulkas*), browned on a tawa or Indian griddle, are the staple of north India. The more wholesome, fat-layered *paratha* is frequently stuffed with *aloo* (potato), *mooli* (turnip), *palak* (greens), *pudina* (mint), and so on.

Eaten with *achaar*, pungent pickle, the feeling is immensely satisfying.

Opposite: Fresh crabs, Goa.

Rumali roti (handkerchief bread), a delicate chappati from the Mughal era, is cooked on a convex tawa and served immediately, before it gets dry and papery. Deep-fried *poori*, puffed to perfection with escaping steam, is also part of the bread repertoire.

The delicious northern leavened breads include the *kulcha*, *bhatura* and *naan*. The *tandoori* naan, a Mughal invention, a boon from the north-west frontier to Indian cooking, is cooked over live coals in a clay oven, or *tandoor*, buried in a mud furnace. Balls of dough are flattened by slapping between the palms, placed on a large, smooth pebble and stuck onto the heated walls of the tandoor. As they cook, the naans fall on the glowing embers and are lifted out with long skewers.

The roadside *dhabas*, that line the national highways in the north and central India, are the best places to view the making of tandoori naan. Moreover, food in these places is always fresh since the truckers they cater to ensure there are no leftovers.

These divine breads are frequently eaten with an enormous variety of *sabzis* (vegetable dishes) and *dals* (split pulses). While dals are prepared in a myriad of different ways to accommodate regional preferences, *ma-ki-dal* made from *urad* dal is a favourite in north India. Dal fry and dal *makhani*, served with a topping of gently melting fresh butter, are other variations. Of Punjabi origin is the *makki-ki-roti* (maize bread) served with *sarson-ka-saag* (mustard greens) and *missy* roti, made from *besan* (chick-pea flour).

Other popular choices with bread are *chole* or *channa*, spicy whole chick-peas with gravy, *paneer* (cottage cheese) dishes with spinach or greens (*palak* paneer/*saag* paneer), peas (paneer *muttar*), or lotus seeds (paneer *phulmakhana*), and *baigan bartha* (brinjal and tomato which has been delicately flavoured with ginger, garlic and fresh coriander).

Southern rice creations

Rice is the chief ingredient of south Indian food. *Iddlis* are steamed rice cakes served with a bland-to-hot coconut chutney and *sambhar*, a traditional sauce of dal, vegetables and spices, piquant with tamarind.

Dosa is a delectable, crisp pancake, a sure-fire favourite. Stuffed with potato *masala*, it becomes a *masala* dosa. Other southern rice creations are *uttappam, appam*, (spongy pancakes with a crisp fringe, fermented with local brew), *iddiappam* (string hoppers) and *uppuma*, a savoury semolina mix of curry leaves and nuts.

Vegetarian delights

To taste the world's finest vegetarian food, visit India. Given the dominance of the Hindu religion and the injunctions of the Buddhist and Jain faiths, all animals are regarded as holy, and meat, fish and even eggs (being the source of life) are strictly avoided. In fact, the Jains avoid all foods considered to be stimulating and to be the beginning of life, like garlic, onions and ginger, to name a few.

Gujarat is a land where vegetarianism rules supreme. Strangely, it is probably the only Indian state with a coastline where the produce of the sea is not consumed. Gujaratis favour sweet foods, and tend to sweeten even their dals.

Outstanding fare like *dhokla* (similar to iddlis), *kandvi* (savoury rolls made from curds and besan) and *undhiyu*, a winter dish of mixed vegetables cooked with coconut are prepared by some of the best vegetarian chefs in the country.

Rajasthan, in northern India, is particularly known for its hot and spicy *gatta* curry. The cooking of Lucknow in Uttar Pradesh is known as *avadh* and is probably immortalized in *dum* aloo, flavourful spuds or quartered potatoes, steamed with aromatic spices; *malai kofta*, cheese balls in cream sauce; and *navrattan korma*, mixed vegetables gently simmered in cream.

Sindhi cooking shows a fondness for *methi* (fenugreek greens) and its best-known dishes are *sai bhajji* (dal and greens), *bhuggha chawal* (onion *pulao*) and Sindhi curry, not unlike sambhar. Much of north India produces versions of the immensely pleasing *karhi*, a buttermilk sauce thickened with besan and garnished with *pakoras* or besan dumplings.

Sumptuous seafood

The coastal districts of the country produce a bewildering array of sumptuous seafood dishes, from the mustardy *macher jhol* of West Bengal to the classic Goan fish curry. Fried Bombay duck, served up from the commercial capital of India, Mumbai, is as delectable as *patra-ni-machhi* and *machhi-nu-saas*, contributions of India's Parsi community. Coconut-based curries are common. The tastiest Indian fish are *surmai, rohu* and pomfret. Crabs, shellfish, shrimp and prawns are other delicacies.

Meat favourites

Pork is probably the favourite of the people of Goa, Mangalore, Coorg and the northeast. However, the culinary gifts of Goa and Mangalore are best savoured in their unrivalled *sorpetel* and *vindaloo*. Goan sausages are spicy and strongly flavoured, and a taste for them is definitely acquired.

What is sold as lamb in India is more likely goat meat. Meat is usually served well done. *Gosht* is the common name for meat in north India as *murgh* is for chicken.

Mughlai cuisine is a world of flavour in itself. Sauces are so rich and delicious, that only a gourmet is a suitable guide into this world of cooking. Malai (cream) and nuts, especially *badam* (almonds), form the basis for most sauces. The eloquent kormas are testimony to this craft, as are koftas, either of meat or vegetables. *Gosht-shahi-korma*, of Persian origin, is a regal offering. *Nargisi* kofta, a hard-boiled egg surprise within a meat ball, is probably the best known. The most impressive is *raan* or leg of mutton, cooked in true Mughlai style and available only in the very big restaurants. *Pasinda* is a heavenly dish of mutton steaks gently simmered in a nut sauce, usually almonds or *piyal* seeds (*chironji*).

Do piazza, literally 'two onions', is yet another finger-licking mutton or chicken creation, spilling over with onions. The Parsi *dhansak*, meat cooked with five different pulses and vegetables, is interesting in its clever use of flavour and texture. A

Above: Fresh produce at a wayside market.

gourmet's choice would easily be the inimitable *biriyani*, the preserve of India's Muslims. This rice and mutton (or chicken and sometimes vegetable) preparation is spicy, aromatic and rich with ghee (clarified butter), saffron, nuts and dried fruit. Less heavy than biriyani is pulao (*pilau/pilaf*). It is perfect with korma or dhansak. Kashmiri Muslims have delighted the continent with their *goshtaba*, airy meatballs in gravy, *al yakhni*, *haleem* and *roghan josh*. Tandoori delights are reasonably bland and utterly enjoyable. The fiery red colour is artificially created, and does not indicate an injudicious use of chilli. They appear on the menu as either *tikkas* or kababs.

Shammi and *sheekh* kababs are marinated minced mutton delicacies, cooked to succulent perfection on skewers stuck into live coals. The marinade drips onto the glowing embers and raises an aromatic vapour that engulfs the meat, sealing in the juices and leaving a lingering smoky flavour. *Boti* kabab (chunks of boneless mutton), *burra* kababs (rib chops) and *kalmi* kababs (chicken) are other tandoori dishes. They are usually served with wedges of lime,

and heaps of salad of onions, turnips, carrots and cucumber which provide an interesting bite to the subtle flavour of the kababs.

Probably the newest entry into Indian cuisine is butter chicken, of unknown origin. Frequently, menu cards sport the cipher B/L beside this dish. It stands for 'boneless' and is one dish guaranteed not to lift anyone's roof. *Chettinad* chicken of south India is really hot, so approach it with caution.

From akoori to achaar

Eggs do not feature in many Indian menus, though *ande ki bhujjia* is the Indian version of scrambled egg, with onions, tomatoes and green chillies. A Parsi variation called *akoori* is equally appealing.

The people of the north-east are partial to pork, soya beans and bamboo shoots. Their chilli-pungent food is mollified with mounds of rice and a lack of tempering fat.

Indians are very fond of salads, usually served with dahi. *Raitas* of the north and *pachadis* of the south are variations of the same thing. They are best ordered with

pungent foods as they help tone the effect, a comfort neither water nor soft drinks will afford. Cucumber, onions, carrots and *boondi* (fried drops of chick-pea flour) are popular choices.

Pappads or *poppadums* are thin, deep fried or toasted, dried pulse or rice circles or wafers. They vary from bland to spiced and are especially liked by children.

No table is considered complete without a full range of Indian pickles — achaars or pungent pickles and *murrabbas* or spiced sweet pickles. The pickles from Andhra Pradesh are very hot. Chutneys, usually made from fresh mint, coriander, mango and coconut, are meant as relishes.

Meals on a leaf

The ubiquitous *thali* (usually vegetarian) is the Indian way of providing a full meal at one go. It is a large steel tray with numerous ramekin-like bowls called *katoris*, which are filled with an assortment of 'dry' and 'wet' vegetables, dal, raita or dahi, pappad and pickle. In the south, they are called 'meals' (always in plural even when you want only one), and in a restaurant, they are likely to be served on a banana leaf. The ritual of cleaning one's banana leaf is best learnt by watching those around you. Most Indian states have a thali on offer, and it is the cheapest way to sample local food. It is extremely filling as well. Frequently, unlimited rice and chappatis are provided at no extra cost, and, among the more generous, the katoris are also refilled often. South Indian thalis might also include a banana/plantain, and in Kerala, *avial*, a coconut-based vegetable stew, is usually featured. The thalis of Andhra Pradesh are only for the daring. With increasing demand, non-vegetarian thalis are getting popular and a meat or chicken dish is served in addition. In some restaurants, it is possible to ask for a de luxe thali, which would include a sweet. Thalis are also served on trains.

Heavenly sweetmeats

It is probably safe to say that no other country can boast the range of sweetmeats

that India has. Non-Indians will find most Indian sweets cloyingly sweet, but in time they will swear there is nothing more heavenly. Sweets fall into two basic categories — those that are milk-based and those that are not. Milk-based sweets are usually created from whole milk solids (*mawa/khoya*) or unmoulded paneer. West Bengal is famed for its sweets, particularly *rosogullas*, *rasmalai*, *sandesh* and *mishti doi*. A number of sweets are first fried (frequently in ghee) before they are immersed in warm, sugar syrup. *Malpuras*, *gulab jamuns*, syrup-filled spirals called *jelabis* and *kesar* and boondi *ladoos* can please an epicurean palate.

During the Ganesh Chaturthi festival in Maharashtra, *modak*, steamed flour and coconut dumplings, are festival fare. The state is also known for *puranpoli*, wheat and sweetened dal pancakes. Rajasthan contributes to the country *lapsi*, a wheat, *gur* (jaggery) and ghee concoction.

Gujaratis are fond of *shrikand*, drained, sweetened and spiced dahi, eaten with pooris. *Kulfi* is the Indian equivalent of Western ice-cream and *phirni* is sweetened milk thickened with rice flour. *Kheer* in the north and *payasam* in the south represent rice pudding, with semolina and vermicelli frequently substituted for rice.

Basundhi and *rabri* are other milk sweets of unsurpassed quality. *Burfi* is made from a base of khoya with every imaginable ingredient stirred into it, even rose petals.

Kaju (cashew) burfi is especially exotic. Most burfis are decorated with *varque,* the impossibly fine and edible silver or gold foil. *Halwas* are also great Indian sweets and come in irresistible red, green, orange and yellow chunks packed with nuts. Famous are Mumbai halwa and the black halwa of Kerala made from rice, coconut milk and gur. Available in most hotels is *gajjar ka halwa* made from carrot. Mysore *pak* is sweetened besan and ghee, while sweet *zaffrani* pulao is served as a dessert.

The dominant spice in Indian sweets is cardamom, a flavour few Westerners appreciate. Almond, *gulab* (rose) and *kewra* are other traditional flavours. *Falooda*, a delicious (and awfully filling) milk drink

Opposite: Spices integral to Indian cuisine.

with vermicelli, flea seeds and ice-cream, comes in a variety of flavours, the most popular being gulab and kesar (saffron).

Sherbets, sweet, cooling drinks and *lassi*, churned, sweetened dahi, are summer refreshers. *Thandai*, a rich, nutty milk drink, is frequently laced with marijuana.

Indian etiquette demands that all Indian food be tackled with the fingers (not beyond the first two digits) of the right hand only. With a little practice, this becomes relatively easy. Most restaurants, however, do provide cutlery, but it takes away from the flavour that hand-fed food imparts.

The Indian meal is usually wrapped up with *paan* (or *beeda* in the south), a proven digestive. A mixture of areca-nut, cardamom, *catechu*, slaked lime, fennel and a host of 'secret' ingredients encased in a betel leaf, this product of the *paanwallah* wizardry is available from *sada* (ordinary) to the highly sophisticated.

Frequently, in India, the bill is presented with sweet, flavoured fennel seeds and *mishree* (sugar candy). The guest is expected to pop a little of each into his mouth to aid digestion.

Tempting snacks
Indians are great people for snacks, which are frequently deep-fried. The range is staggering. Many of these snacks are made from besan — pakoras, *bhajjias* (batter fried vegetables) and *bondas*, and *batata wadas* (a Mumbai speciality) made from potato. Other popular snacks are dal *vada* (or *vadai* — coarsely ground fried chick-pea pats), *dahi* (or *thayir*) *vada*, *kachori* (fried rounds of flour well-stuffed with dal and spices), *samosas* (vegetable and meat triangles of fried dough), *pau* bhajji (spicy potato/tomato mix eaten with local bread — a Mumbai contribution) and *golgoppa* (tiny inflated rounds of dough filled with cooked pulses and cumin/tamarind water, to be eaten whole, also called *pani puri* in western India and *fuchkas* in Calcutta).

Chaat and its Calcutta cousin *jhalmuri* (an amazing blend of sweet, sour and spicy flavours), aloo *tikki* (a potato cutlet with a surprise filling) and *sev puri* are other snacks.

Popular beverages
Tea and coffee are widely available in India. To the non-Indian palate, *chai* (tea) is usually horrendously sweet and milky.

With the advent of tea bags, 'dip chai' is fast becoming popular. Tea is frequently spiced with cardamom or ginger. If you enjoy plain tea and do not wish to experiment, check before ordering if 'special chai' is being offered. The Kashmiri *kahwa* tea is perfect after a heavy meal. In some parts of north India, tea is served in earthen pots, which give it a pleasantly muddy flavour. South Indian filter or decoction coffee is excellent if had in Udipi restaurants.

Some local brews are sold commercially. Cashew *feni* of Goa, one such drink, is a sure knockout. It takes getting used to before one begins to appreciate its finer qualities. Other brews include toddy, the fermented sap of *palmyra* (coconut), which, when distilled, gives arrack. The strong flavoured rice or millet beer called *zu* in the north-east and *asha* in Rajasthan are very popular.

Thankfully, a visitor to India can hope to eat foods from all the regions in most of the big towns and cities even if authenticity is sacrificed a bit. And, as anyone will confirm, partaking of India's vast table can soon become a lifetime fascination.

Above: Simple, rustic fare from Gujarat.
Opposite: A spicy snack made from corn.

Adventure Tourism: from Ocean to Sky

As vast as it is wonderful, the landscape of India is perfect for adventure tourism, a fact that has only now dawned on the concerned authorities. Many African countries have long promoted and cashed in on this feature, and it is, indeed, encouraging to see the flowering of this tourist attraction on the subcontinent. India's forests, rivers, mountains and coastline are the chief lure for the promoters of adventure sports. The state governments are primarily concerned with the advancement of this form of tourism, but, increasingly, privately-run tourist agencies are engaged in arranging special adventure tours. Most importantly, the tourist out for a bit of adventure does not have to be specially trained or fighting fit to dabble in the daring. Most sports have adequate measures built into the system to ensure the safety of the tourist. Incidents of injury, loss or damage generally stem from carelessness and a lackadaisical attitude to warnings and instructions.

Wildlife safaris

By far, wildlife safaris are the most touted form of adventure tourism. Almost every state has its nature reserves, and game can be viewed either from elephant back — a novel and exhilarating experience — or from the seemingly safer option of rather noisy buses. The elephant ride, it cannot be denied, has the added advantage that wildlife tolerate their own better than intrusive mechanized contraptions. The feeling of being almost on top of a snarling tiger guarding its kill can live on in one's memory long after the trip is over.

The best organized wildlife excursions also provide a glimpse of some of the endangered species that animal lovers and naturalists are racing against time to save.

In the south, the Eravikulam National Park near Munnar in Kerala has a sizeable population of Nilgiri tahr, and the Periyar Tiger Reserve near the water reservoir of Thekkady, in the same state, is home to a number of elephants beside other wildlife. Not to be outdone, the Bandipur Tiger Reserve and the Mudumalai Sanctuary in Tamil Nadu offer refuge to a no less impressive list of fauna in its natural habitat.

In the east, the grasslands of the Kaziranga National Park are the last refuge of the Indian one-horned rhino, and the Manas Tiger Reserve protects many endangered mammal species. To the west, in the state of Gujarat, the Gir National Park has on show the Asiatic lion, the only place in the country where it is found. The acres of hardened, saline flats of the Rann of Kutch are perfect for viewing black buck, the dainty chinkara and the Indian wild ass.

Madhya Pradesh in central India has excellent facilities for viewing wildlife in the Karla National Park, a Project Tiger reserve. Outside Khajuraho, the Ken River Lodge, in the village Mandla, offers well organized tours into the Panna National Park besides rafting and fishing trips. The season to visit is between November and June. Bandhavgarh National Park, also within Madhya Pradesh, is home to the tiger and varied bird species.

A virtual haven for birdlife, particularly in the cooler months, when migratory birds flock here, the Keoladeo Ghana National Park at Bharatpur in Rajasthan even boasts the visits of the rare Siberian crane. Sariska and Ranthambore National Park, both in Rajasthan, are well known tiger reserves.

Uttar Pradesh is also home to the big cat, which stalks the forests of the Corbett National Park, also part of Project Tiger conservation scheme.

Two very unusual animal safaris are the white tiger safari in the Nandankanan Biological Park in Orissa, and the camel safari organized by the Rajasthan Tourist Development Corporation across the miles of barren desert outside Jaisalmer. As with all safaris, it is advisable to take sufficient drinking water and food.

Opposite: Kanchenjunga, the third highest mountain in the world.

Angling for fun

Keen anglers will find the swift snow-fed streams of Largi, outside Kulu in Himachal Pradesh, a trout fishing paradise. At 3,400 metres (10,000 feet) in the Garhwal Himalayas, the crystal clear waters of the lake at Dodital, abound in brown trout. Fishing in the Indus is one of the pleasures on offer in the high altitude desert of Ladakh. The Government Tourist Department of Jammu and Kashmir offers valuable advice on fishing in the state, where the Lidder River is sanctuary to trout. Down south, in the Nilgiri district of Tamil Nadu, rainbow and fresh-water trout catch the sun's rays as they leap out of the lakes and streams of Mukurti, Pykara, Emerald, Avalanche, Upper Bhavani, Western Catchment and Carrington. Game fishing for *mahseer (Barbus tor)*, best described as a distant relative of the carp and weighing anything from 5.5 kilos (12 lbs) to 54 kilos (120 lbs), is a popular sport in the fast flowing, rocky rivers of Thannikudy and Munnar in the Iddukki district of Kerala. Deep sea fishing can be pursued off the Kerala coast in Lakshadweep.

Fishing for sport in India requires a licence, issued on request by the local government's forest or fisheries department for a nominal fee.

Trekking

Trekking is organized in a big way. The needs of the young and the not-so-young are increasingly being considered. North India offers treks that pass through vistas of unparalleled beauty, often against spectacular backdrops of snow-clad mountains. The treks of south India are gentler, over rolling grasslands or through thick tropical rain forests.

Treks can fall into the category of well planned, or one can simply follow a trail through the mountains formed by shepherds herding their flocks to reaches of pastureland. The organized tours often arrange halts at tented accommodation, complete with modern-day amenities or comfortable dak bungalows (rest houses).

Trekkers are advised to keep a reliable person or official body informed of their progress as a precaution.

Uttar Pradesh in north India is a trekker's dream. The gentlest and oldest trek is to the Pindari Glacier in Kumaon, ideal for a family endeavour. Also known as Zero Point, the site of the holy *darshan* or vision of divine grace, en route to the glacier, the fabulous peaks of Nanda Kot and Nanda Devi can be glimpsed. The more adventurous can pick out routes from the very well produced trekking map, Kumaon Hills, published by the Survey Department of India. The best season to visit these parts is before or after the monsoon.

While the months of May, June, September and October are recommended, the dazzling display of meadow flowers in the rains will be missed. Pithoragarh, Almora, Kausani and Nainital are other places of note in the Kumaon Hills.

Uttar Pradesh is also the state with two famed pilgrim centres in the mountains, Badrinath and Kedarnath. The trek to Badrinath offers the pleasurable detour to the Valley of Flowers, where the variety and colour of many thousand blooms jolts the mind-weary to an awakening of the senses. Even a moment in this heady atmosphere can leave a lasting impression of what nature has to offer. The flowers are best in July and August.

The trek to the sources of the holy rivers Ganga and Yamuna at Gangotri and Yamunotri, respectively, begins at Uttarakhand. The experienced trekker will find the Tapovan-Nandanvan-Gangotri trek particularly challenging. Tapovan, a grassy plateau at 4,463 metres (14,643 feet), is the base for expeditions penetrating Shivling and the Kedarnath ranges. Rishikesh is the base for most other treks.

The Garhwal Mandal Vikas Nigam Limited at Rishikesh (Tel: 3326620/ 3322251) is responsible for selecting routes and providing information, men and materials to explore these mountains on foot.

On all these treks, the change of fauna and flora with a rise in altitude is dramatic. Particularly staggering are the splashes of colour of rhododendron blossoms, bright red against the blue of the sky, the pristine whiteness of snow-bedecked peaks and fresh green of pine and deodar forests.

The tiny mountainous state of Himachal

Top: Skiing on the mountain slopes of Himachal Pradesh.
Above: White-water rafting in Uttar Pradesh.

Pradesh, north of Delhi, also has similar delights. Kasauli and Chail offer gentle walks through alpine forests on mountain trails. Raison and Katrain, outside Kulu on the main road to Manali, have trekking base camps from where treks are arranged to the great mountain passes. Notable among them is the Rohtang Pass beyond which lies the Lahaul Valley and the Sonapani Glacier, the source of the Beas River. Spiti is for the adventurous, locked in by high mountains, where the locals are still the best guides. However, only tourists with an Inner-Line Permit are allowed here. The weather in these high-mountain regions is unpredictable, and the traveller is warned of sudden snowfalls, which can make these routes impassable. June to November is the time of year to venture into these parts.

The Mountaineering Institute at Manali should be contacted to learn more about trekking through the mountains, and the offices of the government of Himachal Pradesh in the major towns in the country, especially in New Delhi.

In central India, the cool hills of Pachmari, in Madhya Pradesh, are a trekker's delight. Western India offers a gentler pace in the hill-stations of Mahabaleshwar, Panchgani and Matheran.

To the east, the place to head for with your trekking gear is Nagaland, where camping facilities are also arranged. Darjeeling in West Bengal is the start of an adventure to Sandakphu and Phalut through meadows and forests. The trek also holds the excitement of viewing the world's two highest peaks, Everest and Kanchenjunga, in all their majesty, on a cloudless, sunny day.

One of the most thrilling trekking regions is Ladakh, an endless plateau of seeming nothingness. The Tourist Office in the capital Leh is the best place to start. They will provide all information for those keen on getting their pleasure the hard way, including exploring this high-altitude desert by pony and mule. Trekking trails in Ladakh climb into the Zanskar, Ladakh and Karakoram mountains. Kargil and Padum are ideal as base camps before moving into the Zanskar region. Serious

mountaineers, undaunted by these snowy peaks, would be better advised first to stop over at the Indian Mountaineering Foundation at New Delhi to gather complete details of what to expect and how to organize the expedition.

Perhaps, one of the loveliest states for trekking is Jammu and Kashmir. Gulmarg and Pahalgam are the favoured spots.

From Pahalgam, Amarnath Cave, the abode of Lord Shiva, is a three-day trek away. Sheshnag Lake is a place of pilgrimage and the months of July and August are particularly auspicious. Facilities for pilgrims spring up at this time, and unless one is keen to jostle with the religious-minded, it might be wiser to trek in a less crowded season. Outside Srinagar, camping facilities are available at Ganderbal.

Snow, sea and sky
However, Kashmir is better known for its winter sports. In Gulmarg, regular camps are held even for the totally inexperienced when the snows arrive. Skiing is best between January and March. Away from Srinagar, sledging and skiing on the frozen Alpather Lake makes for the perfect holiday. The other ski resorts are at Kufri and Narkanda in Himachal Pradesh, where government-run camps are popular. Board and lodging, also gear, are provided.

Spiti, high up in the mountains, is one of the few places in India that offer hang-gliding facilities to attract tourists.

With the Indian tourist getting more demanding, challenging sports like white-water rafting are beginning to feature on the tourist map. The biggest promoter of this sport is the state of Uttar Pradesh, where the foaming, swirling waters of the Bhagirathi and Alaknanda rivers, rush through narrow gorges, providing the perfect setting for some heart-stopping thrills. The 'Ocean to Sky' rafting expedition can be particularly memorable, an idea that was conceived by none other than Sir Edmund Hillary himself. Rafting amid the turbulence and spray of the Narmada River in Madhya Pradesh can be no less a thrilling experience. The terrain through which the River Indus flows, in the land of Ladakh, is now being exploited for this

Above: Wildlife safari at Kaziranga.

sport. Spiti, in Himachal Pradesh, also has white-water rafting facilities, but it is a place only for those willing to get there.

For a bit of water sporting fun, India's coastline and offshore islands have made a big splash in well loved adventure sports such as snorkelling and deep-sea diving.

The Andaman and Nicobar islands in the Bay of Bengal, and Lakshadweep in the Arabian Sea, promote these sports in addition to the gentler, better known pleasures of water-skiing and windsurfing. However, entry to these islands is restricted, for both Indian and foreign tourists. Foreigners are granted permits to visit the Andaman Islands and only the Bangaram Island in Lakshadweep. Indians may visit the islands of Andaman and Nicobar, though the government controls the flow of traffic to Lakshadweep.

At Corbyn's Cave, the beach closest to Port Blair, the administrative capital of the Andaman and Nicobar islands, windsurfing and water-skiing are major attractions. Snorkelling and scuba-diving excursions are arranged on a daily basis by tour operators to islands outlying Port

Blair. The unhurried pace of Lakshadweep is perfect for leisurely deep-sea diving and fishing, where the play of the forces of nature on one's senses can be an otherworldly experience. More leisurely and less strenuous, windsurfing is another attraction of Bangaram Island.

Responsibility for the future

As with every other tourist spot, litter is often the sad statement that people have passed that way. Since most adventure sports are organized in places not easily accessible to cleaning and clearing arrangements, all visitors should be conscious that they are ultimately responsible for the future of the beauty and welfare of everything around them.

If all travellers pick up their discarded items before they move on, many more generations can engage in the same pleasure-filled pastimes.

Cycle of the Seasons and Power of the Planets

The visitor to India is struck by the colour and exuberance of festivals and fairs celebrated throughout the year. It is a country that celebrates the cycle of the seasons and acknowledges the power of the planets.

The calendar is marked by the passage of the sun and the moon, and each festival has its place, deriving its importance from each phase of the moon. While most of the festivals are marked by the lunar calendar, special significance is attached to the winter solstice, when the sun travels north bringing warmer days, the beginning of the growing season. The 13th and 14th of January are festive days in most parts of India.

Pongal in Tamil Nadu — also called *Makara Sankranti* in other parts of India — is an occasion to offer the winter rice harvest in thanksgiving, and to honour cattle that laboured, tilling the land. Newly harvested rice is cooked in milk that is allowed to boil over as a symbol of abundance. Cattle are decked out with flowers and their horns are painted in garish hues.

Elaborate patterns in rice flour, called *kolams*, decorate the entrance to homes. Similar celebrations take place in other parts of rural India, such as *Bihu* in Assam and the north-eastern states.

In north India, *Lohri* is celebrated on the same day. Bonfires are lit and offerings of sugar and sesame seed are thrown into the fire. Considered the coldest day in the year, it is believed that as the sun grows warm, stimulating growth so, too, will the children of the house be blessed with strength and good health.

Winter can be quite severe in north India, but by the time the moon is full, in February-March, it gets mild and the crops start ripening and the trees begin to bloom. The change in season brings on spring fever, which is given expression in the gay abandon and carnival atmosphere of *Holi*. There are many legends associated with Holi, but beside the religious myth, it is associated with a spirit of renewal. On full-moon night, a bonfire is lit and all things old in the house are burnt, amid much singing and dancing to the rhythm of drums. The morning after, friends and family get together to 'play Holi', boisterously celebrated by dousing one another with coloured water and daubing with many-hued powders. In Mathura, the town associated with the god Krishna, Holi is an occasion for enacting the pranks of Krishna and his friends. The celebration is full of uninhibited fun and wild abandon and is not for the faint-hearted.

The lunar month of *Chaitra* (March-April) brings New Year celebrations to many regions in south and western India. *Ugadi* in Andhra Pradesh and *Karnataka* and *Gudi Padva* in Maharashtra are celebrated with new clothes and special feasts. In the same month, the people of Kerala celebrate *Vishu*, a harvest thanksgiving. Auspicious symbols such as golden sheaves of grain, fruit, flowers and clothing are arranged in front of a mirror the night before. In the morning, the display of the blessings of the past year reflected in the mirror is viewed by members of the family as a token of good things to come in the future. Children receive gifts of money from the eldest member of the family.

Many festivals are connected with the great temples of India. Pilgrims in their thousands gather to catch a glimpse of spectacular processions of deities carried in large, decorated, wooden chariots called temple cars. These are also occasions for trade, barter, amusement and shopping at the fairs that spring up in the temple town. The *Chittrai* festival in Madurai (Tamil Nadu) and the car *Rath Yatra* festival in June-July at Puri (Orissa) are two such occasions.

It is almost a cliché to say that the monsoons awaken the land to life. With the earth flushed green, the occasions for rejoicing are many and varied. Wherever you are in India, the fairs and festivals

Opposite: Ganesh Chaturthi, Mumbai (Bombay).

Above: Devotees at the *Rath Yatra*, Puri.

follow the path of the rain clouds. As cool winds blow over the dusty plains of Rajasthan and Uttar Pradesh, women gather to enjoy themselves at the *Teej* festival. They put up swings in the shade and as the wind rushes through their hair, they sing songs commemorating the wedding of Shiva and Parvati.

The full moon in the lunar month of *Shravana* (July-August) marks the end of the rains. It is a time for prayer and new beginnings. Agriculture is resumed. This day is called *Raksha Bandhan*, a day to honour brothers. Sisters tie a silk thread or decorative bracelet called *rakhi* on the brother's wrist to renew the bonds of affection. The brother promises to protect his sister and gives her a gift.

As the full moon of August begins to wane, the calendar gets crowded with a bewildering number of holidays that confuse those not familiar with the cultural diversity of India.

Eight days after the full moon, *Janamashtami*, the birth of Krishna, is celebrated with religious fervour by devout Hindus. Temples are crowded, as through the night people bring their offerings and come to see tableaux depicting scenes from Krishna's life.

Ten days later, it is *Ganesh Chaturthi*, the festival of the much-loved elephant-headed Ganesh, son of Shiva and Parvati. Clay images of Ganesh are worshipped in the home and in public places, where gigantic stages are erected. At the end of the week, the images are carried in procession followed by large crowds, to be immersed in the sea or river. Pune and Mumbai have particularly grand processions, where people dance in the streets to loud music and the bursting of firecrackers.

Fisherfolk along the coast offer coconuts to Neptune before the start of the fishing season. In Kerala, *Onam* is when the legendary King Mahabali is said to visit his subjects. His coming is greeted with floral decorations, song and dance. Boat races on the canals near Kerala's coast are keenly contested, and crowds gather on the banks and shout encouragement to their teams.

Before one has barely recovered from the excitement of Ganesh Chaturthi and Onam, it is time to count the days to

Above: *Holi* celebrations at Brindavan.

Dusshera. In Bengal, Dusshera is celebrated as *Durga Puja*, the festival of the goddess Kali as Durga, who rides a tiger and destroys evil. It is a festival of colour, as everyone joyfully prepares food and decorations days in advance. Music and dance performances are held. Craftsmen create gorgeous images of Durga in clay, straw and paper. Durga is welcomed as a daughter of the house who has come for a visit.

In addition to the religious aspect, there are special events, entertainment, sales and exhibits. Visitors to Calcutta are overwhelmed by the special spirit of that city at Durga Puja. Similar celebrations, though on a smaller scale, can be seen in all the major cities of India where there are large numbers of Bengalis.

After a week's celebration, the images are immersed in the river accompanied by drums and conches. A sad farewell — until Durga returns another year.

The 10 days of Dusshera are dedicated to Rama in the region along the Ganga plain, where the story of Rama and Sita is narrated and enacted with the interest and excitement never seeming to pall.

Traditional drama groups perform episodes from the *Ramayana* every night and, on the 10th night, the climax of the drama when Rama kills the demon Ravana, giant effigies of Ravana and his brother are set alight, signifying the power of good over evil. Fireworks and the noise and clamour of excited crowds, contribute to the magic of the moment.

The preceding nine nights of Dusshera are called *Navaratri*, special days for the women of western and southern India. The Hindu goddesses and *Saraswati*, in particular, the goddess of creativity and learning, are honoured. Toys and dolls are exhibited in homes, children create special artistic displays, and books and musical instruments are worshipped. Women and children visit one another's homes to view the displays and exchange greetings.

The season for fireworks is just beginning, for the next month, *Kartika* (October to November), is the high point of the festival calendar. The new moon of *Diwali* (or *Deepavali*) is the biggest festival of the year, countrywide. Diwali literally means 'a garland of lights'. The little earthen lamps, or *diyas*, of Diwali bring a cheerful glow to the humblest home, for on this, the darkest night, the lights invite Lakshmi, the goddess of prosperity, to enter the home, bringing good fortune, happiness and wealth. Every home is cleaned and decorated, sweets are exchanged between friends and well-wishers, the family wears new clothes, and special *pujas* (devotional prayers) in honour of Lakshmi commemorate the beginning of a new season. The noise and light of fireworks fill the night sky and, as the festival comes to an end, there is a sense that every day after this is an anticlimax.

The month of *Kartika* is also a season for agricultural fairs in parts of north India. These farmers' gatherings, too, are linked to stories from mythology and take place at temples and places of pilgrimage. Two of the best known and most colourful are the camel fair at Pushkar (Rajasthan) and the *mela* (fair) at Sonepur (Bihar), where large numbers of cattle and elephants are sold.

By and large, the festivals described so far are Hindu celebrations, but India's religious diversity embraces a number of other holy observances. Every major religion of the world is represented in the subcontinent, and each has occasion to consider certain days in the calendar as special.

The lunar month of *Vaisakh* (April-May) is sacred not only to Hindus but also to followers of other faiths.

Buddha Jayanti, the full-moon day of Vaisakh, is thrice-sacred to Buddhists, for on this day the Buddha was born, attained enlightenment and died. The places associated with the Buddha's life and teaching are visited by Buddhists from many parts of the world.

Mahavir Jayanti is the day when the founder of the Jain faith, Mahavir, was born. It is a day of prayer and fasting for his followers.

Guru Nanak, the founder of the Sikh religion, was born on *Kartika Purnima*, when the moon is full in the month of *Kartika*. The celebration of Gurparab is the most important day for Sikhs. Sikhs and Hindus throng the *gurudwaras* (abodes of the gurus), where readings from the holy book, the *Granth Sahib*, continue through the whole day.

The Muslims are the second largest religious group in India. They share common observances with Muslims around the world. The faithful gather in mosques for prayers at *Id-ul-Fitr* at the end of Ramadan, the 30-day fast in the ninth month of the Muslim calendar. Shia Muslims observe *Muharram*, a 10-day-long mourning period for the loss of Hazrat Imam Hussain in the battle of Karbala. Processions of mourners follow *tazias* (large paper and wood models of the tomb of Imam Hussain) through the streets. The large Shia population in Lucknow marks this day with serpentine processions and particularly elaborate tazias. While there are no festivities in mosques comparable to those in temples and churches, the shrines of Sufi saints in many parts of India commemorate the *Urs*, or death anniversaries, of Muslim saints. Groups of Muslims gather for the Urs of the Chisti saints in Ajmer, Delhi and elsewhere. Flowers are offered and groups of male singers sing religious songs. A fair is usually held in the vicinity of the tomb where pilgrims buy souvenirs and food.

The Christians in India observe Good Friday, Easter and Christmas. Catholics, in addition, observe certain other days as special, especially those connected with saints who died and were buried in India. It is believed that Thomas Didymus, one of the twelve apostles of Jesus, came to India in the first century AD and spent his life preaching the gospel in south India, especially in Kerala. He is believed to have been martyred in Chennai and the Cathedral of San Thome on St Thomas' Mount also houses his tomb. The Shrine Festival of St Thomas is held every year.

In Goa, at the Basilica of Bom Jesus, the body of St Francis Xavier, the great Catholic missionary, lies embalmed. Every 10 years the exposition of the relics of St Francis Xavier draws crowds from all over the world. The feast of St Francis Xavier is observed every 3 December.

The small Jewish and Parsi communities observe their holidays traditionally. As these communities are largely in urban areas, the holidays are local events.

Opposite: Bengal's *Durga Puja*.

Indian Music: Sensual and Mathematical

The range and diversity of Indian music is comparable to the geographic dissimilarity of the land. The cultural streams that once flowed through the land, by either conquest or trade, have enriched the people's musical expression. With the impact of technology and the electronic media, a new hybrid of indigenous melody and Western rock has emerged, propagated through cinema and television. From the chants of the *Vedas* and the early hymns to today's compact disc recordings, from simple tribal melodies to sophisticated classical performances on the concert platform, the range is awesome in complexity and depth of cultural expression.

Folk songs to classical forms

The different streams of music, whether classical or folk, are fundamentally alike. From simple folk tunes evolved the later classical forms with highly developed grammar and structure. The tempo of the drums in folk music have been developed by musicians into intricate rhythm through constant improvisation.

The outcome of an agricultural people who sang at marriages, rejoiced at the birth of a child, celebrated the harvest or simply sang to relieve the monotony of work, folk music reflects the cycle of life or the seasons.

Classical music developed into 'pure' tonal arrangements of notes in the major and minor scales. While students of Western music will see a parallel with Greek modes, here the similarity ends. Western music developed harmony and orchestration and drew away from the folk idiom. In India, the solo voice is still the basis of all classical music, for it is believed that the essence of any musical instrument lies in the human voice. Consequently, no musical instrument was developed which produced a pitch and quality beyond the range of the human voice. This is perhaps unusual compared with the music of other cultures.

The earliest codified music was derived from the *Vedas*. The chants were set to a pattern and cadence, reminiscent of Gregorian chants. Stemming from this, different styles with accented notes and time intervals counted with the fingers evolved. This form of music is still heard in schools of religion where priests are taught the Vedic ritual. Between these early musical forms and the classical *ragas* that developed in the 14th to 15th centuries, there is a large gap in our knowledge of how Indian music evolved.

Indian classical music today recognises two systems: Hindustani music, which is practised in northern and central India, and Carnatic music, the preserve of south India. Both styles are based on two fundamental elements: the raga and the *tala*.

Raga is the melodic form or tonal arrangement that is sung or played using the seven main notes with five variants. There are 72 *melas* or generic scales, each with its own ascending and descending structure. Five hundred or more ragas grew out of the generic melas, each a melodic idea governed by its own arrangement of notes.

The order in which these notes are sung, and its accent and emphasis, are defined with scrupulous observance of the rules and restrictions. Within the constraints of a raga's particular definition and structure, a musician is quite free to improvise; therein lies his artistry and skill. The power of a raga lies in an individual's exposition. It is experiential and is recreated with each rendering.

Tala, the second important element, is the organization of time. Tala is not linear as rhythm is in Western music, but repetitive. There is a return to a starting point, in much the same way as Sunday follows the end of each week.

An octave is also cyclical, as is the basic experience of all creation, which is recognised in Indian philosophy as well. The time cycle to which a musician must adhere is precisely set. The sequence is usually measured by clapping, with emphasis on the initial beat and again upon its return to the beginning of another cycle.

Above: Dancer in the Elephanta caves, Mumbai.

The drums accompanying the musician maintain the time. The virtuosity of the percussionist is displayed by the intricate versions improvised within the set tala.

Passages of music may be sung or played without a tala, with the musician improvising introspectively, evoking the unique flavour and mood of a raga. But when the drums strike up, it is the tala which determines the subtleties of time and its organization.

A listener can, therefore, appreciate the music on different planes, either with sensuous delight in the sound or with feeling for the emotion of the mood created. On a third level, the sound of the raga, the mathematical permutations of the tala, and the finely tuned rapport between the musician and the accompanist combine to give the music lover a profound and deeply personal insight into the music.

Between the sophisticated exposition of classical music and the spontaneous and vibrant folk idiom, the gap is bridged by a whole body of devotional religious music called *bhajans* and *kirtans*, romantic poetry and theatre music rendered by entertainers and minstrels. The religious songs composed by saints primarily in the medieval period, at the time of the so-called *Bhakti* Movement, are in various languages and sung all over India by people of different faiths. These are all set to ragas, although there is some freedom in their rendering.

The romantic compositions of singers of the princely courts are also set to traditional ragas in the classical style. The *ragis* (singers) in Sikh temples, and *qawwalis*, sung at the shrines of Sufi Muslim saints, draw on the common thread that weaves the raga system into a unified fabric.

Finally, in the interplay between music, religion and dance, the classical compositions of Carnatic and Hindustani music are interpreted by dancers from the different styles of classical Indian dance.

The appreciation of the dance is heightened when the audience understands the meaning of the songs and the emotion that is conveyed by the dancer through gestures and mime.

For music and dance in India are seen essentially as devotional offerings by artistes in homage of the supreme power.

Indian Dance: a Form of Worship

Indian dance is rooted in antiquity, a religious expression, whose performance is a form of worship. Performances of classical dance formerly took place in temples as part of the daily ritual of worship, but, as patronage shifted to the royal courts, and later to the public auditorium and stage, its repertoire changed. Nevertheless, any performance begins with an invocation and ends with a dedication to the supreme God — an offering and an act of worship.

Dance poses today are reminiscent of ancient carvings and paintings in temples and caves which bear witness to the development of dance through the centuries. Bharata's *Natya Shastra*, a unique treatise on dance and music which codifies the dance forms in minutest detail, was written around the first century AD. It is still the basic reference for contemporary dance.

The classical Indian dancer uses the entire body, an expressive face and hand gestures to project a state of emotion. The language of hand gestures opens up a world of communication that creates a unique link between the dancer and the audience. Together with the music and percussion instruments, the dancer narrates stories from religious mythology through mime.

The four major schools of classical dance are Bharatnatyam, Kathakali, Kathak and Manipuri. In recent years, three more dance forms have been recognized, Odissi, Kuchipudi and Mohiniattam. While each has its own distinctive style, there are common features in rhythmic patterns and music. Three aspects common to all Indian classical dance are the *natya*, *nritya* and *nritta*. The first, natya, is the dramatic aspect, where the dancer uses stage effects and props. The second, nritya, is the interpretive aspect, where the dancer tells a story through movement and facial expression called *abhinaya*. The last, nritta, is pure dance, where the body is used solely for creating beautiful forms, patterns and rhythms without drama or story-telling.

Bharatnatyam is performed by a solo female dancer and was once confined to the temples of Tamil Nadu. She is accompanied by a singer and a percussionist who plays the *mridangam*, a barrel-shaped drum. A *nattuvanar* conducts the performance using cymbals to mark the rhythm, and chants syllables that correspond with the rhythm of the drum and the sound pattern of the bells on the dancer's feet. Bharatnatyam uses both nritya and nritta; some items are interpretations of a song through gestures and facial expression. Others are pure dance, or nritta, conveyed through a skilful use of the feet and graceful body movements.

The most dramatic dance form is, undoubtedly, Kathakali, which combines elements of theatre, opera and dance. Traditionally, an all-male group heavily make up their faces with a paste of rice in green, red and black. The mask colours symbolize the spiritual quality of the character. A traditional Kathakali performance lasts through the night and the bare stage is lit only by two large brass oil-lamps. The dancers' costumes are voluminous cotton skirts, which whirl as the dancers leap, twirling with vigour and agility. The singer and drummer lead the performance by setting the pace, pausing for expression and quickening the rhythm for dramatic effect. The heroes, heroines and villains from episodes in the great Indian epics, the Ramayana and the Mahabharata, are brought alive with unforgettable dramatic intensity.

Kathak is a solo dance, performed by both men and women. Originally, it was a devotional dance, where religious stories were told through mime, while a storyteller, or *kathakar*, recited poems. Later, with the advent of Mughal rule, Kathak moved to the court and took on a different form, full of grace, sophisticated rhythm and brilliant footwork. Both aspects of the dance are now part of the Kathak repertoire.

Opposite: Kathakali, the dramatic dance form from Kerala.

In the north-eastern hill state of Manipur, the dances are mainly devotional. With slow grace and delicate hand gestures, the women trace patterns of movement, describing the story of Krishna and the milkmaids, or *gopis*, with whom he dallied.

Top: Bharatnatyam.
Above: Kathak.
Opposite: Ladakhi dancers at the Hemis festival.
Overleaf: Sunset behind a skyscraper.

The vigorous male dances are performed by drummers who whirl, leap and spin in intricate patterns as they play their drums. Much like Bharatnatyam, the dancers from Orissa were also initially confined to the great temples of Puri and Bhubaneswar. But the dance differs from Bharatnatyam in many ways.

The Odissi dancer sways her body with sensuous grace that brings curved lines to that pattern of movement. The bent head, hip and knees trace an S-shape called a *tribhangi*, or 'three bends'. The repertoire of the Odissi dancer includes songs from the love lyrics of Jayadeva, a 12th-century poet, that describe Krishna's love affair with Radha.

A village in Andhra Pradesh gives its name to Kuchipudi, a form of classical drama and dance with religious themes. Originally performed by men, the dance is now also staged by women. The music is similar to Bharatnatyam, but the rhythm and pace are more fluent and informal.

The temples of Kerala are places where religious dances and drama have been adapted into differing styles. Mohiniattam, performed only by women, assimilates the drama elements of Kathakali and the music and rhythm of Bharatnatyam.

The farm folk of Kerala and Karnataka make admiring audiences for several kinds of dance dramas enacted by all-male professional troupes. Performed in the fields after the harvest, they often go on through the night. Stories of the epics are retold and re-enacted using elaborate costumes and make-up, allowing for improvisation, humour and audience participation.

India's folk dances are many and varied. Elements combine to produce a unique dance to each region, though they express a common spirit — a celebration of nature. Other regional dances include the *bhangra* of Punjab, the *chhau* of Orissa, the *dandiya ras* of Gujarat and *cheraw*, an intricate bamboo dance from the north-eastern state of Mizoram.

Both sophisticated formal performances in urban centres, and the stimulating rhythm of folk instruments and dances nourish the people's creative expression through dance and music.

PART FOUR: BUSINESS INDIA

An Economic History

India possesses the twelfth largest economy in the world in terms of Gross Domestic Product (GDP) measured in US dollars and the sixth largest on the basis of purchasing power parity, according to an International Monetary Fund (IMF) study conducted in 1992. It also has one of the largest industrial sectors in the world. The country has followed a policy of self-reliant economic progress since Independence in 1947, enabling it to evolve from an international basket-case to a self-confident economy that possesses a food-surplus agricultural sector, a well-developed industrial infrastructure and a mature services sector. India follows a mixed economy, but nearly seventy-five per cent of its GDP is generated by the private sector.

The present hallmark of the Indian economy is the economic reform and liberalization programme launched in July 1991. After four decades of industrial development based on active public sector involvement, regulation of industry and restrictions on imports and foreign investment, India has embarked on an ambitious and bold programme of change designed to realize the potential for growth offered by its vast resource base and industrial infrastructure, as well as to improve its international competitiveness. These reforms, together with India's huge market for consumer and industrial products and its tremendous natural and human resources, make the country an extremely attractive investment place.

Having inherited an impoverished colonial economy, independent India's early development policies concentrated on the twin objectives of self-reliance and social equity. For agriculture, the economy's mainstay, the strategy revolved around institutional reforms, state investment to build an infrastructure and promotion of modern agricultural practices. This was attempted through a combination of incentives, subsidies, price support mechanisms and extension efforts.

Industrial development was based on licensing, regulation and protection of domestic industry through import controls and high tariffs. The public sector was responsible for developing the infrastructure sector and industries involving high levels of investment. Nevertheless, the bulk of industrial activity remained in the hands of the private sector which, however, was closely regulated.

Similarly, the financial sector, especially banking and term lending institutions, was largely controlled by the government, which determined the allocation and cost of credit in accordance with development priorities. However, active primary and secondary markets existed for corporate securities, while trade and construction were almost entirely in private hands.

With the accent on financing investment from domestic sources, the policies were aimed at raising the domestic savings rate. The gross savings rate registered a steady GDP growth from 10.4 per cent in 1950-51 to about 24 per cent in 1990-91. External capital has generally financed less than 10 per cent of gross investments in any particular year. So far, external aid and commercial borrowings have constituted the two main forms of external finance, with direct foreign investment playing a marginal role.

This strategy did not yield any dramatic overnight results and many key historical ills of the economy remained neglected. India was, nevertheless, able to achieve agricultural self-sufficiency, set up an extensive infrastructure and create a diverse, modern industrial base. Its pool of scientific, technical and managerial manpower is among the largest and most efficient in the world (with the additional advantage of being English-speaking), while the banking, communications, marketing and distribution sectors have penetrated deep into the rural areas, knitting this huge country into a single modern market with immense potential.

Gradually industry and external trade were freed from control and regulation in the 1980s, culminating in the reform programme launched in July 1991. Regulation of industrial activity has been virtually eliminated and state subsidy to public enterprises progressively removed, reducing the monopoly of the public sector in several areas. Trade barriers are also being removed, while financial sector reforms propose to introduce competition and make allocation and cost of credit flexible.

While the focus remains on domestic savings to finance the bulk of investment, a concerted effort is being made to attract foreign capital in the form of direct investment rather than borrowings.

Economic performance has been satisfactory in recent times. In 1980-81 and 1990-91, the GDP grew at an average annual rate of 5.5 per cent. Measured in terms of gross value added, agriculture grew at an average annual rate of 3.6 per cent, while the manufacturing and services sectors grew at around seven per cent a year. Gross domestic savings averaged 20.75 per cent of GDP during this decade, rising at 6.6 per cent a year in real terms. Gross domestic investment averaged 22.78 per cent of GDP during this period, recording real increases of seven per cent a year. During the same decade, exports grew at an average annual rate of 7.9 per cent from US$8.5 billion to US$18.1 billion. Imports, on the other hand, rose at 4.2 per cent a year from US$15.9 billion to US$24 billion.

However, all was not rosy. Economic growth was accompanied by fiscal and external imbalances leading to mounting government and external debts, excessive liquidity and inflationary pressures, depreciation in the external value of the rupee and a squeeze on development expenditure.

It was in order to tackle these imbalances and push economic growth that the government launched the economic restructuring programme in 1991. This programme was aimed at cutting the fiscal deficit, reducing growth in money supply, allowing greater play of market forces in resource allocation and attracting foreign investment, instead of seeking commercial loans.

The measures included certain demand compression steps which resulted in an initial economic slowdown. The GDP grew by just 1.2 per cent in 1991-92, with both agricultural and manufacturing output registering declines.

But the economy has responded rather well since then to the adjustment programme. After the induced slowdown in 1991-92, it surged the very next year, with estimated growth rates of 4.2 per cent in GDP, 3.6 per cent in industry and 5 per cent in agriculture. The fiscal deficit has come down from 8.4 per cent of GDP in 1990-91 to 5 per cent in 1992-93. Similarly, growth in money supply dropped to 11.2 per cent in 1992-93, while inflation was down to less than seven per cent by March 1993. Official foreign exchange reserves, which were down to US$2.2 billion in March 1991, rose to US$5.5 billion by December 1992. Market forces now determine the exchange rate of the rupee, which remained at 30 to 31 per US dollar for most of 1992-93.

The turnaround was reflected best in investor confidence. Total public issue of capital rose from Rs96 billion in 1990-91 to Rs199 billion in 1991-92, while project assistance sanctioned by financial institutions increased from Rs194 billion in 1990-91 to Rs238 billion in 1991-92. Foreign investment approvals jumped from an earlier average of just Rs2.4 billion a year to Rs38.9 billion between August 1991, and December 1992.

These economic developments over the last 45 years have seen India grow into one of the largest economies in the world. Its huge, rapidly growing market for branded consumer goods is estimated to number 300 million. This market is growing at an average annual rate of eight per cent, with the demand for certain products touching a growth level of 12 per cent. Correspondingly, India possesses a highly trained and adaptable labour force, which is available at extremely competitive rates, and boasts one of the largest pools of scientists, technicians, engineers and managers in the world. Already

familiar with a market-economy infrastructure, the country has developed a sophisticated financial sector, with a vibrant capital market (over 6,500 companies are listed, the second highest in the world) that had a market capitalization worth US$80 billion in December 1992.

The new liberal policy environment and the country's existing economic infrastructure apart, what makes India unique among developing countries as an investment country is its long history of stable parliamentary democracy.

Industry

India has one of the largest manufacturing sectors in the world. A rich mineral base and the policy of self-reliant industrial progress have helped create a large, diversified industrial sector and advanced technological capabilities in the areas of mining and infrastructure, and in the manufacture of machinery, power equipment, metals, metallic and non-metallic components, petroleum and petrochemicals, electronics, software, telecommunication, chemical products, agro-based inputs, transport equipment, packaging and consumer goods.

India's industrial enterprises are classified into factory and non-factory sectors. Units employing 10 or more workers using power, or 20 or more workers not using power, qualify for the 'factory' category. There are some 200,000 such units of which about five per cent are in the public sector. The bulk of the public sector enterprises are in the heavy engineering segment and account for nearly 29 per cent of gross output and 34 per cent of value added in the factory category.

Private enterprise not only plays a big role in the factory sector, but also accounts for roughly 1.94 million smaller industrial units, which employ over 12 million people. Besides, there is a flourishing cottage and household industry.

The gross value added in the industrial sector, including mining and electricity, was Rs 1,301.43 billion in 1990-91, of which Rs 857.9 billion was accounted for by the manufacturing sector. From 1980-81 to 1990-91, electricity generation grew at nine per cent a year, while the manufacturing sector rose at an average annual rate of 7.2 per cent. The engineering industry alone registered an average growth rate of 10 per cent a year, with the electrical machinery industry (average annual growth of 19 per cent) being the star performer. The consumer durables segment registered an impressive yearly growth of about 14 per cent. The production of chemicals and chemical products and electronics also registered substantial increases.

Modern technology made its advent in India in a big way in the mid-1980s, with a wide range of industries investing hugely in modernization and upgrading schemes. These sectors included electronics, telecommunications, computer software, chemicals, electrical machinery, textiles, automobiles, petroleum, petrochemicals and packaging.

However, given its continuing battle with poverty and backwardness, and the predominance of agriculture in the economy, India cannot qualify to be termed 'industrialized'. The contribution of industry to domestic product and employment generation are far below agriculture's even today. However, there is an unmistakable trend towards rectifying the situation. This is evident from the growth in the contribution of the manufacturing and services sectors to the GDP from 15 per cent and 29 per cent, respectively, in 1950-51 to 27.5 per cent and 40 per cent, respectively, in 1991-92.

While the figures may not be all that flattering yet, a qualitative analysis does speak well for a country which began with nothing at all after the colonial power vacated it in 1947. The output generation of basic industries like mining and quarrying, fertiliser manufacture, heavy inorganic chemicals, cement, iron and steel, non-ferrous basic metals and electricity has been impressive. An indication of this is the weight of 32.28 (1985) assigned to this category in the Index of Industrial Production. If we consider along with this the weight of the capital goods industries segment (15.25 in 1985), we get a clear picture of a strong industrial base.

In addition, there has been much diversification of industries, leading to the elimination of dependence on imports of many key items. New industries in the intermediate and consumer goods sectors have displaced traditional industries like sugar and textiles from their pre-eminent position, implying a strengthening and evolution of the industrial base. All these aspects point to the existence of elements that can form the backbone of a strong industrial economy.

Trend-wise, industrial output has grown at an average rate of about six per cent since 1950-51, which is far higher than the growth rates of population (2.5 per cent), agriculture (2.7 per cent) and national income (3.5 per cent). This is remarkable in contrast to the pre-independence trend of a mere two per cent between 1900-01 and 1945-46. In recent years, India's industrial growth rate has been better than that of many developed countries, such as Australia, Canada, France, Germany, Japan and the United States.

Energy

India has a mix of hydroelectric, thermal and nuclear power generation facilities. The generation and distribution of electricity have largely been controlled by government-owned enterprises, but, of late, in keeping with the new economic philosophy, there are moves to give the private sector a much larger role. For example, a substantial portion of the power generation and supply to the metropolises of Mumbai and Calcutta is in private hands, while there are plans to do the same in New Delhi. At the same time, industrial units are being encouraged to set up captive power plants. As such, the power sector has been opened to private investment and the government has outlined a package of incentives to attract private capital, both domestic and foreign.

There has been tremendous investment in this sector, with installed capacity shooting up from a little over 30,000MW in 1980-81 to nearly 80,000MW in 1991-92. An additional capacity of another 30,000MW is proposed to be installed by 1996-97.

Petroleum and its derivatives remain the largest import items for India, but concerted efforts to increase domestic production and refining have enabled the country to meet as much as 60 per cent of its requirements indigenously. The success of the offshore Mumbai High oilfield has resulted in a spurt in the production of natural gas since the early 1980s. A national pipeline grid is now being created for its distribution.

While government-owned enterprises have hitherto carried out the production, refining and distribution of petroleum products, recent policy changes have allowed domestic and foreign private participation in oil and gas exploration and refining, and the marketing of kerosene and liquefied petroleum gas.

Transport and Communications

India has the largest railway network in Asia and the second-largest in the world, with over 62,000 route kilometres (38,440 miles). In 1990-91, the railways moved over 341 million tonnes of freight at an average rate of Re 0.1 per tonne-kilometre and carried 3.8 billion passengers.

The Indian Railways is totally government-owned and, in fact, is the country's largest public sector organization (and the world's single biggest employer). But the private sector is now being permitted to enter some sections of rail transportation.

India has an extensive road network of approximately 1.9 million kilometres (1.178 million miles). It accounts for about half of the total freight movement and 80 per cent of the passenger traffic. In 1990 91, road transport accounted for around 340 million tonnes of freight. The number of goods-carrying vehicles has increased at an annual average of 10 per cent during the last decade.

However, there is a crying need both to extend and to improve the road network. In its current state, it is inadequate to meet both the social needs of the people and the larger requirements of the economy. At the commercial level, there is inadequate co-ordination between the rail and road transportation sectors.

Road building and maintenance is another area that has been entirely in government hands, but there is talk now of involving the private sector in this field as well.

India possesses a large domestic shipping industry, which operates some 6,000 vessels with a total capacity of 6.28 million GRT. However, nearly two-thirds of India's international cargo is carried by foreign shipping companies.

Run by government-controlled trusts, 11 major and 139 minor ports dot India's approximately 7,000-kilometre (4,340-mile) coastline. The most recently developed major port, Nhava Sheva near Mumbai, has been built with state-of-the-art technology and can handle up to three million tonnes of container cargo and 2.9 million tonnes of bulk cargo. It is capable of handling third-generation container vessels and bulk cargo vessels of up to 80,000 DWT.

Foreign investment up to 51 per cent is now permitted in the shipping industry. Controls on the acquisition and sale of vessels have also been greatly eased.

As for air transport, India is conveniently located on the trunk route connecting Europe with East Asia, and its major cities like New Delhi and Mumbai are well-linked to important destinations all over the globe. Air India is the country's international flag-bearer and flies to all the important cities in the world. The total international traffic originating from India was 3,945 million tonne-kilometres in 1990-91, of which sixty-five per cent was handled by foreign airlines.

Besides New Delhi and Mumbai, the other international airports are Chennai and Calcutta, which handle some 20 million passengers and 415,000 tonnes of cargo annually.

The domestic network consists of 88 airports served by the government-owned Indian Airlines as well as a number of privately-run airlines. There was a 7.6 per cent annual increase in domestic air traffic in the 1980s. With the entry of private capital and free competition, domestic air services are bound to improve.

India has its own network of telecommunication satellites which provide quick and easy access to all parts of the country. Some 1,100 places within India and 212 countries are accessible through the direct dialling system.

Over the past decade, much emphasis has been laid on the development of telecommunications, recognized as vital to the growth of the economy. The improvement has been both quantitative and qualitative. Telephone connections rose at the rate of 8.4 per cent a year in the 1980s against the global average of 5 per cent. Most of the major cities and towns now possess electronic switching systems. By 1997, the government plans to triple local switching capacity by installing 11 million additional lines.

The accent on telecommunications has meant that franchises offering fax and long-distance telephone services are now available even in second-class towns.

The private sector, both domestic and foreign, is now being encouraged to manufacture telecommunication equipment. Investments are especially being encouraged in certain value-added services like cellular phones, voice mail, electronic mail and radio paging.

India possesses the largest postal network in the world with nearly 150,000 post offices. Both domestic and international rates are extremely competitive. Besides the government-run postal department, several private courier services function in the country, including a number with international affiliations.

Accompanying the telecommunication revolution has been a television bonanza. A concerted programme in the 1980s of setting up transmission facilities in even the remotest parts of the country has resulted in almost the entire population having access to terrestrial television broadcasts. While both domestic television and radio are owned by the government, much of their software is produced by a vibrant private entertainment industry. The advent of satellite television has resulted in the easy availability of foreign networks, like CNN, the BBC and Star, besides forcing the domestic network to improve and expand the content of its own programmes in the face of competition.

Radio, though not as high-profile as television, remains the main entertainment and news-receiving medium of the common person. The recent introduction of FM channels in Mumbai and New Delhi — owned by the government but run by private agencies — has heralded an exciting new culture which could see a renewed interest in this medium.

Finance and Banking

India's financial sector is marked by its increasing sophistication, extensive banking network and well-developed money and capital markets. The central banking institution and supervisory body is the Reserve Bank of India (RBI), which is the banker to the central and state governments, and is responsible for managing the public debt.

There are 275 commercial banks operating, of which 224 are in the public sector. The 51 private banks include 24 foreign ones with a total of 140 branches. Besides, there are a number of specialized financial institutions catering to industry and trade. The insurance market is well developed with six government-owned corporations currently in the fray. There is talk of opening the market to foreign insurance companies.

India's large capital market — considered among the largest and most dynamic of emerging national markets — is supervised by an autonomous body, the Securities and Exchange Board of India (SEBI). A feature of the market is the presence of professionally managed mutual funds, leasing companies, investment banks and other financial intermediaries. The total market capitalization of Rs2,400 billion in December 1992, places India ahead of other emerging markets, like Brazil and Thailand. Of the 22 stock exchanges, Mumbai is the biggest (it is also the oldest in Asia) with 4,000 stocks listed. It accounts for over two-thirds of the turnover and its average daily total of 70,000 deals gives it one of the highest hourly trading intensity rates in the world. The other important stock exchanges are at Delhi, Calcutta, Chennai, Bangalore and Ahmedabad.

The seminal event in India's banking history was the nationalization of fourteen major banks in 1969. This brought about a sea-change in the nature of commercial banking in India, the most significant feature of which was the rapid expansion of the banking network into the rural and semi-urban areas. As a result, the number of branches has jumped from 8,187 in 1969 to 60,906 in 1992, while the corresponding increase in deposits has been from Rs47 billion in 1969 to Rs2,400 billion in 1992. The State Bank of India, with 8,627 branches, is the largest bank in the world in terms of branch network.

Nationalization, however, also had its drawbacks. Indifferent customer service apart, the identification of a number of priority areas eligible for funds at concessional rates led to a highly complex lending rate structure. This, coupled with other factors, resulted in unsatisfactory financial performance by the banks. An expert committee appointed by the government in mid-1991 to examine these ills has made far-reaching recommendations, some of which have already been implemented. The new liberalization regime is expected to inject fresh dynamism into the banking sector.

Reform has already taken place in the capital market, with Indian companies now allowed to raise equity capital in the international market through Global Depository Receipts, and the domestic stock markets being opened to direct participation by Foreign Institutional Investors (FIIs).

Foreign Trade

Foreign trade stood at roughly 15 per cent of Gross Domestic Product (GDP) in 1990-91, with exports at 6.3 per cent of GDP and imports at nine per cent of GDP. The value of India's exports in 1990-91 was US$18.5 billion compared with US$8.5 billion in 1980-81; for imports, the two figures with US$21.2 billion and US$15.9 billion, respectively. However, while India's volume of trade has grown substantially, it has not expanded in tandem with global trade during the last 20 years. Indeed, India accounts for less than one per cent of world trade.

India's exports have diversified considerably over the years, with manufactured products constituting nearly 72 per cent of exports in 1990-91 as against 56 per cent 10 years earlier. The growth of exports through this decade was sustained largely by chemical products, leather manufactures, engineering goods, gems and jewellery, textiles, iron ore, marine products, transport equipment, tea and garments.

Imports have largely been capital goods, petroleum and its products, edible oils, fertilisers and industrial intermediates. The earlier protective import policy meant a very low influx of consumer goods, while food imports declined two decades ago when India attained self-sufficiency in agricultural products.

India's major trading partners are the United States, the former Soviet republics, the European Community (EC), especially the United Kingdom and Germany, Japan and the Organization of Petroleum Exporting Countries (OPEC).

India has a positive balance in invisibles on current account, though it is tending towards decline because of the pressure of servicing external debt. The major sources of earnings on invisible accounts are tourism (Rs23.9 billion in 1989-90), transportation (Rs15.1 billion in 1989-90) and private inward remittances (Rs38.2 billion in 1989-90). The major sources of outflows are transportation (Rs18.6 billion in 1989-90) and payments of royalties, dividends and interest (Rs55.6 billion in 1989-90).

Unfortunately, India's foreign trade trends have been disquieting. Its negligible presence in the global market-place apart, India has continually experienced unsatisfactory import-export value/volume indices, unfavourable terms of trade and large deficits. While certain indigenous factors are to blame, India, like most developing countries, has suffered in an unequal market where it has had to pay more for its imports and receive less for its exports.

Yet, certain features reflect progress. For instance, well over 300 items that figured on the import list at Independence have disappeared from it as the country became self-sufficient in them. These include food, certain household goods and some key industrial and chemical products. Similarly, the dramatic change in the composition of the very diverse exports list, where engineering goods and consumer durables have a prominent place, testify to India's growing industrial clout and its ability to respond to international requirements.

India's trade policy has been characterized traditionally by strict restrictions on imports in order to protect and develop domestic industry. Another motivation was to conserve foreign exchange which was always scarce. To a certain extent, the policy was successful, as India, while failing to make the dramatic progress of the East

Asian countries, did succeed in establishing a strong industrial base and achieving a measure of self-reliance while other former colonies were, and still are, struggling. But towards the end, this policy began to backfire as Indian industry was denied access to the latest technology and began producing inferior goods.

Currently however, many exciting things are happening on the trade front, thanks to the sweeping changes ushered in by the liberalization policy of 1991. Intended to hasten India's integration into the global economy and reverse the trend of its shrinking share in world trade, the changes have been essentially prompted by the structural balance of payments deficit.

Another simultaneous change taking place is the direction and manner in which India trades. Until recently, the bulk of trade was conducted with the former Socialist Bloc countries through bilateral trade agreements designated in rupees. Now trade with almost all countries is conducted through convertible currencies.

Import Control

Some of the key elements of the changed trade environment are:

The Export-Import Policy (EXIM) will remain stable for 5 years (till 1997), with any emergency or unavoidable changes being made, as far as possible, only once every quarter.

Procedures for export and import have been simplified and made transparent. (These are contained in the *Handbook of Procedures* 1992-97).

Goods can be imported freely, except for those on a short Negative List. Capital goods are no longer on this list, and second-hand capital goods can be brought in subject to certain conditions. The condition of 'actual user' on import of industrial inputs has been removed.

Tariffs have been greatly reduced, ranging from zero to 85 per cent. The maximum import duty on raw materials and components is now 85 per cent. Further reductions are on the anvil. Export of goods is also now free, barring a few items, on the Negative List. Essentially, it is a ban on certain commodities, ceilings on exports of some items required domestically and canalization of certain others.

Foreign equity up to 51 per cent in trading companies and priority industries receives automatic approval. Higher equity participation up to 100 per cent is also permitted. In Export-Oriented Units (EOUs) and Export Processing Zones (EPZs), 100 per cent foreign equity is freely allowed.

EOUs and EPZ units are offered incentives that include a developed infrastructure, a five-year tax holiday, duty-free access to imports, and tax-exemption to income generated through exports.

On 1 March 1993, the trade environment received a further fillip when a single market-determined exchange rate for the rupee was introduced. All export and import transactions are now conducted at the market exchange rate. This rate also applies to other transactions such as inflow of foreign equity for investment and outflow in the event of disinvestment, repatriation of dividends, lump-sum fees, royalties for technical know-how agreements, and for foreign travel.

Foreign investors looking for a strategically located distribution centre in Asia will find India an ideal location for both export and re-export, given its geographical positioning between the Middle East and South-East Asia and its proximity to the new markets of central Asia.

The government is laying special emphasis on EOUs and EPZs. EOUs can be set up anywhere, while there are seven designated EPZs — Kandla (Gujarat), Mumbai (Maharashtra), Chennai (Tamil Nadu), Falta (West Bengal), Kochi (Kerala), Noida (near New Delhi) and Visakhapatnam (Andhra Pradesh). EOUs and EPZ units receive a number of incentives and are even allowed to sell a certain percentage of their output (determined by the proportion of indigenous inputs and the nature of industry) in the domestic tariff area.

Special incentives for EOUs and EPZ units apart, the general incentives to encourage exports include an exemption from income tax proportional to export turnover against total turnover, permission to import capital goods at concessional rates of duty in exchange for a certain export or a foreign exchange-earning obligation, and higher royalty payments on export sales as against domestic sales. Besides, EOUs, EPZ units and other units generating net foreign exchange earnings are allowed to raise, subject to certain conditions, foreign currency loans for capital goods, raw materials, components, technology payments and even to finance local rupee costs of the project.

On the import side, most restrictions have been removed except for certain banned, restricted or canalized items that are enumerated on the Negative List. The tariff system is based on the Customs Cooperation Council (Brussels) Nomenclature. With some exceptions, most tariffs are *ad valorem*. The general philosophy is to charge higher duties on components and parts that can be made in India as well as on consumer goods.

In order to bring down the cost of imported industrial inputs as well as to bring tariffs in line with those prevailing elsewhere, import duties have been significantly lowered in three successive years. The annual budget for 1991-92 reduced the maximum rate on industrial inputs to 150 per cent; the next year this was brought down to 110 per cent; now it is 85 per cent. The duty on project imports and general machinery similarly fell from 80 per cent to 55 per cent and finally to 35 per cent for the same period. The import tariff on capital goods is now generally in the 20-40 per cent range. The government has accepted proposals of a tax reforms committee which has suggested that, by 1997-98, *ad valorem* import duty rates on industrial inputs should range from five to 30 per cent, while the duty on non-essential consumer goods should not be more than 50 per cent.

All these steps represent an essential philosophical shift from import-substitution to export-orientation, setting the stage for India's integration into the global economy. Currently a cipher in world trade, India can ride these changes to become a significant player by matching its inherent advantages of abundant human and natural resources with easy access to modern technology and capital goods.

Foreign Investment

The new industrial policy announced in July 1991, and other related policy changes have opened up the economy to foreign investment and allowed for a much greater role by the private sector. The private sector can now operate in all areas except in such strategic concerns as defence and atomic energy, while an industrial licence is now required in only 15 manufacturing industries. Proposals involving foreign equity up to 51 per cent in high priority areas receive automatic approval from the Reserve Bank of India (RBI) within two weeks.

Incentives

Other policy changes of interest are the removal of the requirement for foreign equity to be accompanied by foreign technology; permission for the use of foreign trademarks and brand names in India; removal of the requirement for dividend balancing against export earnings, except in the case of a specified list of consumer goods; and permission for foreign companies to open branches in the country. Foreign investors have also been given the option of acquiring companies already existing in India. In April 1992, India became a signatory to the Multilateral Investment Guarantee Agency, which provides additional security to foreign investors against non-commercial risks.

All proposals involving foreign investment and technology require approval. On the basis of certain criteria, the approval may be automatically given by the RBI; or it will be considered either by the Foreign Investment Promotion Board (FIPB) or the Secretariat for Industrial Approvals (SIA).

Automatic approval is given when there is up to 51 per cent foreign equity in (a) high priority industries, provided the foreign equity

covers the foreign exchange requirement for the import of capital goods and the capital goods are not second-hand, and (b) trading companies engaged primarily in exports; when there is up to 100 per cent foreign equity in EOU and EPZ units; for all foreign technology agreements involving a lump sum payment of up to 10 million rupees and royalty up to five per cent on domestic sales and eight per cent on exports; to those companies already operating in India that wish to increase their equity holdings from existing levels to 51 per cent.

Applications for automatic approval must be submitted on the prescribed form to the Controller, Exchange Control Department of the Reserve Bank of India, Mumbai.

All proposals other than those qualifying for automatic approval have to be submitted on a prescribed form to the Joint Secretary of the Secretariat for Industrial Approvals in the Department of Industrial Development, Udyog Bhavan, New Delhi, or to the Secretary, Foreign Investment Promotion Board, the Prime Minister's Office, South Block, New Delhi. The latter is a specially empowered board set up to provide quick clearance to proposals that do not fall within the usual policy parameters.

Whether or not one is eligible for automatic approval, applications for EOU and EPZ units, must be submitted to SIA/FIPB for EOUs and to the Development Commissioner of the concerned EPZ for EPZ units.

In addition to the incentives provided by the Central Government (such as an income tax deduction for the first 10 years of operation), most state governments provide their own incentives. These include capital investment subsidies, sales tax exemptions and deferments, and electricity duty and power concessions.

Getting started

Foreign investors can establish a business presence in India by setting up joint venture companies (in collaboration with an Indian partner and/or the general Indian public), wholly-owned companies, liaison or project offices or branches, or by acquiring an existing Indian company.

Formation and operation of companies in India is governed by the Companies Act, 1956. Foreign investors may incorporate either a private or a public company. The main differences between the two relate to the provisions of the Companies Act that are not applicable to private companies. These include provisions concerning raising share capital and restricting the powers of the board of directors.

The first step in the formation of a company is approval of the name by the Registrar of Companies in the state or union territory where the company proposes to have its registered office. There should not be an existing company with the same name, and the last words in the name must be 'Private Limited' in the case of a private company, and 'Limited' in the case of a public company.

Next is the process of incorporation, for which certain documents are to be submitted to the Registrar, the most important of which are the articles and memorandum of association.

The memorandum specifies the objects and scope of activity of the company, while the articles lay down the rules by which the company will achieve them. A public company has the option of not filing the articles, but, in that case, a model contained in the Companies Act will automatically apply. These documents are to be presented with a registration fee, which is proportional to the share capital as stated in the memorandum.

A private company can commence business immediately on receiving the certificate of incorporation, but a public company has the option of inviting the public to subscribe to its share capital. This involves issuing a prospectus that contains information of relevance about itself to potential investors (the Companies Act specifies the kind of information required to be furnished). The prospectus has to be filed with the registrar before being issued to the public. If the company does not wish to approach the public for capital, it must file a 'statement in lieu of prospectus'. Once these requirements are met, the registrar will issue a certificate of commencement of business.

Certain other procedures must be completed before operations can begin. These can be initiated simultaneously or subsequently. These are, at the federal level, registration with Central Excise and approval by the Factories Inspector and the Inspector of Boilers. At the state level, certain municipal and environmental clearances and registration with the Sales Tax Commissioner and Provident Fund Commissioner are necessary.

Foreign nationals are free to travel to India for business and employment. Multiple entry business visas are granted for up to five years and can be renewed thereafter.

Taxation

An industrial unit has to pay taxes at both the federal and state levels. Central taxes include personal income tax (agricultural income is exempt), corporate tax, excise and customs duties. The major state tax is the sales tax. The tax rates may vary from year to year and are announced in the Finance Act passed annually by Parliament. However, of late, there has been an attempt to keep the tax rates stable, at least in the medium term.

A major component of the current liberalization programme is tax reform. The tax laws are being overhauled in order to simplify procedures and to lower and eliminate multiplicity of rates. Thus, vital changes were initiated in personal taxation in 1992, and in the customs and excise regime in 1993. It is widely expected that in 1994 the corporate taxation structure will be thoroughly revised.

The taxable income of corporate bodies is computed as profits or gains from business, capital gains and income from other sources, such as interest and dividends. Resident companies are taxed on their domestic and foreign incomes, while non-resident companies are taxed only on their Indian incomes.

The average taxation rates for a foreign company range from 25 per cent (on dividends and interest on loans) to 65 per cent (miscellaneous income). For widely-held Indian companies, the rate (including a surcharge of 15 per cent on income tax) is 51.75 per cent, while that for closely-held companies goes up to 57.5 per cent.

Tax Treaties

India has comprehensive agreements on avoidance of double taxation with 40 countries, including Australia, Belgium, Germany, France, Great Britain, Greece, Italy, Japan, South Korea, Norway, Sweden, the United Arab Emirates and the United States. The provisions of these treaties override domestic tax laws. The Income Tax Act also provides for the granting of unilateral relief in India in respect of income taxed both in India and in a country with which India has no tax treaty. Relief is allowed at the Indian tax rate or that of the other country, whichever is lower.

Assessing Taxable Income

All expenditure incurred for business purposes is deductible while computing taxable income. This includes interest on borrowing paid during the financial year and depreciation on fixed assets. However, some expenses are disallowed, or their quantum of deduction restricted, such as entertainment expenses, interest, royalties, technical service fees, commissions or any other amounts paid to non-residents without deduction of applicable taxes and provision for expenses not actually incurred.

Depreciation is normally calculated on the declining balance method at varying rates and is available for a full year. However, it is allowed at half the normal rate if the asset is used for less than 180 days in that year. No depreciation is available in the year an asset is sold. Depreciation is not allowed on plant and machinery if the actual cost is being allowed as a deduction under a specific agreement.

In the absence of adequate profits, unabsorbed depreciation can be carried forward without any time limit. Unabsorbed losses can be carried forward and set off against future profits up to a limit of eight years. The wide range of tax concessions include deduction of preoperative expenses incurred in setting up a project, complete tax exemption on profits from exports, full or part exemptions on foreign exchange earnings, five-year tax holidays within the first eight years of operations of EOU and EPZ units, similar tax holidays for power projects and industries set up in certain specified backward states, exemption on income from export of computer technical services and software and so on. Some special concessions are further earmarked for foreign companies working in certain areas.

Foreign individuals are also allowed certain concessions in computing personal income tax and are exempt from wealth tax.

Capital gains taxes, which have been substantially lowered in recent times, are fixed, in the case of long-term capital gains (defined as transfer of an asset held for over three years or one year in the case of equity shares), at 40 per cent for companies, 20 per cent for individuals and 10 per cent for Foreign Institutional Investors (FFIs). In the case of short-term capital gains, companies and individuals pay normal income tax, while FIIs are taxed at the rate of 30 per cent. Expenses incurred in transferring the asset are deductible, while the capital gains of non-residents are computed in the original currency of acquisition. Capital losses can be carried forward for eight years and can be set off only against capital gains.

The financial year is from 1 April to 31 March. Companies are required to pay advance tax in three instalments by 15 September, 15 December and 15 March for the year ending 31 March, and to file tax returns by the following 31 December. Individuals are required to file their returns by the 30 June following the close of the financial year.

The Market

No story about India's economy and business environment can be complete without a word about its market. Despite the low per capita income, there is a large class of consumers (estimated at between 100 and 300 million, depending on the product) for packaged consumer goods, branded ready-made clothing and accessories, home appliances, entertainment electronics, personal transport, radio, television, telecommunication and transport services.

Indeed, one of the most striking features of the Indian economy is the sheer size of the consumer market. Private consumption expenditure was Rs3,418 billion in 1990-91 (at current prices). Nearly 55 per cent (about Rs1,900 billion) was spent on food and beverages. The rest went to clothing and footwear (Rs340 billion), rent, fuel and power (Rs370 billion), transport and communication (Rs360 billion, the bulk of this to purchase of personal transport), furniture, furnishings and household appliances (Rs105 billion), recreation, education and cultural services (Rs113 billion), and other consumer goods and services (Rs230 billion).

Aggregate expenditure grew at an annual rate of 13 per cent in the 1980s, with the highest growth of 21 per cent a year being recorded in the transport and communication sector. Expenditure on household appliances, consumer goods and services rose by 14 per cent a year, indicating a clear shift away from primary products towards manufactured goods and services. The evolution of the consumer market was evident even within the food sector as the share of milk, fruit and vegetables increased while that of cereals declined.

Between 1980-81 and 1990-91, the production and sale of two-wheelers and passenger cars, domestic refrigerators, air-conditioners increased four times. The consumption of mass consumer products, man-made fabric, detergents, toothpaste, shaving blades, and suchlike, saw annual increases of 10 to 15 per cent.

The spectacular growth of the consumer market in the last decade is indicative of a significant rise in income levels and change in lifestyle of large segments of the population. The rural areas, for example, which are home to 75 per cent of the population, are buoyed by rising, untaxed incomes and account for 70 per cent of the sales of portable radio receivers, mechanical wrist watches and bicycles, and between 40 and 60 per cent of the sales of motorcycles, quartz wrist watches, electric irons, soaps and packaged tea.

The apparent contradiction between the low per capita income level (US$350) and the consumer boom is explained by the relatively greater domestic purchasing power of incomes.

A 1992 International Monetary Fund (IMF) study, using the more accurate statistical device of purchasing power parity, put the real worth of the Indian per capita income at US$1,150. Added to this is the comparatively lower price (because of lower local costs) of items like food, clothing, mass consumer goods and services.

The consumer boom has been attributed to the sustained economic growth of 5.5 per cent through the 1980s, a sharp increase in farm incomes (these are not taxed), an increase in urban population, an increase in the number of white-collar workers, professionals and businessmen, the emergence of multiple income households in urban areas, awareness created by the accompanying media boom, increasing literacy levels and the advent of a consumer finance business for durables. The consumer class is anticipated to be 600 million-strong by the turn of the century.

PART FIVE: FACTS AT YOUR FINGERTIPS

Visa and immigration requirements

It is necessary to have a full, not temporary or visitor's, passport for India. Visitors should keep enough pages spare to take the visa, immigration and any liquor permit stamps issued in non-alcoholic Indian states. Do not forget to update your passport well before your holiday.

All foreign nationals require a visa to enter India. Applications should be made to any Indian Consular Office or High Commission abroad. The standard tourist visa is valid for 180 days and the holder is entitled to multiple entries into India within that period. An extension can be obtained from various Foreigners' Registration Offices in India.

Health requirements

As a precaution, and for practical purposes, it is a good idea to be thoroughly examined by a doctor and a dentist before leaving for India. A wide range of inoculations is recommended for personal protection, though a vaccination certificate may not be required as documentary proof. Visitors from Africa and South America must have an International Health Certificate with a valid yellow fever inoculation record (valid for 10 years). Most important, one should remember that immunity becomes effective only 10 days after a vaccination.

Cholera usually occurs in epidemics, so protection against it is recommended for India. A jab is good for six months. Another useful vaccination is TABT, which provides protection against typhoid, paratyphoid (A and B) and tetanus — all prevalent in hot climates. Typhoid and paratyphoid are diseases caused by insanitation, spread by contaminated food. Tetanus is usually caused by an infected cut or wound.

Visitors should consider taking a vaccination against infectious hepatitis, which is spread by contaminated water or food. The vaccine, gamma globulin, should be taken close to departure as it remains effective for a few weeks only.

Vaccination against malaria is not possible, but precautions against it is a must. Malaria is spread by mosquitoes and India sans mosquitoes is unimaginable. Protection is provided by a daily or weekly tablet, depending on what the doctor recommends. Malaria or no malaria, mosquito bites by themselves can be very annoying. Mosquito repellants are widely available in the country in the form of mats, coils and creams.

It is not unusual for visitors to India, on their arrival, to encounter the all too common 'Delhi Belly'. A mere stomach upset, it is often due to a change of diet, a body system unused to spicy food, exhaustion or climate, less often the result of contaminated food or water.

The primary precaution is to avoid getting an upset stomach in the first place. Watch what you eat and drink. Do not rush into sampling the local cuisine, and wait until your body is given a chance to acclimatize. Try to eat only freshly cooked food. Avoid salads and always peel fruit before eating them. Never eat fruit cut open for display. Most pharmacists stock potassium permanganate ($KMnO_4$) crystals — often called 'pinkie' locally — and a pinch in a bowl of water should adequately sterilize fruit left soaking in it for about half an hour. Drink water that has been boiled and filtered, never directly from faucets. When in doubt, use water purification tablets or stick to soda, mineral water or aerated drinks of standard brands. In smaller towns, avoid factory ice as it is often made with unsterilized water. Ice cubes are safe in big hotels and large restaurants, which now sterilize water by ultra-violet radiation.

If avoidance fails and you do get 'Delhi Belly', don't panic! Try to build up immunity by not taking antibiotics. Stick to hot tea, curds and rice, and try not to eat too much.

Here are some additional precautions you have to take to ensure good health in the hot weather. Protect yourself from the sun as much as you can. Due to the dust haze and pollution in big cities, you will not get easily sunburnt, but do not take any chances. In the hills, of course, sunburn is quite possible, so bring some suntan lotion and sunscreen along, as they are not easily available. Keep your liquid intake up to avoid dehydration. Widely available rehydration powder (electral) containing salts and dextrose can be added to water or fruit juice during the summer months or, if one is suffering from diarrhoea, to replace lost fluid and electrolytes.

It is wise to carry a personal medical kit. Anti-diarrhoeal tablets, aspirin and medication for throat infections and allergies should be included. Band-aids, an antiseptic cream, insect repellent, water purification tablets and a small clinical thermometer can be very useful. Take extra care if you are travelling with children.

Most important of all, do not make health your primary concern. Most people survive India with very few problems.

Medical facilities

Modern hospitals and private clinics provide a variety of specialist facilities. In an accident, only a government hospital can provide assistance.

Ambulance services are (usually) not very reliable. Large hotels have doctors on call.

International flights
India is well served by international flights from all around the world to international airports at New Delhi, Mumbai, Calcutta and Chennai. The flying time to New Delhi's Indira Gandhi International Airport from New York is almost 16 hours; from Hong Kong five hours; from London eight hours; from Tokyo 10 hours and from Dubai almost three hours.

Airports
Including the four international airports, the Airports Authority of India manages and maintains 88 airports all over the country. The domestic network is well served by the government-owned Indian Airlines as well as a number of privately-run airlines. All state capitals have quite well maintained airports.

Departure tax
An airport tax of Rs300 has to be paid by all departing visitors.

Customs
Visitors are allowed the usual duty-free bottle of whisky (0.95 litre) and 200 cigarettes into India. Gadgets such as radios, cameras, walkmans, calculators and binoculars are permitted, but some people are required by the Customs Department to register them on a 'Tourist Baggage Re-export' Form (TBRE). This ensures that they are taken back with the traveller.

Currency
The official currency of India is the rupee (Rs). The rupee is divided into paise (p) with 100 paise to a rupee. Denominations of Rs500, Rs100, Rs50, Rs20, Rs10, Rs5, Rs2 and Re1, in addition to 50p, 25p, 20p and 10p are circulated. However, Rs5, Rs2 and Re1 are available as both notes and coins.

Currency regulations
Visitors are not allowed to bring Indian currency into the country or to take any out. They can bring in any amount of foreign currency in cash or travellers cheques but will have to declare anything over US$1,000 on arrival. They will have to fill in a currency declaration form, a useless, yet necessary, activity.

Visitors should buy currency in India from banks or official money-changers. They may be approached by unofficial money-changers as there is a black market for foreign currency, which is best avoided. Most foreign currencies or travellers cheques can be changed in the major cities. When changing money, it is advisable to keep the encashment receipts carefully. These are required when one leaves the country. Visitors staying in India for more than 180 days will have to obtain an Income Tax Clearance,

for which encashment certificates are required. The Foreign Section of the Income Tax Offices in Delhi, Mumbai, Calcutta and Chennai issue these certificates on production of your passport, visa, airline ticket and encashment certificates. Credit cards are now widely accepted in India, particularly Diners Club, American Express and Visa Cards.

Banking
The State Bank of India is the central bank. Other nationalized Indian banks include Punjab National Bank, Bank of India, United Bank of India and other cooperative banks. Foreign banks include Grindlays, American Express and the Banque Nationale de Paris.

Business hours for most nationalized Indian banks and foreign banks are from 1000 to 1400 Monday through Friday, and from 1000 to 1200 on Saturday. Some do business from 0900 to 1300, while others operate evening branches. A few banks remain open on Sundays and take a compensatory day off during the week.

Outward remittance goes through the Reserve Bank of India. It is a difficult and lengthy process, best avoided. It is advisable to remit additional money through a draft or mail transfer and to keep all receipts carefully.

Business hours
Central government offices and most private businesses follow a five-day week, Monday through Friday, from 0930 to 1730. Some state government offices are open on Saturdays, except the second Saturday of the month. Central and state government and private offices are closed on Sundays.

Shops are usually open from 1000 to 1900. Some take an hour's lunch-break, but this could be longer in small cities. Though Sunday is the official holiday, shopping centres in different localities of major cities take different days of the week off, so that some shopping areas are always open. Most restaurants are open up to 2300, with some nightclubs and discothèques closing much later. Hotel coffee shops are often open round the clock.

Post offices are open from 1000 to 1600, Monday to Saturday. In most major cities, at least one branch, usually the General Post Office (GPO), is open 24 hours. Major telegraph offices are also open t24 hours. Most airline offices are open six days a week, from 0930 to 1730. The four major international airports in New Delhi, Mumbai, Calcutta and Chennai are open 24 hours.

Time zones
Despite its enormous size and difference in weather, India has a single time zone applicable throughout the country. Indian Standard Time is five-and-a-half hours ahead of Greenwich Mean Time (GMT) and nine-and-a-half hours ahead of the US East Zone Standard Time.

Language
The national language of India is Hindi, though it is spoken by less than 25 per cent of the total population. Even after 48 years of independence from British rule, English is still the official language, spoken and understood by most. Moreover, a great number of local languages are in use. Each state, more or less, has a language of its own. Major regional languages include Marathi, Malayalam, Punjabi, Urdu, Tamil, Bangla and Assamese. Further, there is a wide variety of dialects and sub-dialects. Hindi is widely spoken and understood except, perhaps, in the peninsula.

Religion
India is a secular state. The majority are Hindus. The other faiths are Muslims, Christians, Jains, Buddhists, Sikhs and Parsis.

Government
The Union of India consists of 26 states and six union territories. After Independence, India decided to adopt the British model of parliamentary democracy. Yet the Indian Constitution is not really a carbon copy of it. The Central (Federal) Government is headed by a prime minister and a council of ministers (Cabinet). Both are jointly responsible to the two houses of Parliament — the Lok Sabha and the Rajya Sabha. The Lok Sabha is the 'Council of the People', directly elected by the people on the basis of adult franchise. The Rajya Sabha, the 'Council of the State', on the other hand, is an indirectly elected body which functions somewhat like the British House of Lords.

Each state and some union territories have their own Legislative Assembly and Government, headed by a chief minister. The president and vice-president are elected by the members of the State Legislature. The Indian president is a figurehead; the prime minister wields the real power.

The division of power and responsibilities between the state and centre is clearly defined in the Constitution. Each state has its own legislature and is responsible for a number of administrative functions, such as health, education, forests and surface transport (except railways).

Elections are normally held every five years but could, in certain situations, be called earlier. India has had nine general elections since it became an independent country in 1947. The country now has a well developed, democratic, political and administrative structure, a large, skilled labour force, and an adequate communication network. Despite the agrarian bias of its economy, industry has grown enormously, placing India among the top 15 industrial nations of the world.

Tipping
Expressing one's appreciation with a small tip is expected every now and then. This could range from two to 10 rupees, depending on the type of establishment and the kind of services rendered. In restaurants, the tip is customarily 10 to 15 per cent of the bill. Leading hotels add a 10 per cent service surcharge and tipping in such places is, therefore, optional. Although tipping taxis and three-wheelers is not an established norm, it is not an unestablished one either. Ten per cent of the fare or leaving the change, if substantial, would be adequate. Better still, acquire a printed fare chart and round the figure off to the nearest rupee.

Communications
Post offices provide a most reliable and efficient service. They are open from 1000 to 1700 on weekdays and on Saturday mornings. The postage rates are relatively cheap compared with elsewhere. Stamps should be franked to avoid theft. Most post offices oblige on request. The postal 'Speed Post' service links over 60 towns in India and abroad. It is quick and very reasonably priced.

India is well served by international courier services and your hotel may be a collection centre. As always, the more advertised, the more reliable. Check beforehand what custom forms have to be processed, if any.

Postes Restantes (General Delivery Offices) are usually located in main (general) post offices (GPOs), with a few exceptions. There are two postes restantes in Delhi, one of which is located on Baba Kharak Singh Marg, near Connaught Place, and the other between Kashmiri Gate and New Delhi Railway Station.

The service is good, but one has to produce some documentary evidence (passport, for example) to prove one's identity before one's mail can be collected. Recording mistakes are common, so check for your name under the initial of the surname and first name as well.

To get mail redirected to some other poste restante, a form should be filled in at the original office (the address left behind at home) and letters will be received at the new destination.

To send parcels home, pop into the nearest post office and send your stuff by registered parcel. Parcels have to be cloth-wrapped and sealed with sealing wax to the satisfaction of the postal department, so half a day has to be set aside to dispatch a parcel.

Telecommunications have so improved that there is no trouble making long-distance calls within India or overseas from almost anywhere.

Visitors should look out for computerized display telephone booths (always manned) marked 'STD/ISD' (Subscriber/International Trunk Dialling) for long-distance calls. The price display allows one to chat for as long as one's budget permits. Avoid making calls from large hotels as the mark-up is tremendous. There are fax facilities also available.

Otherwise, one has to make a long-distance call through the operator. A direct call takes time, and a PP (particular-person) call can tax one's patience. To avoid the invariable time lag, opt for a demand call, which is quick but expensive, or a lightning call, which is very expensive but very fast.

Coin-operated local public call phones are common only in the big cities. If there is no dial tone, dial anyhow, as things might just fall into place. Or else a few sharp raps to the box will set matters back on line.

Telex services are available in most big hotels but could be expensive compared with post office rates.

India now has a fairly sophisticated national and international communications network, including satellite receiving and transmitting ground stations.

Media
There are a number of English-language dailies, like *The Times of India, The Indian Express, The Statesman, The Hindu, The Pioneer,* and *The Hindustan Times,* besides a few weekly news magazines, like *The Sunday Observer* and *The Sunday Mail,* which make for good reading on train or bus journeys. Fortnightly news magazines, like *India Today,* are rich in political reports and analyses. If you are looking for immediate 'spot' world news, then buy a copy of *Time* or *Newsweek,* available in nearly all the major cities. There are a number of magazines in English with matters of interest for everyone.

Driving
Drivers require a valid national or international driving licence. Driving is on the left of the road as in the United Kingdom.

Car hire
Car hire is a relatively new concept. Facilities are available in nearly all the major international airports and big hotels. Hertz and Budget offer cars with or without drivers. Black and yellow-topped cabs or taxis operate by the meter, with a surcharge on the meter-reading in some cities and towns. The percentage mark-up varies. Avoid getting cheated: opt for pre-paid services, as far as possible, from airports and railway stations. Three wheelers are also supposed to charge according to the meter reading, but an additional sum is often indicated on the card. If the driver refuses to take a visitor to a particular place or demands a flat rate, it is advisable to take help from the nearest police officer.

Liquor
Alcoholic drinks in public places are quite expensive, hence it is a wise decision to buy one's own bottle and drink in the privacy of one's hotel room. Indian-Made Foreign Liquor (IMFL) includes all the types familiar to the non-teetotaller. Beer is widely available, both bottled and draught. Indian rum is of a high standard, and vodka, wine, brandy and gin are of good quality in most cases. Indians are avid whisky drinkers, though the quality is not very good. Country brew, like coconut-extract *toddy* and cashew-nut *feni* can be mind-blowing; a taste for them has to be cultivated and they can grow on you like a fungus.

Energy
Electric mains supply 220 to 240 volts on the AC system. Gadgets must have a standard three-point or two-point plug. Power failures and 'load shedding' to conserve electricity are uncomfortably regular.

In Brief

National Parks and Bird Sanctuaries

Throughout the Indian subcontinent numerous parks and sanctuaries have been established to protect the richness and variety of its wildlife. A visit to one or more of these wildlife refuges is a must on any traveller's itinerary.

Some parks offer modern guest-houses with electricity, while in others, only dak bungalows (rest houses) are available. Facilities usually include van and jeep rides. Elephant rides or boat trips allow enthusiasts to approach wildlife more discreetly. Watch towers and hides are frequently available, and provide good opportunities to observe and photograph wildlife at close range. National parks and other protected areas in India are administered at the state level and often promoted as part of each state's tourist attractions. Below are some of the numerous national parks and wildlife sanctuaries and reserves in the country.

Bandhavagarh Sanctuary (Madhya Pradesh)
North-west of the Kanha National Park is the Bandhavagarh Sanctuary, which lies below the historic fort of the same name. The park has the densest tiger population in India. Elephant rides into the forest are an added attraction.

Bandipur National Park (Karnataka)
The Bandipur National Park in the Nilgiri foothills, lies 80 kilometres (50 miles) south on the Mysore-Ooty road. Amid Bandipur's lush 400 square kilometres (154 square miles) of bamboo, teak and rosewood jungle live many elephants, leopards, Indian bison, spotted deer, macaques, and a great variety of birdlife.

Bannerghatta National Park (Karnataka)
The Bannerghatta National Park, 16 kilometres (10 miles) from Bangalore, is a lion safari park, covering 104 square kilometres (40 square miles). It also has a crocodile and snake farm.

Bhitarkanika Sanctuary (Orissa)
The Bhitarkanika Sanctuary on the mouth of the Mahanadi River has salt-water crocodiles and water-monitor lizards. A white crocodile at Dangamala is the second of its kind in the world, the first is at the Thailand Crocodile Research Corridor. The Gahirmatha, 130 kilometres from Bhubaneswar is a breeding ground for Pacific Ridley turtles. More than seven million turtles swim from South America to reach this coast, where they lay over 60 million eggs.

Borivili National Park (Maharashtra)
The Borivili National Park, about 35 kilometres (22 miles) north of south Mumbai, is the only remaining natural forest in the region. A morning hike through the nature trails is invigorating for many city dwellers. It is also India's only national park within a city. The Kanheri Caves are in this park and boast a collection of 109 rock-cut Buddhist temples dating from 200 BC to AD 600.

Corbett National Park (Uttar Pradesh)
The Corbett National Park is a seven-hour drive north-east of Delhi. Apart from an occasional glimpse of a tiger or the more elusive leopard, the park has resident herds of elephants and prey species. Birdlife is also plentiful. There are forest rest houses and a small 'tourist complex' in the park, which can be booked through the Department of Tourism of Uttar Pradesh in Lucknow or New Delhi (Chandralok Building, Janpath).

Dachigam National Park (Kashmir)
Only 23 kilometres (14 miles) from Srinagar and easily visited with permission from the chief wildlife warden at Srinagar, this park is set in a scenic valley with a large meandering river. It is home to the rare Kashmir stag (hangul) and black and brown bears. June and July are the best months to visit.

Desert National Park (Rajasthan)
Near Jaisalmer, the Desert National Park covers over 3,000 square kilometres (1, 158 square miles) of scrub and dune. Permission to visit must be sought from the Forest Department and District Magistrate's office in Jaisalmer. Well known as home to the chinkara gazelle and rare great Indian bustard.

Dudhwa National Park (Uttar Pradesh)
Dudhwa National Park is one of the 19 Project Tiger reserves. Here the visitor has the best chance to see the animal in the wild. Also seen are the barasinghas.

Gir National Park (Gujarat)
Famous for the last surviving Asian lions (under 200), Gir supports a large variety of other wildlife, notably the chowsinghas. This forested oasis in a desert contains Lake Kamaleshwar, full of crocodiles. The lake and other watering holes are good places to spot animals.

Jaldapara (West Bengal)
Wildlife buffs can drive to Jaldapara, 121 kilometres (75 miles) east of Siliguri in Darjeeling, home to one-horned Great Indian rhino. The

sanctuary stretches for 65 kilometres (40 miles) from the River Malangi in the east to the River Torsa in the west. It has a number of perennial streams and acres of grassland. Stay at the Hollong Forest Lodge within the sanctuary.

Kanha National Park (Madhya Pradesh)
The Kanha National Park, one of the most prestigious wildlife sanctuaries in the world, is designated a Project Tiger conservation park. Kanha is haven to swamp deer, an endangered species and nearly 100 varieties of birds.

Kaziranga National Park (Assam)
The Kaziranga National Park, a grassland with marshy areas, lakes and forests, is home to the Indian rhinoceros.

Keoladeo Ghana National Park (Rajasthan)
This bird sanctuary at Bharatpur, 53 kilometres (33 miles) west of Agra, covers only 29 square kilometres (11 square miles) but is host to a number of species of nesting storks, herons, spoonbills, cormorants and ibises.

Thousands of migratory waterfowl, waders and birds of prey arrive from Siberia, the Russian steppes, central Asia and Tibet to winter in the sanctuary. By far the rarest visitor is the Siberian crane.

Manas National Park (Assam)
This lovely area is formed from the watershed of the Manas, Hakua and Beki rivers and borders on Bhutan. The bungalows at Mothanguri, on the banks of the Manas River, offer views of jungle-clad hills.

Besides tigers, the grassland is home to wild buffalo, elephant, sambar, swamp deer and other wildlife; the rare and beautiful golden langur may be seen on the Bhutan bank.

Mudumalai Wildlife Sanctuary (Tamil Nadu)
The Mudumalai Wildlife Sanctuary has a large number of locally migrant elephants. It is also well known as home to the gaur, or Indian bison, one of the most impressive of wild oxen.

Nagarhole National Park (Karnataka)
The Nagarhole National Park, 94 kilometres (58 miles) south-west of Mysore, lies in the beautiful Kodagu district. The park spans 294 square kilometres (114 square miles) of tropical forest, undulating streams and swampland. It's inhabited by tigers, elephants, leopards, sloth bears, wild boar, several species of crocodile and a rich variety of birdlife.

Namdapha Tiger Reserve (Arunachal Pradesh)
The hoolock, a type of gibbon, is the only ape to be found in India. It is best looked for in the Namdapha Tiger Reserve in Arunachal Pradesh.

Nandankanan Biological Park (Orissa)
The Nandankanan Biological Park, which is located near Bhubaneswar, is worth a visit for its white tiger safari.

Panna National Park (Madhya Pradesh)
The Panna National Park, one of the biggest in India, is spread over 546 square kilometres (211 square miles) near Khajuraho. It is home to tigers, panthers, bears, sambars, spotted deer and langurs. Between November and June the Ken River Lodge, Village Mandla, Panna, can organize jeep, pony and elephant rides, boating, rafting, fishing and nature study walks through the park. Accommodation is in a scenically located lodge.

Periyar Wildlife Sanctuary (Kerala)
Due east of Kottayam is the Periyar Wildlife Sanctuary at Thekkady. A gentle cruise on the Periyar Lake at sunset may provide a visual feast of all manner of game — elephant, spotted deer, wild pig, bison and, perhaps, even a tiger or a leopard. Amazing tropical birds, too.

Point Calimere (Tamil Nadu)
Point Calimere along the Coromandel Coast, is a natural haven for 50,000 migratory flamingos. The marshes and salt lagoons are home to a number of other water-birds.

Ranganathittu Bird Sanctuary (Karnataka)
This sanctuary, 35 kilometres (22 miles) from Srirangapatnam, is the breeding ground for thousands of birds and waterfowl — cormorant, shag, white ibis, egret, open-billed stork, spot-billed duck, kingfisher, river tern and even whistling teal.

Ranthambore National Park (Rajasthan)
On the Delhi-Mumbai railway line, 160 kilometres (99 miles) south of Jaipur, the Ranthambore National Park is the smaller of the Project Tiger reserves. Its smaller size makes viewing animals easier. The lake has crocodiles. The best time to visit is from November to May.

Sariska National Park (Rajasthan)
Situated 107 kilometres (66 miles) from Jaipur and 200 kilometres (124 miles) from Delhi, the Sariska National Park is in a wooded valley surrounded by barren mountains. It is home to blue bulls, sambar, spotted deer, wild boar and, above all, tigers. Sariska is noted for night-viewing of game.

Simlipal National Park (Orissa)
The Simlipal National Park is the largest chunk of forest in Orissa, with a rich tribal culture. Its rich wildlife includes the royal Bengal tiger, leopard, elephant, four-horned antelope and deer. It is under the Project Tiger programme.

Sundarbans (West Bengal)
The marshy Sundarbans are home, besides the tiger, to a variety of boar, big cats, crocodiles,

deer and turtles. Strategically located watch-towers are perfect for viewing wildlife. To get there, first take the road to Canning or Sonakhali, from where a launch will take you into the interior.

Vedanthangal Sanctuary (Tamil Nadu)
Bird-watchers are assured of many engrossing hours at the Vedanthangal Sanctuary in Tamil Nadu where more than 100,000 winged Siberian visitors flock.

Velavadar National Park (Gujarat)
This park, 65 kilometres (40 miles) north of Bhavnagar, protects the rich grasslands in the delta region on the western side of the Gulf of Khambhat.

The main attraction is a large concentration of the beautiful blackbuck. A park lodge is available for visitors.

A Demographic Profile

Only second to China in population density, the 1991 census of India recorded a nation of over 800 million people.

India was a country of 25 states and seven union territories in the 1991 census, but since then Delhi has been granted statehood. The most populous state is Uttar Pradesh and the least Sikkim.

The crude birth rate averaged 29.9 in 1990, when infant mortality was 80 per 1,000 live births and family size averaged four people.

Sex, age and marital status
In the census, males outnumbered females by 51.85 per cent to 48.15 per cent. All the states and union territories showed a similar trend, except in Kerala, where 14,802,437 females vied with 14,230,391 males for educational opportunities, jobs and marriage partners. Considering that in male-dominated Indian society this is a state where matriarchal governance is peculiarly strong, this comes as no surprise.

The life expectancy at birth is 58.1 for males and 59.1 for females. The improvement over previous years is due to better infant care, with greater attention being paid to immunization of pregnant women against tetanus, and children below two years of age against infectious diseases.

Age structure
About 61 million (six per cent of India's total population) are elderly, ie, aged 60 and above. A very large percentage of them are poor and destitute because of the increasing urbanization and the disintegration of the joint family system, which has been their time-honoured source of support. Their numbers are bound to increase with increasing longevity.

Marital status
Legally, men and women can marry at the respective ages of 21 and 18. However, tradition still determines the age of marriage, particularly of women, and many marry well before the legal age, in accordance with familial injunctions, which strive to unburden the family of the girl-child at the first opportunity.

Divorce is still frowned on and widowhood a blot in some societies. However, remarriage is an option finding wider acceptance.

Literacy
For the purposes of computation, it is assumed that the age group zero to six years is illiterate. Therefore, seven years or above is the yardstick used to determine the nation's literacy status. The literacy of the entire population rose from 43.56 per cent in 1981 to 52.11 per cent in 1991.

Men are, on average, better educated, and showed a percentage improvement of 63.86 in 1991 as against 56.37 in 1981. Women have always lagged behind, but not without some progress over the 10-year period 1981 to 1991, when their literacy showed an increase from 29.75 per cent to 39.42 per cent.

What is particularly encouraging is that, in all but Rajasthan, female literacy rates rose faster than male literacy rates between 1981 and 1991. This is a positive indication that the girl-child is being allowed to attend school more, instead of the custom-bound rule of old which decreed that she remain at home to mind her younger siblings and do household chores.

However, female literacy is particularly low in Bihar and Uttar Pradesh. Of all the states, Kerala has consistently remained in the forefront, aiming at 100 per cent literacy for both men and women. In 1991, it stood at 90.59 per cent, and recently it has become fully literate.

Bihar, Rajasthan, Arunachal Pradesh and Uttar Pradesh are the least literate states. In states where the population is over 10 million, the literacy rate was maximum in Haryana. Daman and Diu showed the highest increase among the other states and union territories.

Educational attainment
Though education is free in government-aided schools, few children study beyond the primary school level.

From primary school, progress is made through middle and high school. Beyond high school, a period of intermediate studies, called 'Plus Two', determines whether an individual will proceed to tertiary education or pursue vocational training.

University students graduate with either a BA or a BSc degree in the general category, while those choosing professional courses opt for an MBBS for medical studies, or a B Tech/BE for engineering. Further studies for a masters and a PhD interest fewer students, usually only those with academic inclinations.

The government has, since 1950, notified a Scheduled Class and Scheduled Tribe list under the Constitution, which allows persons belonging to these categories to avail themselves of reservation privileges in educational institutions and public sector undertakings.

This is meant primarily to assist the poor in backward regions to gain access to better education and jobs, privileges which have been the domain of the more affluent in urban areas and members of the higher castes.

Language

The official language is Hindi, but English is the lingua franca. In all, sixteen Indian languages are recognized by the government while over 225 dialects are spoken in the country.

However, the south has staunchly resisted Hindi penetration, and few speak the language in Tamil Nadu, Kerala, Karnataka and Andhra Pradesh.

Eastern India has a similar problem, where the mother tongue is still the preferred form of written and spoken communication.

Migration

India's urban population is 25.72 per cent against a population of 70 per cent engaged in rural agricultural pursuits.

Delhi has the highest urban growth rate. Elsewhere in the country, urban populations are expanding because of a natural increase, migration from rural areas and changes in urban territorial jurisdiction.

This is creating a dismal picture of more persons living below the poverty line, which, in 1973-74, was defined as Rs56.64 per capita a month, and 2,100 calories a person in the urban sector, and Rs49.09 per capita a month and 2,400 calories a person in the rural areas. In 1987, 29.9 per cent of the Indian population lived below the poverty line by this definition.

Employment

India still has one of the cheapest labour forces in the world. While 70 per cent of the nation is involved in agriculture and related pursuits, such as fisheries and poultry farming, the rest engage in industrial activities or private entrepreneurship.

Following a liberal economic policy, many government controls, tariffs and levies have been dropped, leading to the flowering of the spirit of enterprise, though the government remains the nation's largest employer.

Festivals and Public Holidays

January

Pongal (Makara Sankranti)

A three-day festival to mark the end of the harvest season. Lively processions, bull fights and beautifully decorated sacred cows symbolize the festival. Best seen in Tamil Nadu and Karnataka. See Listings for 'Hotels'.

Republic Day (26 January)

Important national holiday celebrated all over the country. In New Delhi, this is followed by a big folk dance festival over the next two days. The 'Beating the Retreat' ceremony takes place on 29 January below the magnificent Secretariat buildings.

February

Vasant Panchami (Saraswati Puja)

Marks the first day of spring. Celebrations include colourful kite flying, especially in the north and in West Bengal. Saraswati, the Hindu goddess of learning, is honoured and worshipped.

Float Festival

Commemorates the birth of Thirumalai Nayak, the 17th-century ruler of Madurai, Tamil Nadu. See Listings for 'Hotels' in Madurai.

Desert Festival

Organized in the desert of Jaisalmer, this festival gives an opportunity to listen to the music of the desert, see local craftsmen at work and watch dance performances against the background of the magnificent Jaisalmer Fort. See Listings for 'Hotels' in Jaisalmer.

Shivaratri

Shiva temples are beautifully decorated and jammed with devotees observing all-night vigil and fasts. Chanting processions to the temples conclude the celebrations with ritualistic anointing of the *lingams* (phallic symbols). Important Shiva temples are in Srinagar (Jammu and Kashmir), Khajuraho (Madhya Pradesh), Varanasi (Uttar Pradesh), Mandi (Himachal Pradesh), Chidambaram (Tamil Nadu) and Bhubaneswar (Orissa). See Listings for 'Hotels' accommodation.

March

Holi

It celebrates the end of winter and the advent of spring. Throughout northern India (especially in Mathura in Uttar Pradesh, and Rajasthan) it is a riot of coloured water and powders.

Khajuraho Dance Festival

Khajuraho's temple complex becomes the stage for an exuberance of the performing arts. Not to be missed! See listings for 'Hotels' in Khajuraho (Madhya Pradesh).

Gangaur
The festival is held in honour of Parvati, wife of Shiva, and is a colourful culmination of all marriage ceremonies in Rajasthan, including Udaipur and Jaipur, and West Bengal and Orissa. See listings for 'Hotels'.

Carnival
Very popular in Goa, this is a three-day festival of merriment before the austerities of Lent. See Listings for 'Hotels'.

April
Spring Festival and Baisakhi
Marks the Hindu solar New Year and horticultural themes are emphasized.

Good Friday
A national holiday observed to commemorate the death of Christ (Sometimes occurs in March).

Ramanavami
The birth of the god Rama, hero of the epic *Ramayana*, is celebrated in temples.

Mahavirajayanti
Jains celebrate the birth of Mahavira, the 24th and last *Tirthankara*, who lived in the fifth century BC.

Meenakshi Kalyanam
Excellent music features the annual 10-day, non-stop festival in and around the famous Meenakshi Temple at Madurai (Tamil Nadu) to solemnize Meenakshi's marriage to Shiva.

May
May Day/Labour Day (1 May)
A national holiday.

Buddha Purnima
Commemorative date of Buddha's birth, death and enlightenment. The Buddha is supposed to have gone through each of these experiences on the same day but in different years. Best at Sarnath (Uttar Pradesh) and Gaya (Bihar). See Listings for 'Hotels'.

June
Rath Yatra
The temple chariot festival at Puri, Orissa. Lord Jagannath (Krishna) and his brother, Balaram, and sister, Subhadra, pay a visit to their aunt in Mathura. The crowd and the pilgrims' devotion is to be seen to be believed.

July
Nag Panchami
This festival is dedicated to the serpent, Ananta, upon whose coils Lord Vishnu reclines. Offerings are made to snake images.

August
Independence Day (15 August)
India celebrates her freedom nationwide. A national holiday.

Raksha Bandhan
Across northern India, sisters tie a silk thread or decorative bracelet known as *rakhi* on their brothers' wrists to renew the bonds of affection. The brother promises to protect his sister and gives her a gift.

Jamshed Navroz
Parsis celebrate their New Year in a traditional manner. Best seen in Mumbai.

September
Ganesh Chaturthi
Ganesh or Ganapati, the elephant-headed god of good luck, wisdom and prosperity, is worshipped, and clay images of the deity are taken out in huge processions before they are immersed in the sea.

Ganesh Chaturthi is an important festival of Maharashtra, especially in Mumbai. See listings for 'Hotels'.

Onam Harvest Festival
Celebrated exclusively in Kerala. The famous snake boat races are held during this festival. See listings for 'Hotels'.

Janamashtami
Across northern India, especially in Mathura and Vrindavan (Uttar Pradesh), Krishna's birthday is celebrated with much fun and frolic.

October
Gandhi Jayanti (2 October)
A national holiday to honour the leader of India's freedom movement, Mahatma Gandhi.

Dusshera (Durga Puja)
A 10-day festival of national importance, celebrated almost universally in India. Most colourful and entertaining in Mysore (Karnataka), Kulu (Himachal Pradesh) and West Bengal. See Listings for 'Hotels'.

November
Diwali
A night-long revel of fireworks and illumination, it is the most lively and noisiest of all Indian festivals. It also marks the start of the Hindu New Year in some parts of the country. Best seen in Delhi and the north. See listings for 'Hotels'.

Cattle Fair
A real attraction for tourists on the edge of the desert is the annual cattle fair held at Pushkar (Rajasthan). Pushkar is 11 kilometres (seven miles) from Ajmer. See listings for 'Hotels' in Ajmer.

Nanak Jayanti

The birthday of Guru Nanak, the founder of the Sikh religion, is celebrated with prayer readings and processions. Observed particularly at Amritsar (Punjab) and Patna (Bihar). See listings for 'Hotels'.

December
Christmas Day (December 25)
Celebrated all over India but best in Goa.

Muslim Holidays

Muslim festivals do not have a fixed date as they fall about eleven days earlier each year.

Ramazan
The most important Muslim festival. A 30-day dawn to dusk fast is observed by all Muslims. It was in this month that the Prophet Mohammed had the *Koran* revealed to Him in Mecca.

Id-ul-Fitr
This is the last day of the Ramazan month when the new moon is seen and is celebrated with much fun and frolic.

Id-ul-Zuha
Commemorates Abraham's attempt to sacrifice his son and is celebrated with prayers and presents for children.

Muharram
A ten-day festival to commemorate the martyrdom of Mohammed's grandson, Hazrat Imam Hussain.

The Indian Lunar Calendar

Magha	(January-February)
Phalguna	(February-March)
Chaitra	(March-April)
Vaisakh	(April-May)
Jyestha	(May-June)
Ashadh	(June-July)
Shravana	(July-August)
Bhadra	(August-September)
Ashvina	(September-October)
Kartika	(October-November)
Agrahayana	(November-December)
Pausha	(December-January)

Museums of India

Andhra Pradesh
Amaravati: Archaeological Museum
Noted for its sculptures in marble, caskets and other objects related to the site of the remains of the Buddhist stupa (2 BC-AD 2).

Hyderabad: Sala Jung Museum
Noted for its collection of Indian textiles, wooden artefacts, bronzes, jade, armoury, paintings, European sculpture and oriental art.

Hyderbad: State Museum
Good collection of sculpture from the Buddhist and Hindu periods, decorative arts and copies of paintings from Ajanta.

Nagarjunakonda: Site Museum
Remnants of exquisite sculpture and architectural details from the ancient Buddhist stupa.

Assam
Guwahati: Assam State Museum
Noted for its art and sculptures of the region.

Bihar
Bodhgaya: Archaeological Museum
A site museum, near the place where Buddha attained *Nirvana*. Noted for objects unearthed in archaeological excavations, sculptures in stone and bronze, especially of the Pala period.

Nalanda: Archaeological Museum
At the site of the ancient and famous university area of Nalanda. Noted for its collection of terracotta figurines, pottery and sculptures.

Patna: State Museum
Noted for its exquisite terracottas from the Mauryan to the Gupta period. Bronze Buddhist sculptures and others including the Didarganj Yakshi, the Mauryan chauri bearer.

Goa
Old Goa: Archaeological Museum
Noted for its Goan historical objects.

Gujarat
Ahmedabad: Calico Museum of Textiles
Noted for its brilliant collection of Indian textiles.

Ahmedabad: Gandhi Smarak Sangrahalaya
Dedicated to the memory of Mahatma Gandhi, India's greatest leader.

Ahmedabad: Utensils Museum
A fine collection of Indian utensils, an assortment of metal pots.

Baroda: Maharaja Fateh Singh Museum
Noted for its royal collection of art objects from India and abroad.

Baroda: Museum and Picture Gallery
Opened in 1921. Noted for its Indian paintings, archaeological artefacts and art from Japan, China, Nepal, Tibet and Europe.

Jammu and Kashmir
Jammu: Dogra Art Gallery
Noted for its Pahari paintings and armoury, among other displays.

Srinagar: Sri Pratap Singh Museum
Noted for its miniature paintings, decorative arts, manuscripts and textiles.

Karnataka
Bangalore: Karnataka Government Museum
Specializes in paintings and the traditional arts of Mysore, and sculptures from the Hoysala Chola and Chalukyan periods.

Hampi: Archaeological Museum
A site museum, noted for objects unearthed and preserved from the Hampi excavations.

Mysore: Folklore Museum
An amazing collection of the arts of Karnataka, especially leather shadow puppets, masks and toys.

Srirangapatnam: Tipu Sultan Museum
Collections associated with Tipu Sultan and his family. Paintings, historical documents, textiles, coins and the like.

Kerala
Padmanabhapuram: Palace Museum
Amazing wooden architecture and sculptures, furniture and other articles in the palace. The museum has a fine collection of coins, stone sculptures and an assortment of crafts.

Thrissur: Archaeological Museum
Noted for its exhibits from Harappa civilization. Gandhara sculpture, pottery artefacts from Kerala, megalithic tools, sculptures in wood and metal.

Trivandrum: Government Museum and Art Gallery
Specializes in Indian, Indo-European, Chinese and Japanese paintings.

Maharashtra
Mumbai: Prince of Wales Museum
Noted for its collection of Indian sculpture from the Indus Valley civilization, Gandhara and different medieval schools. Superb Indian miniature paintings, Tibetan and Nepalese art, European paintings and decorative art from the Far East.

Nagpur. Nagpur Central Museum
An old museum, with collections from archaeological excavations, especially the Indus Valley civilization. Paintings, epigraphy, numismatic and armoury sections.

Pune: Museum and Deccan College
This college has conducted several excavations. The museum has a good collection of manuscripts, artefacts, paintings and armoury.

Pune: Raja Dinkar Kelkar Museum
Superb collection of everyday Indian crafts — lamps, woodwork, sculpture and textiles.

Madhya Pradesh
Bhopal: Bharat Bhavan
Tribal arts and contemporary work on display.

Gwalior H H Maharaja Jayaji Rao Scindia Museum
Noted for its kitsch collection of the Scindia royal family.

Gwalior Archaeological Museum
Noted for its paintings, sculptures, sati stones and terracottas.

Khajuraho: Archaeological Museum
Noted for its masterpieces from the temples of the Chandella period in the vicinity.

Sanchi: Archaeological Museum
Noted for its sculpture, coins and tools found during excavations at this famous Buddhist and Hindu pilgrimage centre.

New Delhi
Bahadur Shah Zafar Marg: International Dolls Museum
Collections of dolls from all over the world.

Barakhamba Road: National Museum of Natural History
Interesting galleries on botany, zoology, and collections and dioramas of birds, animals and butterflies. Discovery room for children.

Birla House: The Gandhi Smriti Museum
Dedicated to the memory of Mahatma Gandhi, the Father of the Nation.

Chanakyspuri: Rail Transport Museum
Wonderful collection of vintage locomotives princely saloons, models and photographs. A must for railway buffs.

Jaipur House: National Gallery of Modern Art
Specializes in sculptures and paintings from the post-1857 period and modern art. Garden of sculptures is another attraction.

Janpath: National Museum
One of India's finest. Foundation stone laid in 1955. Specializes in Indus Valley civilization, Mauryan and Gupta period sculptures. Medieval sculptures from different schools and parts of India. Excellent bronze sculptures and galleries displaying paintings, textiles, jewellery, coins and central Asian antiquities.

Pragati Maidan: Crafts Museum
A village complex with replicas of the village houses of India. Demonstrations by craftspeople a feature. Exhibition and sale of these crafts.

Raj Ghak The Gandhi Memorial Museum
Memorabilia of India's greatest freedom fighter.

Teen Murti: Nehru Memorial Museum and Library
Photo-documentation relating to the National Movement, and the life and works of Jawaharlal

Nehru, India's first prime minister.

Old Delhi
Red Fort: Archaeological Museum
Noted for its objects connected with the history of the fort.

Orissa
Bhubaneswar: Orissa State Museum
Specializes in the art of the region. Sculptures from nearby temples, and palm-leaf manuscripts.

Konarak: Archaeological Museum
Noted for its sculptures from the ruins of the famous Sun Temple.

Punjab
Chandigarh: Government Museum and Art Gallery
Excellent collection of Gandhara sculptures, especially the Bodhisattvas paintings of the Mughal, Basholi and Kangra schools.

Rajasthan
Alwar Government Museum
Specializes in paintings, armoury and decorative arts from the maharaja's collection.

Bharatpur Government Museum
Specializes in sculptures from the region, armoury and other crafts.

Bikaner Ganga Golden Jubilee Museum
Noted for its paintings, manuscripts and crafts of the region, especially Mughal textiles.

Jaipur: Government Central Museum
Noted for its stonework from regional architecture, metalware, ivory, armoury and paintings.

Jaipur: Maharaja Sawai Madho Singh Museum
Noted for its collection of textiles, armoury, paintings and manuscripts.

Jodhpur: Sadar Museum
Excellent collection of paintings from the School of Arts in Rajasthan. Specializes in armoury, textiles and pottery.

Udaipur: Government Museum
Noted for its collection of sculptures and art.

Tamil Nadu
Chennai: Fort St George Museum
Noted for its armoury, portraits, coins and manuscripts belonging to the East India Company and the days of British colonial rule.

Madras: Government State Museum
Sculptures from the Buddhist stupa at Amaravati south Indian stone sculptures, musical instruments, natural history section and south Indian bronzes, one of the best collections in India.

Madurai: Sri Meenakshi Sundareshvara Temple Museum
Specializes in south Indian bronzes, paintings, musical instruments, decorative arts and jewellery.

Pudukottai: Government Museum
Noted for its archaeological section, sculptures, epigraphy and numismatics.

Thanjavur: Thanjavur Art Gallery
Exceptional collection of Chola bronzes.

Uttar Pradesh
Allahabad Museum: Allahabad Museum
Noted for its rich collection of sculptures, terracottas, coins and archaeological objects.

Lucknow: State Museum
Excellent collection of Buddhist and Jain sculptures and important Hindu stone sculptures. Paintings, manuscripts and rich coin collection.

Mathura: Government Museum
Noted for its excellent collection of Buddhist sculpture, Kushan art, terracottas and coins.

Varanasi: Bharat Kala Bhavan
Noted for its superb collection of Indian sculpture, paintings, textiles and other arts.

Varanasi: Sarnath Archaeological Museum
Site museum, with an excellent collection of early Buddhist sculptures.

West Bengal
Calcutta: Ashutosh Museum of Art
Noted for its terracottas from Vishnupur, Sena sculpture and arts of Bengal.

Calcutta: Indian Museum
The oldest museum in India, dating back to the 19th century. Amazing Buddhist sculptured railings and sculptures from medieval schools. Karnataka Government Museum.

Calcutta: Victoria Memorial Hall
Noted for its collection of sculptures, paintings, portraits, prints of the British colonial period, armoury and personal items belonging to Britain's Queen Victoria.

Listings

Dialling Codes

Agartala	0381
Agra	0562
Ahmedabad	079
Ajmer	0145
Allahabad	0332
Amritsar	0183
Aurangabad	02432
Bangalore	080
Baroda	0205
Bharatpur	05644
Bhavnagar	0278
Bhopal	0755
Bhubaneshwar	0674
Bikaner	0151
Calcutta	033
Chandigarh	0172
Chennai (Madras)	044
Coimbatore	0422
Darjeeling	0354
Dehradun	0135
Delhi	011
Fatehpur	0518
Gangtok	03592
Gwalior	0751
Hyderabad	040
Imphal	03852
Jaipur	0141
Jaisalmer	02992
Jammu	0191
Jodhpur	0291
Jorhat	0376
Kalimpong	03552
Kanpur	051
Kochi (Cochin)	04841
Kodaikanal	04542
Kota	0744
Kottayam	0401
Kullu	01902
Leh	01982
Lucknow	0522
Madurai	0452
Mamallapuram	04113
Mangalore	0824
Mathura	0452
Mumbai (Bombay)	022
Mussoorie	0135632
Mysore	0821
Nagpur	0712
Nainital	05942
Nalanda	081184
Nasik	0253
New Delhi	011
N Lakhimpur	03752
Panjim	0232
Patiala	0175
Patna	0812
Pondicherry	0413
Port Blair	03192
Pune	0212
Puri	08762
Rajkot	0281
Rameshwaram	04673
Ranchi	0651
Saharanpur	0132
Shillong	0304
Shimla	0177
Siliguri	0353
Srirangapatnam	0194
Thrissur (Trichur)	0487
Thiruvanaphram	0471
Tirupati	08674
Udaipur	0294
Varanasi	0542
Vellore	0416
Vijaywada	0665

Airlines

Bangalore

Air Canada
Hotel Oberoi Towers
Nariman Point
Tel: 2027632/512

Air France
Sunrise Chambers
No 22 Visoor Rd
Tel: 2024818/5021
Airport Tel:
8328070/3072

Air India
Air India Bldg
Nariman Point
Tel: 2024142
Airport Tel: 8366767

Air Lanka
Mittal Towers
Nariman Point
Tel: 223299/599
Airport Tel: 8322829

Air Mauritius
M 7-8
Oberoi Towers
Nariman Point
Tel: 2024723/8474
Airport Tel: 8329666

Air Tanzania
c/o Ethiopian
Airlines
Taj Mahal Hotel
Tel: 2024525

Alitalia
Veer Nariman Rd
Churchgate
Tel: 2207951

Alyemda
Oberoi Towers
Nariman Point
Tel: 2024229

Bangladesh Biman
199 J Tata Rd
Churchgate
Tel: 221339/3342/
4580
Airport Tel: 8320700

British Airways
202 Veer
Nariman Rd
Tel: 220888
Airport Tel: 8329061

Cathay Pacific
Taj Mahal Hotel
Tel: 2029112-3/561
Airport Tel: 8321965

Czechoslovak
Airlines
308/309 Raheja
Chambers
213 Nariman Point
Tel: 2200376/765
Airport Tel: 8366767

Delta
Taj Mahal Hotel
Tel: 2029221/9048
Airport Tel: 6049890

Egypt Air
7 J Tata Rd
Churchgate
Tel: 221415/562
Airport Tel: 6326089

Emirates
Mittal Chambers
228 Nariman Point
Tel: 2871645-50

Ethiopian Airlines
Taj Mahal Hotel
Apollo Bundar
Tel: 2024525
Airport Tel: 6328068

Garuda Indonesian
Raheja Centre
Nariman Point
Tel: 2024525
Airport Tel: 6328068

Gulf Air
Maker Chambers V
Nariman Point
Tel: 2021626/4065
Airport Tel:
8325226/0925

Iran Air
Sundar Mahal
Marine Drive
Tel: 2047070/3524
Airport Tel: 6329977

Iraqi Airways
Mayfair Bldg
79 Veer Nariman Rd
Churchgate
Tel: 221217
Airport Tel: 6327538

Japan Airlines
Raheja Centre
Nariman Point
Tel: 2874941/
233136

Kenya Airways
199 J Tata Rd
Churchgate
Tel: 220064
Airport Tel: 6322577

KLM 198 J Tata Rd
Churchgate
Tel: 221013/185

Kuwait Airways
Chateau Windsor
86 Veer Nariman Rd
Tel: 2041612/5351
Airport Tel: 6327269

LOT
6 Maker Arcade
Cuffe Parade
Tel: 221431

Lufthansa
Express Tower
Nariman Point
Tel: 2023430/0887
Airport Tel:
8321485/0827

Malaysian Airlines
6 Maker Arcade
Cuffe Parade
Tel: 211431/440

Maldives Airways
7 Brabourne
Stadium
Churchgate
Tel: 2029020

PIA
Hotel Oberoi
Towers
Nariman Point
Tel: 2021480/1373
Airport Tel: 6366700

Qantas
Hotel Oberoi
Towers
Nariman Point
Tel: 2026373
Airport Tel: 63290

Royal Nepal Airlin
222 Maker
Chambers V
Nariman Point
Tel: 232438/2443

Sabena
Nirmal Bldg
Nariman Point
Tel: 2023817
Airport Tel: 83299

Saudi Arabia
Express Towers
Nariman Point
Tel: 2020049
Airport Tel: 83299

Singapore Airline
Air India Bldg
Nariman Point
Tel: 2023835/336
Airport Tel: 83270

SwissAir
Maker Chambers
220 Nariman Poi
Tel: 2870121
Airport Tel: 63260

Syrian Arab Airline
7 Brabourne Stadiu
Churchgate
Tel: 232996
Airport Tel: 63202

Thai
15 World Trade
Centre
Cuffe Parade
Colaba
Tel: 2023284

Turkish Airlines
Maker Chambers
V Nariman Point
Tel: 2043605
Airport Tel: 632222

Yemen Airways
7 Brabourne
Stadium
Churchgate
Tel: 204368

Zambia Airways
2/207 Maker
Chambers V

Nariman Point
Tel: 2026942
Airport Tel: 6366700

Bombay: see *Mumbai*

Calcutta
Aeroflot
58 Jawaharlal
Nehru Rd
Tel: 443765/7831
Airport Tel:
572611/395

Air Canada
35-A Chowringhee Rd
Tel: 2477783

Air France
41 Chowringhee Rd
Tel: 296161-2/169

Air India
50 Chowringhee Rd
Tel: 2486012
Airport Tel: 5529685

Alitalia
2/3 Chitrakoot
230 A Acharya
Bose Rd
Tel: 447394

Bangladesh Biman
30-C
Jawaharlal Nehru Rd
Tel: 2492832/43

British Airways
41 Chowringhee Rd
Tel: 293430

Burma Airways
46-C Chawringhee Rd
Tel: 231624
Airport Tel: 572611
Ext: 397

Cathay Pactfic
Jeevan Deep
1 Middleton St
Tel: 447238

Delta
42 Chowringhee Rd
Tel: 2495001

Druk Air
51 Tivoli Court
1-A Dallygunge
Circular Rd
Tel: 434413/444907
Airport Tel: 572611

Gulf Air
5 Chitrakoot Bldg
230-A AJC Bose Rd
Tel: 447783

Japan Airlines
35-A Chowringhee Rd
Tel: 2498370

KLM
1 Middleton St
Tel: 2492451/7466

Lufthansa
30-A/B Jawaharlal
Nehru Rd
Tel: 2499365

Royal Jordanian
Chitrakoot Bldg
230-A AJC Bose Rd
Tel: 447783

Royal Nepal
Airlines
41 Chowringhee Rd
Tel: 2498534
Airport Tel: 572611

Singapore Airlines
18-D Park St
Tel: 2491525/0740

SwissAir
Everest
46-C Chowringhee Rd
Tel: 444643

Thai
18-G Park St
Tel: 249696
Airport Tel: 573937

Yugoslav Airlines
Grosvenor Hse
21 Cama St
Tel: 292323

Chennai (Madras)
Aeroflot
19 Marshalls Rd
Egmore
Tel: 847799/8899
Airport Tel: 431656

Air Canada
733 Anna Salai
Tel: 8250884

Air France
Apex Plaza
3 Mahatma Gandhi
Nungambakkam
Tel: 8250326

Air India
19 Marshalls Rd
Egmore
Tel: 8274488
Airport Tel: 2347064

Air Lanka
142 Nungambakkam
High Rd
Tel: 471195/5332
Airport Tel: 433131

Alitalia
738 Anna Salai
Tel: 860836/1406

Bangladesh Biman
Hardevi Chambers
68 Pantheon Rd
Egmore
Tel: 812775

British Airways
Khaleeli Centre
Montieth Rd
Egmore
Tel: 477559/388
Airport Tel: 434921

Cathay Pacific
Spencer's Bldg
769 Anna Salai
Tel: 869372/7694

Delta
Wellington Estate
Commander-in-
Chief Rd
Tel: 422611/869985

Garuda Indonesian
703 Anna Salai
Tel: 867957/9832

Gulf Air
Hardevi Chambers
68 Pantheon Rd
Egmore
Tel: 867650/872

Japan Airlines
733 Anna Salai
Tel: 867957

KLM
Connemara Hotel
Binny Rd
Tel: 869752

Kuwait Airways
Embassy Towers
55 Montieth Rd
Egmore
Tel: 811810

Lufthansa
167 Anna Salai
Tel: 869197/095

Malaysian Airlines
189 Anna Salai
Tel: 868985/970
Airport Tel: 431656

Sabena
Regency Hse
250 Anna Salai
Tel: 451786

Singapore Airlines
167 Anna Salai
Tel: 862871/1872
Airport Tel: 433860

SwissAir
40 Anna Salai
Tel: 861583/2692

Madras: see *Chennai*

Mumbai (Bombay)
Aeroflot
241/42 Nirmal Bldg
Nariman Point
Tel: 221282/743

Lufthansa
44/2 Dickenson Rd
Tel: 570740/564791

New Delhi
Aeroflot
BMC Hse
N-1 Connought Pl
Tel: 3312843/0426
Airport Tel: 5482331

Air Canada
Room No 1421
Holiday Inn
Crown Plaza
Tel: 3720014-5
Airport Tel: 5452850

Air France
Scindia Hse
Janpath
Tel: 3310407/24
Airport Tel: 5452294

Air India
Jeevan Bharati
LIC Bldg
Connought Circus
Tel: 3311225
Airport Tel: 5452050

Air Lanka
GSA-STIC Travels
and Tours
Tel: 3324789
Airport Tel: 5452011
Ext: 2535

Air Mauritius
GSA-Scindia Hse
Tel: 3311225

Air Ukraine
GSA M/s Flight
International
C-37 Hauz Khas
Tel: 6867545

Alitalia
Surya Kiran
19 Kasturba
Gandhi Marg
Tel: 3311019/20
Airport Tel:
5483140/74

American Airlines
105 Indra Prakash

Building
Barakhamba Rd
Tel: 3325876

Ariana Afghan
Airlines
Surya Kiran
19 KGMarg
Tel: 3311834/1432
Airport Tel: 542173

Austrian Airlines
C-28 Prem Hse
Connaught Circus
Tel: 3321292

Bangladesh Biman
N40 Connaught Pl
Tel: 3325876

British Airways
DLF Centre
Parliament St
Tel: 3327482
Airport Tel: 5452077

Cathay Pactfic
Tolstoy Hse
(Ground Floor)
Tolstoy Marg,
Tel: 3323919/3332

Czechoslovak
Airlines
104 Ansal Bhawan
K G Marg
Tel: 3311833

Delta
Chandralok Bldg
36 Janpath
Tel: 3325222
Airport: 5452093-4

Druk Air
c/o Malbros
Travels
403 Nirmal Tower
26 Barakhamba Rd
Tel: 3322859
Airport Tel: 5452173

Egypt Air
GSA-Esphinx
Travels G-F/1
Ansal Bhawan
Tel: 3318517

Emirates
Kenchenjunga
Bldg 18
Barakhamba Rd
Tel: 3324665/4803
Airport Tel: 5482861

Ethiopian Airlines
Room No 2
Hotel Janpath
Tel: 3329235

Finn Air
303/304 Prakash
Deep Bldg 7
Tolstoy Marg
Tel: 3315454

Gulf Air
G-12
Connaught Circus
Tel: 3327814/4293
Airport Tel: 5452065

Iberia
GSA-STIC
Travels and Tours
Tel: 3324789

Iran Air
Ashok Hotel
Chanakyapuri
Tel: 606471/4397

Iraqi Airways
Ansal Bhawan
K G Marg
Tel: 3318742
Airport Tel: 392185

Japan Airlines
Chandralok Bldg
36 Janpath
Tel: 3324922
Airport Tel: 5452060

Kenya Airways
10-B Scindia Hse
Connaught Place
Tel: 3318502/4796

KLM
Prakash Deep Bldg
7 Tolstoy Marg
Tel: 3315841/1747
Airport Tel: 5482874

Korean Air
303/304 Prakash
Deep Bldg
7 Tolstoy Marg
Tel: 3315454/
3714949

Kuwait Airways
2-C DCM Bldg
16 Barakhamba Rd
Tel: 3314221-3
Airport Tel: 5452295

LOT
G-55 Connaught Pl
Tel: 3324482

Lufthansa
56 Janpath
Tel: 3323310
Airport Tel:
5452063/4

Malaysian Airlines
G-55 Connaught Pl
Tel: 3324308
Airport Tel: 5452395

344

Philippines
GSA-Jet Air
N 40
Connaught Circus
Tel: 3314978/2119

PIA
26 Kasturba
Gandhi Marg
Tel: 3313161-2
Airport Tel: 5452841

Qantas
Mohan Dev Bldg
Tolstoy Marg
Tel: 3321434/9027

Royal Jordanian
G-56
Connaught Circus
Tel: 3320635/7418
Airport Tel:
5452478/2011
Ext: 2517

Royal Nepal
Airlines
44 Janpath
Tel: 3321164/
5483876

Sabena
Himalaya Hse
K G Marg
Tel: 3312701/2928

SAS
B-1 Connaught Pl
Tel: 3325262

Saudi Arabian
Airlines
15 Hansalaya Bldg
15 Barakhamba Rd
Tel: 3310464
Airport Tel: 5481279

Singapore Airlines
G-11
Connaught Circus
Tel: 3326373/0145
Airport Tel: 5484200
Ext: 2398

SwissAir
DLF Centre
Parliament St
Tel: 3325511/7892
Airport Tel: 5452531

Syrian Arab
Airlines
GSA-Inter Globe
Air Transport
66 Janpath
Tel: 3713366

Thai
Ambadeep
14 Kasturba

Gandhi Marg
Tel: 3323608/38
Airport Tel: 5482672

Trans World
Aidines Jet Air
N-40 Connaught Pl
Tel: 3312119/3221

Turkish Airlines
56 Janpath
Tel: 3326661
Airport Tel: 5452021

United Airlines
14 K G Marg
Tel: 3715550

Uzbekistan
Airways
Room No 20
Hotel Janpath
Tel: 3327042/0070
Ext: 2020

Zambia Airways
N-1 BMC Hse
Connaught Place
Tel: 3328129/5521

Thiruvananthapuram
Air Lanka
Geetabali Bldg
Ganpatti
Tel: 63261

Domestic Airlines

Agartala
Indian Airlines
Khosh Mahal Bldg
Tel: 3128/0

Agra
Indian Airlines
Hotel Clarks Shiraj
54 Taj Rd
Tel: 7334
Airport Tel: 61450

Ahmedabad
East West Airlines
Tel: 423311-2
Fax: 423501

Indian Airlines
Airlines Hse
Lal Darwaza
Tel: 391730
Airport Tel: 36277

Jet Airways
Opp Gujarat
Vidyapeeth
Ashram Rd
Tel: 402519/1290
Fax: 429123

Bangalore
Damania Airways
Manipal Centre
Dickenson Rd
Tel: 588736/001
Fax: 588935

Indian Airlines
Flight Information
140-2 (err)
143 (dep)
Tel: 564433

Jet Airways
Sunrise Chambers
22 Ulsoor Rd
Tel: 5588354/8371/
6095
Fax: 224823

Modiluft
Tel: 5592631/651
Airport Tel: 5561136

Baroda
Jet Airways
11 Panorama Bldg
R C Dutt Rd
Tel: 337051-3
Fax: 337054

Indian Airlines
Flight Information
140-2 (err)
143 (dep)
Tel: 6144433

Jet Airways
B-1 Amarchand
Mansion
Madame Cama Rd
Tel: 8386111/
2875090
Fax: 8372396

Modiluft
89 Bhulabhai
Desai Rd
Tel: 3635380/5859/
5960
Fax: 3635384
Airport Tel: 6103807

B-6 Maker
Chambers V
221 Nariman Point
Tel: 2832369/2446
Airport Tel: 6117314

SV Rd
Goregaon (W)
Tel: 8738825/8920
Airport Tel: 6150949

Bombay: see Mumbai

Calcutta
Damania Airways
B-2/5 Sarat Bose Rd
Tel: 4756356/9983
Fax: 4751473

Indian Airlines
29 Chittranjan Av
Tel: 260874/20443
Airport Tel: 552943

Indian Airlines
Flight Information
140-2 (err)
143 (dep)
Tel: 5529433

Modiluft
1 Park Lane
Tel: 299864/29625
Fax: 396257
Airport Tel: 552878

Sahara India
Airlines
101 Mangal Jyoti
Apartments
227/2 AJC Rd
Tel: 401234/247279
Fax: 2475896
Airport Tel: 552844

Cochin: see Kochi

Coimbatore
Damania Airway
Padmavati Twrs
18th June Rd
Panjim
Tel: 55563/31
Fax: 44155

East West Airway
Tel: 46291
Fax: 45237

Jet Airways
102 Rizvi Chamber
Caetano
Albuquerque Rd
Tel: 54476/9
Fax: 43323

Hyderabad
Indian Airlines
Flight Information
Tel: 844433/22

Jet Airways
203 Gupta Estates
5-9-58 Basharbagh
Tel: 230978/1236
Fax: 240831

Jaipur
East West Airlines
Tel: 512961
Fax: 512966

Jammu
Modiluft
Tel: 533470/2972
Airport Tel: 531112

Kochi (Cochin)
East West Airlines
Tel: 355242
Fax: 355639

et Airways
Mootha Centre
Kodambakkam
Iigh Rd
el: 477007/866669

ndian Airlines
9 Marshalls Rd
Egmore
el: 8251677/77888
Airport Tel: 2343131

ndian Airlines
Flight Information
40-2 (arr)
43 (dep)
Tel: 2343131

et Airways
3-5 Gems Court
4 Khadar Nawaz
Khan Rd
Nungambakkam
Tel: 8257914/9817
Fax: 8262409

Modiluft
Omega Reisen
Tel: 8260048/4107
Airport Tel:
2349559/0551
Ext: 4250

Sahara India
Airlines
18 Koddambakkam
High Rd
Lokesh Twrs
Tel 8283180/57509
Fax: 82833180/8
Airport Tel: 2340551
Ext: 4364/5

Mangalore
Jet Airways
Ram Bhavan
Complex
Kodaibail
Tel: 440694/794
Fax: 441328

**Mumbai
(Bombay)**
Damania Airways
17 Nehru Rd
Santacruz (E)
Tel: 6102525
Fax: 6102544

East West Airlines
Lunat Mansion
Mint Rd Fort
Tel: 2620646

Indian Airlines
Air India Bldg
Nariman Point
Tel: 2023031/3131
Airport Tel:

6116633/29534/
2850/6153480/
0063-64

New Delhi
Archana Airways
41-A Friends
Colony (E)
Tel: 638197/7403/
6842001

Damania Airways
UG 26-A
Somdatt Chambers I
Bhikaji Cama Place
Tel: 6881739/6286
Fax: 6877434

East West Airlines
DCM Bldg
15 Barakhamba Rd
Tel: 3755167

Indian Airlines
Kanchenjunga
18 Barakhamba Rd
Tel: 3310071/52

Indian Airlines
Flight Information
140-2 (err)
143 (dep)
Tel: 3014433

Jagson Airlines
12-E Vandana Bldg
11 Tolstoy Marg
Tel: 3711069
Fax: 3324693

Jet Airways
3-E Hansalaya
15 Barakhamba Rd
Tel: 3724727-30
Fax: 3714867
Airport Tel: 3295402

Modiluft
Modiluft Hse
2 Commercial
Complex
Masjid Moth
Tel: 6430689/1128
Fax: 6430929/69658
Airport Tel: 3295568

Sahara India
Airlines
GF Amba Deep Bldg
K G Marg
Tel: 3326851 (8 lines)
Fax: 3326858/
3755510
Airport Tel: 3295715

Rajendra Place
Tel: 5737627/86558
Fax: 5735544

Vayudoot
Safdarjung Airport
Tel: 4693851
Airport Tel: 3295313

Car Hire

Agra
Budget Rent-a-Car
Tel: 64771-2

Bangalore
Hertz Wheels
Rent-a-Car
Tel: 215874/1102

Bombay: see Mumbai

Chennai (Madras)
Hertz Wheels
Rent-a-Car
Tel: 865491/0626

Delhi
Budget Rent-a-Car
G-3 Arunachal
Barakhamba Rd
Tel: 3715657-8/
3318600

Hertz Wheels
Rent-a-Car
Tel: 3318695/0190

Hyderabad
Hertz Wheels
Rent-a-Car
Tel: 242457/1697

Madras: see Chennai

Mumbai (Bombay)
Hertz Wheels
Rent-a-Car
Nirmal 16th floor
Nariman Point
Tel: 2023734/64

Pune
Hertz Wheels
Rent-a-Car
Tel: 56033/54291

Commerce and Industry

**Andaman and
Nicobar Islands**
Andaman Chamber
of Commerce
and Industry
PO Box 119
Port Blair

Andhra Pradesh
Cocanada
Chamber of

Commerce
Commercial Rd
Kakinada

Federation of
Andhra Pradesh
Chamber of
Commerce
and Industry
11-6-841 Red Hills
PO Box 14
Hyderabad

Godavari Chamber
of Commerce
Kakinada

Indian Chamber
of Commerce
PO Box 67
Veer Savarkar Rd
Guntur

Rajahamundry
Chamber of
Commerce
13/236 Khidakotlal
Street
Rajahamundry

Vijayawada
Chamber of
Commerce and
Industry
Chamber Road
Gandhinagar
PO Box 561
Vijayawada

Visakhapatnam
Chamber of
Commerce
and Industry
Visakhapatnam
Stevedores Assoc
Dutt Memorial
Bldg Opp Port
Stadium
Visakhapatnam

Assam
Eastern Assam
Chamber of
Commerce and
Industry
RK Bordoloi Path
PO Dibrugarh
Dibrugarh

Federation of
Northeast India
Chambers of
Commerce and
Industry
Sikaria Bldg AT Rd
Guwahati

Frontier Chamber
of Commerce
GS Rd Shillong

Kamrup Chamber
of Commerce
Kamrup
Chamber Road
Guwahati

Meghalaya
Chamber of
Commerce and
Industry Shalam
Bldg GS Rd
Shillong

National Chamber
of Commerce
Khemka Rd
Tinsukia

North Lakhimpur
Chamber of
Commerce

North Assam
Chamber of
Commerce
and Industry
Tezpur

Sibsagar Chamber
of Commerce
Central Market
Bldg (1st Floor)
JP Agarwala Path
Sibsagar

Upper Assam
Chamber of
Commerce
Chamber Bhawan
Jorhat

Bihar
Bihar Chamber
of Commerce
Judges Court Rd
PO Box 71
Patna

Chota Nagpur
Chamber
of Commerce
and Industry
Main Rd
PO Box 32
Ranchi

North Chota
Nagpur Chamber
of Commerce
and Industry
Bhagwan
Mahavira Marg
Hazaribagh

Palamau Chamber
of Commerce

345

and Industry
PO Box 22
Hotel Koyal Bldg
Zila School Chowk
Daltonganj

Ramgarh Chamber
of Commerce
and Industry
Hotel Park Campus
PO Box 21
Ramgarh
Cantonment
Hazaribagh

Shahabad Chamber
of Commerce
and Industry
Arrah

Singhbhum
Chamber of
Commerce and
Industry
Chamber Bhawan
Main Rd
Jamshedpur

Calcutta
Bharat Chamber
of Commerce
Bharat Chambers
28 Hemanta Basu
Sarani

Calcutta Chamber
of Commerce
18-H Park St
Stephen Court
Eastern Chamber
of Commerce
12 India Exchange
Place

Indian Chamber
of Commerce
India Exchange
Place India
Exchange

Oriental Chamber
of Commerce
6 Dr Rajendra
Prasad Sarani
(Formerly Clive
Row)

Chandigarh
North Indian
Chamber of
Commerce
and Industry
Hse No 714
Sector 14-A

Chennai
Andhra Chamber
of Commerce
Andra Chamber

Building
127 Angappa
Naick St
PO Box 1511

Hindustan Chamber
of Commerce
Hindustan
Chamber Building
8 Kondi Chetty St

India-Sri Lanka
South-East Asia
Chamber of
Commerce
and Industry
Karmuttu Centre
458 Anna Salai

National Chamber
of Commerce
117 Broadway

Southern India
Chamber of
Commerce and
Industry
PO Box 1208
Indian Chamber Bldg
Chennai

Tamil Chamber
of Commerce
Caithness Hall
157 Linghi Chetty
Street

Delhi
Delhi Chamber
of Commerce
Dilbar Bldg
DB Gupta Rd
Paharganj

Dehradun
Doon Chamber
of Commerce
and Industry
PO Box 2

Goa
Goa Chamber
of Commerce
and Industry
Goa Chamber Bldg
Rua De Ommuz
Panaji

Gujarat
Ahmedabad Motor
Transport Assoc
24 Transport Nagar
Narol Crossing
Narol
Ahmedabad

Akhil Gujarat
Truck Transport
Association Near
Idgah Chowki
Opp Rajnagar Mill
Asarv
Ahmedabad

Central Gujarat
Chamber of
Commerce
PO Box 2513
Vanijya Bhawan
Race Course
Baroda

Gujarat Chamber
of Commerce
and Industry
Shri Ambica Mills
Gujarat Chamber
Building
Ashram Rd
PO Box 4045
Ahmedabad

Junagarh Chamber
of Commerce
and Industry
Maharishi
Arvind Marg
Balia Bhavan
Chamber Bldg
Junagarh

Nawanagar
Chamber of
Commerce
and Industry
Shri Digvijaysinhji
Chamber
Grain Market
Jamnagar

North Kanara
District Chamber
of Commerce
Industry and
Agriculture
Sirsi
Karnataka

Porbandar
Chamber of
Commerce and
Industry
Porbandar

Rajkot Chamber
of Commerce
Centre Point
Karansinghji Rd
Rajkot

Shri Soreth
Chamber of
Commerce and
Industry
Vakharia Bazaar
Veraval

Southern Gujarat
Chamber of
Commerce
and Industry
Samruddhi
Nanpura
Surat

Vadodara
Chamber of
Commerce
and Industry
GIDC Industrial
Est Makarpura
Vadodara

Haryana
Haryana Chamber
of Commerce
and Industry
E-23 Industrial
Area Yamuna
Nagar

Karnataka
Belgaum Chamber
of Commerce
and Industry
673 Raviwar Peth
Belgaum

Federation of
Karnataka
Chambers of
Commerce
and Industry
Kempegowda Rd
PO Box 9995
Bangalore

Hyderabad
Karnataka
Chamber of
Commerce
and Industry
Chambers Bldg
Complex
Super Market
Gulbarga

Kanara Chamber
of Commerce
and Industry
PO Box 116
Bunder
Mangalore

Karnataka Chamber
of Commerce
and Industry
Lamington Rd
Hubli

Mysore
Chamber of
Commerce
and Industry
1st Floor
54-D Devraja Urs Rd

Kerala
Ernakulam
Chamber of
Commerce
Chamber Bldg
PO Box 2530
Shanmukham Rd
Ernakulam
Kochi

Indian Chamber
of Commerce
and Industry
PO Box 236
Kochi

North Lakimpore
North Malabar
Chamber of
Commerce
Cannanore

Malabar Chamber
of Commerce
Chamber Hse
Cherooty Rd
Kozhikode

Thrissur Chamber
of Commerce
XXY-782 High Rd

Madhya Pradesh
Association of
Industries
'Lalit Laxmi'
6 Moti Bungalow
Dewas

Bastar Chamber
of Commerce
Jagdalpur
Rani Gadia
Opp Raipur Rd
Jagdalpur

Bhopal Chamber
of Commerce
and Industry
Bhopal

Chhattisgarh
Chamber of
Commerce
and Industry
1st Floor
8 Naveen Bazaar
Raipur

Federation of MP
Chambers of
Commerce
and Industry
Udyog Bhawan
129-A Malviya
Nagar
Bhopal

Madhya Pradesh
Chamber of
Commerce
and Industry
Chamber
Bhawan Gwalior

Mahakoshal
Chamber of
Commerce
and Industry
Makhanlal
Chaturvedi
Bhawan
Ganjipura
Jabalpur

Maharashtra
Mahratta Chamber
of Commerce
and Industry
PO Box 525
Tilak Rd
Pune

Maha Vidarbha
Chamber of
Commerce
and Industry
Homi Hse
Kingsway
Nagpur

Nagpur Chamber
of Commerce
73 Central Ave Rd
Nagpur

Nag-Vidarbha
Chamber of
Commerce
Temple Rd
PO Box 33
Nagpur

Maharashtra
Solapur Chamber
of Commerce
and Industries
Shri Chatrapati
Shivasmarak Bldg
Gold Finch Peth
PO Box 721
Solapur

Manipur
Associated
Manipur Chamber
of Commerce
Thangal Bazaar
Imphal

Mizoram
Mizoram Chamber
of Commerce
General HQ
Upper Bazaar
Aizawl

Mumbai
All India Assoc
of Industries
98 Mittal
Chambers
Nariman Point

Bharat Merchants
Chamber
Bharat Chamber
Bhavan
399 Kalbadevi Rd

Hindustan Chamber
of Commerce
342 Kalbadevi Rd

Indo-American
Chamber of
Commerce
IC Vulcan
Insurance Bldg
Veer Nariman Rd
PO Box 11057

Indo-Italian
Chamber of
Commerce
and Industry
General Assurance
Building
232 Dr DN Rd

Maharashtra
Chamber of
Commerce
Oricon Hse
12-K Dubhash Marg
Fort (Rampart Row)

Western India
Chamber of
Commerce
232/34 Kalbadevi
Road

New Delhi
Indo-Italian
Chamber of
Commerce
and Industry
PHD Hse
Opp Asian Games
Village

Indo-Polish
Chamber of
Commerce
and Industry
PHD Hse

International Fiscal
Association India
Branch
10 Hailey Rd

North Bihar
Chamber of
Commerce

and Industry
4 Community
Centre New
Friends Colony

PHD Chamber of
Commerce and
Industry PHD Hse
Thapar Floor

United Chamber
of Trade Assocs
21 Rex Bldg 4/5
Netaji Subhash
Marg Darya Ganj

Orissa
Rourkela Chamber
of Commerce
and Industry
Uditnagar
Rourkela

Punjab Ludhiana
Chamber of
Industrial and
Commercial
Undertakings Gill Rd

Punjab
Federation of
Commerce
and Industry
Gandhi Gate
Amritsar

Punjab Industry
and Commerce
Association
32 Krishna Market
Chowk Phawara
Amritsar

Rajasthan
Jaipur Chamber
of Commerce
and Industry
Johri Bazaar
Jaipur

Marwar Chamber
of Commerce
and Industry
5 Haider Bldg
Sobti Dwar
Jodhpur

Mewar Chamber
of Commerce
and Industry
Mansinghka Hse
Bhilwara

Rajasthan
Chamber of
Commerce
and Industry
Rajasthan
Chamber Bhawan
MI Rd Jaipur

Udaipur Chamber
of Commerce
and Industry
Rd No 1(P)
Mewar Industries
Area Udaipur

Tamil Nadu
All India Chamber
of Commerce
and Industry
84/2 South Raja St
Tuticorin

Indian Chamber
of Commerce
and Industry
6/83 Avanashi
Coimbatore

Indian Chamber
of Commerce
and Industry
84/5 South Raja St
Tuticorin

Kanchipuram
Chamber of
Commerce
42 Kotrampalayam
Street
Kanchipuram

North Arcot
District
Chamber of
Commerce
2-B Officers Line
Vellore

Pondicherry
Chamber of
Commerce
No 1 Rue Suffren
PO Box 39

Rajapalayam
Chamber
of Commerce
121 Hospital Rd
Rajapalayam

Sattur Chamber
of Commerce
and Industry
Railway Feeder Rd
Sattur

Tamil Nadu
Chamber of
Commerce
and Industry
178-B Kamarajar Rd
Madurai

Tiruchirapalli
District Chamber
of Commerce
167 Madurai Rd
Tiruchirapalli

Tirunelveli District
Chamber of
Commerce
and Industry
Sakthi Complex
25-B Swami
Nellayappar
Tirunelveli

Virudhunagar
Chamber of
Commerce
and Industry
102 Main Bazaar
Virudhunagar

Uttar Pradesh
Avadh Chamber
of Commerce
and Industry
Harbhaj Ram
Kripa Devi Trust
Building
Charbagh
Lucknow

Capital Region
Chamber of
Commerce
and Industry
201 Shivaji Rd
Meerut

Eastern UP
Chamber of
Commerce
and Industry
22 Minto Rd
Allahabad

National Chamber
of Commerce
and Industry
Jeoni Mandi
New Market
Agra

Rohikhand
Chamber of
Commerce
and Industry
95-A Civil Lines
Bareilly

UP Chamber of
Commerce
15/197 Civil Lines
Kanpur

Upper India
Chamber of
Commerce
and Industry
14/113 Civil Lines
Kanpur

Western UP
Chamber of
Commerce
and Industry

PO Box 12
Mumbai Bazaar
Meerut
Cantonment

West Bengal

Asansol Chamber
of Commerce
361 GT Rd (E)
Asansol

Asansol Merchants
Chamber of
Commerce
and Industry
Ghanty Bhawan
(2nd Floor)
173 GT Rd (E)
Asansol

Barakar Chamber
of Commerce
Station Rd
Barakar
Burdwan

Howrah Chamber
of Commerce
and Industry
Sukh Sagar
3 Salikia School
Rd Howrah

Raniganj Chamber
of Commerce
PO Box 5
PO Raniganj
West Bengal

Trade and Industry Associations

Andhra Pradesh

Agricultural
Implements
Dealers
Association
Nav Bharat
Agricultural
Products
Prakasam Rd
Vijayawada

AP Federation of
Chambers of
Commerce
and Industry
Varelaxmi Market
Complex
MG Rd
Secunderabad

Automobile Spare
Parts Dealers Assoc
Prakasam Rd
Vijayawada

Engineering
Products

Dealers Assoc
c/o Advocate
Venkatamaiah
Prakash Nagar
Rajahamundry

Film Exhibitors
Association
Royal Talkies
Hyderabad

Hotel Owners
Association
Khandari
Intemational
Bunder Rd
Vijayawada

Indian Tobacco
Association
GT Rd
Srinivasa Rao
Thota
Guntur

Petroleum Dealers
Association
Ventakeshwara
Commercial
Agencies
Park Rd
Kurnool

Road Transport
Financiers Assoc
Srinivasa Tyre
Prakasam Rd
Vijayawada

Millers Association
67-36 Chinna
Veedhi
Vizianagaram

Vegetable Oil
Traders Assoc
Sadhna Bldgs
Basheer Bagh
Hyderabad

Wholesale Cloth
Merchants Assoc
Eluru

Calcutta

Agro Input Dealers
Association
Bharat Chambers
8 Old Court Hse St

All India Seed
Growers
Merchants and
Nurserymen
Association
14 Thanikachalam
Road

All India Skin
and Hide, Tanners

and Merchants
Association
Leather Centre
53 Sydenhams Rd

Automotive
Manufacturers
Assoc of India
India Exchange
India Exchange Pl

Dye and Chemical
Merchants Assoc
34 Armenian St

Federation of Bidi,
Bidi Leaves and
Tobacco Merchants
1 Rupchand Roy St

Gunny Trades
Association
5 Dr Rajendra
Prasad Sarani
PO Box 573

Indian Chemical
Merchants and
Manufacturers
Association
India Exchange
India Exchange Pl

Indian Coal
Consumers and
Agents Assoc
8/1 Middleton Row

Indian Coal
Merchants Assoc
Indian Mining
Federation
135 Biplabi
Rashbehari Basu Rd

Indian Paint Assoc
India Exchange
India Exchange
Place

Indian Paper
Makers Assoc
6 Netaji Subhash Rd

Indian Paper Mills
Association
India Exchange
India Exchange Place

Indian Produce
Assoc
205 Rabindra
Sarani

Indian Rope
Manufacturers
Assoc
India Exchange
India Exchange
Place

Indian Foundry
Association
India Exchange
4 India Exchange Pl

Indian Strawboard
Manufacturers
Association
Bharat Chambers
6 Old Court Hse St

Indian Wire Rope
Manufacturers
Association
6 Netaji Subhash Rd

Jute Brokers Assoc
India Exchange
India Exchange Pl

Indian Tea Assoc
6 Netaji Subhash Rd

Steel Merchants
Assoc of India
India Exchange
India Exchange Pl

Steel Re-rolling
Mills Association
of India Everest
46-C Chowringhee
Road

Steel Wire
Manufacturers
Assoc of India
Bharat Chambers
28 Hemanta Basu
Sarani

Tea Assoc of India
India Exchange
India Exchange
Place

Textile Merchants
Association
160 Jamnalal Bajaj St

Tool and Alloy
Steels Assoc
648/649 Marshall Hse
25 Strand Rd

Silk Assoc of India
Bharat Chambers
28 Hemanta Basu
Sarani

Chennai

Brick and Tile
Manufacturers
Association
7 Jayammal St
Shenoy Nagar

Society of Auditors
121 Numgambakkam
High Rd

South India Iron
and Hardware
Merchants Assoc
Crescent Court
963 Poonamallee
High Rd

Southern
Handicrafts
Exporters Assoc
c/o Office of the
Development
Commissioner
(Handicrafts)
Shastri Bhawan
26 Haddows Rd

Laminated
Packaging
Manufacturers
Association
Corantla Nilayam
5 Sir Thiagaraja Rc
T Nagar

Tool and Alloy
Steel Dealers Asso
119 Linghi Chetty S

Gujarat

Federation of Sma
Scale Industries
Dadasaheb's Have
Mandvi
Vadodara

Hand Operated
Tin Container
Manufacturers
Association
Tagore Rd
Rajkot

Karnataka

All India Coffee
Production
Merchants Assoc
PO Box 198
Bharatiya Vidya
Bhawan Bldg
Pandeshwar
Mangalore

Automobile Spare
Parts Dealers Assoc
c/o Kasar Auto
and Tyre Centre
J C Rd
Bangalore

Auto Parts Dealers
Association
Kamakshi
Automobiles
Main Rd
Yellapur
North Kanara

Grains and General
Merchants Assoc
Chitra Durga

Grain Merchants
Association
Park Rd (Behind
City Club)
Shimoga

Tyre Retreaders
Association
General Tyres
C Rd
Bangalore

Maharashtra
Mineral Industry
Association
Shell Niwas
PO Box 271
West High Court Rd
Nagpur

Steel and
Hardware
Chamber of
Vidarbha Arihant
(Behind Amandeep
Cinema)
Paithankar Rd
Itwari
Nagpur

Mumbai
All India Alcohol
Based Industries
Development
Association
Narang Hse
34 Chhatrapati
Shivaji Marg

All India Bidi
Industry
Federation
Oricon Hse
12 Kdubhash Marg
(Rampart Row)
Fort

All India Crimpers
Association
515 Churchgate
Chambers
5 New Marine Lines

All India Small
Paper Mills Assoc
109 Shaikh Memon
Street (2nd Floor)

Assoc of Man-made
Fibre Industry
Resham Bhawan
78 Veer Nariman Rd
Churchgate

Assoc of
Merchants and
Manufacturers of
Textiles and
Machinery
Bhogilal
Hargovindas Bldg
(2nd Floor)
18/20 Kaikhushru
Dubash Marg

Assoc of Synthetic
Fibre Industry
Raj Mahal
(Ist Floor)
64 Veer Nariman Rd

Basic Chemicals,
Pharmaceuticals
and Cosmetics
Export Promotion
Council
7 Cooperage Rd

Electrical Cable
Development Assoc
503 Arun Chambers
Tardeo Rd

Grain, Rice and
Oilseeds Merchants
Association
Grainseeds Hse
72-80 Yusuf
Meharall Rd

Indian Drug
Manufacturers
Association
182-E Poonam
Chambers
Dr Annie Besant Rd
Worli

Indian Ferro Alloy
Producers Assoc
18 Shriniketan
14 M Karve Rd

Indian National
Shipowners Assoc
22 Maker Twrs
Cuffe Parade

Indian Non-
ferrous Metals
Manufacturers
Association
Mackinnon
Mackenzie Bldg
Ballard Estate

Indian Soap
and Toiletries
Makers Assoc
Raheja Centre
Room No 614
Backbay
Reclamation

Indian Woollen
Mills Federation
Churchgate
Chambers (7th Floor)
5 New Marine Lines

Iron and Steel Scrap
Assoc of India
Giriraj 301/2
73 Sant Tukaram Rd

Steel Chamber
of India
418 Loha Bhawan
P D'Mello Rd

Textile Machinery
Manufacturers
Assoc of India
53 Mittal
Chambers
Nariman Point

Travel Agents
Assoc of India
2-D Lawrence
and Mayo Hse
276 Dr DN Rd

Silk and Art Silk
Mills Assoc
Resham Bhawan
78 Veer Nariman Rd

New Delhi
All India
Airconditioning
and Refrigeration
Association
PHD Hse

All India Brick and
Tile Manufacturers
Federation
1-E/21 Swami
Ram Tirth Nagar
Jhandewalan
Extension

All India Distillers
Association
805 Siddharth
96 Nehru Place

All India
Federation of
Master Printers
E-14 (3rd Floor)
NDSE Market
Part-II

All India Garments
Manufacturers and
Wholesalers Assoc
327 Lajpat Rai
Market

All India Industrial
Gases Manufacturers

Association
9-A Connaught Place

All India Metal
Forging Assoc
2-E/14 Jhandewalan
Extension

Automotive
Component
Manufacturers
Assoc of India
203-205 Nirti Deep
Building
Nangal Raya
Business Centre

Automotive Tyre
Manufacturers
Association
9-A Connought Pl

Cement
Manufacturers
Association
Vishnu Kiran
Chamber 2142-47
Gurudwara Rd
Karol Bagh

Consumer
Electronics and TV
Manufacturers
Association
J-13 Jangpura
Extension

Directorate
of Export
Promotion
Khadi and Village
Industries
Commission
K Block
Chaudhary Bldg
Connaught Pl

Electronic
Component
Industry
Association
407 Sahyog
58 Nehru Place

Federation of All
India Automobile
Spare Parts Dealers
Association
207 Nandheri
Chambers
9/54 Desh Bandu
Gupta Rd
Karol Bagh

Federation of Biscuit
Manufacturers of
India
Phelps Bldg
9-A Connaught Place

Federation of
Engineering
Industries of India
B-30 Tilak Marg

Federation of
Hotel and
Restaurant
Association
of India
406/75-76 Nehru
Place

Federation of Indian
Export Organizations
PHD Hse (3rd Floor)
4/2 Siri Fort
Institutional Area
Hauz Khas

Federation
of Indian
Mineral Industries
301 Bakshi Hse
40/41 Nehru Place

Federation of Indian
Plywood and
Panel Industries
Indra Place H-Block
Connaught Circus

Indian
Confectionery
Manufacturers
Association
Sugar Hse
39 Nehru Place

Indian Transformer
Manufacturers
Association
303 South Delhi Hse
18 Community
Centre
Zamrudpur

Indian Vanaspati
Producers Assoc
908/909 Padma
Tower-I
5 Rajendra Place

Overseas
Construction
Council of India
Himalaya Hse
23 Kasturba Gandhi
Marg

Pesticides Assoc
of India
1202 New Delhi Hse
27 Barakhamba Rd

Roller Flour Millers
Federation of India
Thapar Chambers II
Flat Nos 29-33

349

Opp Kalindi Colony
6-B Ring Rd

Steel Furnace
Assoc of India
3-D Vandhana
11 Tolstoy Marg

Indian Sugar Mills
Association
Sugar Hse
39 Nehru Place

Vanaspati
Manufacturers
Assoc of India
903 Akashdeep Bldg
26-A Barakhamba Rd

Punjab
Cottage Industries
Association
Jallianwala Bagh Rd
Amritsar

Uttar Pradesh
All India Sports
Goods
Manufacturers
Federation
Surajkund Sports
Colony
Meerut

Merchants Assoc
Shyam Ganj
Bareilly

Small Oil Industries
Association
Choraha Marwari
Ganj
Bareilly

Tamil Nadu
Management Assoc
of Southern India
1/4 Devjee
Mansion Melur Rd
Madurai

United Planters
Assoc of
Southern India
Glenview
PO Box 11
Coonoor
The Nilgiris

Foreign Diplomatic Missions

Bombay: *see Mumbai*

Calcutta
Austria
96/1 Sarat Bose Rd
Tel: 752795

Germany
1 Hastings Park Rd
Alipore
Tel: 711141/2
Fax: 713028

Norway
Call and Hse
Chitrakoot
230-A Acharya
JC Bose Rd
Tel: 2474757
Fax: 401953

Philippines
Mercantile Bldg
Block-E/10 Lal
Bazaar St
Tel: 2481507/7102
Fax: 2486960

Poland
3-B Albert Rd
Tel: 497144

Turkey
2 Nazar Ali Lane
Ballygunge
Tel: 2471601

United Kingdom
1 Ho Chi Minh
Sarani
Tel: 2425171
Fax: 2423435

United States
of America
5/1 Ho Chi Minh
Sarani
Tel: 2425757/3611
Fax: 2422335

Chennai (Madras)
Austria
20 Nungambakkam
High Rd
Tel: 476036/8739
Fax: 825718

Germany
22 Commander-in-
Chief Rd
Tel: 8271747/3593
Fax: 473542

Malaysia
No 287 TTK Rd
Tel: 453580/99

Norway
Harbour Gate Hse
PO Box 1396
44/45 Rajaji Rd
Tel: 517950/3
Fax: 519931

Philippines
SPIC Centre
97 Anna Salai
Tel: 2350593
Fax: 2352163

Turkey
18/19 Bawa
Rowther Rd
Alwarpet
Tel: 459101/452

United Kingdom
24 Anderson Rd
Tel: 8273136-7
Fax: 8269004

United States
of America
Anna Salai
Tel: 8273040
Fax: 8250240

Mumbai (Bombay)
Austria
210 DN Rd
Taj Bldg Fort
Tel: 2042022

China
90 Cuffe Parade
Colaba
Tel: 2188738
Fax: 2188737

Germany
Hoechst Hse
Nariman Point
193 Backbay
Reclamation
Tel: 232422/1517
Fax: 2025493

Hungary
11-A WodeHse Rd
Tel: 2020224/0329
Fax: 2020429

Ireland
Royal Mumbai
Yacht Club
Chambers
Apollo Bunder
Tel: 2872045/1441
Fax: 2871087

Malaysia
Rahimtoola Hse

Homji St
Tel: 296056/
2660056

Norway
Nowroji Mansion
31 Nathelal Parekh
Marg
Tel: 242098/042
Fax: 2046576

Philippines
116 Free Press Hse
215 Nariman Point
Tel: 2024792/0375
Fax: 2020295

Poland
Manavi
Apartments
36 BG Kher Marg

Turkey
Mistry Court
Flat No 25
208 Dinshaw
Vacha Road
Tel: 240992

United Kingdom
Maker Chambers
IV 222 Jamnalal
Bajaj Rd
Box 11714
Nariman Point
Tel: 2830517/2330
Fax: 2027940

United States
of America
Lincoln Hse
78 Bhulabhai
Desai Road
Tel: 3633611
Fax: 3630350

New Delhi
Afghanistan
Plot No 5
Block 50-F
Shantipath
Chanakyapuri
Tel: 606625/3331
Fax: 6875439

Afro-Asian Rural
Reconstruction
Organization
A-2/31 Safdarjang
Enclave
Tel: 672084/687783

Algeria
E-12/4 Vasant Vihar
Tel: 6882029/14
Fax: 6882289

Angola
C-12 Anand

Niketan
Tel: 600055/688859
Fax: 6884839

Argentina
B-8/9 Vasant Viha
Paschimi Marg
Tel: 671345/8
Fax: 6886501

Asian African
Legal Consultative
Committee
27 Ring Rd
Lajpat Nagar-IV
Tel: 6415280/4265

Australia
1/50-G Shantipath
Chanakyapuri
Tel: 6872035/8823
Fax: 6885088

Austria
EP-13
Chandragupta Marg
Chanakyapuri
Tel: 601112/607
Fax: 6886929

Bangladesh
56 Ring Rd
Lajpat Nagar-III
Tel: 6834668/9205
Fax: 6839237

Belgium
50-N Shantipath
Chanakyapuri
Tel: 6876500
Fax: 6885821

Belize
D-5/17 Vasant
Vihar
Tel: 6888457
Fax: 674546

Benin
Consulate General
Weston Hse
43-A Okhla
Industrial Estate
Tel: 630052/6831048
Fax: 6842307

Bhutan
Chandragupta Marg
Chanakyapuri
Tel: 609217/8
Fax: 6876710

Brazil
8 Aurangzeb Rd
Tel: 3017301
Fax: 3015086

Brunei Darussalam
A-42 Vasant Marg

...asant Vihar
...el: 6888341/1545
...ax: 6881808

...ulgaria
...P-16/17
...handragupta Marg
...hanakyapuri
...el: 607716/413
...ax: 6876190

...ambodia
-47 Soami Nagar
...el: 6423782/5363
...ax: 6425363

...anada
/8 Shantipath
...hanakyapuri
...el: 6876500
...ax: 6876579

...hile
/13 Shantiniketan
...el: 671363
...ax: 6876424

...hina
...0-D Shantipath
...hanakyapuri
...el: 600328-9
...ax: 6885486

...olombia
...2-D Malcha Marg
...hanakyapuri
...el: 3012771/3
...ax: 3792485

...uba
4 Munirka Marg
Vasant Vihar
Tel: 6882463/3849
Fax: 6883846

...Cyprus
106 Jor Bagh
Tel: 4697503/8
Fax: 4628828

...Czech
50-M Niti Marg
Chanakyapuri
Tel: 601015/9205
Fax: 673829

Denmark
11 Aurangzeb Rd
Tel: 3010900/0722
Fax: 3010961

Dominica
48 Friends
Colony (E)
Tel: 6845695

Egypt
1/50-M Niti Marg
Chanakyapuri
Tel: 608904/2074
Fax: 6885355

Estonia
M-2 Hemkunt
Tower
98 Nehru Place
Tel: 6431067/49808
Fax: 6444642

Ethiopia
7/50-G Satya Marg
Chanakyapuri
Tel: 604407/411
Fax: 6875731

European
Community
65 Golf Links
Tel: 4629237/8
Fax: 4629206

Finland
E-3 Nyaya Marg
Chanakyapuri
Tel: 605409/40
Fax: 6885380

Food and
Agriculture
Organization (FAO)
55 Lodi Estate
Tel: 4628877/7702
Fax: 4620115

France
2/50-E Shantipath
Chanakyapuri
Tel: 604004/37
Fax: 6872305

Gambia
Consulate
General Weston
House
Okhla Indusrial Est
Tel: 6847725/9976
Fax: 6842307/7080

Germany
No 6 Block 50-G
Shantipath
Chanakyapuri
Tel: 604861-2
Fax: 6873117

Ghana
50-N Satya Marg
Chanakyapuri
Tel: 6883340/38/15
Fax: 6883202

Greece
16 Sunder Nagar
Tel: 4617800/54

Holy See (Vatican)
50-C Niti Marg
Tel: 606921/520
Fax: 6874286

Hungary
2/50-M Niti Marg
Chanakyapuri
Tel: 608414-5
Fax: 6886742

Iceland
Consulate General
Speedbird Hse
41/2 M Block
Connaught Circus
Tel: 3321122/72
Fax: 3321275

Indonesia
50-A, Chanakyapuri
Tel: 602352/4
Fax: 604865

International
Committee of the
Red Cross (IRC)
84 Golf Links
Tel: 4698385/22338
Fax: 4631723

International
Crops Research
Institute for the
Semi-Arid
Tropics (ICRISAT)
23 Golf Links
Tel: 4615931

International
Labour
Organization (ILO)
Habitat Centre
East Court
Tel: 4602101-4

Iran
No 5 Barakhamba Rd
Tel: 3329600
Fax: 3325493

Iraq
169-171 Jor Bagh
Tel: 4618011/3
Fax: 4620996

Ireland
13 Jor Bagh
Tel: 4617435/5485
Fax: 4697053

Israel
Gopaldas
Varma Bhavan
28 Barakhamba Rd
Tel: 3755389-90
Fax: 3716798

Italy
50-E
Chandragupta
Marg
Chanakyapuri
Tel: 600071

Fax: 6873889

Ivory Coast
Punj Hse
M-13 Connaught Pl
Tel: 3323621
Fax: 3326087

Japan
4 and 5/50-G
Shantipath
Chanakyapuri
Tel: 6876581/64

Jordan
1/21 Shanh
Niketan
Tel: 606678/7732
Fax: 6883763

Kazakhstan
EP-16/17
Chandragupta
Marg
Tel: 6881461/8252/
8459
Fax: 3018668

Kenya
E-66 Vasant Marg
Vasant Vihar
Tel: 6876538-9
Fax: 6876550

Kirghistan
Block A 9/32
Vasant Vihar
Tel: 6886890/1868
Fax: 6876823

Korea (North)
B-11 Pamposh
Enclave
Greater Kailash-I
Tel: 6466357

Korea (South)
9 Chandragupta
Marg
Chanakyapuri
Tel: 6885374/6
Fax: 6884840

Kuwait
5-A Shantipath
Chanakyapuri
Tel: 600791

Lao P D R
A-20 Friends
Colony (E)
Tei: 634013/3459

Latvia
48/11 Commercial
Centre, Malcha
Marg
Tel: 3010471/5457/
2931
Fax: 3013753

League of Arab
States Mission
A-137 Neeti Bagh
Tel: 6852183/62138
Fax: 6852182

Lebanon
10 Sardar Patel
Marg
Tel: 3013174/637

Libya
22 Golf Links
Tel: 4697717/8027
Fax: 463305

Luxembourg,
Grand Duchy
Consulate General
2 Panchsheel Marg
Tel: 3015855/1569
Fax: 6431929

Malaysia
50-M Satya Marg
Chanakyapuri
Tel: 601291/7
Fax: 6881538

Malta
Consulate General
1 Hailey Rd
Tel: 631050/6831718
3329090/9393

Mauritius
5 Kautilya Marg
Chanakyapuri
Tel: 3011112-3
Fax: 3019925

Mexico
10 Jor Bagh
Tel: 4697991-2
Fax: 4692360

Monaco
Consulate General
DLF Centre
Sansad Marg
Tel: 3719202-4
Fax: 3719233

Mongolia
34 Archbishop
Makarios Marg
Tel: 4631728/17989
Fax: 4633240

Morocco
33 Archbishop
Makarios Marg
Tel: 4636920-4
Fax: 4636925

Myanmar
3/50-F Nyaya
Marg
Chanakyapuri
Tel: 600251-2
Fax: 6877942

Nauru
Consulate General
C-5/4 Safdarjung
Development Area
Tel: 6863427/3906
Fax: 6862502

Nepal
7 Barakhamba Rd
Tel: 3329969/7594/
8066/8191
Fax: 3326857

Netherlands
6/50-F Shantipath
Chanakyapuri
Tel: 6884951/5852
Fax: 6884956

New Zealand
50-N Nyaya Marg
Chanakyapuri
Tel: 6883170
Fax: 6872317

Nigeria
21 Olaf Palme Marg
Vasant Vihar
Tel: 6876228/646
Fax: 6876641

Norway
50-C Shantipath
Chanakyapuri
Tel: 605982/003
Fax: 6873814

Oman
16 Olaf Palme Marg
Vasant Vihar
Tel: 671704/4798

Pakistan
2/50-G Shantipath
Chanakyapuri
Tel: 600601/905
Fax: 6872339

Palestine
D-1/27 Vasant Vihar
Tel: 676605/2859
Fax: 6872943

Panama
25 Vasant Marg
Vasant Vihar
Tel: 6872051/677065
Fax: 6872051

Peru
D-6/13-C
Vasant Vihar
Tel: 674085/3937
Fax: 6876427

Philippines
50-N Nyaya Marg
Chanakyapuri
Tel: 601120/3511
Fax: 6876401

Poland
50-M Shantipath
Chanakyapuri
Tel: 608321-2
Fax: 6872033

Portugal
13 Sunder Nagar
Tel: 4602695
Fax: 4602694

Qatar
G-5 Anand
Niketan
Tel: 601240/741
Fax: 6882184

Romania
A-52 Vasant Marg
Vasant Vihar
Tel: 670700/4447

Russia
Shantipath
Chanakyapuri
Tel: 6873799/606026
Fax: 6876823

Sahrawi Arab
Democratic
Republic
E-16 East of Kailash
Tel: 6435804
Fax: 6466433

San Marino
Consulate General
15 Aurangzeb Rd
Tel: 3015850/3793549
Fax: 6466784

Saudi Arabia
D-12 South
Extension-II
Tel: 6442470-1

Senegal
30 Paschimi Marg
Vasant Vihar
Tel: 6873720/5808
Fax: 6875809

Singapore
E-6 Chandragupta
Marg
Chanakyapuri
Tel: 6885659/77939
Fax: 6886789

Slovak
50-M Niti Marg
Chanakyapuri
Tel: 609205/318
Fax: 6877941

Somalia
A-17 Defence
Colony
Tel: 4619277/559

South Africa
B-18 Vasant Marg
Vasant Vihar
Tel: 6119411/20

Spain
12 Prithviraj Rd
Tel: 3792085/2
Fax: 3793375

Sri Lanka
27 Kautilya Marg
Chanakyapuri
Tel: 3010201/3
Fax: 3015295

Sudan
F-63 Poorvi Marg
Tel: 6873185/746
Fax: 6883758

Surinam
83-C Himgiri
Apartments
Kalkaji Extension
Tel: 6469015

Sweden
Nyaya Marg
Chanakyapuri
Tel: 604961/6875760
Fax: 6885401

Switzerland
Nyaya Marg
Chanakyapuri
Tel: 604225/323
Fax: 6873093

Syrian Arab
Republic
28 Vasant Marg
Vasant Vihar
Tel: 670233/85

Tanzania
27 Golf Links
Tel: 4694351-2
Fax: 4616054

Thailand
56-N Nyaya Marg
Chanakyapuri
Tel: 605679/985

Trinidad and
Tobago
131 Jor Bagh
Tel: 4618186-7
Fax: 4624581

Tunisia
23 Palam Marg
Vasant Vihar
Tel: 6885346/9
Fax: 6885301

Turkey
50-N Nyaya Marg

Chanakyapuri
Tel: 601921/701
Fax: 6881409

Uganda
C-6/11 Vasant Vihar
Tel: 6877687/4412
Fax: 6874445

Ukraine
176 Jor Bagh
Tel: 4616086/19
Fax: 4616085

United Arab
Emirates
EP-12
Chandragupta Marg
Chanakyapuri
Tel: 670830/945

United Kingdom
Shantipath
Chanakyapuri
Tel: 6872161
Fax: 6872882

United Nations
Children's Fund
UNICEF Hse
73 Lodi Estate
Tel: 4690401/31401
Fax: 4627521

United Nations
Development
Programme
(UNDP)
55 Lodi Estate
Tel: 4628877
Fax: 4627612

United Nations
Educational
Scientific and
Cultural
Organization
UNESCO Hse
8 Poorvi Marg
Vasant Vihar
Tel: 677310/6886205
Fax: 6873351

United Nations
High Commission
for Refugees
(UNHCR)
14 Jor Bagh
Tel: 4699302/16038
Fax: 4620137

United Nations
Industrial
Development
Organization
55 Lodi Estate
Tel: 4628877
Fax: 4627612

United Nations
Information Cent
55 Lodi Estate
Tel: 4623439/887
Fax: 4620293

United Nations
International Dru
Control
Programme
55 Lodi Estate
Tel: 4625782/336!
Fax: 4620127

United Nations
Military Observer
Group in India
and Pakistan
1-AB Purana Qila R
Tel: 386661/4052
Fax: 384052

United Nations
Population Fund
55 Lodi Estate
Tel: 4628877
Fax: 4628078

United States
Agency for
International
Development
28-B Institutional
Area
Near Qutab Hotel
Mehrauli
Tel: 6865301

United States
of America
Shantipath
Chanakyapuri
Tel 600651 (50 lines
Fax: 6868594/8601!

Uzbekistan
D-2/5 Vasant Viha
Tel: 673752
Fax: 6873246

Venezuela
N-114
Panchshila Park
Tel: 6436535/783
Fax: 6471686

Vietnam
17 Kautilya Marg
Chanakyapuri
Tel: 3018059/0532

World Bank
69/70 Lodi Estate
Tel: 4617241/0210
21 Jor bagh
Tel: 4619491

World Food
Programme (WFP)
53 Jor Bagh
Tel: 4694381/4
Fax: 4627109

orld Health
rganization (WHO)
draprastha Estate
l: 3317804/23
x: 3318607

men
70 Greater
ailash-I
l: 6414623/51348
x: 6451346

ugoslavia
50-G Niti Marg
hanakyapuri
l: 6872073/3661
x: 6885535

aire
0 Jor Bagh
l: 4619455/6

ambia
8/22 Vasant Vihar
l: 6877681/848
x: 6877928

imbabwe
8 Anand Niketan
el: 6872063/85060
ax: 6886073

anjim
ermany
are Cosme
latias
ua de Ourem
el: 43261/4
ax: 43265

Hotels

gra
larks Shiraz
4 Taj Rd
el: 361421
ax: 361420

Hotel Agra Ashok
-B Mall Rd
el: 361223/31
ax: 361620

Hotel Amar
ourist Complex
atehabad Rd
el: 360695/9

Hotel Mumtaz
atehabad Rd
el; 361771

Mayur Tourist
Complex
atehabad Rd
el: 360310

Taj View Hotel
aj Ganj
el: 361171
ax: 361179

Welcom Group
Mughal Sheraton
Mall Rd
Tel: 361701
Fax: 361730

Ahmedabad
Cama Hotel
Khanpur
Tel: 305281
Fax: 305285

Hotel Klassic Gold
42 Sardar Patel
Nagar
Tel: 445594-5
Fax: 445195

Rivera Hotel Pvt Ltd
Khanpur Rd
Tel: 24201

Ajmer
Hotel Mansingh
Palace
Vaishali Nagar
Tel: 50855

Hotel Regency
Delhi Gate
Tel: 30296/32439

Allahabad
Presidency
19-D Sarojini
Naidu Marg
Tel: 623306/9

Amritsar
Amritsar
International Hotel
Tel: 31991-2

Mohan
International Hotel
Albert Rd
Tel: 227801-8
Fax: 226520

Ritz Hotel
42 The Mall
Tel: 226606/266027

Aurangabad
Ajanta, The
Ambassador Hotel
Jaina Rd
Tel: 82211/5

Holiday Resort
Railway Station Rd
Tel: 23298

Hotel Aurangabad
Ashok
DR Rajendra
Prasad Marg
Tel: 20520-9
Fax: 31328

Hotel Rajdhani
Railway Station Rd
Tel: 27562-3

Welcomgroup
Rama International
Tel: 82241
Fax: 83468

Bangalore
Ashok Hotel
Kumara Krupa
High Grounds
Tel: 269462/82
Fax: 260033

Gateway Motel
Residency Rd
Tel: 584545
Fax: 584030

Holiday Inn
Bangalore
Sankey Rd
Tel: 269451
Fax: 267676

Hotel Ajantha
Mahatma Gandhi Rd
Tel: 584321

Hotel Harsha and
Convention Centre
Park Road
Tel: 565566
Fax: 563249

Nilgiris Nest
171 Brigade Rd
Tel: 588103

Oberoi-Bangalore
Mahatma Gandhi Rd
Tel: 585858
Fax: 585960

Taj Residency
Mahatma Gandhi Rd
Tel: 584444
Fax: 584748

Welcomgroup
Windsor Manor
Sheraton and
Towers
Sankey Rd
Tel: 2269898
Fax: 2264941

West End Hotel
Racecourse Rd
Tel: 2269281
Fax: 2200010

Woodlands Hotel
Private Ltd
Sampangi Tank Rd
Tel: 225111

Baroda (Vadodra)
Best Western
Rama Inn
Tel: 300131
Fax: 333523

Express Alkapuri
Tel: 325744/960

Express Hotels
R C Dutt Rd
Tel: 33700
Fax: 330980

Hotel Aditi
Tel: 327722/88

Hotel Rama Inn
Tel: 330131
Fax: 33523

Hotel Surya Palac
Tel: 329999
Fax: 336504

Hotel Surya
Sayajigunj
Tel: 328282/13
Fax: 336504

Hotel Utsav Pvt Ltd
Tel: 551415

Sayaji Hotels
Limited
Tel: 330088

Welcomgroup
Vadodara
Tel: 330033
Fax: 330050

Bharatpur
Bharatpur Forest
Lodge
Tel: 22760/22

Bhavnagar
Blue Hill
Tel: 26951/4

Hotel Apollo
Tel: 25249 (7 lines)
Fax: 27791

Jubilee Hotel
Tel: 20045-6

Welcomgroup
Nilambag Palace
Tel: 24241

Bhopal
Hotel Lakeview
Ashok
Tel: 541600

Hotel Ramsons
International
Hamidia Rd
Tel: 75298-9/73331

Bhubaneshwar
Hotel Kalinga
Ashok
Gauatam Nagar
Tel: 53318

Hotel Prachi
Tel: 402366/52689

Hotel Swosti
Pvt Ltd
103 Jampath
Tel: 404178-9
Fax: 407524

Kenilworth, The
Gautam Nagar
Tel: 54330/56543
Fax: 56147

Oberoi Deluxe, The
Tel: 56116

Bikaner
Hotel Lallgarh
Palace
Tel: 61963
Fax: 23253

Tara Hotel
Tel: 27180

Bodhgaya
Hotel Bodhgaya
Ashok
Tel: 227080

Bombay: *see Mumbai*

Calcutta
Fairlawn Hotel
Tel: 2444460/1835
Fax: 2441835

Great Eastern Hotel
Tel: 2482311/31

Hotel Airport
Ashok
Tel: 569111-29
Fax: 5529137

Hotel Hindustan
International
Tel: 2472394
Fax: 2472824

Hotel Rutt Deen
Tel: 401691/1878
Fax: 2475210

Hotel Shalimar
Tel: 2485016

Kenilworth
Tel: 2421373
Fax: 2425136

Lindsay Guest
House and Hotel
Tel: 248639

Lytton Hotel
Tel: 2491875/9

Oberoi Grand
Tel: 292323/0181
Fax: 291217

Park Hotel
Tel: 297336/941
Fax: 297343

Ouality Inn
Tel: 2486817
Fax: 293381

Taj Bengal
Tel: 2483939
Fax: 2481766

Chandigarh
Hotel Chandigarh
Mountview
Tel: 45882/41773

Hotel Maya Place
Tel: 532118/3277

Hotel Pankaj
Tel: 41906/25083

Hotel President
Tel: 40840/33233

Hotel Rikhy's
International
Tel: 26764/40033

Hotel Shivalik
View
Tel: 67131
Fax: 32094

Hotel Sunbeam
Tel: 41335/32057

Piccadily Hotel
Tel: 32223-7

Chennai (Madras)
Ambassador, The
Pallava
Tel: 8262061
Fax: 8268757

Connemara Hotel
Tel: 8260123
Fax: 8260123

Fisherman's Cove
Tel: 2304
Fax: 2303

Hotel Atlantic
Pvt Ltd
Tel: 8260461/3

Hotel Blue
Diamond
Tel: 6412244
Fax: 64128903

Hotel Dasaprakesh
Tel: 8255111

Hotel Kanchi
Tel: 8271100

Hotel Maris
Tel: 8255924

Hotel Palmgrove
Tel: 8271881

Hotel Peninsula
Tel: 8252770
Fax: 4725

Hotel President
Tel: 832211/842211
Fax: 832299

Hotel Swagarth
Tel: 828466/22

Madras Hotel
Ashoka Pvt Ltd
Tel: 8253377

Madras
International Hotel
Tel: 8261811
Fax: 8257412

New Victoria Hotel
Tel: 8253638

New Woodlands
Hotel Pvt Ltd
Tel: 473111

Sindoori Hotel
Tel: 8271164
Fax: 8275838

Taj Coromandel
Hotel
Tel: 827827
Fax: 8257104

Tourist Homes
Pvt Ltd
Tel: 8250079

Trident, The
Tel: 2344747
Fax: 2346699

VGP Golden Beach
Resort Ltd
Tel: 4926445

Welcomgroup
Chola Sheraton
Tel: 473347
Fax: 478779

Weolcomgroup
Park Sheraton
Tel: 452525
Fax: 455913

Cochin: *see Kochi*

Coimbatore
Corbet National
Park
Tel: 85230

Hotel Alankar
Tel: 35461 (6 lines)

Hotel Surya
International
Tel: 217751

Shri Aarvee Hotels
Tel: 43677/422

Sree Annapoorna
Tel: 47722 (10 lines)

Dalhousie
Aroma-N-Claire
Tel: 2199

Grand View Hotel
Tel: 8928/2123

Darjeeling
Bellevue Hotel
Tel: 54075

Central Hotel
Tel: 2033/2746

Hotel Sinclairs
Tel: 3431-2/54355

New Elgin Hotel
Tel: 3314/6

Windamere Hotel
Pvt Ltd
Tel: 54041
Fax: 54043

Dehradun
Hotel Madhuban
Tel: 24094-7

Hotel Prince
Tel: 27070/26678

Hotel Relax
Tel: 27776

Motel Kwality
Tel: 27001

President Hotel
Tel: 27386/082

Delhi
Ambassador Hotel
Tel: 4632600

Ashok Relax
Tel: 600121/412
Fax: 6873216

Centaur Hotel
Tel: 5452223
Fax: 5452256

Claridges Hotel
Tel: 3010211
Fax: 3010625

Connaught Palace
Tel: 344225
Fax: 310757

Hans Plaza
Tel: 3316868
Fax: 3314830

Holiday Inn
Crowne Plaza
New Delhi
Tel: 3320101
Fax: 3325335/16163

Host Inn
Tel: 3310431/523

Hotel Alka
Tel: 344328

Hotel Bhagirath
Palace
Tel: 236223

Hotel Broadway
Tel: 3273821

Hotel Diplomat
Tel: 3010204
Fax: 3018605

Hotel Fifty Five
Tel: 3321244/78

Hotel Flora
Tel: 3273634-6

Hotel Imperial
Tel: 3325332
Fax: 3324542

Hotel Janpath
Tel: 3320070

Hotel Kanishka
Tel: 3324422

Hotel Marina
Tel: 3324658

Hotel Metro
Tel: 3313856/05

Hotel Neeru
Pvt Ltd
Tel: 3278522/756

Hotel Rajdoot
Pvt Ltd
Tel: 699583

Hotel Ranjit
Tel: 3311256

Hotel Regal
Tel: 2526197/
2915254

Hotel Samrat
Tel: 603030
Fax: 6887047

Hotel Shiela
Tel: 525603/516692

Hotel Siddharth
Tel: 5712501
Fax: 5781016

Hotel Sobti
Tel: 5729035

Hotel Sofitel Surya
Tel: 6835070
Fax: 6837758

Hotel Vasant
Continental
Tel: 678800
Fax: 6873842

Hotel Vikram
Tel: 6436451

Hyatt Regency
Delhi
Tel: 6881234/609⁹
Fax: 6886833

Le Meridien
Tel: 3710101
Fax: 3714545

Lodhi Hotel
Tel: 362422

Manor Hotel
Tel: 6832171/511

Nest, The
Tel: 526614/429

Nirula's Hotel
Tel: 3322419

Oberoi, The
Tel: 4363030
Fax: 4360484

Oberoi Maidens
Tel: 2525464
Fax: 2929800

Qutab Hotel
Tel: 660060

Sartaj Hotel
Tel: 667759/3277
Fax: 6864240

Taj Mahal Hotel
Tel: 3016162
Fax: 3017299

Taj Palace Inter
Continetal
Tel: 3010404
Fax: 3011252

Tera Hotel and
Restaurant Pvt L
Tel: 239660-1

York Hotel
Tel: 3323769/019

YMCA Tourist
Hotel
Tel: 311915

Welcomgroup
Maurya Sheraton
Hotel and Tower
Tel: 3010101
Fax: 3010908

Gangtok
Hotel Nor-Khill
Tel: 23186-7

Hotel Tashi Dele
Tel: 203592/2299

Hotel Tibet
Tel: 22523/23468

oa
guada Hermitage
el: 276201
ax: 276044

idade de Goa
el: 3301-8
ax: 43303

ort Aguada
each Resort
el: 87501-7
ax: 7733

otel Baia Do Sol
el: 6084/5

otel Fidalgo
el: 46291-9/43330

otel Golden Goa
el: 6321

otel La Paz
ardens
el: 512121/6
ax: 513302

otel Mandovi
el: 6270-4

otel Metropole
el: 21169/552

otel Nova Goa
el: 6231

otel Solmar
el: 6555-6

otel Zuari
el: 2121-6/2738

eni's Hotel
el: 4581-3

eela's Beach
el: 6363-70
ax: 426352

Majorda Beach
esort
el: 20751/203

Noah's Ark
el: 7321-4

beroi, The
ogmalo Beach
el: 45/3291

rainha Cottages
y the Sea
el: 44162/004/
5917
ax: 3433-4

amada
enaissance Resort
el: 4/23611/2

ea Queen Resort
el: 22986

aj Holiday Village
el: 47514

Gopalpur on Sea
Oberoi Palm Beach
Tel: 81221/3

Guwahati
Coronet Dynasty
Tel: 24353/23322

Hotel Belle Vue
Tel: 28291-21
28639-41

Hotel Brahmaputra
Ashok
Tel: 32632/15/446

Hotel Nandan
Tel: 32621-9

Hotel Prag
Continental
Tel: 33785-7/33275

Hotel Samrat
Tel: 41657

Gwalior
Welcomgroup
Usha Kiran Palace
Tel: 323993

Hassan
Hotel Hassan
Ashok
Tel: 68731-7

Hyderabad
Asrani
International Hotel
Tel: 842267
Fax: 811529

Bhasker Palace
Ashok
Tel: 226141

Gateway Hotel
on Banjara Hill
Tel: 222222
Fax: 222218

Hotel Ashoka
Tel: 230105

Hotel Balwas
Intercontinental
Tel: 39938/21815

Hotel Baseraa
Tel: 823200

Hotel Deccan
Continental
Tel: 840981

Hotel Dwaraka
Tel: 237921

Hotel Emerald
Pvt Ltd
Tel: 202836
Fax: 233901

Hotel Jaya
International
Tel: 232929

Hotel Nagarjuna
Tel: 2377201

Hotel President
Tel: 432858
Fax: 32230

Indore
Hotel Shreemaya
Tel: 34151-6

Indotel Manor
House
Tel: 31645-8

Jabalpur
Ashok Hotel
Tel: 22167/22267

Jackson's Hotel
Tel: 21320

Krishna Oberoi
Tel: 222121
Fax: 223079

Rajdhani Hotels
Pvt Ltd
Tel: 557571

Ritz Hotel
Tel: 233571

Taj Mahal Hotel
Tel: 237988

Jaipur
Arya Niwas
Tel: 73456/68524

Hotel Broadway
Tel: 41765/254

Hotel Clarks Amer
Tel: 822616-9

Hotel Jaipur Ashok
Tel: 75171-5
Fax: 67923

Hotel Khetri House
Tel: 69183

Hotel Mangal
Tel: 75126

Hotel Mansingh
Tel: 78771
Fax: 77582

Hotel Meru Palace
Tel: 371111
Fax: 563767

Jai Mahal
Palace Hotel
Tel: 371616
Fax: 365237

LMB Hotel
Tel: 565844

Rambagh Palace
Tel: 3652254

Jaisalmer
Gorbandh Palace
Tel: 2749

Narayan Niwas
Palace
Tel: 2408/2753/
2601

Jammu
Asia Jammu Tawi
Tel: 47749/48261

Hotel Jammu
Ashok
Tel: 43127/864

Jodhpur
Ratanada Polo
Palace
Tel: 31910-4
Fax: 331118

Welcomgroup
Umaid Bhawan
Palace
Tel: 33316/30460

Jorhat
Hotel Paradise
Tel: 321521/366

Kalimpong
Hotel Silver Oaks
Tel: 296/368

Kanpur
Hotel Maghdoot
Tel: 211999

**Katra
(Vaishnodevi)**
Hotel Ambica
Tel: 2062

Hotel Asia
Vaishnodevi
Tel: 2061/2161

Khajuraho
Hotel Chandela
Tel: 2054/2102
Fax: 2095

Hotel Khajuraho
Ashok
Tel: 24

Jass Oberoi
Tel: 66

Khimsar
Welcomgroup
Royal Castle
Tel: 28

Kochi (Cochin)
Bharat Hotel (BTH)
Tel: 353501/361415
Fax: 364113

Casino Hotel
Tel: 66822/69521
Fax: 668001

Dwaraka Hotel
Tel: 352706 (9 lines)

Gaanam Hotel
Limited
Tel: 367123 (8 lines)

Hotel Abad
Tel: 28211

Hotel Abad Plaza
Tel: 361636
Fax: 370729

Hotel Presidency
Tel: 363100

Hotel Sangeetha
Tel: 368487

International Hotel
Tel: 353911/560

Malabar Hotel
Tel: 666811
Fax: 69497

Sealord Hotel
Pvt Ltd
Tel: 352682/368040

Woodlands
Tel: 351372/368900

Willingdon Island
Tel: 668352

Kodaikanal
Carlton Hotel
Tel: 426063
Fax: 4170

Hotel Kodai
International
Tel: 649/767/794
Fax: 753

Hotel Tamilnadu
Tel: 481

Kohinoor
Executive
Tel: 55059/58938

Kota
Brijraj Bhawan
Palace Hotel
Tel: 25203

Hotel Aida
Tel: 61391 (8 lines)

Hotel Ambassodor
Tel: 3293/4

Hotel Greenpark
Tel: 563311

Kottayam
Anjali Hotel
Tel: 563661

Kovalam
Ashok Radisson
Beach Resort
Tel: 68010
Fax: 62522

Hotel Samudra
Tel: 465153

Kullu
Span Resorts
Tel: 38

Leh
Hotel Shambha La
Tel: 67

Kang Lha Chan
Tel: 267

Lonavla
Fariyas Holiday
Resort
Tel: 3852
Fax: 472080

Lucknow
Carlton Hotel
Pvt Ltd
Tel: 244021-4
Fax: 249793

Clarks Avadh
Tel: 240131/236501
Fax: 237507

Madurai
Hotel Madurai
Ashok
Tel: 42531

Hotel Prem Nivas
Tel: 37531/31521

Hotel Tamil Nadu
TNDC
Tel: 23001

Taj Garden Retreat
Tel: 522300

Mammalapuram
Silversands
Tel: 2280
Fax: 2280

Temple Bay Ashok
Beach Resort
Tel: 251-7
Fax: 2257

Manali
Ambassador
Resort Hotel
Tel: 173 (5 lines)

Apple Valley
Resort
Tel: 5270
Fax: 4116

Mandawa
Castle Mandawa
Tel: 324/371
Fax: 382214

Mangalore
Hotel Srinivas
Tel: 440061

Moti Mahal
Tel: 22211

Welcomgroup
Manjarun
Tel: 31791

Mathura
Hotel Madhuvan
Tel: 5058/6414

Mount Abu
Hotel Hilltone
Tel: 3112-5
Fax: 3115

Palace Hotel
(Bikaner House)
Tel: 3121/33

Mumbai (Bombay)
Ajanta Hotel
Juhu Tara Rd
Tel: 6124890/8936

Ambasador
Hotel, The
Tel: 2041131
Fax: 2040004

Ascot Hotel
Garden Rd
Tel: 240020
Fax: 2871765

Astoria Hotel
Tel: 2852626

Centaur Hotel
Tel: 6116660
Fax: 6113535

Centaur Hotel
Juhu Beach
Juhu Tara Rd
Tel: 6113040
Fax: 6116343

Citizen Hotel
Tel: 6117273
Fax: 6117170

Damjis
Tel: 6152922
Fax: 6116741

Fariyas Hotel
Tel: 2042911
Fax: 234992

Garden Hotel
Tel: 241476/700
Fax: 2871592

Grand Hotel
Tel: 2618211/3211
Fax: 2626581

Grand Hotel
137 Station Rd
Tel: 364014

Holiday Inn
Tel: 6204444
Fax: 6204452

Hotel Accord
Tel: 6145624/992
Fax: 6115237

Hotel Airlink
Tel: 6148310
Fax: 6105186

Hotel Airport
Kohinoor Pvt Ltd
Tel: 634548-9
Fax: 8382434

Hotel Apollo
Tel: 2020223
Fax: 2871592

Hotel Avion
Pvt Ltd
Nehru Rd
Tel: 6113220
Fax: 6116956

Hotel Caesars
Palace
Tel: 542311-3

Hotel Diplomat
Tel: 2021661

Hotel Galaxy
Tel: 6125223/44980

Hotel Godwin
Tel: 241226/
2862050
Fax: 2871592

Hotel Heritage
Tel: 371489 (6 lines)

Hotel Hilltop
International
Tel: 4930860/2/4

Hotel Horizon
Pvt Ltd
Tel: 6117979
Fax: 6116715

Hotel Jal
Tel: 6123820 (8 lines)
Fax: 6369008

Hotel Kemps
Corner
Tel: 3634646

Hotel King's
Tel: 6149776/29726
Fax: 6132474/10059

Hotel Mayura
Tel: 6494416/19/21

Hotel Metro
International
Tel: 6341229/5395
Fax: 2873348

Hotel Metro Palace
Pvt Ltd
Tel: 6427311/022

Hotel Midtown
Pritam
Tel: 4145555
Fax: 4143388

Hotel Nagina
Tel: 3717799

Hotel Nataraj
Hetaji Subhash Rd
Tel: 2044161
Fax: 2043864

Hotel Park Lane
Tel: 448241
Fax: 2871592

Hotel Parkway
Tel: 453361

Hotel Parle
International
PO Box 16867
Tel: 6144335/8361
Fax: 6146685

Hotel President
Tel: 2150808
Fax: 2151201

Hotel Rajdoot
Tel: 851442-4
Fax: 2873348

Hotel Rosewood
Tel: 4940320

Hotel Royal Garden
Tel: 6130050/252

Hotel Sahil
Limited
Tel: 3081421

Hotel Samraaj
Tel: 6349311

Hotel Sands
Tel: 620451/21/42

Hotel Sea Princess
Tel: 6122661
Fax: 6113973/45054

Hotel Singh's
International
Tel: 6496806-10
Fax: 545503

Hotel Suresha
Tel: 6321198/8989

Hotel Transit
Pvt Ltd
Tel: 621087/
6129325/26

Hotel Tunga
International
Pvt Ltd
Tel: 6366010/46666

Kumaria
Presidency Hotel
Tel: 6042025/56
Fax: 8373850

Leela Kempsinki
Tel: 86363636
Fax: 86360606

Oberoi
Tel: 2025757
Fax: 2041505

Oberoi Towers
Tel: 2024343
Fax: 2043282

Ramada Hotel
Palm Grove
Tel: 6112323
Fax: 6113682

Resort
11 Madh Marve l
Tel: 6823331
Fax: 6820738

Ritz Hotel Pvt Lt
Jamshedji Tata R
Tel: 285000
Fax: 2850494

Royal Inn
Tel: 6495151

Rupam Hotel
Tel: 2618298/364

Sea Green Hotel
Tel: 222294

Sea Green
South Hotel
Tel: 221613/62/7

Sea Palace Hotel
Tel: 241828

Sea Side Hotel
Tel: 6200293/5

Shalimar Hotel
Pvt Ltd
Tel: 36313
Fax: 3631317

South End Hotel
Tel: 612523

Sun-n-Sand Hotel
Pvt Ltd
Tel: 6201811
Fax: 6202170

Taj Mahal Hotel
Tel: 2023366
Fax: 2872711

Taj Mahal
Inter-Continental
Tel: 2023366
Fax: 2872711

West End Hotel
Tel: 299121
Fax: 2864091

elcomgroup
arock Sheraton
el: 2042286
ax: 6408046

ussoorie
unsvirk Court
el: 2680
ax: 2680

ackman's Grand
otel
el: 2559/2959

otel Filigree
el: 2380

otel Shiva
ontinental
el: 2980
ax: 2780

otel Solitaire
aza
el: 2164
ax: 2166

avoy Hotel
el: 2010/2620

ysore
shok Radisson
alitha Palace
otel
el: 26316/27650
ax: 33398

otel Dasaprakash
el: 24444/55

otel
rishnarajasagar
el: 22

otel Metropole
el: 20681/871
ax: 20681

uality Inn
outhern Star
el: 27217
ax: 32175

agpur
otel Jagsons
el: 48611-4

awell Continental
el: 523845/5611

ainital
rand Hotel
ol: 2406

otel Arif Castle
el: 2801/2

hervani
illtop Inn
el: 3298

wiss Hotel
el: 3013

Vikram
Vintage Inn
Tel: 3177/9

Nasik
Hotel Panchavati
Tel: 71273-4

Wasan's Inn
Tel: 77881/6

Nilgiris (Ooty)
Fernhill Palace
Hotel
Tel: 3910-5

Hotel Dasaprakesh
Tel: 2434/5

Hotel Tamil Nadu
(TNTDC)
Tel: 3910

Ritz Hotel
Tel: 20084/484

Savoy Hotel
Tel: 4142/3

Taj Garden Retreat
Tel: 20021/131
Fax: 3318

Patna
Hotel Chanakya
Tel: 223141-2

Hotel Pataliputra
Ashok
Tel: 226270/9

Hotel Republic
Tel: 655021

Welcomgroup
Maurya-Patna
Tel: 222061

Pondicherry
Hotel Pondicherry
Tel: 460-8

Port Blair
Aasiana
Tel: 20937

Andaman Beach
Resort
Tel: 21462-5

Hotel Shompen
Tel: 20360/425

Welcomgroup
Bay Island
Tel: 20888/110
Fax: 21389

Pune
Blue Diamond
Tel: 663775
Fax: 666101

Hotel Amir
Tel: 661840-9

Hotel Ashirwad
Tel: 668989

Hotel Deccan Park
Tel: 345065

Hotel Executive
Ashok
Tel: 324567

Hotel Gauri
Tel: 778855
Fax: 660909

Hotel Gulmohr
Tel: 661773-5

Hotel Nandanvan
Tel: 321111
Fax: 660909

Hotel Regency
Tel: 669411

Hotel Sagar Plaza
Tel: 661880/585

Hotel Sheetal
Tel: 51165-7

Hotel Srimaan
Tel: 662367

Hotel Sunderban
Tel: 661919/78 Fax:
641199

Hotel Suyash
Tel: 439377

Hotel Woodland
Tel: 661111
Fax: 660909

Shalimar Hotel
Tel: 69191

Puri
Hotel Nilachal
Ashok
Tel: 3639/3551

Toshali Sands
Tel: 2888/2999
Fax: 57365

Rajgir
Centaur, The
Hokke Hotel
Tel: 5231/45
Fax: 5231

Rajkot
Hotel Arya
Tel: 31791-3

Ranchi
Hotel Arya
Tel: 20355/77

Hotel Yuvraj
Tel: 300403/514/
358

Ranikhet
West View Hotel
Tel: 61/196

Rishi Kesh
Garhwal Mandal
Vikas Nigam
Tourist
Tel: 371-2

Hotel Ganga Kinare
Tel: 30566/31645

Hotel Mandakini
International
Tel: 30781/31081

Sariska
Hotel Sariska
Palace
Tel: 322

Sasangir
Lion Safari Lodge
Tel: 21/28

**Sawai Madhopur
(Ranthambore)**
Sawai
Madhopur Lodge
Tel: 2541/2247
Fax: 381098

Shillong
Hotel Alpine
Continental
Tel: 25361
Fax: 25199

Hotel Pinewood
Ashok
Tel: 23116

Shimla
Asia the Dawn
Tel: 5858/6464

Himland Hotel
(East)
Tel: 3595/6

Oberoi, The Clarkes
Tel: 212991

Shirdi
Hotel Goradia's
Pvt Ltd
Tel: 5249

Hotel Nikki Palace
Tel: 5239

Hotel Sai Leela
Tel: 39
Fax: 2080404

Pilgrim's Inn
Tel: 5194

Shivpuri
Tourist Village
Shivpuri
Tel: 2600

Siliguri
Hotel Sinclairs
Tel: 22674-5

Srinagar
Centaur Lake
View Hotel
Tel: 75631-3

Hotel Broadway
Tel: 75621-3
Fax: 3325122

Oberoi Palace
Tel: 71241-2

Surat
Hotel Sheetal
Tel: 29229/33333

Thanjavur
Femina Hotel
Tel: 41551
Fax: 40615

Hotel Aristo
Tel: 41818/40004

Hotel Parisatham
Tel: 21801
Fax: 21844

Hotel Sangam
Tel: 44700

Tiruchirapalli
Rajali Hotel
Pvt Ltd
Tel: 41301

Thekkady
Spice Village
Tel: 2314
Fax: 668001

Thrissur (Trichur)
Casino Hotels Ltd
Tel: 24699
Fax: 27097

Hotel Elite
International
Tel: 21033
Fax: 27077

**Thruvanantapuram
(Trivandrum)**
Hotel Horizon
Te: 66888
Fax: 68569

Hotel Luciya
Continental
Tcl: 73443
Fax: 73347

Mascot Hotel
Tel: 68990

Tirupati
Bhimas Deluxe
Hotel
Tel: 20121

Hotel Mayura
Tel: 20901

Udaipur
Chandralok Hotel
Tel: 60011/32

Hotel Hilltop
Palace
Tel: 28708-9

Hotel Lakend
Tel: 23841/25944
Fax: 23898

Lake Palace
Tel: 23241
Fax: 25804

Laxmi Vilas
Palace Hotel
Tel: 29711-5

Shikarbadi Hotel
Tel: 83200
Fax: 23823

Shivniwas Palace
Tel: 28239-40
Fax: 23823

Ullal
Summer Sands
Beach Resort
Tel: 6400-7

Varanasi
Diamond Hotel
Tel: 310696

Hotel Clarks
Varanasi Ltd
Tel: 46771-5

Hotel de Paris
Tel: 46601-8

Hotel Hindusthan
International
Tel: 57075-82
Fax: 55030

Hotel Taj Ganges
Tel: 42481
Fax: 322067

Hotel Varanasi
Ashok
Tel: 46020-30

Pallavi
International Hotel
Tel: 54894
Fax: 322119

Vellore
Hotel River View
Pvt Ltd
Tel: 22349/25251

Vijayawada
Dolphin
Hotels Ltd
Tel: 64811
Fax: 63737

358

Hotel Apsara
Tel: 64811

Hotel Daspalla
Tel: 64861/63141
Fax: 62043

Hotel Kandhari
International
Tel: 471311

Hotel Manorama
Tel: 77221-30

Hotel Matma
Tel: 61251

Hotel Raj Towers
Tel: 61311

Hotel Sea Pearl
Tel: 64371-9
Fax: 63470

Ocean View Inn
Tel: 54828
Fax: 63234

Visakhapatnam
Park Hotel
Tel: 54181
Fax: 54488

Tourist Information Centres

(Government of India)
Agra
191 The Mall
Tel: 363377/959

Aurangabad
Krishna Vilas
Station Rd
Tel: 331217

Bangalore
KFC Bldg
48 Church St
Tel: 5585417

Bhubaneshwar
B/21
B J B Nagar
Tel: 432203

Bombay: *see Mumbai*

Calcutta
Embassy
4 Shakespeare
Sarani
Tel: 2421402/1475
Fax: 2423521

Chennai (Madras)
154 Anna Salai
Tel: 8524295/4785
Fax: 3522193

Cochin: *see Kochi*

Guwahati
B K Kakati Rd
Ulubari
Tel: 547407

Hyderabad
3-6-369/A 30
Sandozi Bldg
2nd Floor,
26 Himayatnagar
Tel: 630037

Imphal
Old Lambulane
Jail Rd
Tel: 221131

Jaipur
State Hotel
Khasa Kothi
Tel: 372200
Fax: 372200

Khajuraho
Near Western
Group Temples
Tel: 2047-8

Madras: *see Chennai*

Mumbai
123 M Karve Road
Tel: 2033232/3144
Fax: 2014496

Naharlagun
Sector C
Tel: 4328

New Delhi
88 Janpath
Tel: 3320005/8
Fax: 3320342

Domestic Airport
Counter
Tel: 3295296

International
Airport Counter
Tel: 3291171

Panaji
Communidade
Building
Church Square
Tel: 243412

Patna
Sudama Palace
Kankar Bagh Rd
Tel: 345776
Fax: 345776

Port Blair
VIP Rd
No 189
Jungli Ghat
Tel: 21006

Shillong
Tirot Singh
Syiem Road
Police Bazar
Tel: 225632

Thiruvananthapuram
Airport Counter
Tel: 451498

Varanasi
15-B The Mall
Tel: 43744

Travel Agencies and Tour Operators

Agra
Argee Tours
Opp Hotel
Howard Palace
Fatehabad Rd
Tel: 360456/529
Fax: 360456

SITA World Travel
(India)
A-2 Shopping
Arcade
Taj Rd
Tel: 363376/922

Taj Travels
Taj Ganj
Tel: 360457/363
Fax: 360128

Travel Bureau
Near Taj View
Hotel
Tel: 360118/719
Fax: 436

Travel Corporation
(India)
Taj Rd
Tel: 361121-3

Ahmedabad
Darshan Tours
Khanpur Rd
Tel: 302086
Fax: 300802

Express Travels
Behind Ashram Rd
Police Chowki
Tel: 448602/440265
Fax: 469101

SITA World Travel
(India)
Suflam Flats
Ashram Rd
Tel: 409105/401592

TPH Travel
Services
Stadium
5 Rasta
Navrangpura
Tel: 445761/4753

Aurangabad
TPH Travel
Service
Railway Station F
Tel: 26553-4

Bangalore
Apollo Travels
and Tours
KG Rd
Tel: 264771-2

Arman Tours
and Travels
Palace Rd
Tel: 267725/3729
Fax: 625893

Beleast Travels
Lady Curzon Rd
Tel: 592746-7

Cosmopol Travels
3 Queens Rd
Tel: 281591-2
Fax: 200154

Durga World
Travels
Kamaraja Marg R
Tel: 563122/57524
Fax: 587337

Globe Express
Travels
Richmond Rd
Tel: 213733/172

Imperial Travels
Cunnigham Rd
Tel: 264383/2843
Fax: 260174

Marco Polo
Travels and Tours
2 Residency Rd
Tel: 214441-3/84
Fax: 214438

Passage (India)
Residency Rd
Cross
Tel: 581294-7

Ram Mohan and
Kempegowda Rd
Tel 266885-7/3995

SITA World Travel
1 St Mark's Rd
Tel: 588482/892

TPH Travel
Service
Queens Rd
Tel: 205252
Fax: 564163

Triway Travels
Richmond Rd
Tel: 217587-8

UVI Holidays
St Mark's Rd
Tel: 217658

Bhopal
Radiant Travels
PO Box 24
Tel: 555460-1
Fax: 554773

Travel Bureau
Qaziyat Campus
Tel: 530210
Fax: 360006

Bhubaneshwar
Devi Tours
and Travels
Ashok Nagar (E)
Tel: 408001
Fax: 400599

SITA World Travel
14-A Bapuji Nagar
Tel: 404408

Swosti Travels
and Exports
Janpath
Tel: 408526/738
Fax: 407524

Travel Link
Satya Nagar
Tel: 402310/403424
Fax: 403778

Travel Wings
Bapuji Nagar
Tel: 400898/405898
Fax: 400599

Bodhgaya
Shashi Travels
and Tours
Tel: 81449
Fax: 236000

Bombay: *see Mumbai*

Calcutta
Charson Tours
and Travel Service
6 Jawaharlal
Nehru Road
Tel: 2489384/1509
Fax: 2481509

Everett Travel
Service
4 Government Pl
Tel: 2486295/9583
Fax: 2489583

Lionel Edwards
(Head Office)

Old Court Hse St
Tel: 2489864/1171-9
Fax: 280589

Minnie Pan Travel
Acharya Jagdish
Chandra Bose Rd
Tel: 2471052/3262
Fax: 293381/
294476

Orient Express
1 and 2 Old Court
Hse Corner
Tel: 201911/207004

Peerless Holidays
Hotels and Travels
1 Chowringhee Sq
Tel: 2487181
Fax: 293381

Sinclairs Hotel and
Transportations
56-A Mirza Ghalib
Street
Tel: 292925/5261
Fax: 293109

Travel Bureau
SN Banerjee Rd
Tel: 2450428
Fax: 360006

Chennai (Madras)
Aries Travel
Nandanam
(Anna Salai)
Tel: 455149
Fax: 836644

Binny Travel Srvc
LIC Bldg
Anna Salai
Tel: 841875/7024
Fax: 589034

Chalukya Group
Tours
4/8 Kasturi
Apartments
Dr Radhakrishnan
Road
Mylapore
Tel: 8265854

Diana World
Travel
45 Montieth Rd
Egmore
Tel: 8261716/5579

Eastman Travel
and Tours
(Chennai)
4 Sheshadri Rd
Alwarpet
Tel: 459086/5135
Fax: 76867

Lionel Edwards
(Branch)
Deshbandhu Plaza
Royapettah
Tel: 8259700

Mercury Travels
191 Anna Salai
Tel: 8269993/8995/
2840

Orient Express
19 GN Chetty Rd
Tel: 8261823/9616
Fax: 8263432

Shibi Travels
1-A
Nungambakkam
High Rd
Tel: 8279428/2153
Fax: 8263653

SITA World Travel
(India)
Commander-in-
Chief Rd
Tel: 478861
Fax: 473536

Swagatam Tours
and Travels
45 Montieth Rd
Tel: 8265721/56616

UVI Holiday
Gopala Puram
Tel: 8279440

Delhi
Adventure World
(India)
26 Rajendra Place
Tel: 5737320
Fax: 5751536

Alpine Travels and
Tours Gole Market
Tel: 344599/311410
Fax: 350722

American Express
Bank (Travel
Related Services)
A Block Wenger
Hse Connaught
Place Tel: 3324119

Ashok Travels
and Tours
19 Ashok Rd
Tel: 3325035/4511/
3715917

Avis Travels
3 Bhikaji Cama
Place
Tel: 674575
Fax: 6876357

Beckon Tours
Lajpat Nagar-I
Tel: 6843002/23546
Fax: 6823546

Business and
Tourist Services
KG Marg
Tel: 3317133/5876
Fax: 3712254

Charson Tours and
Travel Service
40 Shahpur Jat
Tel: 6436191/46745
Fax: 6436191/
6864714

Cosmopolitan
Tour Operators
and Travel Agents
Chanakyapuri
Tel: 676631/6882072

Cox and Kings
(India)
H Block Indra Place
Connaught Circus
Tel: 3320067/90
Fax: 3317373

CTI Travels
21 Barakhamba Rd
Tel: 3723122/11217
Fax: 3723255

Discover India
Tours
D-21 Kalkaji
Tel: 6465600/50600
Fax: 6439221/50600

Dynamic Tours
Gulmohur Enclave
Tel: 666770/
6853760
Fax: 6865212

Ekta Tours
and Travels
Gulmohur Enclave
Tel: 6868812/655034
Fax: 6868829

EMPL Tours
95 Nehru Place
Tel: 6412501/28310
Fax: 6428311

Essdee
Travexpress
Safdarjung Enclave
Tel: 6875433
Fax: 6875433

Eternal India
Travel
89 Nehru Place
Tel: 6453874/69910
Fax: 6463547

Everett Travel
Service
11-C Connaught Pl
Tel: 3321117/217
Fax: 3326748

Exotic India (Tours
and Travels)
5 Bhikaji Cama Pl
Tel: 602682/6875320
Fax: 6884847

General Travel
23 KG Marg
Tel: 3312391-3
Fax: 6475847

Great Adventure
Travels
80 Scindia Hse
Janpath
Tel: 3323619/7
Fax: 3320151

High Points
(Expeditions
and Tours)
Vasant Vihar
Tel: 601224/5849
Fax: 6884797

Holiday India
Kalkaji Main Rd
Tel: 6474227/21352
Fax: 6461896

Holiday Maker
Qutab Hotel, Rd
Tel: 6864236-7/
8630
Fax: 6853425

Ibex Expeditions
G-66 East of
Kailash
Tel: 632641/6846403
Fax: 6846403

India Vision Tours
and Travels Ranjit
Nagar Complex
Tel: 5702828/7272
Fax: 5702929

Indian Tourism
Cooperative
East of Kailash
Tel: 6441019/34
Fax: 6475085

Indiana Travel
124 Yashwant
Place
Chanakyapuri
Tel: 671991/76
Fax: 671790

Indo Asia Tours
NDSE-I
Tel: 4628596/9361
Fax: 4620533

Indus Tours
and Travels
Bhikaji Cama Place
Tel: 605741/674505
Fax: 4620533

Inpac Tours
SU-5 Bhikaji Cama
Bhawan
Bhikaji Cama Place
Tel: 671442/4772
Fax: 6886389

Intel Travel
77 Nehru Place
Tel: 6446789/64557

Jetair Tours
Connaught Circus
Tel: 3321292
Fax: 3328593

Kash'Venture
Travels (KVT)
Pahar Ganj
Tel: 7522407/
731311
Fax: 7522407

Lawrence (India)
Tour and Travels
36 Janpath
Tel: 3323628/
3722899

Lionel Edwards
(Branch)
Asaf Ali Rd
Tel: 7521050/0954
Fax: 7520954

Mercury Travels
Jeevan Tara Bldg
Parliament St
Tel: 312008/
3732866
Fax: 3732013

Minar Travels
(India)
14/2369
Gurudwara Rd
Karol Bagh
Tel: 5731946/81950
Fax: 5781952

Nova Travel
6 Bhikaji Cama
Place
Tel: 672188/
6881523
Fax: 6875470

Nu Travel Bureau
Jhandewalan
Extension
Tel: 7510709/32695
Fax: 73821

Orient Express
70 Janpath
Tel: 3322142

360

Oriental Travels
Hotel Marina
Connaught Circus
Tel: 3327214/4015
Fax: 3327127

Paradise Tour
(India)
Vasant Vihar
Tel: 678597/606712
Fax: 6875112/7122

Peak Adventure
Tours
Kailash Colony
Tel: 6432894
Fax: 6440866

Peerless Holidays
Hotels and Travels
7 Tolstoy Marg
Tel: 3329399/
3747138
Fax: 343239

Perfect Travels
and Tours
26 Rajendra Place
Tel: 5724462/1861
Fax: 5751536

PTC Travel
and Tour
17-B Vasant Lok
Vasant Vihar
Tel: 6877701/7506
Fax: 6877497

Raaj Overseas
Travel
6/90 P Block
Connaught Circus
Tel: 345762/351340

Rainbow Travels
(India)
Room No 3
Janpath Hotel
Tel: 3326327/8453
Fax: 3325735

Rama Tours
and Travel
19 Barakhamba Rd
Tel: 3323459/7154
Fax: 3327138

Razdan Travel
Service
M-6 Magnum Hse I
Karampura
Commercial
Complex
Tel: 5467019/
536463
Fax: 549190

Reshu Boktoo and
Sons 37 Shaheed
Bhagat Singh Marg
Tel: 344603
Fax: 344952

Senator Travels
16 Barakhamba Rd
Tel: 3713435 (4
lines)
Fax: 3713848

Services
International
Old Rajinder
Nagar
Tel: 5782636/42
Fax: 5749797

Shah Travel
36 Janpath
Tel: 3716433/3525
Fax: 3713409/
6447347

Shashi Travels
and Tours
Behind Stayan
Cinema
Tel: 5701246/326
Fax: 5701246

SITA World Travel
(India)
F-12 Connought Pl
Tel: 3311122
Fax: 3324652

Span Tours
N Travel
36 Janpath
Tel: 3328510/2332
Fax: 3713036

STIC Travels
Room Nos 4 and 5
Imperial Hotel
Janpath
Tel: 3324789/7582
Fax: 3712710

Swagatam Tours
and Travel
Arya Samaj Rd
Tel: 5744500/4411
Fax: 5752776

Thomas Cook
(India)
Rashiya Mook Bldg
Panchkuin Rd
Tel: 344152/
3747404
Fax: 3746735

TPH Travel
Services
13/29 East Patel
Nagar
Tel: 5747810
Fax: 5752563

Tradewings
60 Janpath
Tel: 3321822/1623
Fax: 3324005

Trans India
Travels
17 Barakhamba Rd
Tel: 374259/23731
Fax: 3723517

Travel Planners
Connaught Place
Tel: 3322933/
3713047
Fax: 3712707

Travelite (India)
11 Tolstoy Marg
Tel: 3313541/6493
Fax: 3319511/
3712245

Triveni Travels
6 Tilak Marg
Tel: 383631-3
3782667
Fax: 3782696

UNI Tours (India)
Barakhamba Bldg
Tel: 3711569-70/
3327747
Fax: 3329401

UVI Holidays
Karol Bagh
Tel: 5732569/82050
Fax: 5752701

Vacation Travels
and Tours
B-2 Taj
Apartments
No 2 Factory Rd
Ring Rd
Tel: 6866583/
662297
Fax: 6866765

Vasco Travel
Lajpath Nagar-II
Tel: 6843680/5382
Fax: 6847424

Ventours India
Bhikaji Cama Place
Tel: 671817
Fax: 6882789

Wanderlust
Travels
Opp Hyatt
Regency
Tel: 6875200/
602180
Fax: 6885188

Goa
Aero Mundial
Hotel Mandovi
PO Box 88
Panaji
Tel: 44813/43773

SITA World
Travel (India)
101 Rizvi
Chambers Caetan
Albuquerque
Road Panaji
Tel: 54418-9
Fax: 54419

Syndicate Tours
and Travels
G-5 Noreen
Apartments
St Inez Panjim
Tel: 47098/42187
Fax: 43433

TPH Travel
Services
GS-7 Padmavati
Towers
Panaji
Tel: 55524

UVI Holidays
Orav's Guest Hse
Cunha Gonsalves R
Panjim
Tel: 44896/43819
Fax: 44129

Guwahati
BSS Travel Service
SRCB Rd
Fancy Bazaar
Tel: 41205-6/3167
Fax: 42198

Gwalior
Travel Bureau
Lashkar
Tel: 24765/340103
Fax: 360006

Hyderabad
MN Tours and
Travels
6-3-855/10-A
Ameerpet
Tel: 213223/291601
Fax: 831344

Satellite Travels
Matrusri Bldg
3-5-873 Hyderguda
Tel: 240174/2879

SITA World Travel
SITA Hse
3-5-874 Hyderguda
Tel: 233642/628

Jaipur
Aravali Safari
and Tours
Bhandari
Chambers
MI Rd
Tel: 373124/8057
Fax: 363833

Group and
individual
Travel Service
Tilak Nagar
Tel: 46129/78771-8
Fax: 40909

Registhan Tours
Sardar Patel Marg
C Scheme
Tel: 380824

SITA World
Travel (India)
O Villa
Station Road
Tel: 68226/66809

Khajuraho
Orient Express
Hotel Chandela
Tel: 49

Travel Bureau
34 Sewagram
Tel: 2037

Kochi (Cochin)
Chalukya Group
Tours
Willingdon Island
Tel: 667500

Chanakya Group
Travels
Marine Drive
Tel: 362061/667521
Fax: 370944

Kerala Travels
Koithara Bldgs
JOS Junction
Tel: 367738/9279

UVI Holidays
Banerjee Rd
Tel: 364350

Ladakh
Peerless Holidays
Hotels and Travels
Kanglachen
Shopping Complex
Leh
Tel: 2267

Lucknow
Travel Bureau
A-8/3 Paper Mill
Colony
Tel: 385046
Fax: 360006

Madras: *see Chennai*

Mangalore
Albion Travels
10 Kumudavathi
Building
Balmatta
Tel: 31460/22025

Globe International
Travels
Al-Fareed Centre
Hampankatta
Tel: 35500-3
Fax: 31903

Mumbai (Bombay)
Adarsh Trading
Malabar Hill
Tel: 3625209/8993

Ador Travels
Dubash Marg
Tel: 2870740/
242480
Fax: 2851770

Aero Agencies
Nagindas Master Rd
(Meadows St)
Tel: 274425/2801

Asiatic Travel
Service
Fort
Tel: 204815
Fax: 2873355

Bulch and
Travels Service
Opera Hse
Tel: 3880758/66248

Cosmos Travels
Nariman Point
Tel: 221659/3103

DBS World Travels
213 Nariman Point
Tel: 2872641/
244949
Fax: 2872640

Designer Holidays
19 Peddar Rd
Tel: 4924415
Fax: 4939534

Elbee Travel
Services
Vile Parle (E)
Tel: 6124449/14404
Fax: 6116727/0328

Everett Travel
Service
Nariman Point
Tel: 245339/127
Fax: 2024893

Forvol Tours and
Transport Services
Ballard Estate
Tel: 2616751/1531
Fax: 2619404

Futura Travel
Nariman Point
Tel: 2832929/2378
Fax: 2832769

Game Garden
Tour and Travel
Mahim
Tel: 465281/458072
Fax: 464151

Great Escape
(Division of
Cambata Aviation)
Churchgate
Tel: 8251583-4/
221044
Fax: 2853763

Hermes Travel
and Cargo
9 Hazarimal
Somani Marg
Tel: 2040666-9
Fax: 2873521

Indwest Travels
Nanda Patkar Rd
Tel: 6126845/42561
Fax: 6152306

Jetair Tours
Nariman Point
Tel: 2040221/223275
Fax: 2046861

JM Mehta and Co
(Travel Division)
Santacruz (E)
Tel: 6125152/224
Fax: 6113720

Lionel Edwards
Ballard Estate
Tel: 2617123/98
Fax: 2610335

Orient Express
DN Rd
Tel: 2871047/2965
Fax: 2834653

Peerless Holidays
Hotels and Travels
5 New Marine
Lines
Tel: 2624808
Fax: 2624808

Preferred Holidays
Santacruz (E)
Tel: 6100515/0624
Fax: 6236189/
6100624

Ramniranjan Kedia
Tours and
Travels Worli
Tel: 4371112/2046
Fax: 4361682

SOTC Travels and
Tours (Mumbai)
Churchgate
Tel: 2855797

Swagatam Tours
and Travels
Juhu
Tel: 6133980/28942

Syrisa Travels
Fort
Tel: 220615/2831674

Treasure Tours
and Travels
Nariman Point
Tel: 244086/
2044287
Fax: 2851953

TPH Travel
Services)
Santacruz (W)
Tel 6480233/0318
Fax: 6491580

Trimurti Holidays
Nariman Point
Tel 2854866 (5
lines)
Fax: 2871780

UVI Holidays
Chembur
Tel: 5554714/7
Fax: 5564342

Vensimal World
Travel Agents
PO Box 2112
Tel: 2084233
Fax: 2060470

Ventours India
Nariman Point
Tel: 2040910/
2874760
Fax: 2040160

Wilco Ship
Management and
Travels
Nariman Point
Tel: 2045716/6511
Fax: 2022671

Mysore
Triway Travels
Dr Radhakrishnan
Avenue
Tel: 26321/27548

Patna
Travel Bureau
Grand Hotel
Fraser Rd
Tel: 221456
Fax: 360006

Pune
Asiatic Travel
Service
175 Dhole Patil Rd
Tel: 662546/8493
Fax: 667934

SITA World Travel
(India)
Hotel Blue
Diamond
11 Koregaon Rd
Tel: 668707/2638

Shimla
Span Tours N
Travels
4 The Mall
Tel: 5279/201360/
5222
Fax: 201300

Siliguri
Help Tourism
66 Bidhan Rd
Tel: 27941/20476
Fax: 27941

Rajat Traveller
Hill Cart Rd
Tel: 967/9
Fax: 27120

Srinagar
Shah Travels
AUQAF Bldg
Dal Gate
Tel: 74641/76865/
77293/72384

SITA World
Travel (India)
Hotel Broadway
Maulana Azad Rd
Tel: 78891/77186

Thiruvananthapuram
Aries Travel
Press Rd
Tel: 65417/67964/
61163
Fax: 77702

Chalukya Group
Tours
Kunnukuzhy
Tel: 444618

Chanakya Group
Travels
St Joseph's Bldg
Cotton Hill
Tel: 65498/64498
Fax: 370944

Kerala Travels
LMS Bldg
Tel: 434712/286
Fax: 434286

South India
Expeditions
NPP Nagar
Peroorkada
Tel: 61163
Fax: 77702

UVI Holidays
GPO Lane
Statue
Tel: 77702
Fax: 77702

Tiruchirapalli
SITA World Travel
(India)
Hotel Sangam
Complex
Tel: 44700/480

Varanasi
Shashi Travels
and Tours
53 Patel Nagar
Tel: 45211
Fax: 45211

SITA World Travel
(India)
Hotel Clarks
Tel: 43421/42945

Travel Bureau
Hotel Clarks
Tel: 45512/46621/
771
Fax: 360006

Vellore
SITA World Travel
(India)
St Luke's Centre
Vethiyar St
Tel: 26711

Youth Hostels Association of India

NORTHERN REGION
Amritsar
Grand Trunk Rd
Tel: 48165

Bhopal
Tel: 63671

Dalhousie
Tel: 89

Delhi
5 Nyaya Marg
Chanakyapuri

Haryana
837 Sector 14
Sonepat

Jaipur
Tel: 69084

Nainital
Tel: 513

Pachkula
Tel: 155

Patni Top
Patni Top 180001
Jammu and
Kashmir

NORTH EASTERN REGION
Arunachal Pradesh
Syndicate Press
Building
Bomdila

Assam
111/92 Bonngaon
Beltola
Guwahati

Meghalaya
Ryngi Rynjai
Near East End
Chambers
School Umpling
Shillong

Mizoram
Electric Hebron
Veng
Aizawl

EASTERN REGION
Bihar
66/4 Near Stadium
TELCO Colony
Jamshedpur

Darjeeling
Tel: 2290

Orissa
Rang Mahal
Marchikot Puri

Puri
Tel: 424

West Bengal
62/3 Nabin
Senapati Lane
Howrah

SOUTHERN REGION
Andaman and
Nicobar Islands
31 Mahatama
Gandhi Rd
Port Blair

Andhra Pradesh
LIG 10
APHB Colony
Visakhapatnam

Karnataka
39 8th Cross
Swimming Pool
Extension
Ma lleswa ran
Bangalore

Madras
Tel: 412882

Pondicherry
Solai Nagar

Tamil Nadu
24 II St
Balaji Nagar
Royapettah
Chennai

Trivandrum
Tel: 424

WESTERN REGION
Aurangabad
Tel: 23801

Gandhinagar
Tel: 2364

Gujarat
Seth Bhavan
Seth Kantilal Sheri
Dhari

Madhya Pradesh
F-83/32 Tulsinagar
Bhopal

Maharashtra
20/154 Unnat
Nagar No 3
Behind Filmistan
Studio
Goregaon (W)
Mumbai

Panaji
Tel: 2433

Rajasthan
B-5 New Colony
Jaipur

Bibliography

Ali, Salim *The Book of Indian Birds*, Natural History Society, Mumbai, 1979.

Allen, Charles *Lives of the Indian Princes*, Century, London, 1984.

Anand, M R *The Hindu View of Art*, London, 1933.

Archer, W G *Indian Miniatures*, Victoria and Albert Museum, London, 1960.

Basham, A L *The Wonder That Was India*, Sidgwick and Jackson, London, 1954.

Chaudhari, N C *Hinduism*, Chatto and Windus, London, 1979.

Commaraswamy *The Dance of Siva*, Ananda Kentish reprint, New York/Dover, 1985.

Craven, Roy C *Indian Art: A Short History*, Thames and Hudson, London, 1976.

Davies, Philip *The Splendours of the Raj*, John Murray, London, 1984.

Monuments of India, Vol II: (Islamic, Rajput and European), Viking, London, 1989.

Durrans, Brian *India — Past into Present*, BMP, London, 1982.

Gandhi, MK *My Experiments with Truth*, Penguin India reprint, New Delhi, 1982.

Grewal, Bikram *Birds of India*, The Guidebook Company, Hong Kong, 1993.

Harle, J C *The Art and Architecture of the Indian Subcontinent*, Penguin India reprint, New Delhi, 1986.

Jayakar, Pupul *The Earth Mother: An Introduction* to the Ritual Art of Rural India, Penguin India, New Delhi, 1981.

Lanoy, Richard *Speaking Tree*, Oxford University Press, New York, 1971.

Michell, George *Monuments of India, Vol 1: "Buddhist, Jain, Hindu"*, Viking, London 1989.

Mookerjee, Ajit *Arts of India*, Oxford University Press, London, 1966.

Nehru, Jawaharlal *The Discovery of India*, Oxford University Press, New Delhi, 1916.

O'Flaherty, *W Hindu Myths*, Penguin India, New Delhi 1975.

Prater, S H *The Book of Indian Animals*, Natural History Society, Mumbai, 1948.

Punja, Shobita *Museums of India*, The Guidebook Company, Hong Kong, 1990.

Monuments of India, The Guidebook Company, Hong Kong, 1994.

Randhava, M S *Indian Painting*, Vakils, Mumbai 1968.

Spear, Percival *A History of India Vol 11*, Penguin India reprint, New Delhi, 1990.

Thapar, Romila *A History of India Vol 1*, Penguin India reprint, New Delhi, 1990.

Woodcock, Martin *Guide to the Birds of the Indian Sub-continent*, Collins, London, 1980.

Zimmer, H *Myths and Symbols in Indian Art and Civilization*, Boston, 1962.

The Art of Indian Asia, Princeton, 1955.

Index

(Illustrations are indicated in bold.)